Georg Lukács and Critical Theory

Georg Lukács and Critical Theory

Aesthetics, History, Utopia

Tyrus Miller

EDINBURGH
University Press

Edinburgh University Press is one of the leading university presses in the UK. We publish academic books and journals in our selected subject areas across the humanities and social sciences, combining cutting-edge scholarship with high editorial and production values to produce academic works of lasting importance. For more information visit our website: edinburghuniversitypress.com

© Tyrus Miller 2022, under a Creative Commons Attribution-NonCommercial licence

Edinburgh University Press Ltd
The Tun – Holyrood Road
12(2f) Jackson's Entry
Edinburgh EH8 8PJ

First published in hardback by Edinburgh University Press 2022

Typeset in 10.5/13pt Adobe Sabon LT Pro
by Cheshire Typesetting Ltd, Cuddington, Cheshire

A CIP record for this book is available from the British Library

ISBN 978 1 3995 0241 2 (hardback)
ISBN 978 1 3995 0242 9 (paperback)
ISBN 978 1 3995 0243 6 (webready PDF)
ISBN 978 1 3995 0244 3 (epub)

The right of Tyrus Miller to be identified as the author of this work has been asserted in accordance with the Copyright, Designs and Patents Act 1988, and the Copyright and Related Rights Regulations 2003
(SI No. 2498).

Contents

List of Figures	vi
Acknowledgments	viii
1. Georg Lukács and Critical Theory: The Long Goodbye	1

Part I Georg Lukács

2. Matthew, Mark, Lukács, and Bloch: From Aesthetic Utopianism to Religious Messianism	31
3. Lukács's Theatres of History: Drama, Action, and Historical Agency	55
4. The Non-Contemporaneity of Lukács and Lukács: Cold War Contradictions and the Aesthetics of Visual Art	81

Part II Theodor W. Adorno

5. Adorno and/or Avant-Garde: Looking Back at Surrealism	105
6. Avant-Garde *and* Kitsch, or, Teddy the Musical!	124
7. Remediating Opera: Media and Musical Drama in Adorno and Kluge	144

Part III Critical Theory

8. Perversion and Utopia: Sade, Fourier, and Critical Theory	169
9. Interdisciplinary Legacies: Critical Theory and Authoritarian Culture	195
10. Prophecies of Mass Deception: Dewey, Trotsky, and the Moscow Show Trials	225
11. Tell-Trials, or, Gyuri the Radio Play	258
Index	263

Figures

2.1 Károly Kernstok, *Nude Boy*, c. 1909. Private collection. Photographic source: bankaustria.kunstforum.at. Public domain.   44

2.2 Lajos Tihanyi, *Main Square in Nagybánya*, 1908. Private collection. Photographic source: Szilas. Public domain.   45

4.1 László Lakner, *My George Lukács-Book/Mein Georg-Lukács-Buch*, 1970. Foto/Siebdruck, 70 × 50. László Lakner. Permission for use by Creative Commons Attribution Share-Alike 3.0 License.   97

9.1 *Zeitschrift für Sozialforschung 1* (1932), table of contents.   200

9.2 Attila F. Kovács set from András Jeles, *Dream Brigade*, 1983. Film still.   214

9.3 Central foyer of Terror Háza Muzeum, Budapest. Fred Romero, 2017. Permission for use by Creative Commons Attribution Generic 2.0 License.   216

9.4 Statues in courtyard of Memory Point, Andrassy Street 34, Hódmezővásárhely. Unnamed photographer ("Globetrotter19"), 2021. Permission for use by Creative Commons Attribution Share-Alike 3.0 License.   216

9.5 Exterior view of Terror Háza Muzeum, Budapest. Fred Romero, 2017. Permission for use by Creative Commons Attribution Generic 2.0 License.   218

9.6 Permanent installation at Terror Háza Muzeum, Budapest. Unnamed photographer ("n1207"), 2017. Permission for use by Creative Commons Attribution Share-Alike 3.0 License.   220

10.1	Trotsky "Whitewash" Cartoon, *The Daily Worker*, April 26, 1937.	231
10.2	Cover of Leon Trotsky, *I Stake My Life!*, 1937.	233
10.3	Bukharin scene at Moscow trial, *Mission to Moscow*, 1943. Film still.	240
10.4	James Rorty as William Randolph Hearst's Trained Seal, *The Daily Worker*, June 11, 1937.	243

Acknowledgments

In researching and writing this book, I received assistance from many people, through their discussion of ideas, their sharing of difficult-to-access materials, and their invitations to present parts of it in progress. These include: Edit András, David Ayers, Erik Bachman, Jonathan Beecher, Hunter Bivens, Sascha Bru, Sebastian Budgen, James Clifford, Annalisa Coliva, Kelly Donahey, Steve Edwards, Aleš Erjavec, David Féher, Peng Feng, Éva Forgács, Péter Forgács, Paul Fry, Samir Gandesha, Jianping Gao, Péter György, Johan Hartle, George Hoare, Alex Hochuli, David Hoy, George Legrady, Catherine Liu, Angelina Lucento, Stefano Marino, Mena Mitrano, Judith-Frederike Popp, István Rév, James Robertson, Glyn Salton-Cox, Tamás Scheibner, Catherine Soussloff, James Steintrager, Miško Šuvaković, Zsuzsanna Szegedi-Varga, Alberto Toscano, Hedvig Turai, Lioudmila Voropai, Barrett Watten, the late Hayden White, and Naoki Yamamoto.

I feel special gratitude for the late Géza Kállay, who, on my arrival in Budapest in 2001, escorted me to the Lukács Archive for the first time. I also want to thank the archivists there as well, who were always generous and accommodating to visiting researchers.

I wish especially to thank my wife, Deanna Shemek, who is my ideal reader and best editor as well as my partner in opera, movies, cooking, and other accoutrements of the good life we share.

This book is dedicated to Lilliane Weissberg, who a long time ago tended to an awkward intellectual sprout. I hope that this late bloom may go a little way in answering her constant generosity and kindness.

Parts of this book have appeared in earlier versions; the revised and expanded chapter versions include reprinted parts by permission of the publishers:

For Chapter 4: "The Non-Contemporaneity of György Lukács" appeared in *Acta Historiae Artium* 56, 2015. Published with permission of the Akadémiai Kiadó.

For Chapter 5: "Remediating Opera: Music and Musical Drama in Adorno" appeared in *Adorno und die Medien*, 2022. Published with permission of Kulturverlag Kadmos.

For Chapter 7: "Blindspots in the Rearview Mirror: Surrealism in Adorno's *Aesthetic Theory*" appeared in *The "Aging" of Adorno's Aesthetic Theory*, eds. Samir Gandesha, Johan F. Hartle, and Stefano Marino, © 2021. Published with permission of Mimesis International.

For Chapter 8: "Perversion and Utopia: Sade, Fourier, and Critical Theory" © 2018 Johns Hopkins University and West Chester University. This article first appeared in *College Literature*, volume 45, issue 2, Spring 2018, pages 330–59. Published with permission of the Johns Hopkins University Press.

Chapter 1

Georg Lukács and Critical Theory: The Long Goodbye

"When something has once become problematic . . . then salvation can only arise by accentuating the doubtfulness, by a radical taking of that problematic to its limit."

—Georg Lukács, *Soul and Form* (1911)[1]

Lukács (Missing)

In his interview with the Lukács scholar Rüdiger Dannemann in *Lukács and 1968*, the Frankfurt School philosopher Axel Honneth observed the peculiar position that Lukács had occupied in the original Frankfurt School:

> Horkheimer, Adorno and Marcuse . . . possessed an apparently both politically and personally conditioned tendency to underplay or even to ignore the powerful experience that *History and Class Consciousness* must have represented for them all. The most dramatic is certainly in the relation of Adorno to Lukács. . . . Adorno stands presumptively in debt to Lukács and always was strongly inclined to deny this legacy.[2]

Honneth notes that this tendency increased in the post-war period with the dismissal of Lukács as a Stalinist and the Frankfurt School's retrospective baptism of the economist-philosopher Alfred Sohn-Rethel as the "actual progenitor" of their Marx-influenced theory of society. And, Honneth concludes, that represents "a denial of history at the core of the Frankfurt School."[3]

Honneth's work in critical theory builds upon the communicative action theory of Jürgen Habermas, who sought to reconstruct Lukács's theory of reification in connection with social rationalization in the first volume of *Theory of Communicative Action*, remarkably one of the few direct engagements with Lukács's work in decades of Frankfurt School critical theory. Despite Adorno's own disavowals, Habermas drew a direct link from Lukács to Frankfurt School theory, as his chapter title "From Lukács to Adorno: Rationalization as Reification" indicates.[4] Of major Frankfurt School figures after Habermas, only Honneth has trained much critical attention on Lukács, first with his 1995 essay "A Fragmented World: On the Implicit Relevance of Lukács' Early Work,"[5] then in a more thoroughgoing reconstructive critique in his 2005 Tanner Lectures at the University of California, Berkeley, published as *Reification: A New Look at an Old Idea.*[6] Honneth's engagement with both Lukács and Adorno, however, starts from a still firmer rejection of the social-theoretical bases of their work than even Habermas, although following his lead. In particular, Honneth rejects Lukács's ascription of the negative epistemic, existential, and practical effects of capitalist modernity to the commodity form, as well as the Hungarian Marxist's favored response to reification through revolutionary proletarian consciousness and action organized by a Leninist party. Adorno, he argues, further generalizes Lukács's problematic to the whole of society and nature and extends it backwards in historical time as well with his totalizing concept of instrumental reason. Lukács and Adorno, according to Honneth, similarly partake in a speculative philosophy of history and a discredited philosophical anthropology, giving short shrift to the more diverse dynamics by which societies are actually integrated.[7] Lukács's work and, by extension, Adorno's as well are no longer of interest for their "paradigmatic theoretical core." At most, they may still serve as a "seismographic aid for critical theory," "a sensor . . . able diagnostically to indicate disturbances in an era's patterns of cultural integration."[8] In keeping with his reorientation of critical theory towards questions of social recognition and the "social pathologies" that failures of recognition produce,[9] Honneth views Lukács and Adorno as relevant primarily as sensitive indicators of social and cultural *problems* of modernity, while critical explication and analysis of the questions they raise call for other social-theoretical and sociological frameworks.

Honneth's attempt to reconstruct Lukács's and Adorno's notion of reification as an exceptional form of social pathology rooted in problems of recognition is complex and controversial, and I will not take up the specifics of those arguments here.[10] My point is rather to underscore what I have called "the long goodbye" of critical theory in Lukács's regard: the lengthy delay and the theoretical and practical distance traversed by the Frankfurt School before any direct reckoning with Lukács appeared possible. In Habermas's case, it waited until 1981, while for Honneth until the 1990s and 2000s. By this point, the theoretical work of the Frankfurt School had been drastically redirected by Habermas, while its fraught relation to Marxism had slackened to little more than a memory. Honneth treats Lukács's concept of reification exclusively as a (superseded) precursor of his own critical *moral* philosophy, which is indebted as much to Martin Heidegger, John Dewey, and Stanley Cavell as to Marx, Lukács, and Adorno.

Yet aside from Honneth's moral-philosophical reconstruction of the theory of reification, there has also been a recent wave of new exegetical scholarship on Lukács's thought as well as application of his work to new contexts including neo-liberalism, political ecology and environmentalism, cinema, contemporary art, and queer sexualities.[11] Additionally, publications and English translations of previously unknown works by Lukács have appeared, such as his response to the events of the Prague Spring of 1968, *The Process of Democratization* in 1991, his *A Defence of History and Class Consciousness: Tailism and the Dialectic* in 2000, and my own recent translation of Lukács's post–World War II Hungarian writings on culture in "people's democracy."[12] After a long lag following the political changes of 1989, new work on Lukács has also begun to appear in Hungary, which, it is to be hoped, will enrich the international discussion of Lukács as well.[13]

With the notable exception of Fredric Jameson's writing on realism and modernism, which sympathetically draws upon Lukács's later realism theory as well as a range of his early writings, much of the new Anglophone writing, both theoretical and applied, focuses heavily on Lukács's concept of reification and hence on (a few essays within) *History and Class Consciousness*. In this book, while Lukács's reification concept certainly appears in different contexts, I have nonetheless displaced *History and Class Consciousness* from the center of my discussion so as to tease out other threads of Lukács's work and related motifs in Frankfurt School critical writing; for example, the dramaturgical and musical-dramatic mediations of historical action or the question of democratization. In its reception of Lukács, the New Left, influenced by the Frankfurt School, selectively emphasized the theory of reification to the exclusion of other motifs of Lukács's work, a focus that in the Anglophone world was further narrowed by the limited number of works in English translation. Overemphasis of the theory of reification also derived from and reinforced the assumption that after 1930 Lukács had become a petrified Stalinist whose work henceforth—for the next forty years—could be of no further interest: a narrative in which Adorno, with his unwarrantedly authoritative "Extorted Reconciliation" essay, played no small role in elevating into dogma. Unquestionably, Lukács's post-1920s relation to Stalinism is uncomfortable and complex, with notable instances of both adaptive conformity and courageous criticism. In my view, however, it is long past time to call in question the polarized Cold War frameworks that marked the reception of Lukács by even such an otherwise discerning thinker as Adorno. I take inspiration from Jameson's view that new, revitalized readings of Lukács—and, I would add, of Frankfurt School's theory and criticism as well—are possible by engaging with a more ample corpus of writings beyond the playlist of theoretical greatest hits. We can, as Jameson suggests, begin to sketch a new "picture of Lukács that is . . . less Stalinist, dogmatic, and one-dimensional" than we have possessed till now.[14] But before opening a new horizon, we must close an old one, taking "the problematic to its limits" by retracing the long goodbye of infelicitous encounters between Lukács and the Frankfurt School, and particularly his collisions with Adorno.

Passages in a Long Goodbye

In May 1923, a gathering of socialist intellectuals took place in Geraberg, Germany, for a Marxist Study Week. It included, along with Lukács and the philosopher Karl Korsch, also the future members of the "Frankfurt School" (Institut für Sozialforschung), Karl August Wittfogel and Friedrich Pollock. The event was sponsored by Felix Weil, who would bankroll the founding of the Institut and bring on its first director, Carl Grünberg. Weil also financed the leftist Malik Verlag, run by Wieland Herzfeld, which had earlier published the Berlin Dadaist pamphlet *Every Man His Own Football* and the magazine *The Bankruptcy*, and subsequently, after the Dada tempest had cooled, also Lukács's *History and Class Consciousness* in 1923. Herzfeld's brother John Heartfield, who had put together the famous Dada photomontage of the football-everyman, designed the sober modern typography for Lukács's historic work of Marxist philosophy. Grünberg, for his part, was a Social Democratic academic who in 1910 had founded the journal *Archiv für die Geschichte des Sozialismus und der Arbeiterbewegung* (Archive for the History of Socialism and the Worker's Movement). It would publish Lukács and close followers of him such as József Révai[15] and would, after a brief hiatus from 1930 until 1932, become the *Zeitschrift für Sozialforschung*, the Frankfurt School's house journal.

Rolf Wiggershaus points to the 1923 gathering in Geraberg as the embryonic form of the Frankfurt School itself:

> Almost half of the participants in the Geraberg meeting were later to be connected with the Institute of Social Research in one way or another. In fact, the meeting was clearly the "first seminar on theory" held by the Institute for Social Research, the most astonishing and momentous of Felix Weil's undertakings as a patron of the left.[16]

Yet while eagerly read by key figures of the Frankfurt School such as Adorno and Marcuse, Lukács would not be one of these Geraberg attendees invited into the offices of the Institute (though he did publish one review in the *Zeitschrift für Sozialforschung* in 1933, on a newly published volume of Marx and Engels writings).[17] Rather, he would spend a quarter century in exile in Austria, Vienna, Berlin, and the Soviet Union before returning after World War II to an often precarious intellectual and political life in Budapest until his death in 1971. The Frankfurt School intellectuals would, of course, have their own trajectory of exile, taking them to Paris, London, New York, and Los Angeles before the return in 1949 of Horkheimer and Adorno to Frankfurt and the reestablishment—on the opposite side of the "Iron Curtain" from Lukács's Hungary—of the Institut für Sozialforschung the following year.

Lukács and Adorno, who would set the direction for post–World War II Frankfurt School theory, met in person only once, on June 14, 1925, in Lukács's quarters in Vienna, where he had been in exile since the collapse of the Hungarian Revolution in 1919 and where Adorno had come to study with Alban Berg after completing his dissertation on Edmund Husserl. The meeting, on Adorno's own account, did not go well. As he reported in brief to his teacher Alban Berg:

> In Vienna I immediately got into a discussion with the Marxist thinker Lukács . . . whom, as you know, I greatly revere; he made a strong impression upon me on a personal level, but in intellectual terms communication proved impossible, which of course pained me particularly in the case of Lukács, who has had a more profound intellectual influence on me than almost anyone else.[18]

To his friend and mentor Siegfried Kracauer, Adorno expounded at greater length his conversations with Lukács in his Hütteldorf abode, where, Adorno noted, Lukács lived "on the ground floor in a decidedly scruffy little room." Finding Lukács "the personification of the ideal of unobtrusiveness and also, of course, intangibility," Adorno writes, "I sensed at once that he was beyond any kind of possible human relationship during our conversation, which lasted over three hours."[19] Adorno promised to write up the conversation for Kracauer, which, he notes, was really like an interview. If he did send his protocol of the conversation, it has not been preserved. His letter, however, indicates some of the topics of discussion, including Lukács's disagreement with Ernst Bloch's review of *History and Class Consciousness*[20] and his vehement rejection of Kierkegaard, which, Adorno recounts, modulated to an attack on Kracauer and Adorno himself as his defender.

Ironically, given his own later history, Adorno appears rather insensitive to his interlocutor's conditions of exile. In his memoirs Victor Serge described the indigence of the Hungarian exiles from the counterrevolution in Hungary: "Several of [Béla Kun's] opponents were starving to death in Vienna. Of these, I held Georg Lukács in the greatest esteem ... He was engaged in writing a number of books that would never see the light of day."[21] In a diary entry of December 1919, three months after Lukács's escape from Hungary to Vienna, Béla Balázs wrote of his friend:

> The most heart-rending sight; deathly pale, drawn face, nervous and sad. Watched and followed, he walks around with a revolver in his pocket ... From time to time in conversation, like a bloody geyser his philosophy will shoot high, in testimony to its henceforth having further developed and expanded beneath his self-consciousness, yet this just props up, stirs up, and ruins his soul.[22]

And in his taped interviews with István Eörsi recorded from 1969 to 1971, Lukács described his straitened material circumstances in Vienna as follows:

> Int: What did you live on in Vienna?
> G.L.: I wrote this and that, sold old things—I still owned all sorts of things. Somehow we got by.
> Int.: There was at that time no party support ...
> G.L.: At the start for a short time, one could say that I was in a miserable state. Then, for three years I was the editor of the Russian embassy's trade magazine, *Torgovij Bülten*, for which I got a hundred dollars a month, and on that we lived well. In 1928 my father died ... and I finally managed to get hold of my inheritance. We lived on that until my departure for Russia.[23]

Adorno notes only Lukács's "scruffy little room," registering a certain muted distaste for the austerity of the exile's living conditions.

Nor does Adorno show greater understanding of Lukács's troubled relation to the communist movement as the Stalinist "Bolshevization" of the international parties progressed in the mid-1920s. At the time of Adorno's visit, the Bolshevik leader Grigory Zinoviev had the year before attacked Lukács and Karl Korsch as "ultra-left and theoretical revisionist" "professors" in a speech before the Fifth Congress of the Comintern, setting off the obligatory round of echoes in the communist press and related journals. As we now know, too, Lukács was at this time writing his unpublished defense of *History and Class Consciousness*, *Tailism and the Dialectic*, unpublished until 1996.[24] Adorno concludes his letter to Kracauer by noting that Lukács "did shock me ... when he declared to me that, in his conflict with the Third International, his opponents were in the right, in actual terms, and in dialectical ones all that was required of him was an absolute approach to dialectics. His human greatness and the tragedy of his reversal of fortune are rooted in this nonsensical error."[25] But if only from Ernst Bloch's review of *History and Class Consciousness*, "Actuality and Utopia," in *Der Neue Merkur* early in 1924, Adorno might also have recognized that Lukács was under heavy pressure for the perceived heresies of *History and Class Consciousness* and that the personal and political stakes of those polemics were high. Bloch's review, which Adorno says Lukács repudiated, scornfully refers to Russians who, purporting to be philosophers, would act like dogs and sniff out garbage in Lukács's pages.[26] Lukács himself would remark in his autobiographical notes that when the matter came to a head in the International a few years later, "[P]olitically, an annihilating defeat. Danger: expulsion for the Comintern. [Karl] Korsch's fate. Impotence at a time when the fascist threat was at its greatest."[27]

Adorno's correspondent, Kracauer, may in fact have helped deepen his intellectual estrangement from Lukács following this disillusioning encounter, because of Kracauer's own increasingly negative view of Lukács. Kracauer had reviewed *Theory of the Novel* sympathetically in 1921,[28] but rejected *History and Class Consciousness* as idealist in its understanding of dialectics. In two long letters exchanged with Bloch, accordingly, Kracauer offered a stringent critique of Lukács's Marxism. In the first letter, from May 27, 1926, Kracauer writes that—

> L[ukács] ... has consciously refused the incorporation of facts indicated by theology on the basis of his conception of our current situation in the dialectical process, as I know from the conversations of my friend Wiesengrund [Adorno] with him. ... Now, he has indeed picked up an idealism that has run out and run empty, but he has not transcended it. ... Instead of saturating Marxism with realities [*Realien*], he brings to it the spirit and metaphysics of a tapped-out idealism. ... Rudas and Deborin, as horribly shallow as they are, unconsciously are right in much that they say against Lukács.[29]

Parenthetically, Adorno would repeat this judgment by Kracauer forty years later in *Negative Dialectics*, even repeating the ironic rhetorical twist of taking the side of Lukács's opponents against him, which in his 1925 letter to Kracauer, we may recall, he dismissed as Lukács's "nonsensical error." "There is a good deal of irony," Adorno writes in 1966, "in the fact that the brutal and primitive functionaries who more than forty years back damned Lukács as a heretic, because of the reification chapter in his important *History and Class Consciousness*, did sense the idealist nature of his conceptions."[30]

On June 29, 1926, Kracauer resumed his discussion of Lukács with Bloch. He notes that in the meantime he has had the opportunity to discuss Lukács with Korsch, who, he claims, agrees with Kracauer's arguments against Lukács and is only holding back his own criticisms publicly on tactical grounds; just two years earlier, Korsch had positively reviewed *History and Class Consciousness* in *Die Internationale*.[31] Kracauer grants one positive aspect of Lukács's book, his method, about which he notes:

> I affirm his connection to our factically given spiritual situation. In that, he meets the demands of the real dialectic, in that he takes up idealism itself and in essence allows no other terminology than the idealistic and to a modest extent the materialistic. His banishment of theological vocabulary is certainly very profoundly intended. If the contents to which theological thinking directs itself are present in his work . . . they have to be able to be presented without any mythological vocabulary. The question is only whether his works do this. I can . . . only to a very limited extent answer this question affirmatively.[32]

Kracauer concludes with a damning judgment, consigning Lukács to the company of the pre-Marxist Young Hegelians. Lukács's dialectic, writes Kracauer, "represents a step back with respect to Marx . . . L[ukács] is in some ways, of course finer and more profound, a Bruno Bauer redivivus."[33]

Adorno returned to the topic of Lukács with Kracauer in 1930 and, as in his face-to-face meeting with Lukács, to Kierkegaard, about whom Adorno was now writing his own *Kierkegaard: Construction of the Aesthetic*, published in 1933.[34] Adorno's study begins by dismissing the attempt to read Kierkegaard's philosophy as "poetic." Adorno quotes Lukács's *History and Class Consciousness* about how one-sided, false concepts can be brought to their true meaning by relating them dialectically to the totality—but attributes the passage only to an unnamed "contemporary materialist interpreter of Hegel" (4). He goes on to extrapolate from this concept of dialectical mediation his own methodological premise:

> Not even totality is required to confer on dialectical concepts the ability to reveal the content of phenomena. If, however, philosophy as "subjective" thought has renounced totality altogether, it is the newly emerging that is most likely to confer on it the questionable reputation of being poetic . . . As soon as this type of philosophy is tolerantly accepted as poetry, the strangeness of its ideas . . . is neutralized along with the seriousness of its claim. . . . Philosophy is thereby depreciated; poetry in philosophy means everything that is not strictly relevant.[35]

Adorno here already grapples with the methodological problems of the dialectic he would eventually formulate as "negative dialectics": a dialectics taking inspiration from both Walter Benjamin and Lukács, as he suggests in his letter to Kracauer, a non-totalizing dialectics that maintains a regulative orientation towards totality, so as to remain philosophy and not lapse into poetic pseudo-philosophy.[36] In his letter to Kracauer, however, Adorno heaps scorn on Lukács, perhaps in flattery of his friend's own negative view: "I have taken on Lukács, *Die Seele und die Formen*, in which there is a very poor essay about Kierkegaard, and *Geschichte und Klassenbewußtsein*, which leaves a shocking number of loose ends and diffuses a kind of Heidelberg local color in an unbearable fashion; it is only a step to Mannheim, most of all in the wholly abstract conception of the concept of ideology which cannot be handled in this schematic way of deducing it in idealistic terms" (140). Adorno finally does condescend to admit that "In spite of this there are a few outstanding passages in his work" (140). In a related connection, Adorno employed, along with Benjamin's allegory concept, the notion of "second nature" from Lukács's *Theory of the Novel*, for his 1932 lecture, "The Idea of Natural History"[37]—though notably not the controversial discussions of nature in *History and Class Consciousness*.[38] Robert Hullot-Kentor has argued that the concepts Adorno explored in this lecture were eventually integrated into Adorno's revision of the Kierkegaard manuscript for publication—yet he never published the lecture itself during his lifetime.[39]

Along with Kracauer, Adorno's other senior mentor Max Horkheimer may also have discouraged him from more openly recognizing his intellectual debts to Lukács. Adorno had corresponded with Sohn-Rethel beginning in 1936, and in 1937, along with Benjamin, met with him in Paris for theoretical conversations, one of which Adorno reported to have extended for seven hours.[40] Adorno was enormously impressed with Sohn-Rethel and confessed to him in a letter of November 17, 1936 that their correspondence had moved him no less than his first encounter with Benjamin's work in 1923.[41] He might have added, of course, that he had been similarly moved by Lukács, when, in his teens, Adorno had read *Theory of the Novel*. As Kracauer testified to Leo Lowenthal, along with Kracauer himself, Lukács had become his young protégé's intellectual master.[42] Adorno now sought to persuade Horkheimer to support Sohn-Rethel's work and publish it in the Institute's journal. However, after Horkheimer and Marcuse had reviewed Sohn-Rethel's exposé, Horkheimer sent Adorno a harsh critique, including his detection of "an undigested memory of the phenomenon of reification, which Sohn-Rethel has retained from reading Lukács."[43]

Sohn-Rethel's specific appropriation of Lukács's reification concept, diverging in important ways from *History and Class Consciousness*, became consequential in Sohn-Rethel's eventual displacement of Lukács in Adorno's subsequent thinking. In his "Paris Exposé," written March–April 1937 and entitled "Towards the Critical Liquidation of Apriorism: A Marxist Investigation," Sohn-Rethel wrote:

> We have in common with Georg Lukács the application of Marx's concept of fetishism to logic and epistemology ... We differ from him in that we do not conclude from the conditioning of rational thought through reification and exploitation that this thinking is merely false consciousness. Neither logic nor reification will, with the elimination of exploitation, that is, in a classless society, disappear, even if they will also be altered in a way that we cannot anticipate.[44]

In addition, Sohn-Rethel rejected Lukács's explanation of reification as a phenomenon traceable to the capitalist commodity fetish and instead linked it to much older forms of direct exploitation: "The historical origin of reification is exploitation. The product of work originally becomes a thing not as commodity but as the object of direct, one-sided appropriation" (195). Sohn-Rethel's projection of reification back to early class societies (he refers, for example, to the ancient Egyptian rulers' taxation of their subjects) and his derivation of it from pre-capitalist forms of domination lent theoretical fodder to Adorno and Horkheimer's *Dialectic of Enlightenment*, which traced the genesis of contemporary total reification far back to archaic forms of mastering nature through myth.

Adorno, for his part, also saw in Sohn-Rethel a congenial critique of idealism that did not depend on the non-philosophical externality of practice—the revolutionary activity of the working class—as both Marx and Lukács had demanded. In his enthusiastic letter to Sohn-Rethel of November 17, 1936, Adorno writes: "I believe now with certainty what for a long time I took on with my attempt: that we will succeed in concretely blowing up idealism: not through the 'abstract' antithesis of praxis (as still with Marx), but rather out of the antinomic nature of idealism itself."[45] Already early in his intellectual career, Adorno thus affirms the methodological bracketing of Marxism's moment of practice, in order to draw out more profoundly the immanent dialectical contradictions of philosophical systems of thought and, correlatively, of works of art and literature as well. In fact, in seeking to reestablish strictly *immanent* philosophical parameters to critique rather than open them out onto praxis, Adorno recurs to the early, pre-Marxist Lukács, for whom, as Alberto Asor Rosa noted, heightened consciousness of irreconcilable contradictions and the loss of a worldly space of practice in which to resolve them are constitutively intertwined. "The concept of bourgeois totality is founded on the concept of loss," Asor Rosa writes, "and is indissociable from it. Also, thus, the totality in the bourgeois universe can do nothing but reproduce the conditions under which its actualization is *materially* impossible."[46] The young Lukács's self-conscious diagnosis of the tensions within subjectivity against a world that appears to allow no practical way forward or out—captured in his characterizations of the poet Endre Ady as a religious poet without religion and a revolutionary in a country without the possibility of revolution (discussed in the next chapter)—is adopted by Adorno as axiomatic for his work from the 1930s on.

Fighting Words: Lukács and Adorno

As with the early Lukács, this orientation leads Adorno especially to problems of aesthetic form, which, along with philosophy, constitutes for him one of the sole spaces for critical practice left in this world of "absolute sinfulness," as Lukács puts it in *Theory of the Novel*. Art allows the externalization of the irreconcilable contradictions between the individual and a reified, alien world. Insofar as Adorno early on diagnosed a regression of Lukács's thought under the shadow of official Communism, he raised Lukács's pre-Marxist writings as the standard from which Lukács himself had retreated. This is explicit in Adorno's overrated polemic "Extorted Reconciliation," directed against Lukács's 1957 *Wider den misverstandenen Realismus* (in English, *The Meaning of Contemporary Realism*), in which Lukács attacked the "ideology of avant-gardism," criticized the schematism of current socialist realism, and notoriously parried Thomas Mann off against Franz Kafka. In response, Adorno accuses Lukács of applying a double standard of judgment to literature, alternating between consistent application of standards of artistic quality and standards of conformity to a philosophy of history in which socialist realism as a whole, if not in its individual instances, must necessarily constitute a higher form of literature than its precursors. With respect to modernist literature, Adorno writes, however, that—

> once [Lukács] explains that solitude is inevitable . . . and at the same time . . . becomes aware of its objective illusory character, then the inference is compelling . . . that when the solitary consciousness reveals itself in the literary work to be the hidden consciousness of all human beings, it has, potentially, to sublate itself. This is precisely what we see in works that are genuinely avant-garde. They become objectified through unqualified monadological immersion in their own formal laws, that is, aesthetically, and thereby mediated in their social basis as well.[47]

For Adorno, artistic objectification of this dialectic precludes direct social effect—indeed, it *demands* that the artist carry on her practice as if any other socially meaningful action beyond artistic form-giving were impossible. Adorno particularly rejects any organized *political* intervention to mitigate the total reification of society. Yet as I discuss later, Adorno also restricted authentic artistic activity to a limited set of individual artists, works, and media, thus leaving out of consideration much of the twentieth-century avant-gardes' explosive pursuit of new publics, media, and modes of action through art.

It has long been a matter of belief among readers of Adorno that "Extorted Reconciliation" offers a definitive critique of the later Lukács. Even the usually contrarian Slavoj Žižek pronounces gleefully that "Adorno was fully justified in sarcastically designating . . . Lukács as someone who misread the clatter of his chains for the triumphant march forward of World Spirit,"[48] and more generally suggests that after about 1930, characterized as Lukács's "personal Thermidor," he wrote nothing more worth reading or thinking about. I believe, on the contrary, that "Extorted Reconciliation" is one of Adorno's least insightful essays, not least because it is marred by his near-complete unwillingness to read or consider Lukács's actual views. Undoubtedly, Lukács's short book is flawed by many weak arguments and questionable critical judgments, which gives Adorno ample opportunity to provide correction and wag a schoolmasterly finger at the stylistic lapses in Lukács's awkward prose. (Lukács himself once quipped that he recognized literature by the secret criterion of its being that which he could not himself write.) But about Adorno's essay, I am tempted to turn around Lukács's much-quoted maxim that even if all of Marx's individual theses proved wrong one would not need to renounce Marx's method, to say that on the contrary even if all of Adorno's arguments against Lukács proved to be correct, his misrepresentation of Lukács's basic assumptions and methods remains painfully wrong. Lukács's argument, in any case, is by no means as vulgar and apologetic as Adorno made it out to be, nor beyond the pale of serious discussion and debate.

From the start Adorno ignores the considerable upheaval in the East Bloc after the death of Stalin, including the glaring fact of the 1956 uprising in Hungary. He assumes a Cold War view of state socialism as totalitarian and thus incapable of significant historical change, a situation for which he takes Lukács's text to be the hapless mouthpiece.[49] Moreover, as Žižek points out (despite his wholesale endorsement of "Extorted Reconciliation"), the Frankfurt School on the whole was marked by an "almost total absence of theoretical confrontation with Stalinism . . . in clear contrast to its permanent obsession with Fascist anti-semitism"

("Georg Lukács as the Philosopher of Leninism," 157). Including Marcuse's 1958 study *Soviet Marxism*, which Žižek accurately characterizes as negligible, there is no Frankfurt School analysis of the Soviet Union comparable to Franz Neumann's magisterial analysis of the Nazi state in his 1942 book *Behemoth: The Structure and Practice of National Socialism* nor, beyond the Frankfurt School, with the historical breadth and theoretical boldness of Hannah Arendt's *Origins of Totalitarianism*.[50] Similarly, Kracauer's proposed study of "totalitarian propaganda"—a project commissioned by the Institut für Sozialforschung in 1936–37 and hence concurrent with the Moscow trials, though eventually rejected for publication—was to have dealt exclusively with Italian and German fascism; there was no hint of extending the concept of totalitarianism comparatively to Stalin's USSR, as was typical in Cold War totalitarianism theory.[51] Adorno, who was pushing the reluctant Horkheimer to pursue the project, wrote Kracauer of his personal interest, implying also his approval of its delimited focus and scope: "A work about propaganda and the problem of today's masses—between us!—has in any case for a long time belonged to my program."[52]

Žižek goes on to suggest that Stalinism remained a traumatic topic for the Frankfurt School, since it too openly touched the wound of the unresolved relation of its theoretical commitments to any realization through political practice. Vagueness about the actual history, social psychology, and cultural products of state socialist societies allowed the Frankfurt School to maintain its implicit sympathy with Western liberal anti-communism without dispelling its "radical aura" of leftist critique ("Georg Lukács as the Philosopher of Leninism," 158). Žižek's impolite suggestion helps, in fact, to understand better both the vehemence of Adorno's denunciations of Lukács and their distortions, which in places are no less glaring than those of Rudas or Deborin back in the day. For Adorno, Lukács presented the uncomfortable spectacle of dissent and change, of historicity, *within* the communist bloc, belying the ahistorical Cold War mythology on which Adorno uncritically depends. Adorno reacted defensively to Lukács, mimetically adopting, we might say, the very style of the aggressive functionary he feared.

The preface to *The Meaning of Contemporary Realism* itself bears poignant testimony to the historicity of Lukács's own writing. There he remarks that he had begun composing the text back in September 1956 and was only able to complete it in April 1957. In between, of course, the 1956 uprising had interceded, leading to Lukács's arrest and transportation to Romania after the fall of Imre Nagy's reform-communist government. Lukács was released and returned to Budapest only months later on April 11 1957, after which he got to finishing his preface![53]

The eventual trial and execution of Nagy and his closest associates in 1958 still lay ahead, creating an ongoing atmosphere of uncertainty and danger for the seventy-two-year-old Lukács.

Lukács's book reflected his increasingly overt critique of Stalinism, including its literary manifestations in the dictates of socialist realism. It also, however, explicitly directed his conception of literary realism not, as Adorno claims, to "photographically" reproducing the Soviet status quo, but rather towards the politics of the international peace movement within a nuclear-armed Cold War. Lukács takes up in his book the aspiration to "peaceful coexistence" between the socialist and capitalist countries put forward by Khrushchev in February 1956 at the Twentieth Congress of the Communist Party of the Soviet Union, the same that heard Khrushchev's "secret speech" exposing the personality cult and crimes of Stalin. Khrushchev's attempt to reorient Soviet domestic and foreign policy was a key factor in the Sino-Soviet split, which led the Soviet leader to cancel deliveries of atom bombs to China because of fears that Mao's desire to retake Taiwan might provoke a war.

In 1963, Lukács himself wrote "Reflections on the Sino-Soviet Split," in which he continues to uphold the Twentieth Congress's historical importance, emphasizing above all its contribution to de-Stalinization and the avoidance of nuclear war. Lukács even writes the following parenthetical remark, reminding readers of the connection he had made in *The Meaning of Contemporary Realism* between pessimistic literary worldviews and the disabling of resistance to war:

> It would be interesting to inquire, in those cases where the Chinese position evokes sympathy among certain small groups of the Western intelligentsia, whether their position is always really founded upon politics only or whether it is not perhaps founded also upon that response to reality which largely sustains the popularity of such contemporary authors as Beckett. Well worth the while in its own right as this question is, we cannot pursue it here.[54]

Although this remark is unwittingly hilarious in context for its obsession with poor Beckett, we should recall that at its writing in 1963, Lukács could have known nothing yet of the later Maoist follies of the *Tel Quel* avantgardists, nor seen the situationist graffiti that designated Jean-Luc Godard "le plus con des suisses pro-Chinois" (the dumbest of the pro-Chinese Swiss), nor savored the Beckett criticism of the former "Marxist-Leninist" Alain Badiou.[55] In light of these later developments, I am tempted to suggest, after Adorno, that in Lukács's criticism "only the exaggerations are true."

Reorientation away from Stalinism and towards peaceful coexistence would entail, Lukács argues, a fundamental shift in the context of

Marxist critique as well. While the struggle of socialism and capitalism may in the long run remain formative, the "new principle determining human alliances" must be the antithesis of war and peace. Along with the more obvious reasons—such as the threat of "mutually assured destruction" through nuclear weapons—Lukács believed that as long as the communist and capitalist blocs stood on a permanent war footing, the possibility of reforming and democratizing state socialism remained very slender. (More dubiously, he would also retrospectively justify his opposition to Trotsky in 1930s on the same basis, that Trotsky's continuing calls for world revolution would have provoked war and invasion of the Soviet Union.) Lukács thus seeks to diagnose cultural conceptions and attitudes towards the current moment that support action towards peace or, in contrast, help discourage and disable such action. Towards a new sort of Popular Front alliance fostering solidarity among individuals and movements dedicated to averting war, Lukács suspends Marxism's traditional accent on class-based ideological conflict in favor of new, alliance-based orientations of social action (a position that may also have been motivated by his need, after his release from Romania, to avoid anything smacking of direct party politics):

> [T]he polarization of opinion brought about by the Peace Movement is not without its ideological elements. But these elements are ideological only in the narrow sense of the word. They are simply the common denominator which people of differing, even opposed, attitudes of mind must share if they are determined to act together. It may imply no more than a superficial awareness of certain problems and a practical reaction to them. This awareness itself may be expressed in terms of different, even contradictory, philosophical or religious systems.[56]

Adorno, for his part, completely ignores Lukács's intention to identify and strengthen practical action-orientations in the context of the Peace Movement, which included the communist-founded World Peace Council, of which Bertrand Russell (who had lobbied on behalf of Lukács's release) was the president; and the proximate establishment of the British Campaign for Nuclear Disarmament in November 1957. In fact, the whole question of peace and war goes without any explicit mention in Adorno's essay. Instead, Adorno spends considerable time harping on Lukács's supposed failure to recognize that art is different from, indeed "antithetical to," empirical reality (which Adorno tendentiously equates with "the status quo") because of its intrinsic quality of semblance ("Extorted Reconciliation," 224). Adorno even marshals his philosophical arch-enemy Heidegger against Lukács, arguing that art manifests its "aesthetic difference" from existence, "in analogy to a current philosophical expression"—that is, to the ontological difference between Being and beings that Heidegger explicated in *Sein und Zeit*.⁵⁷ He suggests that Lukács fails to understand that art mediates empirical reality with subjective intentions, which lends it an "autonomous constitution." Lukács is thus, Adorno argues, guilty of reducing art to readymade sociological theses:

> Lukács simplifies the dialectical unity of art and science so that it becomes a pure identity, as though works of art merely anticipated something perspectivally which the social sciences then diligently confirmed. What essentially distinguishes the work of art as knowledge *sui generis* from scientific or scholarly knowledge is that nothing empirical remains unaltered, that the contents become objectively meaningful only when fused with subjective intention. (227)

Lukács, however, expounds at length his theory of creative subjectivity and its mediation by the objectivity of the artwork, focusing on the formative process by which a given author becomes capable of creating an artistically authentic work. He notes that while "subjective aim and objective achievement" may diverge, this divergence "is not something abrupt and irrational, a distinction between two metaphysical entities. Rather it is part of the dialectical process by which a creative subjectivity develops, and is expressive of that subjectivity's encounter with the world of its time (or possibly of its failure to come to terms with that world)" (*The Meaning of Contemporary Realism*, 54). The key mediating moment for Lukács, however, is the writer's commitment to a "teleological pattern of his own life," which forms the principle of the "selection and subtraction" from its historically factitious materials and "constitutes the most intimate link between a writer's subjectivity and the outside world" (55). As I argue in Chapter 3, this teleological remediation of experience finds its model in drama, as Lukács argued in his early drama theory; he subsequently extended these dramaturgical categories to his realist conception of the novel as well. The selective/subtractive reordering of the writer's life and experience in light of a teleological goal represents a "dialectical leap from the profound inwardness of subjectivity to the objectivity of social and historical reality" (55). Lukács is careful to underscore that this ordering teleology should not be understood as a narrowly ideological perspective or political outlook to be represented, but rather as a broad orientation towards the future that projects the author's subjective vision beyond her immediate understanding of everyday events and the contemporary scene (56–57). Given the connection of *The Meaning of Contemporary Realism* to the politics of peaceful coexistence in the Cold War context, Lukács implies that commitment to action for peace might constitute such a formative teleology for otherwise ideologically diverse contemporary authors, allowing subjective experiences and historical objectivity to be mediated in authentically new ways.

One can, of course, question whether Lukács's theory of authorial subjectivity is adequate, or whether he applies it consistently in his various interpretations and judgments of works. But to ascribe to him a reductive sociologism that recognizes neither subjective authorial intentions nor the special semblance-reality of the artwork—a view that Adorno steadfastly asserts throughout his essay—appears simply a failure to read and an instance of the very stereotypical sloganizing he diagnoses in Lukács. Adorno's uncharacteristically crude handling of Lukács's work is, as he himself suggests, rooted in fear: fear of a regression to barbarism already in train. Adorno leaves unresolved whether this threatening barbarism should be understood as the traditional variety of uncultured non-Europeans knocking at the gates of Europe or as a more abstract barbarism of the collapse of theory itself, under the boot of a practice too urgently concerned with staving off late-civilizational disaster:

> It remains an open question whether the regression that one senses in Lukács ... is an objective expression of the shadow that the underdeveloped nations throw across the more developed ones, which are already beginning to align themselves with the former; or whether it reveals something of the fate of theory itself—a theory that is not only wasting away in terms of its anthropological presuppositions, that is, in terms of the intellectual capacities of the theoreticians, but whose substance is also objectively shriveling up in a state of existence in which less depends on theory than on a practice whose task is identical to the prevention of catastrophe. ("Extorted Reconciliation," 235)

Though Adorno does not rule out that the regression of theory may be blamed on the ethnicized bearers of intellectual underdevelopment to the developed nations of the world,[58] he appears inclined to assign guilt to practice itself, to social action such as that urged by Lukács in the cause of peace. Practice appears as theory's misfortune, puncturing its dialectical immanence and rendering it incapable of keeping its distance from the contingencies of contemporary history. As Adorno presents it, practice is not the necessary complement to theory, but rather its looming *catastrophe*.

Hotel Grand Abyss?

This formulation is consistent with others that Adorno put forward subsequently, including in *Negative Dialectics* and in his late "Marginalia to Theory and Practice," which was directly focused on the question of the relation of theory and practice to one another. The opening paragraph of *Negative Dialectics* famously reverses Marx's eleventh thesis on Feuerbach to reassert the necessity of philosophy's interpretation of the world. "A practice indefinitely delayed is no longer the forum for appeals against self-satisfied speculation," Adorno wrote. "It is mostly the pretext used by executive authorities to choke, as vain, whatever critical thoughts the practical change would require."[59] In the latter essay, Adorno conceives practice as a negative epistemological moment within theory itself, a phantom presence that can manifest itself only symptomatically, through a significant, if risky, overestimation of the particular: "Praxis . . . appears in theory merely, and indeed necessarily, as a blind spot, as an obsession with what is being criticized. . . . This admixture of delusion, however, warns of the excesses in which it incessantly grows."[60] More than any moralizing about bourgeois comfort that Lukács injects into his condemnation in 1962 of Adorno as a resident of the "Hotel Grand Abyss"[61]—a phrase that dates back as far as an unpublished essay of Lukács from 1933 and that he associated originally with Schopenhauer in *The Destruction of Reason*[62]—it was unquestionably this fundamental difference on the question of practice that motivated Lukács's intemperate designation. Indeed, Lukács probably included this swipe at Adorno in his preface to the 1962 reissue of *Theory of the Novel* precisely because he perceived that Adorno's stark separation of dialectical thought and artistic forms from the domain of collective action reprised a position he himself had earlier exhaustively explored and abandoned.

Jameson has noted the pedagogical aim of much of Lukács's later work. Lukács conceived of his criticism as an aid to orienting writers and other intellectuals in the public sphere. He wanted to help educate the younger generations for anti-fascism, popular democracy, and ultimately, socialism. As Jameson suggests,

> one of the ways that one has to look at Lukács's life work is as a contribution to socialist pedagogy . . . [H]e was not merely making critical judgments or writing literary criticism, but he was thinking about what in Ernst Bloch's rather different terms one talks about as the use of the heritage, *das Erbe*, and the role that that should play in socialist formation, socialist education.[63]

I would likewise argue that the most consequential matter at issue between Lukács and Adorno was not the ad hominem questioning who had a more comfortable apartment or who enjoyed better food and wine; nor even was it their more principled clash over the relative merits of modernism and realism. Rather, the pivotal issue of their debate was how they conceived the relation of critique and pedagogy, the function they ascribed to a critical education that neither believed, it is worth underscoring, was being realized in their respective societies. Underlying their heated polemic was a quieter and more serious argument about the educative function of culture and critique. We can sum up the fundamental terms of that debate as the confrontation of two conceptions of education, which literary criticism and theoretical reflection should serve: "education into maturity," which Adorno advanced with both Kantian and Weberian accents,[64] or education as preparation for historical action, as Lukács after his turn to Marxism persistently believed. We still stand today before a more dialectical answer to that unresolved question dividing them.

Star Friendship: Lukács and the Frankfurt School

"We were friends and have become estranged. . . . There is probably a tremendous but invisible stellar orbit in which our very different ways and goals may be *included*. . . . Let us then believe in our star friendship even if we should be compelled to be earth enemies."
Friedrich Nietzsche, *The Gay Science*[65]

The chapters that follow this introduction take up the work of Lukács, Adorno, and other critical theorists in specific topical contexts which, I hope, may reveal new aspects of their thought left invisible by the "actually existing" record of their encounters in person and print. The problems I discuss are rooted in the theoretical and critical texts of Lukács and the Frankfurt School, along with their historical and discursive contexts, though sometimes perhaps in unanticipated configurations. Yet however thickly I immerse my observations in the original texts and contexts, I do intend for them to illuminate more general theoretical issues concerning how aesthetics relate to history and utopia in this critical theory tradition. Ultimately, I view this book through Benjamin's and Adorno's notion of theoretical "constellations" constructed through discrete and detailed arguments, which across more comprehensive spans disclose larger patterns of conceptual convergence and difference indiscernible at more proximate scale. The major themes, including various concepts of utopia, the relations of theoretical critique to practice, the critical function of art, the dramaturgical mediation of history, problems of Stalinism and other forms of twentieth-century authoritarianism, and the question of democratization in both capitalist and socialist societies, unfold organically from issues raised in the first section, dealing with Lukács. Yet they also quickly segue onto unexpected terrains, including opera, musical kitsch, surrealist aesthetics, Sade and Fourier, post-socialist art, and political trials.

The first major section of the book following this introduction comprises three chapters on Lukács. In Chapter 2, I discuss the relations between the early Lukács and the early Bloch in their divergent conceptions of utopia and its connection with art. Both Lukács and Bloch pose in stark ways the relations between the "utopian" status of the artwork and explicitly religious hope for a coming redemption, highlighting the interaction between a projected horizon of the future in their philosophies of history and the particular conceptions of art in their aesthetics. Yet Bloch and the early Lukács do not offer compatible theories of art, despite a shared terminology of utopia. By focusing on the question of the *future* of the aesthetic—how does the aesthetic relate to the future and what sort of future does the aesthetic imply, foreshadow, or project?—I tease apart problematic threads of the general concept of art's utopian function in the work of these two key thinkers.

In Chapter 3, I discuss how, despite Lukács's renown as a theorist of the novel, it was in the apparatus of *drama* specifically that he discerned one of the most concrete, legible sites in which to grasp the dialectics of historical action in the formalized world of the artwork. By revealing the regulative anthropological conditions of human action, Lukács suggests, the drama also has a close proximity to the philosophy of history. I discuss three specific moments in Lukács's work in which he lays bare the dramaturgical underpinnings of his conception of historical action. The first is his early work on drama, especially his *Developmental History of Modern Drama* and his important essay on Paul Ernst in *Soul and Form*, "The Metaphysics of Tragedy." The second centers on Marx and Engels's critical remarks and correspondence with the German Social Democratic leader Ferdinand Lassalle about *Franz von Sickingen*, his five-act historical tragedy set in the German Peasant Wars and published in 1858. The final example is Lukács's major essay on the historical novel and historical drama, which dates from early in his Moscow years and is included in his important book on *The Historical Novel*.

Chapter 4 considers the complex relations of Lukács to visual art and aesthetics, from his early writings through his engagement with artistic politics in the post–World War II "people's democracy" transitional period and during the Stalinist dictatorship. In one sense, Lukács seems untimely for contemporary art and aesthetics, as a philosopher and critic with an out-of-fashion aesthetic theory, justifying a canon of works opposed to even mainstream twentieth-century modernism, and deployed in the service of a cultural politics of Soviet and East Bloc socialism now historically discredited. Yet in another sense, Lukács's non-contemporaneity may been seen through the dispersed reception of his work, particularly across the Cold War East–West divide, in which different moments of Lukács's oeuvre were picked up and developed in divergent ways. Given these multiple contexts of reception, the author and thinker "György/Georg Lukács" could never be wholly contemporary with himself, but always signified a contradictory complex of current writing with belated reception of his earlier work.

The second major section of the book focuses on the work of Adorno. Chapter 5 takes up the question of surrealism as an avant-garde incompatible with Adorno's aesthetic theory and basic critical precepts, because of its violation of the immanence of the artwork and its projection of a general life-transforming praxis as its aim. Adopting Peter Bürger's seemingly paradoxical characterization of Adorno's aesthetics as "anti-avantgardist," I explore some of the implications of that stance for his *Aesthetic Theory*. Surrealism, I argue, is particularly notable as an instance of Adorno's more general anti-avantgardism, given its early significance in Adorno's formative arguments with Benjamin. I return to Adorno's "Looking Back on Surrealism," from the 1950s, as a key instance in which he diagnosed the avant-garde's "aging" and neutralization and go on to discuss surrealism's subsequent importance for younger critical theorists such as Bürger and Elisabeth Lenk, who after 1968 sought to renew the utopian spark between surrealism and critical theory, following its post-war eclipse under Adorno's long shadow.

Chapter 6 explores the interstices of Adorno's arguments about the Culture Industry, which were sharply critical of popular, light, low-genre music. In certain moments in his musical criticism, however, Adorno also surprisingly blurs and shades the gap between innovative experimental music and popular music, including commercial forms. He thus complicates his own apparently binary schema with a more nuanced dialectic between popular and technically advanced art forms, allowing us to see avant-garde and kitsch not merely dichotomously, but also as dialectical complements of one another: avant-garde *and* kitsch.

In Chapter 7, I discuss Adorno's and Alexander Kluge's writings on opera, which invite comparison with Lukács's historicizing treatment of drama. For Adorno, the question of opera's changing public was closely tied to problems of its *mediation*, including its evolving relations to media of production and reproduction, from live performance in opera houses to its dissemination through the technical media of radio, film, and recording. Adorno also considers opera's mediations within the framework of what we could characterize as an ecology of media, reflecting his postulate that the differentiation of media is a dynamic and historically developing process and that individual media receive their significance not just immanently, through internal formal developments, but also relationally in their collisions and interactions with one another.

Indebted to Adorno's arguments, Kluge's engagements with opera go beyond Adorno to trace out, in a critical-theory-inspired media archeology, the communicating vessels that connect opera and film culture with the traumas of historical moments in which they were composed and performed.

The third major section broadens the view beyond Lukács and Adorno to other topics and thinkers in critical theory. Chapter 8 considers a tradition of writing and theory that links perversion, utopia, and the philosophical critique of modern forms of rationality. Stimulated by the eighteenth- and early nineteenth-century writings of Sade, whose works were rediscovered and reinterpreted in the twentieth century, the Frankfurt School theorists Benjamin, Horkheimer, Adorno, and Marcuse, as well as the French writers Blanchot, Bataille, and Klossowski, confronted the challenge put forward by Sade's works, sometimes juxtaposing them to the explicitly utopian writings of Fourier. This chapter explores the various configurations of perversion, utopia, and the critique of reason that these writers advance, and also the implicit and explicit theories of perverse/utopian reading they adumbrate.

In Chapter 9, I take up the Frankfurt School's conception of interdisciplinary research and its relation to interdisciplinary research in the humanities and interpretative social sciences today. I focus particularly on the case study of an explicitly interdisciplinary project of the Institut für Sozialforschung published in 1936 as *Studien über Authorität und Familie*, which engaged a wide range of expertise across disciplines and demonstrated the methodological implications of the pre–World War II Frankfurt School's vision of interdisciplinary research. In the latter part of the chapter, I depart from the Frankfurt School framework to consider a contemporary counterpoint to the Frankfurt School's interdisciplinary study of authoritarianism: the post-socialist musealization of "totalitarianism" and terror by digital artist George Legrady (*An Anecdoted Archive of the Cold War*, 1993) and film designer and architect Attila F. Kovács (Budapest's House of Terror, 2002).

Chapter 10 concludes the book with an extended look at a traumatic historical episode from the 1930s: the falsifications of legality perpetrated by Stalin's regime in the show trials of the 1930s, and the concomitant justifications given by American liberals at the time for accepting or remaining agnostic about the "facts" put forward in the Soviet courts and communist press as evidence of an infamous Trotskyite conspiracy. I constellate original sources from the Moscow trial protocols; documents of the Dewey Commission's fact-finding trial of Leon Trotsky; editorials and reports from the contemporary press; relevant writings by John Dewey, Trotsky, and Sidney Hook; the 1961 study *Political Justice: The Use of Legal Procedure for Political Ends* by the Frankfurt School legal scholar Otto Kirchheimer; Lukács's late writings on democratization; and writings by the contemporary philosophers Hilary Putnam and Axel Honneth on Dewey's conception of democracy, to shed light on this crucial event in the history of socialism and of the left internationally.

My conclusion takes up again Lukács's dramaturgical nexus of theatre and history at the end of the history of state socialism in Eastern Europe. The radio-drama *The Interview*—written in the 1980s by István Eörsi, Lukács's friend, translator, and, at the end of the philosopher's life as he was dying of cancer, also his interviewer—was first performed in 1989, concurrent with the accelerating political changes in the socialist bloc. Incorporating both documentary materials from historic interviews, personal memories, and fantasy conversations with Lukács even beyond his death, Eörsi reckons with the complex legacy of his master and mentor. Eörsi's play, however, goes beyond a personal settling of accounts. It dramatizes an unresolved work of mourning regarding that vision of the future to which Lukács had dedicated his life and work, and a retrying, one more time, of the "case of Lukács" in light of the end of socialism as it had to date "actually existed."

Notes

1. Georg Lukács, *Die Seele und die Formen* (Berlin: Egon Fleischel & Co., 1911), 33. This passage does not appear in the 1910 Hungarian original, but was added by Lukács in his German edition. Throughout this book I consistently prefer the German spelling of Lukács's name except when referring to Hungarian-language texts that utilize the Hungarian "György."
2. Axel Honneth, interview with Rüdiger Dannemann, "Auf Augenhöhe mit Heidegger," in *Georg Lukács und 1968: Ein Spurensuche*, ed. Rüdiger Dannemann (Bielefeld: Aisthesis Verlag, 2009), 262.
3. Honneth, "Auf Augenhöhe mit Heidegger," 263.
4. Jürgen Habermas, *The Theory of Communicative Action, Volume 1: Reason and the Rationalization of Society*, trans. Thomas McCarthy (Boston: Beacon Press, 1984), 339–99.
5. Axel Honneth, "A Fragmented World: On the Implicit Relevance of Lukács' Early Work," in *The Fragmented World of the Social: Essays on Social and Political Philosophy*, ed. Charles Wright (Albany: State University Press of New York, 1995), 50–60.
6. Axel Honneth, *Reification: A New Look at an Old Idea*, with Judith Butler, Raymond Geuss, and Jonathan Lear, ed. Martin Jay (Oxford: Oxford University Press, 2008).
7. For Honneth's critique of Adorno and the early Frankfurt School more

generally, see "Critical Theory" and "From Adorno to Habermas" in Honneth, *The Fragmented World of the Social*, 61–91 and 92–120.
8. Honneth, "A Fragmented World," 58.
9. Axel Honneth, *Pathologies of Reason: On the Legacy of Critical Theory*, trans. James Ingram (New York: Columbia University Press, 2009).
10. Along with the responses in Honneth's book by Butler, Geuss, and Lear, see also: Andrew Feenberg, "Reification and Its Critics," in *Georg Lukács Reconsidered: Critical Essays in Politics, Philosophy and Aesthetics*, ed. Michael J. Thompson (London: Continuum, 2011), 172–94; Timothy Hall, "Returning to Lukács: Honneth's Critical Reconstruction of Lukács' Concepts of Reification and Practice," in ibid., 195–210; Konstantinos Kavoulakos, "Reifying Reification: A Critique of Axel Honneth's Theory of Reification," in *Axel Honneth and Critical Theory of Recognition*, ed. V. Schmitz (London: Palgrave Macmillan, 2019), 41–68; Matthew J. Smetona, "Reification: A Defense of Lukács's Original Formulation," *Angelaki* 23/5 (2018): 32–47.
11. See, for example, Timothy Bewes, *Reification, or the Anxiety of Late Capitalism* (London: Verso, 2002); Kevin Floyd, *The Reification of Desire: Toward a Queer Marxism* (Minneapolis: University of Minnesota Press, 2009); *Georg Lukács: The Fundamental Dissonance of Existence: Aesthetics, Politics, Literature*, eds. Timothy Bewes and Timothy Hall (London: Continuum, 2011); *Georg Lukács Reconsidered*, ed. Thompson; Ian Aitken, *Lukácsian Film Theory and Cinema: A Study of Georg Lukács' Writing on Film, 1913–1971* (Manchester: Manchester University Press, 2012); Andrew Feenberg, *The Philosophy of Praxis: Marx, Lukács and the Frankfurt School* (London: Verso, 2014); Anita Chari, *A Political Economy of the Senses: Neoliberalism, Reification, Critique* (New York: Columbia University Press, 2015); *The Spell of Capital: Reification and Spectacle*, eds. Johan F. Hartle and Samir Gandesha (Amsterdam: Amsterdam University Press, 2017); Konstantinos Kavoulakos, *Georg Lukács: Philosophy of Praxis: From Neo-Kantianism to Marxism* (London: Bloomsbury, 2018); Richard Westerman, *Lukács's Phenomenology of Capitalism: Reification Revalued* (Cham, Switzerland: Palgrave Macmillan, 2019); Daniel Andrés Lopez, *Lukács and the Absolute* (Amsterdam: Brill, 2019); *Confronting Reification: Revitalizing Georg Lukács's Thought in Late Capitalism*, ed. Gregory R. Smulewicz-Zucker (Chicago: Haymarket Books, 2020); *Georg Lukács and the Possibility of a Critical Social Ontology*, ed. Michael J. Thompson (Chicago: Haymarket Books, 2020).
12. Georg Lukács, *The Process of Democratization*, trans. Susanne Bernhardt and Norman Levine (Albany: State University of New York Press, 1991); Georg Lukács, *A Defence of History and Class Consciousness: Tailism and the Dialectic*, trans. Esther Leslie (London: Verso, 2000); György Lukács, *The Culture of People's Democracy: Hungarian Essays on Literature, Art, and Democratic Transition, 1945–1948*, ed. and trans. Tyrus Miller (Amsterdam: Brill, 2013).
13. These include, for example, János Weiss, *Lukács Örökség: Helyzetfelmérés a kommunizmus bukása után* (Budapest: Gond-Cura Alapítvány, 2011); Tibor Szabó, *Lukács György: Az Autonóm Filozófus: Kritiká, Viták, Téoriák* (Budapest: Gondalat Kiadó, 2017); *A Forradalom Végtelensége:*

Lukács György Politka- és Tarsadalomelmélete, ed. Balázs Böcskei (Budapest: L'Harmattan, 2017); and Éva Fekete's new biography, *Lukács György: Késleltetett Életrajz* (Budapest: Pesti Kalligram, 2021).
14. Fredric Jameson, interview with Eva L. Corredor, in Corredor, *Lukács after Communism: Interviews with Contemporary Intellectuals* (Durham, NC: Duke University Press, 1997), 94.
15. See, for example, Lukács's reviews of Nikolai Bukharin's *Theory of Historical Materialism* and Karl August Wittfogel's *The Science of Bourgeois Society* in *Archiv für die Geschichte des Sozialismus und der Arbeiterbewegung* 11 (1925): 216–24 and 224–27. This same issue contained Révai's positive review of Lukács's *History and Class Consciousness* just following Lukács's two reviews, 227–36.
16. Rolf Wiggershaus, *The Frankfurt School: Its History, Theories, and Political Significance*, trans. Michael Robertson (Cambridge, MA: The MIT Press, 1994), 16.
17. Georg Lukács, review of Karl Marx and Friedrich Engels, *Werke und Schriften von Mai 1846 bis März 1848*, in *Zeitschrift für Sozialforschung* 2 (1933): 280–81. The most extensive study of Lukács's relation to the Frankfurt School is A.H. Dmitriev's Russian-language *Marksizm Bez Proletariata: Georg Lukach U Rannyaya Frankfurtskaya Shkola (1920–1930 e rr.)* [Marxism Without the Proletariat: Georg Lukács and the Early Frankfurt School (1920–1930s] (St. Petersburg: European University, 2004).
18. Theodor W. Adorno to Alban and Helene Berg, June 21, 1925, in Adorno and Berg, *Correspondence, 1925–1935*, ed. Henri Lonitz, trans. Wieland Hoban (Cambridge: Polity Press, 2005), 9.
19. Theodor W. Adorno to Siegfried Kracauer, June 17, 1925, in Adorno and Kracauer, *Correspondence 1923–1966*, ed. Wolfgang Schopf, trans. Susan Reynolds and Michael Winkler (Cambridge: Polity Press, 2020), 50.
20. Ernst Bloch, "Aktualität und Utopie: Zu Lukács' *Geschichte und Klassenbewusstsein*," in Bloch, *Philosophische Aufsätze zur objektiven Phantasie* (Frankfurt am Main: Suhrkamp Verlag, 1969), 598–621.
21. Victor Serge, *Memoirs of a Revolutionary*, trans. Peter Segwick and George Paizis (New York: New York Review Books, 2012), 220.
22. Béla Balázs, *Napló 1914–1923* (Budapest: Magvető Könyvkiadó, 1982), 353.
23. Georg Lukács, *Record of a Life: An Autobiography*, ed. István Eörsi, trans. Rodney Livingstone (London: New Left Books, 1983), 70. I have translated the quote from the Hungarian original, which differs somewhat from the English text: György Lukács, *Megélt Gondolkodás: Életrajz magnószalagon* (Budapest: Magvető Könyvkiadó, 1989), 174.
24. For Zinoviev's speech, see *Fifth World Congress of the Communist International: Abridged Report of Meetings Held in Moscow, June 17th to July 8th, 1924* (London: The Communist International, 1924), 37. For the Lukács debate, see Andrew Arato and Paul Breines, *The Young Lukács and the Origins of Western Marxism* (New York: The Seabury Press, 1979), 163–79; Lukács, *A Defence of History and Class Consciousness*; and Oskar Negt, "Marxismus als Legitimationswissenschaft. Zur Genese der stalinistischen Philosophie," in *Kontroversen über Dialektischen und*

Mechanistichen, ed. Oskar Negt (Frankfurt am Main: Suhrkamp Verlag, 1969), 7–48. For Lukács's main attackers, see Abram Deborin, "Lukács und seine Kritik des Marxismus," in *Arbeiterliteratur* 10 (1924): 615–40; and Ladislaus (László) Rudas, "Orthodoxer Marxismus?" *Arbeiterliteratur* 9 (1924): 493–505; Rudas, "Die Klassenbewußtseinstheorie von Lukács," *Arbeiterliteratur* 10 (1924): 669–97 and *Arbeiterliteratur* 12 (1924): 1064–1089.

25. Adorno to Kracauer, June 17, 1925, in *Correspondence*, 51. For further on this encounter of Lukács and Adorno, see Heinz Steinert, *Adorno in Wien: Über die (Un-)Möglichkeit von Kunst, Kultur und Befreiung* (Vienna: Verlag für Gesellschaftskritik, 1989), 159–60.
26. Bloch, "Aktualität und Utopie," 601.
27. Lukács, *Record of a Life*, 163.
28. Siegfried Kracauer, "Georg von Lukács' Romantheorie," *Neue Blätter für Kunst und Literatur* (October 4, 1921): 1–5.
29. Siegfried Kracauer to Ernst Bloch, May 27, 1926, in Bloch, *Briefe 1903–1975*, Bd. 1, eds. Karola Bloch et al. (Frankfurt am Main: Suhrkamp Verlag, 1985), 272–73.
30. Theodor W. Adorno, *Negative Dialectics*, trans. E.B. Ashton (New York: Continuum, 1983), 190.
31. Karl Korsch, "Über materialistische Dialektik," *Die Internationale* (June 2, 1924): 376–79.
32. Siegfried Kracauer to Ernst Bloch, June 29, 1926, in Bloch, *Briefe 1903–1975*, Bd. 1, 282.
33. Siegfried Kracauer to Ernst Bloch, June 29, 1926, in Bloch, *Briefe 1903–1975*, Bd. 1, 283.
34. Theodor W. Adorno, *Kierkegaard: Construction of the Aesthetic*, trans. Robert Hullot-Kentor (Minneapolis: University of Minnesota Press, 1989).
35. Ibid., 4.
36. Adorno to Kracauer, May 12, 1930, in *Correspondence*, 140.
37. Theodor W. Adorno, "The Idea of Natural History," trans. Robert Hullot-Kentor, *Telos* 60 (1984): 111–24.
38. See, for example, Georg Lukács, *History and Class Consciousness*, trans. Rodney Livingstone (Cambridge, MA: The MIT Press, 1971), 128 and 136.
39. For the connection of this essay to Adorno's Kierkegaard book, see Robert Hullot-Kentor, "Introduction to 'The Idea of Natural History'," *Telos* 60 (1984): 100.
40. Theodor W. Adorno to Max Horkheimer, December 15 1936, quoted in Theodor W. Adorno and Alfred Sohn-Rethel, *Briefwechsel, 1936–1969*, ed. Christoph Gödde (Munich: Edition Text + Kritik, 1991), 34.
41. Theodor W. Adorno to Alfred Sohn-Rethel, November 17, 1936, in Adorno and Sohn-Rethel, *Briefwechsel*, 32.
42. Siegfried Kracauer to Leo Lowenthal, quoted in Wiggershaus, 66.
43. Max Horkheimer to Adorno, quoted in Adorno and Sohn-Rethel, *Briefwechsel*, 40.
44. Alfred Sohn-Rethel, "Zur kritischen Liquidierung des Apriorismus: Eine Marxistische Untersuchung," in Sohn-Rethel, *Geistige und körperliche Arbeit: Zur Epistemologie der abendländische Geschichte* (Weinheim: VCH Acta humaniora, 1989), 157–58.

45. Adorno to Sohn-Rethel, November 17, 1936, in *Briefwechsel*, 32.
46. Alberto Asor Rosa, "Il Giovane Lukács Teorico dell'Arte Borgese," *Contropiano* 1 (1968): 72.
47. Theodor W. Adorno, "Extorted Reconciliation: On Georg Lukács' *Realism in Our Time*," in Theodor W. Adorno, *Notes on Literature, Volume 1*, trans. Shierry Weber Nicholsen (New York: Columbia University Press, 1991), 230–31.
48. Slavoj Žižek, "Georg Lukács as the Philosopher of Leninism," postface to Lukács, *A Defence of History and Class Consciousness*, 156.
49. Even Hannah Arendt admitted in her preface to the 1959 second edition of *The Origins of Totalitarianism* that the 1956 uprising "is important enough to require a reexamination of what we know, or think we know, about totalitarianism," and dedicated a lengthy epilogue to the topic. Hannah Arendt, *The Origins of Totalitarianism*, 2nd edition (New York: Meridian Books, 1958), xi and 480–510.
50. A partial exception is the work of Otto Kirchheimer, discussed in Chapter 10, who extensively analyzed the legal system of communist East Germany.
51. Siegfried Kracauer, *Totalitäre Propaganda*, ed. Bernd Stiegler (Frankfurt am Main: Suhrkamp Verlag, 2013). See also Kracauer, *Selected Writings on Media, Propaganda, and Political Communication*, eds. Jaeho Kang, Graeme Gilloch, and John Abromeit (New York: Columbia University Press, 2022).
52. Adorno to Kracauer, November 9, 1936, quoted in *Totalitäre Propaganda*, 319.
53. Arpad Kardarkay, *Georg Lukács: Life, Thought, and Politics* (Cambridge: Blackwell, 1991), 438.
54. Georg Lukács, "Reflections on the Sino-Soviet Split," trans. Lee Baxandall, in Lukács, *Marxism and Human Liberation: Essays on History, Culture and Revolution*, ed. E. San Juan, Jr. (New York: Delta Books, 1973), 77.
55. For detailed treatment of Maoism among the French intelligentsia, see Richard Wolin, *The Wind from the East: French Intellectuals, the Cultural Revolution, and the Legacy of the 1960s* (Princeton: Princeton University Press, 2010).
56. Georg Lukács, *The Meaning of Contemporary Realism* (London: Merlin Press, 1963), 15.
57. Ibid., 225. In an unpublished text entitled "Ad Lukács," Adorno criticizes Lukács's critique of Martin Heidegger, about whom Lukács had published "Heidegger Redivivus" in *Sinn und Form* in 1949. Adorno argues that the proper way to bring out the "political-social implications of the fascistic cult of being would be to develop them out of the determination of its own inconsistency. Instead . . . Lukács . . . takes up a reified standpoint in which the categories of being and consciousness appear unmediated and given in advance." See Theodor W. Adorno, "Ad Lukács," in Adorno, *Gesammelte Schriften* 20, ed. Rolf Tiedemann (Frankfurt am Main: Suhrkamp Verlag, 1986), 252. Lukács's essay appears in *Existentialismus oder Marxismus?* (Berlin: Aufbau-Verlag, 1951), 161–83.
58. Adorno blurts out this racially tinged fear less guardedly in his 1956 discussions with Max Horkheimer: "I have the feeling that, under the banner of Marxism, the East might overtake Western civilization. This would mean

a shift in the entire dynamics of history. Marxism is being adopted in Asia in much the same way as Christianity was taken up in Mexico at one time. Europe too will probably be swallowed up at some point in the future." See Theodor Adorno and Max Horkheimer, "Towards a New Manifesto?" *New Left Review* 65 (2010): 41.
59. Adorno, *Negative Dialectics*, 3.
60. Theodor W. Adorno, "Marginalia to Theory and Practice," in Adorno, *Critical Models: Interventions and Catchwords*, trans. Henry W. Pickford (New York: Columbia University Press, 1998), 278.
61. Georg Lukács, "Preface" (1962) to *Theory of the Novel*, trans. Anna Bostock (Cambridge, MA: The MIT Press, 1971), 22.
62. Georg Lukács, "Grand Hotel 'Abgrund'," manuscript text, MTA Lukács Archiv, http://real-ms.mtak.hu/21580/ (accessed December 28, 2021); Georg Lukács, *Die Zerstörung der Vernunft* (Neuwied am Rhein: Luchterhand, 1962), 219.
63. Jameson, in Corredor, *Lukács after Communism*, 90.
64. See Theodor W. Adorno, *Erziehung zur Mündigkeit: Vorträge und Gespräche mit Helmut Becker, 1959–1969*, ed. Gerd Kadelbach (Frankfurt am Main: Suhrkamp Verlag, 1970). Maturity for Adorno involves, among other things, resisting the false reconciliation of contradictions, a resistance maintained at the cost of subjective suffering. In this ethical imperative, he echoes the young Lukács, who, as Peter Bürger notes, upheld "mature manliness" as the ethical disposition of enduring "the modern world's loss of meaning." See "Essayismus und Ironie beim frühen Lukács," in Bürger, *Prosa der Moderne* (Frankfurt am Main: Suhrkamp Verlag, 1988), 420. See also, on this theme, David Owen, *Modernity and Maturity: Nietzsche, Weber, Foucault and the Ambivalence of Reason* (London: Routledge, 1994).
65. Friedrich Nietzsche, *The Gay Science*, trans. Walter Kaufmann (New York: Vintage Books, 1974), 225–26.

Part I

Georg Lukács

Chapter 2

Matthew, Mark, Lukács, and Bloch: From Aesthetic Utopianism to Religious Messianism

> The essayist . . . is a John the Baptist who goes out to preach in the Wilderness about another who is still to come. . . . And if that other does not come—is not the essayist then without justification?
> —Georg Lukács, 1910[1]

This chapter explores how concepts in aesthetics in the Lukácsian and critical theory traditions implicate broader notions of historical time and historicity. When we speak of "realism" and "modernism" or "art's utopian function" or the "artistic avant-garde," to make sense of such expressions, I would argue, we must seek to explicate the framework of time—the specific constellation of past, present, and future—in which artworks are thought to stand. I consider this question in relation to a particular historical case, that of the early Lukács and Bloch, focusing on the years from about 1910, the date of their first contact as well as of the publication of Lukács's essay collection *Soul and Form*, to about 1923, the publication date of *History and Class Consciousness* by Lukács and the second, significantly revised edition of Bloch's *Spirit of Utopia* (the first edition being in 1918).

My reasons for this focus are twofold. On the one hand, in Lukács's and Bloch's early work the relations between the status of the artwork as a utopian entity and religious hope for a coming redemption are posed in particularly stark, even extreme ways. So we can see in clear outline the interaction between a projected horizon of the future in their theo-philosophies of history and a particular conception of art in their aesthetics. On the other hand, Lukács's and Bloch's utopian conceptions of the artwork have, for different theoretical and political motives, been regularly conjoined, first by Bloch, then by the Budapest School followers of Lukács in the German-Hungarian context, by Michael Löwy's influential historical work in the French context, and in the theoretical and critical work of Jameson in the United States.[2]

Bloch himself set the tone for this identification in a well-known interview with Michael Löwy in which he strongly insists on the substantive unity of their views up until around 1921: "I was as much the apostle of Lukács as he was mine. There was no difference between us."[3] Yet the asserted connections between them are often very blurry or abstract. Thus for example in his otherwise penentrating article exploring the premise that Bloch and Lukács had *conflicting*, even antinomical "world-views," Sándor Radnóti concludes that "The final basis of the two philosophies—the rejection of the existing world . . . and the necessity to transcend the world—is the same."[4] Similarly, Thomas Bremer argues that for all their differences, Lukács and Bloch converge in their common rejection of a contemplative stance and their "basic conviction" that the present should be grasped as "becoming" and therefore changeable—an unimpeachable view, to be sure, but hardly of great critical value in understanding the relation of their ideas.[5] Despite a shared terminology of utopia, I would argue that Bloch and the early Lukács in fact offer incompatible theories of art and utopia even at the moment of their closest dialogue, and hence too, differing conceptions of art's relation to utopia. By posing emphatically the question of the *future* in the aesthetic—how does the aesthetic relate to the future, and what sort of future does the aesthetic imply, foreshadow, or project?—I believe we can begin to tease apart the problematic threads of this general concept of art's utopian function.

Historicity in Lukács's Aesthetic

One critic who early on highlighted the problem of historicity in relation to Lukács's work was Paul De Man, in a short essay on *Theory of the Novel* in *Blindness and Insight*. De Man noted that underlying Lukács's account of the historical changes in epic form is "a presupposition about the nature of historical time."[6] He sees Lukács's account as employing two contradictory frameworks of temporality, an existential-intentional temporality of the subject that registers itself in the narrative discontinuities and breaks of irony and a linear, continuous chronological flow that De Man claims Lukács sees as the essence of time. Through his focus on literary irony, De Man writes, Lukács came close to uncovering a more basic philosophical truth: the discontinuous, non-chronological nature of time. Yet Lukács was supposedly blind to his own insight, so that in writing literary history he fell back on what Heidegger calls the "vulgar" conception of time.

De Man bases his judgment, above all, on what he sees as the shortcomings of Lukács's chapter on Flaubert's *Sentimental Education*. By concentrating on the issue of time, De Man puts his finger on a crucial problem in interpreting Lukács's conception of aesthetics and its relation to his philosophy of history, whether religious-messianic as in his early work or Hegelian-Marxist and realist as in the later work. However, De Man's particular judgment of Lukács is in my view untenable. De Man isolates a few remarks that Lukács makes that suggest temporal continuity is the dominant principle of Flaubert's novel. In fact, he all but ignores Lukács's overall argument, which ascribes the artistic achievement of Flaubert's novel to its complex syncopation of discontinuity and temporal extension, particularly as memory and longing give temporal shape to the seemingly formless drift of the present that the characters experience.

Moreover, after Lukács's death in 1971, well after De Man published his essay, there was a major philological find that radically revised the view of the early Lukács: a suitcase of letters, diaries, notebooks, and manuscripts that had languished in a Heidelberg bank vault for over fifty years suddenly made its reappearance. These included manuscripts of Lukács's two attempts to write an aesthetics in Heidelberg during the 1910s, and his plans that revealed that the published text of the *Theory of the Novel* formed part of a much more ambitious philosophy of history that would have continued where *Theory of the Novel* had broken off: with the transcendence of novelistic form and the historico-philosophical world of the novel in the religious sphere adumbrated, in Lukács's view, by Dostoevsky.

Referring to these materials found in Heidelberg, I will mention three points on which De Man would surely have had to revise his view of *Theory of the Novel*. First, the chapter entitled "Historicity and Timelessness of the Artwork" in the *Heidelberg Philosophy of Art*, drafted between 1912 and 1914, reveals Lukács's rich, layered concept of artistic time and suggests how thoroughly critical of linear-chronological time he was in this period. Whatever the validity of Lukács's specific interpretation of *Sentimental Education*, when one sees the philosophical writing that accompanies its composition, it simply will not do to ascribe a crude notion of chronology to *Theory of the Novel*. In addition, in this same chapter of the *Heidelberg Philosophy of Art*, Lukács makes a careful methodological distinction between art history and philosophy of history of art. These have, he argues, not only different approaches, but even different objects. The temporal order given to the categories of the *philosophy of history* of the novel—which, crucially, is how Lukács characterized *Theory of the Novel*, not as literary history—must not be conflated with the empirical temporality of history. De Man, however, accuses Lukács of doing just that: conceiving the virtual succession of epic forms as an actual linear history by which one form of the novel succeeded its predecessor. Finally, the Dostoevsky notes reveal that far from being linear and chronological-objective in the sense that De Man suggests, Lukács's temporal conception of the philosophy of history at this time is likewise punctuated by radical breaks, subjective decisions and hesitations, and leaps from sphere to sphere referrable only to the non-conceptual, authentic acts of individual subjects. Properly speaking, his conception of historical time bears marks of both the existential temporality of Kierkegaardian decision and a messianic temporality dominated by the question of how human action might accelerate or delay redemption.

Mysticism and Messianism in the Early Lukács

The title of my chapter refers to a well-known anecdote recounted by Karl Jaspers in his *Heidelberg Memoirs* (and elsewhere by Helmut Plessner), about Lukács and Bloch during their years of study at Heidelberg starting in 1912. The posturing and fervor of these "messianic young men,"[7] as Max Weber's wife Marianne described them, moved the philosopher Emil Lask to quip, "What are the names of the four evangelists? Matthew, Mark, Lukács, and Bloch."[8] In the texts of both Bloch and Lukács in the years between 1910 and 1918, one indeed finds abundant evidence of their bent towards heterodox religiosity, from mysticism to interest in religious community to messianic-apocalyptic philosophies of history. Similarly, there is ample testimony from their contemporaries that both were strongly animated by religious ideas and desires. Thus, for example, Anna Lesznai wrote that "Bloch is a young man from Berlin who is so Talmudic that he verges on Catholicism."[9] The Hungarian-born art historian Arnold Hauser, describing Lukács's Budapest "Sunday Circle" that met between 1915 and 1918, reported that "Lukács ... was interested in philosophy and religion, having come back from Heidelberg a kind of mystic. ... The guardian saints of the group in those early times were Kierkegaard and Dostoevsky."[10] In an analogous vein, Lesznai and Tibór Gergely observed that the Sunday Circle gave a lot of attention to Dostoevsky and German mystics such as Meister Eckhardt, and that "the group had more in common with a religious meeting than with a political club: there was a ceremonial, quasi-religious tone to the meeting" ("Culture and Revolution," 59).

Let us take for a moment Lask's ironic designation of Lukács and Bloch at its word—an evangelist is a harbinger of good news, an "eu-angelos." In its religious sense, the evangel has a tropism towards the future, even when recounting a set of events that has happened in the past. The story recounted takes on its meaning in the light of a redemption yet to come; the story points towards the fulfillment of its promise. During their Heidelberg period, the promised redemption that Lukács and Bloch sought to prefigure was not, in the first instance, a proletarian revolution that would inaugurate humanity's entry into the realm of freedom, but rather a religious revolution that would bring about something like a Dostoyevskian religio-anarchic community of goodness, making unnecessary secular law and the state. Marianne Weber thus characterizes the orientation of Lukács and Bloch during the teens as follows:

> These young philosophers were moved by eschatological hopes of a new emissary of a extraworldly God, and they saw in a socialistic order of society founded on brotherhood the precondition of salvation. For Lukács, the dominance of this-worldly culture, above all aesthetic culture, represented something against God, "Luciferian" competition against God's effectiveness. But the complete development of this domain *should* take place, for the choice of the individual between it and the transcendent must not be made easier. The final struggle between God and Lucifer is still coming and depends on humanity's decision. The final goal is redemption *from and of* the world. Not, as for [Stefan] George and his circle: fulfillment *in it*.[11]

Weber accurately characterizes a number of features of Lukács's early thought. Two things to highlight for later discussion, however, are: 1) his rigorous *opposition* of the religious to the aesthetic, and 2) his articulation of a set of Kierkegaardian and neo-Kantian spheres of being that are coexistent but *essentially separate*. The inner-worldly sphere of the aesthetic, the transcendentally oriented but empirically realized realm of socialist ethics and politics, and the extraworldly religious sphere of redemption can come in contact only through a series of spiritual "leaps" or "decisions" that ultimately *confirm* their separation. Notably, during the heady days of the Hungarian Soviet Republic in 1919, Lukács's Marxist engagements with artistic and political questions still aimed towards the farther religious horizon of redemption, beyond the scope of the aesthetic and the ethico-political. As he noted in an interview with István Eörsi in 1971, almost at the end of his life, Lukács and his close comrades were dissatisfied that—

> the dictatorship had failed to take the giant strides we had expected towards that earthly paradise which we thought of as communism. When I say earthly

paradise, this must be understood in a very sectarian, ascetic way. There was absolutely no thought in our minds of a land flowing with milk and honey. What we wanted was to revolutionize the crucial problems of life.[12]

Lukács hoped in 1919 that the revolution would soon begin to abolish its own "provisional" political institutions and inaugurate a thoroughgoing transformation of life in its totality.[13]

As already mentioned, for many English-language readers of *Theory of the Novel*, even today it is little known that Lukács planned a third, uncompleted section of the book on Dostoyevsky, notes to which were found in a bank vault in Heidelberg along with other manuscripts left behind during World War I when he returned to Budapest.[14] As the basis of this third section of his study, dedicated to a post-bourgeois philosophy of history, Lukács intended a thorough critical examination of Dostoyevsky, interpreted as inaugurating a new religious worldview in his books. Dostoyevsky, Lukács believed, heralded a new age beyond the alienation and "transcendental homelessness" of the epoch of the novel, the "age of absolute sinfulness" known as bourgeois individualist modernity. Even as late as December 1918, in the midst of a revolutionary process that would shortly usher Lukács into his life-long commitment to Marxism, Lukács favored Dostoyevsky over Lenin in his essay "Bolshevism as a Moral Problem," while he hesitated on the threshold of conversion to communism.[15] Notably, even in his early Marxist period, in which he was involved with various practical aspects of the short-lived Hungarian Soviet Republic, Lukács retained this religious orientation as a superethical and superpolitical horizon, for which the ethical and political commitments of his communist activity were only preparatory. In *Visegrád Street*, a memoir-novel of the 1919 uprising and the foundation of the Hungarian Communist Party, the novelist József Lengyel disparagingly referred to Lukács and his followers as the "spirituals/intellects" and "ethicals" who, in the swirl of armed revolutionary conflict, were apt to ponder injunctions from Kierkegaard and Dostoyevsky alongside Lenin and Béla Kun.[16]

Lukács, Bloch, and Utopia

Analogously, in his 1918 book *Spirit of Utopia*, Ernst Bloch gave his final chapter a title that virtually calls for an allegorical woodcut: "Karl Marx, Death, and the Apocalypse." Bloch concludes this chapter and his book as a whole by arguing that only the bad are *created* by their God, whereas the just name the God that they then mirror in their goodness.

The task of the revolution-apocalypse, then, is to name and thus bring forth God anew into the fallen world. In Lukács's personal copy of Bloch's book, the 1918 edition, one of the limited number of underlined passages includes the following:

> And finally, these days, it is no particular philosophical service ... if Marxism remains consistently atheistic, in order to provide the human soul nothing other than a more or less eudaemonistically furnished "heaven" on earth without the music that might have sounded out of this effortlessly functioning mechanism of the economy and social life. About this one can say that precisely the sharp emphasis on all economic aspects, as well as the present, but still hidden latency of all the transcendental moments, bring Marxism in the vicinity of a critique of pure reason for which no critique of Practical reason has yet been written.[17]

Both Lukács's and Bloch's Heidelberg-period religious messianism and its transfiguration in the early activist Marxism of *History and Class Consciousness* and *Spirit of Utopia* are deeply marked by what Hans Blumenburg called, in *The Legitimacy of the Modern Age*, the horizon of immediate eschatological expectation.[18] However, as Blumenberg notes, even the felt need to seek more precise theoretical or philosophical definition for such expectation already indicates that it is in retreat: "In acute situations of immediate expectation, the promised salvation can remain extremely undefined; everything is going to be different, and he who asks how has already lost his chance to participate" (67). Lukács's recorded testimony about the communist milieu in Hungary in 1919 suggests that it was pervaded by just such a combination of passionate enthusiasm and obscurity that marks such a moment of—as yet unreflective—immediate expectation:

> I was not the only one who could not see my way clearly. The position was very complicated. On the one hand, we were convinced that this was the only way out of the situation as it existed, not just in Hungary, but for the whole of mankind. On the other hand, we had not the faintest idea about the theoretical grounding or the specific stages of this solution. Modern historians of the party cannot imagine that there are matters on which party officials are completely ignorant. Hence this situation does not exist for them. (*Record of a Life*, 55–56)

We can see Bloch's and Lukács's theoretical work of the early 1920s, including the former's *Thomas Münzer als Theologe der Revolution* (1921) and *History and Class Consciousness* (1923), as attempts to reflect on and give theoretical mediation to the events that had transpired in 1918 and 1919 in Central Europe, as well as indices that the messianic intensity of immediate expectation for redemption through communism had "retreated" to the more distant future.

Bloch's sense of the retreating eschatological horizon entailed ever greater enrichment and detailing of the utopian motif in his theoretical writing, his burgeoning ontologization of "the principle hope" in a vast range of philosophical, cultural, and religious contexts. Whereas, in contrast, the preponderance of Lukács's life-long work pursued another, more sobering question: what are the possibilities for redemption once the horizon of revolutionary expectation retreats, and world-historical movements precicipate into parties, states, publishing houses, and other institutions dedicated to managing and articulating historical time rather than being sublimated in its pure transcendence-yearning dynamism? Put otherwise, after the extreme acceleration of historical experience he had undergone in the "Event" of 1918–19,[19] Lukács's work subsequently comes to constitute a series of answers to the question of what a *decelarated* path to socialism might mean: a socialism that will have to coexist for decades, perhaps centuries, alongside capitalism, a socialism that may take a long time to arrive. For this one needs, Lukács concludes, not ethical leaps of transcendence, but an immanent understanding of constrained action in restricted action-contexts, insight into the opaque motivations and consciousness of actors, and attention to the many-sided dynamics of character formation and deformation—all of which means that Lukács's embrace of realism and attention to literature were not simply matters of his avowedly classical aesthetic tastes, but also expressions of his most fundamental theoretical and practical concerns. Already in his pre-Marxist writings, moreover, Lukács has prepared the conceptual ground for this experience of an extended historical vigil. For he identified here the problem of historical *prematurity* as an immanent problem for a work's form, or even for the whole oeuvre of an author or thinker, which might sketch the boundaries of a greater, synthetic unity without ever taking the decisive step into it. Lukács thus characterized the essayist as "the pure type of the precursor," who he doubts "could lay claim to any value or validity," "independent from the fate of that other of whom he is the herald"—an other who, he noted, might not ever actually arrive ("On the Nature and Form of the Essay," 16–17).

Since Löwy's historical studies of "revolutionary romanticism" and "libertarian messianism," it should be less surprising to us that two young philosophers of Central European-Jewish extraction should gravitate at this time towards radical religious ideas and messianic hopes for redemption. Such a gravitation forms, in Löwy's view, an "elective affinity" between a whole range of thinkers and writers of the period, including Martin Buber, Franz Rozenzweig, Franz Kafka, Gershom Scholem, Gustav Landauer, Benjamin, Bloch, Lukács, and many others. It is not even startling that Bloch and Lukács should have come to articulate an idealist, activist, utopian, and messianically tinged version of *Marxism* on the basis of such religious ideas and aspirations. Yet still surprising and insufficiently clarified in the large body of exegetical and biographical literature on Lukács and Bloch is that their religious messianism and its Marxist offshoots should be so closely bound to a focus on art and artistic culture. In other words, to return to my title, we should not take it for granted that their religious messianism should be so closely connected to an aesthetic utopianism.

Their conceptions of "utopia," hence of the utopian dimension of art, were, however, quite distinct. I will recall that in naming his ideal society, Thomas More employed an etymological pun: "utopia" was at once the "eu-topia" or "good place" against which the present evils of English society could be measured, and the "u-topia" or "other-place" of an island that existed only on the imaginary seas of a work of literary art. In a complementary way, the metahistorian Reinhold Koselleck has noted the shift of utopia's "other place" from a location in space to a location in time, a "temporalization of utopia" that took place in the later eighteenth century.[20] Bloch's aesthetic utopianism emphasized the temporally "eu-topic" aspect of art, its adumbration of "goodness," of a redeemed world of which the artwork is an intimation and anticipation. If art is also "u-topic" for him, an "elsewhere," it is only thus insofar as it is everywhere and nowhere in Bloch's pan-cultural, mystically indifferentiated system. He draws no essential distinction between art and all other expressions of utopian striving, including play, daydreaming, love, and philosophy. Thus, despite countless references in *Spirit of Utopia* to everyone from Dante to Kandinsky, art has no specificity and no autonomy for Bloch, but rather flows into a utopian continuum urging towards future salvation. Jameson accurately notes that:

> Bloch's hermeneutic . . . finds its richness in the very variety of its objects themselves, while its initial conceptual content remains . . . relatively unchanging: thus little by little wherever we look everything in the world becomes a version of the same primal figure, a manifestation of that primordial movement toward the future and toward ultimate identity with a transfigured world which is Utopia. (*Marxism and Form*, 120)

The primal figure to which Jameson refers is the subjective ego striving for realization and redemption. Notably, Bloch characterizes his discussion of art in the first half of *Spirit of Utopia* not as an aesthetic, but as an "ego-metaphysics" (*Ich-Metaphysik*), a self-encounter (*Selbstbegegnung*).

Lukács, in contrast, has a more complex conceptualization of the utopian aspect of art, in which the emphasis falls on art's utopian *separation* from everyday life as well as from the spheres of ethics, logic, and religion—a separation that is both ontological and institutional, in terms of spaces of presentation and reception, from concert halls and theatres to exhibition spaces to the library to which one retreats to read a novel. Art is utopian, precisely insofar as it renounces efficacy in the spheres in which the essential contradictions of life may be confronted. The "goodness" of the artistic utopia is indeed a transfigured expression of the suffering and frustration that the artist and the audience experience in the other spheres. The artwork's utopia, however, remains at most an index of the irresolution and chaos that continues to dominate "life." Put otherwise, for Lukács, the aesthetic has no future, for the artwork utopically withdraws from the domains in which the future must be decided—in which decision is called for ethically, politically, or religiously. And yet, he suggests, its inefficacious perfection may play a negative, dialectical role in shaping the existential resolve to leave art and aesthetic culture behind for a leap into future goodness.

I would like briefly to summarize the basic argument of Lukács's *Heidelberg Philosophy of Art*, where he develops this view of the utopian status of the artwork, and then more briefly refer to a number of Lukács's essays and reviews from the 1910s, presenting key themes for his uncoupling of aesthetic utopianism and religious messianism. These will include his critique of aestheticism (or what he called "aesthetic culture" or "impressionism"), his development of the paradoxical concept of a "revolutionary without a revolution" and "a religious poet without God" around the Hungarian poet Endre Ady, and his considerations on non-tragic drama as transcending the ethical sphere of tragedy towards the religious domain of grace. Finally, I compare the antithetical parallelism between Lukács's surviving diary of his personal crisis around the suicide of his one-time lover Irma Seidler and Bloch's memorial diary for his wife Else Bloch-von Stritzki, who died in 1921 after a long illness.

Lukács's starting point in his *Philosophy of Art* was the existence of the artwork. The crucial questions of aesthetics, in his view, derive from the artwork's very possibility. Given the undeniable fact that there are artworks, how are they possible? And what implications follow from this possibility? Keeping the artwork at the center of his account, Lukács stresses the autonomy of the work from the lived experience of either the artist or receiver of the work and its distinction from the products of other spheres such as ethical norms or logical theories. Yet unlike ethics or logic, which gain their coherence and autonomy from their removal from the world of subjective lived experience, the aesthetic sphere manifests a fundamental paradox in this respect: the experience of the artwork is irreducible to either the artist's or the receiver's lived inner experience, yet its realization is inseparably bound to both. Moreover, in further complication and paradox, the inner experiences of the artist and that of the receiver are essentially solipsistic and cannot in any way be assumed to be similar. Lukács argues that artistic *form* is the means by which the paradoxes of lived experience are spanned in the aesthetic. The autonomous objectivity of the formed artwork, however, cannot assure a communication from artist to receiver such that an identical experiential content is preserved. Any attempt to overcome the gap between artist and receiver by some sort of assumed identity of experience exceeds the realm of the aesthetic and verges into metaphysics.

Yet the aesthetic, Lukács argues, does not require the success of communication on these terms; quite the contrary. It is not understanding, but rather *mis*understanding that proves productive in the aesthetic sphere. The artwork becomes an open locus for the historical accumulation and transformation of meanings and experiences, precisely insofar as the artwork *differs* from the stream of lived experience of both artist and receiver. Thus, Lukács writes, "The more significant and timeless an artwork is, the more its interpretation, as the intellectualized explication of misunderstanding in receptive experience, is subjected to the changes of time: only a work that is misunderstandable in unlimited variability may be effective in every time and to everyone" (*Heidelberger Philosophie der Kunst*, 204). In this idea of a double misunderstanding between the artist's conception and the receiver's experience, mediated by the artwork's form, Lukács had been inspired by his close friend Leo Popper, who left behind at his death in 1911 a short note towards a "theory of misunderstanding"; Lukács and Popper also refer to this theory in their correspondence.[21] It is the hermeneutic openness of the artwork, the artwork's disposition towards being *mis*understood—rooted in the necessarily imperfect mediation by form between the artist's inner experience and the viewer's receptive experience—that also ensures artworks' durability and renewability in time. The great works of Shakespeare, for example, have been the occasion for productive misunderstandings by generation after generation of writers and scholars.

Such variability, however, requires that works of art retain their distinction from the lived reality of artists and receivers of artworks. They occupy a utopic space that *can* affect life (by occasioning new misunderstandings), but only insofar as a constitutive distance is maintained between the work and life. Hence, the utopian aspect of the artwork is itself paradoxical. From one side, this utopian distance resides in the ornamental self-referentiality and formal immanence that regulates, as an ideal, all artworks. As Lukács writes:

With this concept of the ornament, the synthesis of order and play and the ornamentally formed surfaces of things, in which every irrationality can be taken up and everything closed round with strict laws, but where the rigidity of laws has been dissolved, without relinquishing necessity, and the indissoluble becomes bright and light without losing itself in flat graspability, the goal of this formation is achieved and all its paradoxes are dissolved: the image of every utopian reality has come into being.[22]

Yet this ornamental image (or the artwork qua ornament) is not a *model* of utopia to be realized, but is rather itself a realization of utopia, yet in a space distinct from that of life. As Lukács puts it, it is not a matter of reality becoming utopia and the artwork's being a prefiguration or foreshadowing of this utopic fulfillment. This would, in contrast, be closer to Bloch's view of utopia's latent immanence in artworks and other objects and practices. Rather, for Lukács, the artwork realizes utopia as *present reality* with no direct relation to the future in its extra-aesthetic dimension. The realized utopian perfection of the artwork demonstrates only that utopia *already exists* in the real world, but only aesthetically. At the same time, thus, the artwork also indexes its own inefficacy with respect to the future and to the solution of the problems of life. The artwork does not need the redeemed future; it is utopian in the present. But by implication, to employ a rather colloquial translation of "utopia," its goodness is *neither here nor there* with respect to the dimension in which we live, love, suffer, and struggle. Relatedly, in *Spirit of Utopia*, Bloch criticizes Lukács's concept of tragedy as too immanent and self-enclosed; Bloch believed that such "externals" as blood and suffering were not contingent features of tragedy. Yet if this is so, then Lukács's sharp separation of tragic form from the contingency of the life-world could not, in Bloch's view, be valid (*Geist der Utopie*, 67–74).

The Artwork According to Lukács

This strongly autonomized sphere of the artwork and Lukács's attempt to articulate an aesthetic theory on its basis constrast starkly with another way in which the "aesthetic" appears in his work, although ultimately I think these views are the recto and verso of the same coin. In the essays collected in his 1911 volume, *Esztétikai kultúra* (Aesthetic Culture), which unlike his previous essay volume *Soul and Form* was published only in Hungarian, Lukács developed his criticism of a culture that had lost all transindividually valid points of orientation, and hence had fallen back on an impressionistic psychology of lived experience and mood. Key for Lukács is that aesthetic culture dissolves the object as the basis of artistic making and reception, substituting instead the succession of subjective moods. This has two crucial implications, both of which are opposed to a consequential, realized utopian art in the sense I outlined above. The first is that mood no longer recognizes the exteriority and autonomy of the artwork that is the basis of Lukács's view of art's utopian function:

> The mood is merely a work of art's creative, transient contact with the soul of the beholder. If the endless succession of moods is caused by something else, then its effect is more valuable and quite different from the sum total of the random, chaotic, endless succession of moods. This something, present nowhere and yet apparent everywhere, makes art an art ... It is precisely this, the dynamic nature of art, which had perished under the onslaught of "aesthetic culture."[23]

Second, mood recognizes no difference between spheres. A mood can just as easily be triggered by a random play of light or a revolution or the thought of God as by a work of art. This indifference ultimately destroys any basis for specific valuation and leads to nihilism:

> Aesthetic culture owes its birth to the very moment when man's spiritual activity expands and encompasses the whole of life, in other words, the moment when life itself is seen as an endless sequence of transient moods. It was born when objects ceased to exist, because everything was merely an occasion for the mood; when all that was permanent disappeared from life, because the mood proved intolerant of what was permanent and recurrent. It was born when life was stripped of all values, and it now values the products of moods, that is to say, the products of fortuitous circumstances devoid of any necessary correlation with values. ("Aesthetic Culture," 148)

Further essays in this volume spell out concretely the hazards of aesthetic culture, particularly Lukács's contribution to a show of the post-impressionist painter Károly Kernstok and other painters of the modernist painting group "A Nyolcak" ("the Eight"), "The Parting of the Ways,"[24] and his tribute to August Strindberg on the occasion of his sixtieth birthday (Figures 2.1 and 2.2).[25] In Kernstok's case, Lukács praises his rejection of impressionism, his displacement of the "I" from the center of aesthetic discourse, and his return to an emphatic sense of the medium and the finished painted work. In Strindberg's more complicated case, Lukács notes the mastery that Strindberg achieved in any genre he attempted and, at the same time, the vast centerless quality of his autobiographical works. Strindberg's greatness, Lukács concludes, is the skill and large scale with which he realizes in his person and writings an uncomfortable representativeness of our time. He writes large the intransitiveness of our development, our centerlessness, our goallessness, our lack of form ("August Strindberg," 223–24). Strindberg thus

Figure 2.1 Károly Kernstok, *Nude Boy*, c. 1909. Private collection. Photographic source: bankaustria.kunstforum.at. Public domain.

symbolizes for Lukács a giant figure hovering over the low plains of aesthetic culture, but nevertheless a prodigy scarred by the historical environment of aesthetic culture itself.[26]

Even the greatest contemporary writers, in Lukács's view, struggle with the lack of a binding source of cultural values, for which acts of individual creative will, no matter how heroic, can scarcely substitute. The source of value in the past was above all religious, while current writers necessarily grapple with the disjunction between aesthetics and religiosity, and their works become indices of a problematic lack of relation between art and the higher spheres. The forms that result from individualistic strivings to overcome a crisis rooted precisely in secular individualism—forms that in Lukács's view are characteristic of modern art and literature—always bear the scars of their inconsequentiality, their status as mere "aesthetic culture" (which clearly for Lukács is not coterminous with art as such). This basic framework—a cunning dialectic by which modernity undermines its greatest and most ambitious writers—shapes Lukács's reading of two contemporary authors who

Aesthetic Utopianism to Religious Messianism   45

Figure 2.2   Lajos Tihanyi, *Main Square in Nagybánya*, 1908. Private collection. Photographic source: Szilas. Public domain.

are crucial for his early work and thought, the poet Endre Ady and the playwright Paul Ernst.

Ady, considered one of the most outstanding figures in modern Hungarian lyric poetry, is for Lukács exemplary in two respects, politically and religiously. Politically, Ady is the revolutionary poet of a Hungary that, in Lukács's view, is incapable of carrying out a revolution. Linked directly and inseparably to Ady's socialist and anarchist leanings, however, are his spiritual and religious yearnings, and this religiosity is of a similarly paradoxical nature as that of Ady's revolutionary politics. We might say that if "re-ligio" implies a set of ties between past, present, and future dynamically maintained by repeated observance and celebration, then Ady is a poet who finds himself ever anew trying to *religare* the broken ties of the Hungarian present, to reforge the connection between himself and God and among the members of the community through singular acts of poetic creation. But first and foremost, he also must rebind the fragments of the self, torn by moods and desires in a way familiar to us from Lukács's discussion of "aesthetic culture." In verses such as Ady's "I Believe Disbelievingly in God," included in his 1910 collection *The Poetry of All Secrets*, Lukács sees the problem of aesthetic culture raised to a peak of crisis, which may be the precondition for a Kierkegaardian leap of ethical and religious decision:

> I believe disbelievingly in God,
> Because I want to believe,
> Because never was it so necessary
> For both living and dead.
> * * *
> Everything is a secret in this wide world
> And the Lord too, if he exists
> And I am the secret of secrets,
> Poor hunted me.
> God, Christ, Virtue, and everything
> In turn, what I yearn for
> And why—this too is
> Alas, an even greater secret than I.[27]

According to Lukács, Ady's religiosity is, in fact, detectable not solely in the verse that explicitly uses religious rhetoric, but everywhere in his writing:

> It is not necessary to refer to those poems where religion and revolution are blended, only for those who have to see God's name to recognize the religious in something; every poem of Ady is religious verse. To formulate briefly what all of his poems have most profoundly in common: they are religious verses, and the effusion of great mystical, religious feeling in every way and in all directions.[28]

Yet if Ady is a great mystic, he nevertheless has the problem of being a *modern* mystic, a mystic who has to invent religious content out of himself poetically: "Today's mystic does not have a space in which to find any form, he must cultivate everything out of himself: God and the devil, the earth and the heavens, the Redeemer and the Antichrist, the saints and the damned; he has to write the Bible himself" ("Új Magyar Líra," 251). Poetically, Ady achieves something analogous to the great mystics of the past: the perception of the sublimity of every single thing. Yet unlike past mystics, who could rely on a background of religiosity, Ady as the mystic of today "only has moments ... only the manifestation of a million, particular atoms of mood complete in themselves and contrary to others standing in contiguousness. Only thus can these verses take form, but to a mystic it is never enough if he writes a few or even a complete, long series of 'beautiful' verses" (253). Ady, finally, for Lukács, is the exemplary modern Hungarian poet. He is, as Lukács puts it, "the poet of Hungarian revolutionaries without a revolution" (248). Bereft of revolution, his socialism is permeated by apocalyptic longing, mystical communion, and religious diction. But also bereft of any genuine religious foundation, his religiosity shoots high in the air but ultimately falls as scattered aesthetic precipitate. As artistic utopia rather than actual socialism or religiosity, this great poetry that gestures desperately towards the future is in fact foreclosed from it. This, for Lukács, is the tragedy of the revolutionary without revolution and the mystic in a world without God.

Lukács employs a similar set of critical tropes in his analysis of the playwright Paul Ernst. In two reviews of plays by Ernst, *Brunhild* and *Ariadne auf Naxos*, Lukács develops his critique of the limits of tragedy, which in his earliest writing on drama and in essays such as "The Metaphysics of Tragedy" in *Soul and Form* he had originally championed as the highest literary form. In his review of *Brunhild*, Lukács notes the way that tragic guilt is taken on by the tragic hero, against the urging of those around him, as a way of individuating himself, delimiting his individuality from those around him, and giving his existence a hard, monumental form. In the review of *Ariadne auf Naxos*, however, he notes that the play has a metatragic aspect, insofar as it confronts Ariadne with the heroic form of Theseus and finds him wanting. Lukács sees Ernst as considering whether there might not be a still higher form than that ethical apex that the tragic hero represents, namely the religious form of grace. He thus speaks of "Ariadne's devastating disappointment" in her experience that "the highest man—and Theseus is that—is nevertheless only a hero."[29] Lukács sees a similar confrontation of inner heroism and grace in Dostoyevsky's confrontation of Stavrogin and Prince Myschkin, Ivan Karamazov and Aloysha. But he also diagnoses an essential limitation to the success of any modern dramatist to give form to a new drama of grace. For what is lacking in the modern age is precisely any positive grounding of religious grace:

> It is the religious drama of an age without religion ... in which the absolute, God, is not only the object but also the subject of desire. The drama of grace of earlier ages always had gods of being; here instead the non-being of God, his distance from us takes form. (61)

Ultimately, then, the trans-individual solution of religious grace remains an act of aesthetic will on the playwright's part, which is nevertheless not an artistic failing, but rather a profound registration of a historical and theological situation:

It is only a feeling, that of a formation, not a fullness of forms, that awaits order here. So with both of these two great works of poetry [*Brunhild* and *Ariadne auf Naxos*] everything expressible has become eternal: their uniqueness in the life of a poet is the most complete historico-philosophical expression of the poverty of our age and the realisation of its sole dramatic possibilities. (61)

Similar to Ady, Ernst embodies the paradox of a modern aesthetic of grace, which nevertheless points to the absence of grace in modernity, because of the artwork's utopic foreclosure from the redeemed future that grace would imply.

Irma and Else

To return to the comparison of Lukács and Bloch, I would like to consider a peculiar parallelism between a biographical event that marked both of their lives and work in important ways: both experienced the death of a beloved woman and muse figure at a crucial moment in their lives and careers. In 1911, while in Florence, Lukács was informed that the painter Irma Seidler, with whom he had carried on an ambivalent love relationship and correspondence even after her marriage, had committed suicide. Ten years later, in 1921, Bloch's first wife, Else Bloch-von Stritzki, died in surgery after many years of illness and medical treatment. Both Lukács and Bloch produced diaristic texts in which these deaths were the central focus. In Lukács's case, this was the diary written from 1910 to 1911 that was posthumously discovered in the Heidelberg bank vault in 1971. In Bloch's case, the relevant text is his "Gedenkbuch für Else Bloch-von Stritzki," written immediately after his wife's death and included as the opening essay of his late collection on the concept of utopia, *Tendency-Latency-Utopia*.[30] Notably, Bloch also dedicated to Else both editions of *Spirit of Utopia*, in 1918 and in 1923, thus both before and after her death. *Tendency-Latency-Utopia*, in which the memorial book for Else Bloch appears, is in turn dedicated to Bloch's second wife, Karola Bloch, who is thanked for "saving husband and work from the Nazis." Among the entries of the memorial book, Bloch notes that he has completed the composition of his study of *Thomas Münzer as Theologian of the Revolution*, which he himself characterized as a sequel to *Spirit of Utopia*. So the relationship to his dead wife Else is deeply intertwined with his articulation of a messianic theory of utopia and his concept of art and culture as prefigurations of a redeemed future.

Thanks to studies by Agnes Heller, Lee Congdon, Mary Gluck, Massimo Cacciari, Thomas Harrison, and others, the case of Lukács and Irma Seidler has been extensively discussed.³¹ Less well known is the Bloch text. While I cannot explore these works in depth, I want to suggest that the strong divergence between Lukács's and Bloch's responses to the deaths of these women, who are at once lovers and imagined muses of their philosophical work, also highlights their basic difference with respect to the problem of artistic utopia and future salvation.

In the relationship with Irma, Lukács had early on hesitated over committing to her and offering marriage; perhaps, among other things, as an ernest reader of Kierkegaard, he feared that realizing happiness in love and erotic life might prove constraining for his writing and thought. However, he kept up a correspondence that reveals his working through of his own personal and intellectual identity against, as it were, the projective screen of his female interlocutor. Thinking in terms that anticipate his theory of productive misunderstanding in the relations between artist, artwork, and receiver—and reflecting the fraught gender relations of the fin-de-siècle Austro-Hungarian bourgeois that Freud and his contemporaries likewise explored—Lukács thus considers the love relationship between an intellectual man and his beloved muse as one of creative *misunderstanding* as well:

> How ridiculous the philologists are that make of Frau von Stein a goddess, in order to make her effect on Goethe understandable! But still more ridiculous are the psycho-philologists that subtly prove how little she understood Goethe! Of course she didn't understand him: Fr[iedrich] Schlegel understood him, and W[ilhelm] v[on] Humboldt—but out of that misunderstanding Iphigenie was born; from being understood, nothing. No! It's a matter of something mystical here: to be able to believe that someone can work a miracle[.]³²

Yet when Lukács heard of Irma's suicide, he was thrown into a moral crisis about his own culpability in her fate and the possibility that what he had thought was creative self-fashioning was no more than a frivolous, aesthetic game—as if he had thought he were a character in Kierkegaard's ethical and religious works, only to discover that he was the author of the "Diary of a Seducer." For many months, even before the blow of hearing of Irma's death, he had contemplated suicide, going as far as to buy a pistol. But after her suicide, he couldn't manage to do it:

> Should one make an end of it? Yesterday—before I had the news—I thought about it almost uninterruptedly. But it's no solution. For Irma, yes. Her tragedy lay in the vital sphere of life, where death is really the dialectical opposite of life, where an absolute homogeneity of death and life are encompassed. But what can death be for me? (43)

Like the artwork in his aesthetic theory, Lukács felt as if he lived not in life, but only in and through his work. Only an *actual* life can have death as a *consequent* future; he who is not really alive, but dwells only in the utopian haven of his work, cannot embrace death as a solution or consolation. Moreover, to die now would only eternalize the triviality and frivolousness of his previous actions. And as a passionate reader of Ibsen—Lukács, we should recall, at age fifteen asked his father for money to visit the playwright in Norway!—he feared above all the fate of Peer Gynt, whose trivial soul was not worthy even of damnation but only of being melted down in the Buttonmaker's ladle.

Lukács in turn eventually comes to a resolution that is indicative of his early thought: a strict division of work and life, in which the possibility of redemption in either sphere can only be awaited and by different means. First, Lukács wonders whether at least the work can be "saved," even if he cannot: "The—very deep—feeling that one can possess the holy *for the work* even if one does not have it oneself ... that one does not oneself have to fall to ruin in the redeeming system" (47–48). However, if this is not the case, then there is only a kind of Kierkegaardian absurd faith preconditioned by an absolute exhaustion of all intellectual means to mitigate the certainty of one's damnation: "It lies with God to redeem me from my being; so long as I am to live in it, to be damned, I will remain faithful to him" (49).

Bloch's beautiful text for Else, in contrast, reveals an almost antithetical orientation. If Lukács's diary is permeated by the sense of separation and horizonlessness, personal and spiritual, Bloch's memorial book for Else is filled with a sense of communion, fusion, and the latent presence in this life of the utopian and sacred. Curiously, he quotes in the book a letter that he wrote to Lukács, who by 1921 had become more distant from Bloch, in which Bloch recalls their one-time fusion of interests and foretells a future continuation of their spiritual communion: "I feel, since Else's death, that my life is closed. ... You, our friendship, our unique spiritual relationship, indeed identity, stereoscopic identity, belongs to the old complex of life and is the only thing that from it continues as life, as spiritual life, not only as memory" ("Gedenkbuch," 14).

But above all, it is Else herself who is presented as a kind of divine messenger who has allowed Bloch to discover the truth of his personal, intellectual, and spiritual mission and understand through direct experience the anticipatory presence of utopia and salvation *in this world*. For the angelically transfigured Else herself is the hidden subject-object of Bloch's work, insofar as he projects, even across the division of death, a fusion of spirit with her:

Else firmly believed in the absolute truth of my philosophy. To her it came from the same blood and from the same region as the Bible; she explained the Bible through my philosophy and my philosophy through the Bible. . . . Her esteem, her honor of my work was as unconditional and unbounded as her love; the difficult, religious-metaphysical passages and domains of my philosophy were the ones she understood the most easily and were the most familiar to her. (17)

In Else, Bloch finds a spiritual continuum, running without break from the objects of everyday life in which, still mourning, he feels her presence, through the communion with the many friends from whom he quotes letters of consolation and memory, through the hope for personal and collective salvation. Bloch writes: "Else has done for me perhaps the greatest thing that one can do for a person: to illuminate heaven, she gave me a feeling for death, so that I can grasp it, so that I understand it boundlessly" (24). The message of salvation Else bears is a consolation for her loss, since it allows Bloch to believe that death does not divide them, as well as a spur to realize his work in this life, since it will be through his messianic philosophy that the salvational hope to rejoin Else may pass from present latency to future actuality.

In discussing these two texts, I have not intended any psycho-biographical speculation on the origins of Lukács's and Bloch's philosophical and political views in their personal lives. My point is rather that these thinkers connected their aesthetics, ethics, politics, and religiosity with a demand for individual decision and existential transformation that would be efficacious at both large and small scale. They sought to lend coherence to their work at each level, even where, in the case of Lukács, such coherence entailed drawing rigorous *distinctions* between the different spheres in which thought and action were to be engaged. What the relations of Lukács with Irma and Bloch with Else reveal is the divergent existential temporalities with which they faced the totality of these problems.

Both men confronted the challenge of continuing to write in a state of grief, in a time after the death of their beloveds. For Lukács, however, this implies a kind of exile to a space without relation to a lived future, at once a utopian preserve and a desert of words. If there is to be a future, it will come suddenly, as a salvation *from* the present, and it cannot be worked towards or wished for, only faithfully awaited without expectation. Prior to his embrace of Marxism, Lukács can only possess the future as an apocalyptic event that will arrive from outside his sphere of time, the time of work and of the work. Bloch, in contrast, sees everywhere in the present the latency of the future. The work—the work of art, the work of philosophy, the work of love—is continuous preparation and passage of that latency into actuality. Thus, for Bloch, the work's meaning in the strongest sense *resides* in the future, a time in which its still-indistinct meaning today will at last be fulfilled—or perhaps, from the anticipatory perspective of the present, in that future in which its promised meaning is already turning, in hope, towards the light.

Notes

1. Georg Lukács, "On the Nature and Form of the Essay: A Letter to Leo Popper," in Lukács, *Soul and Form*, trans. Anna Bostock (Cambridge, MA: The MIT Press, 1974), 16.
2. See Michael Löwy, *Georg Lukács: From Romanticism to Bolshevism*, trans. Patrick Camiller (London: New Left Books, 1979); Michael Löwy, *Redemption and Utopia: Jewish Libertarian Thought in Central Europe, A Study in Elective Affinities* (Stanford: Stanford University Press, 1988); and Fredric Jameson, *Marxism and Form: Twentieth-Century Dialectical Theories of Literature* (Princeton: Princeton University Press, 1971). See also Ivan Boldyrev, *Ernst Bloch and His Contemporaries: Locating Utopian Messianism* (London: Bloomsbury, 2014).
3. Ernst Bloch, "Interview avec Michael Löwy, 24 March 1974," in Löwy, *Pour une sociologie des intellectuels révolutionnaire: L'évolution politique de Lukács, 1909–1929* (Paris: Presses Universitaires de France, 1976), 296.
4. Sándor Radnóti, "Lukács and Bloch," in *Lukács Reappraised*, ed. Agnes Heller (New York: Columbia University Press, 1983), 72. See also Miklós Mesterházi, *Ernst Bloch, Avagy, Az Örökség Műveszete* (Budapest: Akadémiai Kiadó, 1991), who treats at length the critical debate between Lukács and Bloch over more than two decades.
5. Thomas Bremer, "Blochs Augenblicke: Anmerkungen zum Zusammenhang von Zeiterfahrung, Geschichtsphilosophie und Ästhetik," *Text + Kritik* (Ernst Bloch Sonderband), ed. Heinz Ludwig Arnold (Munich: Edition Text + Kritik, 1985), 86. See also: Günther K. Lehmann, "Stramin und Totale Form: Der Kunstphilosoph Georg Lukács und sein Verhältnis zu Ernst Blochs Ästhetik der Hoffnung," *Weimarer Beiträgen: Zeitschrift für Literaturwissenschaft, Ästhetik, und Kulturtheorie* 31 (1985): 533–57; and Werner Jung, "The Early Aesthetic Theories of Bloch and Lukács," *New German Critique* 45 (1988): 41–54.
6. Paul de Man, "Georg Lukács's Theory of the Novel," in *Blindness and Insight: Essays in the Rhetoric of Contemporary Criticism*, 2nd edition (Minneapolis: University of Minnesota Press, 1983), 55.
7. Mary Gluck, *George Lukács and His Generation, 1900–1918* (Cambridge, MA: Harvard University Press, 1991), 151.
8. Karl Jaspers, "Heidelberger Erinnerungen," *Heidelberger Jahrbuch 1961* (Berlin: Springer Verlag, 1961), 5; see also Helmut Plessner, quoted by Vincent Geoghegan, *Ernst Bloch* (London: Routledge, 2008), 12.
9. Anna Lesznai, quoted by Gluck, *George Lukács and His Generation*, 160.

10. David Kettler, Memorandum of conversation with Arnold Hauser, quoted in "Culture and Revolution: Lukács in the Hungarian Revolutions of 1918/1919," *Telos* 10 (1971): 59.
11. Marianne Weber, *Max Weber: A Biography*, ed. and trans. Harry Zohn (New Brunswick: Transaction Publishers, 1975), 466.
12. Georg Lukács, *Record of a Life: An Autobiographical Sketch*, ed. István Eörsi, trans. Rodney Livingstone (London: Verso, 1983), 59.
13. Löwy, *Redemption and Utopia*, 150.
14. For the notes and drafts for this project see Georg Lukács, *Dostojewski: Notizen und Entwürfe*, ed. János Kristóf Nyíri (Budapest: Akadémiai Kiadó, 1985). For critical discussion of this project, see Andreas Hoeschen, *Das "Dostojewsky" Projekt: Lukács' neukantianisches Frühwerk in seinem ideengeschichtlichen Kontext* (Tübingen: Max Niemeyer Verlag, 1999); and Michele Cometa, "Postfazione" to the Italian edition of Lukács's Dostoyevsky materials, in György Lukács, *Dostoevskij*, ed. Michele Cometa (Milan: SE, 2000), 133–64.
15. Georg Lukács, "Bolshevism as a Moral Problem," in *The Lukács Reader*, ed. Arpad Kadarkay (Oxford: Blackwell, 1995), 216–21.
16. József Lengyel, *Visegrádi Utca* (Budapest: Magvető Kiadó, 1972), 137–38.
17. Ernst Bloch, *Geist der Utopie: Erste Fassung, Faksimile der Ausgabe von 1918* (Frankfurt am Main: Suhrkamp Verlag, 1971), 407–8; Lukács also inscribed marginal notes in this section on 414–15. Lukács's copy of the book is catalogued as 0000601 DB III/1 in the Catalogue of the Lukács Heritage Library in Budapest.
18. Hans Blumenberg, *The Legitimacy of the Modern World*, trans. Robert M. Wallace (Cambridge, MA: The MIT Press, 1983).
19. In his postface to Lukács's unpublished 1926 defense of *History and Class Consciousness*, "Georg Lukács as the Philosopher of Leninism," Žižek connects Lukács's conception of the dialectic with Alain Badiou's notion of "fidelity to the Event," understood as an "intervention that cannot be accounted for in terms of its pre-existing 'objective conditions'" See Žižek in Lukács, *A Defence of History and Class Consciousness*, 164. Jameson and (more skeptically) Jay also consider *History and Class Consciousness* as an "Event" with a long, unfinished afterlife in reception: Fredric Jameson, "*History and Class Consciousness* as an Unfinished Project," in *Valences of the Dialectic* (London: Verso, 2009), 201–22; and Martin Jay, "Fidelity to the Event? Lukács's *History and Class Consciousness* and the Russian Revolution," in *Genesis and Validity: The Theory and Practice of Intellectual History* (Philadelphia: University of Pennsylvania Press, 2022), 106–23.
20. Reinhold Koselleck, "The Temporalization of Utopia," in *The Practice of Conceptual History: Timing History, Spacing Concepts*, trans. Todd Samuel Presner (Stanford: Stanford University Press, 2002), 84–99.
21. Leó Popper, "Félreértési Elmélet," in Popper, *Esszék és Kritikák* (Budapest: Magvető, 1983), 116–17; see also Lukács's letters to Popper, [mid-June] 1909 and May 19, 1911, in *Georg Lukács: Selected Correspondence, 1902–1920*, eds. Judith Marcus and Zoltán Tar (New York: Columbia University Press, 1986), 88–89 and 161.
22. Georg Lukács, *Heidelberger Philosophie der Kunst (1912–1914)*, eds.

György Márkus and Frank Benseler (Darmstadt and Neuweid: Luchterhand, 1974), 100.
23. Georg Lukács, "Aesthetic Culture," in *The Lukács Reader*, 149.
24. Georg Lukács, "The Parting of the Ways," in *The Lukács Reader*, 167–73.
25. György Lukács, "August Strindberg Hatvanadik Születése Napján," in György Lukács, *Ifjúkori Művek (1902–1918)*, ed. Árpád Tímar (Budapest: Magvető Kiadó, 1977), 222–26.
26. For the broader intellectual and artistic context of Lukács's critique of impressionism and aesthetic culture, see also: Györgyi Földes, *"Hädüzenet minden impressionizmusnak . . .": Impresszionizmusellenség a Vasárnapi Körnel és a Magyar Avantgardistáknál* (Budapest: Széphalom Könyvműhely, 2006); Károly Kókai, *Im Nebel: Der Junge Georg Lukács und Wien* (Vienna: Böhlau Verlag, 2002); Gyula Hellenbart, *König Midas in Budapest: Georg Lukács und die Ungarn* (Vienna: Passagen Verlag, 1995).
27. Endre Ady, "Hiszek hitetlenül Istenben," in Ady, *Összes Versei I*, eds. József Láng and Pál Schweitzer (Budapest: Osiris Kiadó, 2004), 345–46.
28. György Lukács, "Üj Magyar Líra," in Lukács, *Ifjúkori Művek*, 250.
29. Georg (von) Lukács, "Ariadne auf Naxos," in Paul Ernst and Georg Lukács, *Dokumente einer Freundschaft*, ed. Karl August Kutzbach (Emsdette: Verlag Lechte, 1974), 60.
30. Ernst Bloch, "Gedenkbuch für Else Bloch-Von Stritzki," in Bloch, *Tendenz-Latenz-Utopie* (Frankfurt am Main: Suhrkamp Verlag, 1978), 11–50.
31. Agnes Heller, "Georg Lukács and Irma Seidler," in *Lukács Reappraised*, 27–62; Lee Congdon, *The Young Lukács* (Chapel Hill: University of North Carolina Press, 1983); Gluck, *Georg Lukács and His Generation*; Massimo Cacciari, "Metafisica della Gioventù," in György Lukács, *Diario 1910–1911*, ed. Gabriella Caramore (Milan: Adelphi, 1983), 69–148; Thomas Harrison, *1910: The Emancipation of Dissonance* (Berkeley and Los Angeles: University of California Press, 1996).
32. György Lukács, *Napló-Tagebuch (1910–1911). Das Gericht (1913)*, ed. Ferenc L. Lendvai (Budapest: Akadémiai Kiadó, 1981), 33.

Chapter 3

Lukács's Theatres of History: Drama, Action, and Historical Agency

I take my point of departure for this chapter from a question posed to me after a presentation about Lukács's Hungarian essays of 1945–48, which I translated and edited in *The Culture of People's Democracy*. In presenting my translation, I had observed that in the writings of this period, Lukács gave surprisingly sparse attention to the classic Marxist theme of the dialectic of labor and capital. Instead, I argued, he emphasized a populist-republican dialectics of action, a "Machiavellian moment" traceable from Machiavelli through the French Jacobins, the 1848 revolutionaries and national independence movements, up to Lenin and the Russian Revolution.[1] In answering my colleague's question—"So what does 'action' look like for Lukács?"—after a moment of reflection, I responded, "Action for Lukács is what happens in realist novels. His theory of literary realism *is* his theory of action." I still believe this was not bad for quick thinking at the lectern. But subsequently, I have come to believe it only partially captures the nature of action in Lukács, not least because it suggests that the *novel* is the destined site of Lukács's reflections on historical action. Equally important for uncovering Lukács's theory of action, however, are his extensive writings on *drama*, which span from his very earliest work through his mature writings of the 1930s, and up to key writings late in his life.[2]

Dramatizing Lukács

To offer a hint of the surprising perspective shift that attention to drama may occasion even in the most familiar and apparently unlikely of Lukács's texts, I begin with a brief venture into his best-known work, *History and Class Consciousness*, published in 1923. In the most influential section of the book, his essay on "Reification and the Consciousness of the Proletariat," Lukács discusses how the proletariat's engagement with apparently immediate historical happenings or circumstances points, in an anticipatory way, towards a synthetic grasp of more remote factors that in turn informs its historical action. He writes that "For the proletariat . . . this ability to go beyond the immediate in search of the 'remoter' factors means the *transformation of the objective nature of the objects of action*. . . . [I]t holds the immediate objects of action firmly and decisively in its grip so as to bring about their total, structural transformation and thus the movement of the whole gets under way."[3] In the paragraph that follows, Lukács makes explicit that he is talking about the relation of the proximate space of action to the horizon of totality, which takes up partial, disconnected acts and relates them dialectically in a transformational or developmental process: "The category of totality . . . operates by ensuring that actions which seem to confine themselves to particular objects, in both content and consciousness, yet preserve an aspiration towards the totality, that is to say: action is directed objectively towards a transformation of totality" (175). This dialectical relation of proximate action, which at a subjective level has not yet revealed its more remote objective meaning in a totality still in the process of emerging, is crucial for the special historical role that Lukács ascribes to the proletariat in *History and Class Consciousness*. On the one hand, it provides a point of contrast to the consciousness of the bourgeoisie, which remains unable to connect surface and partial social phenomena into a more comprehensive totality through its own transformative praxis. On the other hand, it allows Lukács to acknowledge a proletarian consciousness that is still inchoate and incipient, but which may take on historical coherence as the horizon of totality comes ever more clearly into view.

In expounding this conception of emergent self-conscious proletarian action, we may be surprised to discover, Lukács turns to the example of *tragic drama* to illustrate this crucial theoretical point. "When," Lukács writes,

> the theory and practice of tragedy from Aristotle to the age of Corneille regard family conflicts as providing the most fruitful subject-matter for tragedy, we glimpse lying behind this view . . . the feeling that the great changes in society are being revealed here with a sensuous, practical vividness. This enables their contours to be drawn clearly whereas it is subjectively and objectively impossible to grasp their essence, to understand their origins and their place in the whole process. Thus an Aeschylus or a Shakespeare draws pictures of family life that provide us with such penetrating and authentic portraits of the social upheavals of their age that . . . only now, with the aid of historical materialism, . . . it has become . . . possible for theory to do justice to those artistic insights. (175–76)

Dwelling for a minute on what Lukács has asserted here, we see that he has suggested that the proletariat's historical praxis has, in its relation of vivid, concentrated action to a wider horizon of significance, an isomorphism with the dramaturgical structure of action in great tragic drama and as analyzed by the classical theorists of tragedy from Aristotle to Hegel (with perhaps some nod to the younger Lukács himself). Lukács moreover suggests that the theory and practice of tragic drama, as it has come down to us in literary tradition, can be understood precisely as a pre-theoretical form of the Marxist theory of action in the epoch of proletarian revolution, with great drama constituting a kind of literary drill field for budding Leninists.

Shifting back a few years to 1919, in Hungary in early spring a real-live moment of revolutionary proletarian action was taking place. On March 21, 1919, the president of the republic that had been declared in November 1918, Mihály Károlyi, stepped down, giving way to the 133 days of the Hungarian Commune (the *Tanácsköztársaság*, or Council Republic), which was led by the foreign minister and returned prisoner of war Béla Kun, who took directions on the Bolshevization of Hungary via radiotelegraph from Lenin in Moscow. What was Lukács, who had recently converted to communism, doing in these early days of the revolution?

We have a report in the March 30–April 5 1919 issue of *Színházi Élet* (Theatre Life) that on March 27th, six days after the commencement of the Commune, Lukács named the Committee for the Communalization of the Theatres, with an overall director, Béla Reinitz, and section leaders for the following subdivisions: 1) the Opera and National Theatres, 2) the Comic Theatre, the Hungarian Theatre, the Bárdos Theatre, and the Madách Theatre, 3) the King's Theatre, the People's Opera, the City Park Theatre, and the Medgyasszay Theatre, along with the cabarets, and 4) the music halls, nightclubs, etc. Somewhat later this committee morphed into the Committee of Socialized Theatres and Nightclubs, the second department of the Eighth People's Committee for Education, which included sections for dramatic theatre, musical theatre, and circus, variety, and other collective entertainment. A report by László Kalotai quotes a speech by Lukács at the government assembly in which he addressed the matter of theatre under the Hungarian Soviet order:

> If we are communalizing the theatre, it is above all … to open a viewing space into the places of culture for the proleteriat, the working masses: our theatres will no longer be the monopoly of the well-heeled. Provisionally then for a limited portion of the tickets the theatres will still charge their normal prices, but the eventual situation will be that all the tickets will be at the disposal of the trade unions, and the prices will be reduced to a minimum.

> As far as the matter of the theatre personnel, at the outset we will keep everyone in their previous place, even the theatre producers, of course as paid employees. We don't want to cause the least disturbance, but of course later there will be changes in personnel as well.
>
> With reference to the theatre programming a transitional situation will be in place, until our theatre committee helps to form a truly high quality program worthy of proletarians. In the dramatic theatres we will present serious pieces representative of the best international literature. For this transformation of the programming we will take into account those experiences that we gained during the period of the communalization of the Moscow theatres, in which the total reshaping succeeded perfectly within a year.[4]

The reporter asks: "And what about the musical theatre?" Lukács responds:

> As far as this goes, we will for the time being turn the operetta theatres towards the cultivation of older classic composers such as Offenbach and Planquette, until the new direction, which will probably aim towards comic opera, can be definitively given shape, after which the music halls, which likewise remain as they always were, will see radical reform. (214)

In an interview for the *Neues Wiener Journal* published in German and Hungarian in the latter half of April, Lukács amplified upon some of the above positions in light of developments in the following weeks. Revealing further steps in the direction of communalization, Lukács notes:

> The tying of actors to a single theatre must cease, because the collective theatrical forces should in the future belong to a single organized group. We want to bring to an end the monopolizing of the best actors by a single theatre. The star system will no longer exist, and we need to give shape to performances of the whole group. The direction of the theatres will be in the hands of the writers and stage directors.
>
> What will happen with the fantastic payments of single female and male primadonnas ... has not yet been definitively decided, but in principle the Soviet government takes the view that the payment of actors should not be any higher than any other kind of intellectual work. (224)

We can also note that Lukács was occupied with related questions of the nationalization of the cinema as well during the Hungarian Commune. As Tom Levin notes, the journal *Vörös Film* reported in April 1919 that Lukács's cultural proposals included an institute for supporting the development of film and film workers.[5]

These two examples, one from Lukács's *History and Class Consciousness*, the other from his activity as a cultural and educational commissar in the Hungarian Revolution of 1919, may of course just be singular instances. But I would suggest more generally that we pay heed to the role of drama and dramatic concepts in Lukács, who has been read with almost exclusive focus on his early Marxist philosophy and critical writings on prose narrative. In the United States and Britain at least, there has been selective emphasis on only two of Lukács's works, which, though highly important, are rather exceptional in his overall corpus: *The Theory of the Novel* (1916) and *History and Class Consciousness* (1923). Both works stake out the main themes of the English-speaking reception of Lukács: the relation of the novel to history, and the concept of reification. Through the lens of these two works, Lukács was envisioned as the avatar of the New Left's activist, cultural, non-mechanistic, and anti-economistic Marxism. His own later work, as I have already discussed, appeared a self-betrayal in the interest of accommodating himself to the Stalinism of the East Bloc.

Along with other criticisms we might raise about this simplified view of Lukács's oeuvre, we might also complicate these commonplace perspectives from a *generic* point of view: by refocusing our picture of him such that the drama and dramatic concepts come to the fore. No one, surely, would want to deny that Lukács is a formidable and justly celebrated theorist of the novel and that this focus is a powerful component of his legacy for subsequent literary criticism. However, as I trace out in what follows, his narrative criticism stands in an intimate relationship to his writings on drama, especially his early work, both in his introduction of modern European theatre to Budapest and in his early dramatic criticism and theory. Moreover, while somewhat eclipsed by his writings on prose narrative, drama continued as an important thread of interest for Lukács throughout his sixty-year career.

Dramatic Typology

Both before his conversion to Marxism and in every phase of his Marxist development, Lukács's criticism drew parallelisms between literary genres and philosophies of history, seeing in generic structures the expression of larger social frameworks, whether pre-capitalist, bourgeois, socialist, or fascist. This in turn was undergirded by an implicit theory of social types, which are defined by modes of their action and interaction with other types. Within literary works, these type-actions constitute the mimetic foundations of characterization and plot, expressing how characters, as vehicles of action, are shaped by the constraints of milieus and in interaction with other characters. The theory of types is a crucial element of most theories of literary realism, up to and including Lukács's own "critical realism" and also the various "socialist realisms" he opposed. In the long run, this typological theory derives from Aristotle's *Poetics*, which takes "men in action" as the "object of poetic imitation," categorizes these objects of imitation according to moral types (goodness or badness), which in turn relate to social role and standing (it makes a difference regarding appropriate action and diction whether you are a king or a servant). Aristotle's mimetic theory also provides philosophical justification for applying analogous conceptual frameworks to both poetics and ethics, because *action*—in literary works in the former, in social life in the latter—is their common object. Thus, for example, Aristotle underscores that "Tragedy is essentially an imitation not of persons but of action and life. . . . Character gives us qualities, but it is in our actions that we are happy or the reverse. In a play accordingly they do not act . . . to portray the characters; they include the characters for the sake of action."[6] For Lukács, this encompassing Aristotelian presupposition of action as the object of representation dovetailed in complex ways with notions of contradiction and praxis derived from Hegel and Marx. Yet his later conception of action never definitively left behind its roots in dramatic action as he had theorized it in *Developmental History of Modern Drama*.

To take a typical example of his later application of such notions, we find in his study *The Young Hegel*, which purports to offer "studies in the relations between dialectics and economics," a discussion of Hegel's chapter on "tragedy in the realm of the ethical" from his early writings on natural law. While considering Hegel's conception of tragedy and comedy with respect to the law, Lukács also applies these generic notions to the structure of action in his favorite nineteenth-century novelist, Balzac: "Balzac, the great realist of the age, creates in his *Human Comedy* a compendium of the tragic, tragi-comic, and comic contradictions growing out of the soil of bourgeois society and manifesting themselves in the relations between men."[7] Lukács sees the forms of action in the field of social relations as already generic in nature: tragic, tragi-comic, and comic. There are, as it were, objective social-ontological forms of action that preexist and provide the infrastructure for the generic basis of literary representation. Notably, even when Lukács discusses novels, this action-field is conceived in dramatic terms and is described in traditional terms of dramatic genre theory. Of course, we know that there is a broad tradition of applying modal concepts to works that are outside the dramatic genre, such as Dante's *Divina Commedia* and Balzac's *Human Comedy* ensemble of novels. Likewise, there is a powerful critical tradition dating back to German idealist philosophy that conceptualized tragedy as an ontological, moral, or existential human modality, as for example Peter Szondi's study *The*

Poetics of Tragedy and the Philosophy of the Tragic and others have expounded.[8]

What is distinctive to Lukács, however, is his extension of this philosophical and literary tradition well beyond his early aesthetics, formulated under the influence of Kant, Kierkegaard, and Simmel, into his mature Marxist phase and using historical materialist categories of analysis. Thus for example in the aforementioned chapter of *The Young Hegel*, Lukács takes his obligatory distance from the idealism of Hegel's discussion of tragedy in relation to natural law, his hypostatizing of the specifically modern problem of "tragedy in the realm of the ethical" into an "eternal human conflict" (405), thinking perhaps of Hegel's celebrated discussion of tragedy in the *Phenomenology of Spirit* and the *Philosophy of Right*.[9] But he goes on to admit that "even this exaggeration contains a grain of truth since it anticipates a genuine conflict between the real potential of mankind and the limitations placed upon it by the economic activities of class society as such" (406). Later in the chapter, Lukács refers to Hegel's discussion of Aeschylus's *Oresteia*, representing the tragic conflict of the representatives of natural law with the legal order of the state, to the subsequent reflections on this same body of tragic drama by Bachofen and Engels, granting Hegel "profound intuitions" about the "real historical co-ordinates" of the problem of the family (411). He refers in this case to the arguments for a pre-patriarchal primitive communist matriarchy in Bachofen's 1861 study *Mother-Right*; Engels's 1891 preface to the fourth edition of *The Origin of Private Property, the Family, and the State*, in which he discusses the *Oresteia*; and implicitly also the 1886 articles by Karl Marx's son-in-law Paul Lafargue entitled "Le matriarcat: Étude sur les origines de la famille," published in the paper *Le socialiste*.

I will point to a couple of additional examples in evidence that this is a consistent feature of Lukács's work. His 1940 essay "Tribune or Bureaucrat?"—a prime example of his "high Stalinist" critical mode—takes up Lenin's conceptions of spontaneity and conscious organization to discuss the comportments of the artist under capitalism and socialism and the ways these comportments open or block access to sociohistorical truth in literary representation. The third of four subsections of this lengthy essay is entitled "Tragedy and Tragicomedy of the Artist under Capitalism."[10] Here Lukács traces a developmental trajectory from the tragedy of the artist—the key example being Goethe's play about the sixteenth-century Italian poet Torquato Tasso[11]—in which the artist's role has become "problematical," through such transitional nineteenth-century figures such as Baudelaire, Flaubert, and Ibsen, up to the full-blown contemporary "tragedy of art" itself. As Lukács writes:

"These writers [Baudelaire, Flaubert, and Ibsen] experienced the modern tragedy of the artist and expressed it as a confession of faith. The real modern tragedy ... the tragedy of art itself, remained ... unknown to them; only here and there do outlines of it begin to dawn. ... They scarcely saw that art itself was falling to pieces" (223). So too in 1948, when Lukács would write of Thomas Mann's *Joseph* trilogy and his *Künstlerroman Doktor Faustus*, he would entitle his essay "The Tragedy of Modern Art." In characterizing the latter, he applies the categories of drama to Mann's novel (which, after all, itself alludes to the dramatic tradition of Marlowe and Goethe in allegorizing as Faustian the scions of late German culture from Nietzsche to Schoenberg and Hitler):

> The intellectual *dramatis personae* of his writing are the disintegrating bourgeois humanism and the reactionary, mystifying, demagogic powers which utilize this disintegration on behalf of monopoly capitalism. But since he has thought through this tragedy more deeply and experienced it more painfully than any of his bourgeois contemporaries, what he sees on the horizon is enough artistically to give his conflict a conclusive and comprehensive *finale*.[12]

In answer to the tacit question about why then read Mann's work about the disintegrating world of bourgeois art at all—recall that 1948 was the cusp of the Cold War and the imposition of socialist realist artistic policy throughout the occupied East Bloc—Lukács responded by comparing Mann to Shakespeare:

> Mann may not be able to give concrete embodiment to the "great world" which the people ... are building. Nevertheless, it is sufficiently manifest everywhere for him to fulfill his tragedy of the declining world. ... In Shakespeare's greatest tragedies ... the light of a new world gleams in the tragic darkness at the end. Who has the right to ask Shakespeare to provide an accurate social description of this new world? Does not the vision itself lend the light and shade of the tragedy their right proportions and emphases? (96–97)

Form and Historicity

This presupposition of the historical expressiveness of artistic forms, for which genre constitutes the mediating pivot between historical context and individual artistic works, is indeed nothing less than the conceptual linchpin of Lukács's whole body of literary-critical thought. For Lukács, Peter Demetz suggests, "Type and genre are torn away from the intent of the writer and declared to be a function of historical reality itself. It is history itself that immediately brings forth epic and drama out of epic situations and dramatic conflicts."[13] This basic idea animates

Lukács's later Marxist literary criticism, in which his own typological theory of realism draws sustenance from his critique of Soviet literary theory, which emphasized *regulative* types and action, the presentation of positive heroes acting in ideologically topical situations of labor, technological innovation, political action, or combat. Yet it also receives complex treatment in the pre-Marxist *Theory of the Novel*, which is not an empirical history of the development of the forms of epic, but a consideration of the changing *historicity* of those forms, the problematic nature of empirical instances of these forms to express history's transcendental structures as disclosed by the philosophy of history.

In his methodological observations early in *Theory of the Novel*, "The Problems of a Philosophy of the History of Forms," Lukács postulates an alignment of empirical history and philosophy of history among the ancient Greeks, which in turn allowed their literary genres to express, in their empirical-historical development, the "philosophical periodicity" of history. Genres and literary instances of them were for the Greeks, Lukács states, "born only when the sundial of the mind showed that its hour had come, and had to disappear when the fundamental images were no longer visible on the horizon."[14] The necessity of a critical approach such as Lukács himself deploys in *Theory of Novel* indicates that such "philosophical periodicity" has been disrupted, untuning genre and history and making necessary the analytic reconstruction of the syncopated relations between the history of categories (genres and generic subtypes) and empirical instances of the genre as they emerge contingently in history. Lukács's implication is that new generic forms may be "ahead of their time" (as defined by their actual position vis-à-vis their imputed stages of the philosophy of history), thus giving them a prefigurative, utopian character. But also, as Lukács makes explicit, genres that are "early" within the philosophy of history may persist, residually, in empirical literary history. It is precisely distance from the immediate currents of empirical history that allows an early genre to persist, with its generic essence relatively undisturbed by historical change. "That is why," he writes, "tragedy, although changed, has nevertheless survived in our time with its essential nature intact, whereas the epic had to disappear and yield its place to an entirely new form: the novel" (41). Although a materialist revision of these historico-philosophical presuppositions required many changes in Lukács's theory, he persistently returned to this basic valuation of genre as the pivot between literary history and history at large, and it animated in discernible ways his interpretative strategies in reading key authors and works. In his 1960 preface to the English edition of *The Historical Novel*, for example, he explains the intention of that important study from his Moscow exile as follows: "What I had in mind was a theoretical examination of the interaction between the historical spirit and the great genres of literature which portray the totality of history."[15]

In the apparatus of *drama* specifically, Lukács discerned one of the most concrete, legible sites in which to grasp the dialectics of historical action in the formalized world of the artwork. He extends fundamentally Aristotelian ideas about dramatic character, social representativeness, and action beyond the dramatic genre to more general problems of narrative form as well. In particular, Lukács's notorious theory of literary-historical decadence, which considered bourgeois novelistic characters as increasingly unable to sustain representative, "realist" epic forms, dated back, as Ferenc Fehér has demonstrated, to his very early, pre-Marxist *Developmental History of Modern Drama* (written 1906–08; published in revised form in 1911), in which the emergence of "non-representative," problematic characters was analyzed as a defining feature of modern, bourgeois drama.[16]

In his early writings on theatre, Lukács emphasized the analogy of drama's dependence on real time, embodied presence, and mass effect, which makes it a particularly appropriate artistic evocation of historical action. In a remarkable essay from 1913 on the aesthetics of cinema, Lukács thus noted that the transient quality of theatrical performance is not an unfortunate weakness to be overcome by registration on film; rather, it constitutes a productive limitation within the dramatic medium that is an artistic analogon to the force of fate. Indeed, it is the "tangible expression" of fate's necessity within the dramatic medium itself.[17] By extension, then, drama may thus serve the sociologically and historically minded critic as a crucial means for evoking and communicating to a mass audience the objective necessity of a particular epoch or moment in history.

From the *Developmental History of Modern Drama* to "The Metaphysics of Tragedy"

Lukács's early work on drama dates to the early years of the twentieth century, during which he directed the Thalia Theatre in Budapest between 1904 and 1907, which introduced modern European drama to Hungary. He also wrote numerous theatre reviews and in 1908 submitted a prize-winning essay on modern drama that would eventually be published as a book in 1911; a long section was excerpted in the *Archiv für Sozialwissenschaft und Sozialpolitik* in 1914, which included among its editors Max Weber, Werner Sombart, and Robert Michels.

Already in a theoretical essay published in Hungarian in 1906 ("The Form of Drama"), long before his conversion to Marxism, Lukács had sketched a dialectics of action, character, form, and time that extended well beyond his initial point of departure in the narrower question of dramatic form: "This is the goal—character and action are indivisible ... The action is nothing other than the development of the characters; the character is the prime mover of the action."[18] For the young Lukács, this synthesis of theatrical agent and action had to occur within the formalized generic context of the dramatic artwork, insofar as it was performed within the symbolic medium of dialogue. The task of his study of the *Developmental History of Modern Drama* was to establish in general theoretical terms how this was so, and how the development of a specifically modern drama inflected dramatic form with the problematic nature of modern life.

I cannot offer here anything like a full exposition of Lukács's study, but I will underscore a few key points from his book, because Lukács continued to assume its conceptual framework even decades later and across the ideological and geographical divide that separates his early Hungarian period from his Moscow exile. Lukács argues that the drama is essentially defined by two major features: its concentration on interactions that occur between people and its evocation of a strong, immediate effect for a mass audience. Other additional defining characteristics follow from these two. For example, drama has a strong impulse towards reduction and generalization, concentrating on key collisions or conflicts between a limited number of characters. In addition, it has a strong impulse towards typicality and exemplarity in representation, reciprocally defined as typicality of a certain human type experiencing a typical fate. All this, in turn, leads Lukács to see tragedy as the purest manifestation of this essence of drama:

> Drama is ... a struggle carried out between forces pushed to their utmost degree of tension, symbolizing the total life of a man. ... The consistent thinking through of the material challenge of drama must lead to tragedy. ... Drama always achieves its pinnacle in tragedy; a consummate drama can be nothing other than a tragedy. For the tragic feeling, however, there can be no more adequate medium of expression than drama.[19]

I have already mentioned how later, through the lenses of Hegel and Marx, Lukács will establish a relationship between the genre of tragedy and "tragic" experience of historical contradictions, which in turn correlates forms of literary and historical agency through representative acts of typical historical actors. Notably, then, in the *Developmental History* Lukács goes on to hypothesize that the great historical periods of drama are the periods in which tragedy comes to the fore, which legitimates the search for objective historical conditions of such great tragic-dramatic ages:

> It can also be no accident that the great dramatic epochs (the Greek, the English, Spanish, French epochs) are at the same time also the periods of great tragedies. We know of no epoch, even, in which drama was really flourishing that didn't also experience the dominance of the tragic form and for which the end of tragic feeling was not also the end of the period in which drama could flourish. (25–26)

Lukács also embraces at this early date a sociologically informed perspective—temporarily suspended in his more metaphysical and mystically tinged writings of the midteens—that relates tragic drama to the becoming-problematical of the worldviews of the previously dominant class—"all feelings, thoughts, and evaluations of this class," as he writes. He goes on to postulate that tragedy emerges from the heroic experience of class decline: "It is the epoch in which a class (that of the predominating mass in the audience of drama) apprehends through the men and the heroic types that represent its main capabilities the tragic decline of the typical experiences and events that symbolize its whole life" (47). He specifies that in the case of classic European tragedy—that of Shakespeare, Calderon, Lope de Vega, Corneille, and Racine—the specific historical collision that animates the dramatic epochs of various countries is the decline of the medieval aristocracy in the face of the new monarchs and the emerging bourgeoisie, although still while that declining class's value-system and worldview is substantially intact and has not been reduced to a mere ornament of the absolutist courts (50).

Lukács connects the question of agency or type-action, its possibility in history and in literary characterization, with problems of dramatic form and style. For Lukács, specifically modern drama is defined by two intertwined, but opposed worldviews in bourgeois life more generally: on the one hand, the tendency towards historicism, to see the present as a product of historical experiences and legacies; and on the other, individualism, which sees any limitation of the sort that historical legacy represents as illegitimate and calling forth a struggle for individual liberation from its ties. These tendencies generate pressures on dramatic form, among them a new emphasis on character that *cannot* be reduced to a few essential, typical, and symbolically encompassing acts, but which rather holds open a problematically unlimited field of naturalistic details about the character's relation to its milieu, its psychological and interior life, and the contingent histories that have made it what it is. Lukács also brings to bear a critique of bourgeois life, echoing Simmel and Weber, that sees in the processes of modern secularization and demythification an undermining of proto-dramatic typicality in bourgeois society. Asserting that "Life as material is no longer dramatic, as it was in earlier times" (113), he goes on to expound: "The new life has no pathos" (113). If in earlier ages myth preformed the material of life poetically, "The new life has no mythology, which means that the themata of tragedies must be kept at an artificial distance from life" (114). Lukács ascribes the experimental, form-breaking and new form-inventing impulse of modern drama to authors' attempts to adapt to these features of bourgeois life, but also the increasingly problematic nature of these forms and their attenuated capacity to evoke representative experiences in audiences composed of disenchanted, psychologically involuted, and individualist members of modern society. What Lukács had not yet decided at this point, however, as György Márkus and Fehér have noted, is whether this problematic situation of bourgeois life and modern culture, and its impact on artistic forms, reflected a fundamental existential ontology that the conditions of modernity disclosed or a contingent, hence potentially correctable historical situation.[20]

Lukács's essay "The Metaphysics of Tragedy" was originally published in 1911 in the journals *Szellem* (Spirit) and *Logos*; in the latter German-language version, notably, it appeared alongside Georg Simmel's important essay "The Concept and the Tragedy of Culture."[21] Lukács recaps in brief the theory of drama and modern drama that he had expounded at length in the *Developmental History*. But now, along with his discussion of the tragedies of the neo-classicist contemporary dramatist Ernst, with whom Lukács conducted an extensive correspondence, he also offers new observations about the relation of tragedy and history, which he sees as embodying a paradox. Amplifying his previous emphasis on the reductive, typifying nature of tragedy, Lukács focuses on the temporality of the tragic, which, he argues, involves compression into a durationless moment. He writes: "The tragic experience ... is a beginning and an end at the same time. Everyone at such a moment is newly born, yet has been dead for a long time; and everyone's life stands before the Last Judgment. Any 'development' of a character in drama is merely apparent.... The dying heroes of tragedy ... are dead a long time before they actually die."[22] Tragedy thus stands in a contradictory relation to history, which is defined by duration and contingency. The paradoxical attempt to write historical tragedy represents a desire to find an underlying meaning in the apparently accidental detail and extensiveness of history and give it essential, typical expression. But, Lukács concludes, the metaphysical dissonance between tragedy and history—their radically different temporalities and the nature of the actions related to these modes of time—cannot be concealed or artistically harmonized. Historical tragedy, in his view, is an intrinsically problematic form. As Lukács sums up:

> [T]he technical paradoxes of historical tragedy spring from the metaphysical paradox of the relationship between tragic man and historical existence.... The historical view of life does not allow of any abstraction of place or time or the other principles of individuation: ... the characters of historical drama must "live" and the events portrayed must show all the colorful variegation of life. (195)

From this analysis, too, we can see better why the bourgeois worldview of historicism appeared to Lukács as problematical for dramatic form. Its assumption of a historical definition of a character or the circumstances of action militated, in Lukács's view, against the essentializing and typifying principle of dramatic form itself, carrying into the form of modern drama this metaphysical dissonance between tragedy and history as modes of human existence. But this then raises the question of how Lukács accounts for his own embrace of historicism, already in the association of drama with periods of class decline in the *Developmental History*, and still more emphatically in the full-scale Hegelian-Marxist problematic of his writings of the 1930s on.

Marx, Engels, and Lassalle's *Franz von Sickingen*

Lukács worked in collaboration with Mikhail Lifshitz in Moscow in the 1930s to unearth a Marxist aesthetics out of freshly available writings and correspondence of Marx and Engels.[23] One of Lukács's key essays from this work, dating back to a German manuscript written as early as 1930, "The Sickingen Debate between Marx-Engels and Lassalle," centers on Marx and Engels's critical remarks and correspondence with the German Social Democratic leader Ferdinand Lassalle about *Franz von Sickingen*, Lassalle's five-act historical tragedy set in the German Peasant Wars and published in 1858.[24] In addition to this longer essay on the discussions of Lassalle, Marx, and Engels, Lukács offered a shorter treatment for the sixth volume of the Soviet *Lityeraturnaja Enciklopegyija* (1932), "A Critique of Lassalle's Literary Theory," which explicitly situates the work in relation to the current political conjuncture established by Stalin's 1931 letter to the Editorial Board of *Proletarskaya Revolutsia*, "Some Questions Concerning the History of Bolshevism,"[25] which called for a definitive rupture with "opportunist" Social Democrats and "Centrist" Trotskyists in all areas of Communist

Party and Comintern policy. Lukács dutifully provides historical justification for this position dating all the way back to the 1850s, in which an authentic "Marxist" (leading to a Bolshevist, Lenin-Stalin) conception of literature can already be opposed to the "Lassallean" (leading to a Second International, Centrist, Menshevik and Trotskyist) conception of literature).[26] In this essay, Lukács also references his own programmatic essay, "Tendency or Partisanship?" published in the journal *Linkskurve* in 1932, which advocated continuing application of Lenin's term *partynost* (party spirit, partisanship)[27] and which explicitly traces this current socialist literary debate back to German radical writers of Marx's context such as Heinrich Heine, Ernst Moritz Arndt, Georg Herwegh, and Ferdinand Freiligrath and forward to figures such as the Social Democratic literary historian and Marx biographer Franz Mehring and the exiled oppositionist Trotsky. Yet another version of this material, "Marx and Engels on Problems of Dramaturgy," was published in English and French in 1934 in the international editions of *The International Theatre/Le Théatre International*,[28] suggesting the topicality that Lukács and the organs of communist literary politics found in this otherwise seemingly arcane cultural-historical topic during the mandated "Bolshevization" of literary policy against Social Democratic and Trotskyite tendencies.

In *Franz von Sickingen*, Demetz notes, Lassalle gives the Reformation adventurer "the qualities of a national revolutionary of 1848"[29] and makes his tragedy a prefiguration of later revolutionary struggles to come. While it is true that the historical Franz von Sickingen offered refuge to figures such as Luther and to men of science who were part of the Reformation struggle against Rome, he might just as well be described as a military adventurer and extortionist than as the proto-Enlightenment humanist and would-be populist that Lassalle makes him out to be. In the play, he is given to anachronistic speechifying in Kantian terms about "interest" and "disinterestedness" with simultaneous economic, moral, and aesthetic connotations, leading to tendentious set pieces such as this passage in which the knight expounds how the beauty of Renaissance art is creating stirrings of humanistic this-worldliness that threaten the mystifying power of the Church:

> When with the city's fall,
> The city of Constantine, the fleeing Greeks
> Arrived, transplanting, 'mong us spreading
> The ruins of their Arts and Sciences—
> That was the evil's start! With baneful fascination seized,
> Upon its neck hung, God-intoxicated,
> The Bembos, Medicis, the flow'r of all Italy;

> The serpent young they suckled into strength;
> And from th'eternal laws, with beauty's lines
> Instinct, there flowed a sense of *Now* and *Here on Earth*.
> [...]
> From Raphael's Madonnas there peers forth
> Old heathendom's superb-divine grimace;
> And swellingly a disposition new
> Is preached by Titian's flesh-tints! (*Franz von Sickingen*, 51–52)

Marx and Engels's exchange of letters about Lassalle's play, with its clunky iambics and bombastic speeches, was unusually polite for this usually scathing duo. While Demetz has suggested that they were both somewhat calculating about their response (110), seeing in Lassalle a political friend and in Marx's case also a supporter in getting his *Contribution to the Critique of Political Economy* published, Engels at least got seriously into the questions of dramatic form in relation to the history of early modern German revolutionary conflict and carried it on in some depth. Among the topics Marx and Engels bandied about were the relative value of different models for historical drama, including Shakespeare's history plays, Goethe's *Egmont* and *Götz von Berlichingen*, and Schiller's *Don Carlos* and *Wallenstein* trilogy. Marx ribbed Lassalle that he should "Shakespeare-ize" (*Shakespearisieren*) more and do less Schiller-izing (*das Schillern*), a wordplay that puns on the name of Schiller and the verb *schillern* (to shimmer, sparkle, dazzle, change color). Marx specifies the sense of his pun, however, as Lassalle's tendency, like Schiller, to change "the individual into the mere mouthpiece of the spirit of the age."[30] Engels for his part had direct interest in this historical material dating back at least to his 1850 history *The Peasant War in Germany*, and as late as 1885, he was still discussing questions of drama in a letter to Minna Kautsky in which he claimed that Schiller's play *Cabal and Love* could be considered the first German "tendency-drama." Engels's use of the "tendency" concept surely drew Lukács's attention to this passage because of the latter's own struggles with "tendency" in socialist writing of the late 1920s and 1930s.[31]

Lukács faithfully follows Marx's lead in applying his own critical concept of "schematism" to the debate, a concept he also used to criticize current socialist literature, including documentary reportage literature and the idealizing plots and characters of an emerging socialist realism, extremes at which, in his view, abstract formalism and undigested positivism meet.[32] As Lukács writes, "The drama's basic conception, the tragic conflict, does not achieve its poetic formation from the authentic historical process, but rather—to the contrary—the author's subjective and readymade opinions are arbitrarily *imported into history*. The plot thus merely illustrates the poet's thesis, while the characters are examples, symbols of the writer's own views."[33] Lukács also, however, claims that the focus of these three great socialists on the dramatic genre and its problems was no mere happenstance, but followed from the nature of the historical events of the period, in which "the revolution became the central theme of dramatic literature and the theory of drama"—noting that this was also true for the liberal aesthetics of Theodor Vischer and for the conservative position of Christian Friedrich Hebbel as well (70). In his related essay on "Marx and Engels on Problems of Dramaturgy," Lukács evokes the urgent need to study Marx's discussions of drama closely so that drama can reappropriate its own millennia-long history and "on the path of socialist realism" experience a "new flowering."[34]

Almost two decades earlier, before the correspondence with Lassalle (around 1840–41), the young Friedrich Engels had himself tried writing a historical drama on the fourteenth-century Roman political leader Cola di Rienzo. Cola had led an uprising against the nobles and empowered the populace, who then turned against him and burned the Capitol with him and his last followers inside.[35] Through the popular novel *Cola di Rienzo, the Last of the Roman Tribunes*, published in 1835 by Edward Bulwer-Lytton,[36] and in derivative works such as a tragedy by Julius Mosen[37] and the early opera of Richard Wagner,[38] Cola circulated in pre-1848 radical political circles as an exemplum, akin to the Anabaptist Thomas Münzer in Germany and the Digger Gerrard Winstanley in England, of tragically premature anticipations of the coming democratic and socialist revolutions. Following this chain out one step further, it has been suggested that Hitler's enthusiastic viewing of Wagner's *Rienzi* in his youth was an inspiration for his plebian politics[39] and as Chancellor he requested and kept in his possession the original manuscript of the opera.[40]

This same early Wagner opera was also staged in both Moscow and St. Petersburg in the early 1920s, including the 1923 Zemin Opera production with Georgi Yakulov's avant-garde set design. Yakulov was, in fact, to have collaborated with Meyerhold on a staging of *Rienzi* already in 1920 for the Comintern's Third Congress.[41] Meyerhold (as Valentine and Jean-Claude Marcadé note) was attracted to the revolutionary romanticism of Wagner's opera,[42] but in the end, due to political and financial issues of the theatre, it was not performed. In his 1925 book on the new theatre in the Soviet Union, Huntley Carter described the 1923 staging as "revolutionary":

> Here a treatment that was more left wing than the home of classic opera had ever known, presented itself in the form of the circus ideas with which the Proletcult theatre had definitively associated itself. The scene, as designed by

the painter, Yikylov [Yakulov], was shaped like a circus arena with steps at all angles and all levels, with suggestions of a trapeze and hoops and the rest of the objects and agents of circus representation.[43]

I evoke these various connections to suggest a wider matrix in which to think of the intersections of drama (including musical drama) and political action in the nineteenth- and early twentieth centuries, and to note that Lukács's critical interest in the Lassalle-Marx-Engels debates over historical drama indicates his awareness of how deeply dramaturgical concepts had figured in the development of socialist thought and practice.

Historical Novel and Historical Drama

I turn now to Lukács's essay on historical drama and the historical novel in his study *The Historical Novel*, written during his exile in Moscow, partially published in the journal *Literaturnyi Kritik* between 1937 and 1938, and unsuccessfully submitted for publication in Russian in 1937; it eventually saw German-language publication in 1955.[44] As Jameson writes in his preface to the English translation, "*The Historical Novel* is perhaps the single most monumental realization of the various programs and promises of a Marxist and a dialectical literary criticism."[45] Notably, a full quarter of the book is dedicated primarily not to the novel but to its generic-dialectical counterpart, the drama. Though Jameson in his preface does not take up at length Lukács's engagement with drama, he does note the pages that Lukács dedicates to drama in *The Historical Novel* represent a crucial theoretical move on Lukács's part. Jameson writes, "Not the least striking feature of Lukács's book, indeed, is the grand moment in which the formal specificity of the historical novel (and prose narrative itself) requires a turn of the theorist's attention, in elaborate and achieved detail, to the dialectical *other* of this genre, namely, the historical *drama*" (2).

I cannot treat in detail this rich chapter, and in particular, I leave aside its main focus, which is the *comparison* of two generic modes of representing historical reality, in favor of briefly discussing the specific account of the dramatic genre that Lukács articulates. My first preliminary observation, before passing to more specific points, is that Lukács, almost three decades after the publication of his *Developmental History of Modern Drama*, clearly recurs to the theory of drama already formulated there, which defined drama with reference to its essentializing drive; its focus on intensive relations between human individuals rather than on interactions of characters with an extensive totality of things; its use of dialogue as its primary means of expression with a concurrent minimizing of exposition; its aim to produce immediate and direct mass effect on its audience; the dramatic primacy of tragedy because of its reduction to the central collision of opposed forces; its literary-historical assumption that the conditions of great drama exists only under particular circumstance and that there are intermittently dramatic and non-dramatic periods in literary history; the relationship it draws between tragedy and periods of class decline; and the increasingly problematic status of drama under modern bourgeois society which puts dramatic form under various sorts of pressure. These all reappear anew in this chapter. The second preliminary observation derives from Lukács's conclusion to the chapter, which suggests that the question of the historical novel and the historical drama is really a question of the novelistic and dramatic genre as such, since as he argues, the novel and drama in themselves, independent of a specific historiographic theme, are paradigmatic ways in which human beings mediate history to themselves. As he concludes:

> If one treats the Marxist problem of genre seriously, acknowledging a genre only where one sees a peculiar artistic reflection of peculiar facts of life, there is not a single fundamental problem one can adduce to justify the creation of a specific genre of historical subject-matter either in the novel or in drama. Naturally a preoccupation with history will always produce its individual and special tasks. But none of these specific problems is or can be of sufficient weight to justify a really independent genre of historical literature. (170)

This is a rather surprising thing to say in the midst of a book entitled *The Historical Novel*, that perhaps the book really should just be called *The Novel*. But Lukács's point about both the novel and the drama is that their historicity, their capacity to represent and communicate historical experience, lies not with their historical subject matter, much less with their positivistic accuracy and detail, but rather with their ability to give literary form to a human experience which is *already* socially and historically *preformed*. Fictionality is not the contrary of historicity—it is a necessary modality of history as mediated through art and literature.

I will add here a few specific points. The first is that Lukács assumes that dramatic art can be realistic—therefore also realistic with respect to the representation of history—because life itself produces experiences that might be thought of as dramatic or proto-dramatic. There are basic "forms of life" that derive from the sharpening of social contradictions to the point of collision between opposed individuals, and of these forms of life, Lukács writes, "it is clear that the social-historical concentrating of contradictions in life necessarily demands a dramatic embodiment ... The contradictoriness of social development, the intensification of these contradictions to the point of tragic collision is a *general* fact of life" (99). Lukács goes on to suggest that there are general topoi in which life takes proto-dramatic shape. He discusses, by way of example, the "parting of ways" topos, in which a radical decision is called for. Remarkably, he relates this to Lenin's political maxim to grasp a particular link in the chain that allows access to the whole chain. Lukács writes:

> Lenin not only describes incomparably an important principle of political action, especially in periods of necessary change, but at the same time a feature of human behavior in general. ... [T]he act of choosing and grasping the link in the chain is closely related to the parting-of-the-ways problem. ... What is specific to the link-in-the-chain problem is, above all, the stress given to the chosen link, which is made central. Thereby, life, to further its own ends, simplifies and generalizes itself. This simplification and generalization gives life a pulsating, vigorous character, forming contrasts and driving them to extremes. (102)

Lukács suggests, then, that dramatic form's delimitation of the field of literary representation to a central collision is isomorphic with more general dramatic structures of life. Even more striking, however, is a further implication: that the underlying structure of Lenin's political thought and characteristic form of political action, as represented by his famous chain-link metaphor, is *dramaturgical*. Time after time, Lenin concentrated political action at points where a central political collision could be condensed, clarified, and heightened to a dialectical extreme, just as the great tragedians did in their dramatic works.

A second dramatic topos Lukács names "the calling to account," in which the implications of past actions come to the fore in a concentrated moment of action and passion. Lukács notes that "History is full of such facts. ... The great French Revolution, in particular, is full of such catastrophes which are already dramatic in life itself" (101).[46] A third such topos for Lukács is an individual's passionate attachment to his work. He writes:

> If we have already seen in the complete personal devotion to a task a dramatization of life in life itself ... such a supreme case of involvement represents a high point dramatically both in life and art. In life, too, this basic personal unity between the individual, his life-work and its social content sharpens the concentrated sphere in which the "world-historical individual" moves, drawing it around significant collisions which are materially linked with the realization of this life-work. The "world-historical individual" has a dramatic character. He is destined by life itself ... to be the central figure in drama. (104)

There would be much more to say about Lukács's subsequent discussion of the interrelations of the generic features of drama and historical subject matter; his discussion of crucial works and theoretical arguments by Shakespeare, Alfieri, Goethe, Schiller, Manzoni, and Pushkin; and his dialectical exposition of the divergences and intertwinings of the historical drama and the historical novel. In closing my discussion of *The Historical Novel*, however, I will underscore just one further conclusion that Lukács comes to in his comparison of the historical novel and drama. Lukács argues that because of the concentration of key historical collisions in individual characters acting and expressing themselves through dialogue in the present, however deep in the past the represented events are, historical drama tends to represent relative constants within historical life. Or, as Lukács puts it, citing the nineteenth-century German dramatist and critic Otto Ludwig, it presents history in an "anthropological light." Lukács connect this anthropological orientation of historical drama to a seeming paradox, the fact that we must experience past history as taking place in the present and as referring directly to us. Thus, he writes:

> While the essence of a collision must remain historically authentic, historical drama must bring out those features in men and their destinies which will make a spectator, separated from these events by centuries, feel himself a direct participant of them. . . . [D]rama draws out those features in all men which in the course of history have been relatively the most permanent, general, and regulative. (152)

Drama, we might say, in revealing the regulative anthropological conditions of human action, has a close proximity to the *philosophy* of history.

Heller has suggested that Lukács's two late attempts at systematic philosophy, *The Specificity of the Aesthetic* and *The Ontology of Social Being*, express his desire, in the face of the failures of actually existing socialism, to go back to first principles of Marxist theory, to elucidate two interrelated but independently important modalities of praxis: the principles of mimetic action (human interaction with each other) and the principles of labor (human interaction with material nature).[47] If Heller is correct, then we can glimpse here the enduring significance that drama played for Lukács. It formed in the *Developmental History* a crucial object of his earliest attempt, and in the *Aesthetics* one of his latest attempts, to grasp the very structure of human action in history.

The Tragedy of Lukács?

> "Just as it is essential for the statue to be the work of human hands, so is the actor essential to his mask . . ."
>
> G.W.F. Hegel, *The Phenomenology of Spirit*[48]

I will conclude on a more speculative note, but on an issue important to consider when speaking of the broad significance of drama in Lukács's life and work. When Lukács, at key points in his career—after the defeat of the Blum Theses in 1929, in the anti-Lukács campaign of 1949–50 under the Hungarian Stalinist dictatorship, and again following the suppressed 1956 Hungarian uprising—was forced by historical circumstances to retreat from his more practical political engagements to literary criticism, writing about literary artworks and aesthetics became for him a space in which to reflect on the problem of historically significant action and to "act out" or "rehearse," in the virtual "theatre" of critical discourse, a historical role barred to him elsewhere.[49] By the late 1920s, Lukács had recanted the activist notion of class consciousness dominating *History and Class Consciousness* in favor of an underlying Marxist philosophical anthropology and a "realist" exploration of social action in its historical contexts. He found, as Heller has suggested, his most important examples in works of art: "Some entity has to be found that already represents in itself the unity of individual and species and provides that, through its adoption, it will give to all the possibility of rising to true, defetishized consciousness. This entity, according to Lukács, is art itself" ("Lukács' Late Philosophy," 184).

In subsequent work, and in partial return to earlier themes about the relation of "form" and "soul," Lukács sought to explain the dynamics determining which symbolic forms can mediate the actions through which humans manifest their essence in and as history. In making this shift, however, Lukács was not, I would suggest, simply putting forward a new theoretical position in his attempt to replace class with the mediations of human species-being in cultural forms. He was also reflexively justifying his own, still engaged, but now necessarily more mediated relation to "History": philosophically legitimating the necessity of detouring his own action through the symbolic indirection of a philosophical and critical discourse.

Notes

1. See J.G.A. Pocock, *The Machiavellian Moment: Florentine Political Thought and the Atlantic Republican Condition* (Princeton, NJ: Princeton University Press, 1975).
2. A small sample of these writings, along with critical discussions, appears in the recent volume *Georg Lukács: Texte zum Theater*, eds. Jakob Hayner and Erik Zielke (Berlin: Verlag Theater der Zeit, 2021).
3. Georg Lukács, *History and Class Consciousness: Studies in Marxist Dialectics*, trans. Rodney Livingstone (Cambridge, MA: The MIT Press, 1971), 175.
4. György Lukács, *Forradalomban: Cikkek, Tanulmányok, 1918–1919* (Budapest: Magvető Kiadó, 1987), 213–14.
5. Tom Levin, "From Dialectical to Normative Specificity: Reading Lukács on Film," *New German Critique* 40 (1987): 35–61.
6. Aristotle, *Poetics* 1450: 16–21, in *The Complete Works of Aristotle: The Revised Oxford Translation, Volume 2*, ed. Jonathan Barnes (Princeton, NJ: Princeton University Press, 1984), 2320.
7. Georg Lukács, *The Young Hegel: Studies in the Relations Between Dialectics and Economics*, trans. Rodney Livingstone (Cambridge, MA: The MIT Press, 1976), 400.
8. Translated as Peter Szondi, *An Essay on the Tragic*, trans. Paul Fleming (Stanford: Stanford University Press, 2002). See also on this point: Raymond Williams, *Modern Tragedy* (Stanford: Stanford University Press, 1966); Denis Schmidt, *On Germans and Other Greeks: Tragedy and Ethical Life* (Bloomington: Indiana University Press, 2001); Agnes Heller, *The Time Is Out of Joint: Shakespeare as Philosopher of History* (Lanham, MD: Rowman and Littlefield, 2002); Terry Eagleton, *Tragedy* (New Haven, CT: Yale University Press, 2020).
9. G.W.F. Hegel, *Phenomenology of Spirit*, trans. A.V. Miller (Oxford: Oxford University Press, 1977), 433ff.; G.W.F. Hegel, *Philosophy of Right*, trans. T.M. Knox (Oxford: Oxford University Press, 1952), 114–15.
10. Georg Lukács, "Tribune or Bureaucrat?" in *Essays on Realism*, trans. David Fernbach, ed. Rodney Livingstone (Cambridge, MA: The MIT Press, 1980), 213ff.
11. Johann Wolfgang von Goethe, *Torquato Tasso: Ein Schauspiel* in Goethe, *Werke*, Bd. 2, eds. Friedmar Apel et al. (Frankfurt am Main: Insel Verlag, 2007), 301–95.
12. Georg Lukács, "The Tragedy of Modern Art," in *Essays on Thomas Mann*, trans. Stanley Mitchell (London: Merlin Press, 1964), 96.
13. Peter Demetz, *Marx, Engels, and the Poets: Origins of Marxist Literary Criticism*, trans. Jeffrey L. Sammons (Chicago: University of Chicago Press, 1967), 212.
14. Georg Lukács, *The Theory of the Novel: A Historico-Philosophical Essay on the Forms of Great Epic Literature*, trans. Anna Bostock (Cambridge, MA: The MIT Press, 1971), 41.
15. Georg Lukács, *The Historical Novel*, trans. Hannah and Stanley Mitchell (Lincoln, NE: University of Nebraska Press, 1983), 13.

16. Ferenc Fehér, "A dráma történetfilozófiája, a tragédia metafizikája és a nem-tragikus dráma utópiája: Válaszutak a fiatal Lukács drámaelméletében," in *A Budapesti Iskola: Tanulmányok Lukács Györgyről* I, ed. András Kardos (Budapest: T-Twins Kiadó, 1995), 78. See also: L. Ferenc Lendvai, "Lukács' So-Called 'Essay' Period and the Concept of History in His Book on Drama," in *Hungarian Studies on György Lukács* I, eds. László Illés et al. (Budapest: Akadémiai Kiadó, 1993), 42–65; Tamás Bécsy, "György Lukács' Theory of Drama," in *Hungarian Studies on György Lukács* II, eds. László Illés et al. (Budapest: Akadémiai Kiadó, 1993), 357–84.
17. Georg Lukács, "Thoughts on an Aesthetics of Cinema" (1913), in *German Essays on Film*, eds. Richard W. McCormick and Alison Guenther-Pal (New York, London: Continuum, 2004), 17–22.
18. György Lukács, "A Dráma Formája," in *Ifjúkori művek (1902–1918)*, ed. Arpád Tímár (Budapest: Magvető Kiadó, 1977), 109.
19. Georg Lukács, *Entwicklungsgeschichte des modernen Dramas*, ed. Frank Benseler (Darmstadt and Neuwied: Luchterhand, 1981), 25.
20. György Markus, "Life and the Soul: the Young Lukács and the Problem of Culture," in *Lukács Reappraised*, ed. Agnes Heller (New York: Columbia University Press, 1983), 4–5; Fehér, "A dráma történetfilozófiája," 71, citing Markus.
21. György Lukács, "A Tragedia Metafizikája," *Szellem* 1/1 (March 1911): 109–29; "Metaphysik der Tragödie," *Logos* 2 (1911): 80–92. Cf. Georg Simmel, "Der Begriff und die Tragödie der Kultur," 2–26; cf. Georg Simmel, "On the Concept and the Tragedy of Culture," in *The Conflict in Modern Culture and Other Essays*, trans. K. Peter Etzkorn (New York: Teachers College Press, 1968), 27–46.
22. Georg Lukács, "The Metaphysics of Tragedy," in *Soul and Form*, trans. Anna Bostock, eds. John T. Sanders and Katie Terezakis (New York: Columbia University Press, 2010), 182.
23. For the products of this research, see *Karl Marx, Friedrich Engels. Über Kunst und Literatur. Eine Sammlung aus ihren Schriften*, ed. Mikhail Lifschitz (Berlin: Henschel Verlag, Berlin 1948); Georg Lukács, *Karl Marx und Friedrich Engels als Literaturhistoriker* (Berlin: Aufbau Verlag, 1952); Mikhail Lifshitz, *The Philosophy of Art of Karl Marx* (1933), trans. Ralph B. Winn (London: Pluto Press, 1973). For context of Lukács's activities in mid-1930s Moscow and work with Lifshitz, see also: Mikhail Lipshitz and László Sziklai, *Moszkvai évek Lukács Györggyel: Beszélgetések, Emlékezések* (Budapest: Gondolat, 1989); Katerina Clark, *Moscow, the Fourth Rome: Stalinism, Cosmopolitanism, and the Evolution of Soviet Culture, 1931–1941* (Cambridge, MA: Harvard University Press, 2011).
24. Ferdinand Lassalle, *Franz von Sickingen: A Tragedy in Five Acts*, trans. Daniel de Leon (Honolulu: The University of the Pacific Press, 2001). For Lukács's essay, see "Die Sickingendebatte Zwischen Marx-Engels und Lassalle," in Lukács, *Karl Marx und Friedrich Engels als Literaturhistoriker*, 5–43. For further detail concerning Marx and Engels's engagement with Lassalle and the question of historical tragedy, see S.S. Prawer, *Karl Marx and World Literature* (London: Verso, 2011), 197–231.
25. J.V. Stalin, "Some Questions Concerning the History of Bolshevism"

(1931), https://www.marxists.org/reference/archive/stalin/works/1931/x01/x01.htm (accessed December 31, 2021).
26. Hungarian translation in György Lukács, *Esztétikai írások, 1930–1945*, ed. László Sziklai (Budapest: Kossuth Könyvkiadó, 1982), 65–77.
27. See Lenin's 1905 essay "Party Organization and Party Literature," https://www.marxists.org/archive/lenin/works/1905/nov/13.htm (accessed December 31, 2021).
28. Georg Lukács, "Marx and Engels on Problems of Dramaturgy," *The International Theatre* 2 (1934): 11–14.
29. Demetz, *Marx, Engels, and the Poets*, 109–09.
30. Karl Marx to Ferdinand Lassalle, April 19, 1859, in Ferdinand Lassalle, *Nachgelassene Briefe und Schriften, Volume 3*, ed. Gustav Mayer (Berlin: Julius Springer, 1922), 174.
31. Friedrich Engels to Minna Kautsky, November 26, 1885, quoted by Lukács, "Marx és Engels a dramaturgia kérdéseiről," in *Esztétikai írások, 1930–1945*, 44.
32. Margaret A. Rose suggests an alternative reading of the significance of the Lassalle-Marx-Engels Sickingen debate in Marx's aesthetic thinking than that of Lukács, who elevates the correspondence to central importance for illumination of the conditions of literary realism and the representation of history—that is, his own dominant theoretical concerns both in the 1930s and throughout most of his career. Rose notes that the debate in 1859 follows Marx's 1857 introduction to the *Grundrisse*, in which, she argues, Marx is "concerned as much with the role of art in materialist production as with the reflection of historical reality in art." See Margaret A. Rose, *Marx's Lost Aesthetic: Karl Marx and the Visual Arts* (Cambridge: Cambridge University Press, 1984), 94–95.
33. Lukács, "Lassalle irodalomelméletének kritikája," in *Esztétikai írások, 1930–1945*, 70.
34. Lukács, "Marx és Engels a dramaturgia kérdéseiről," in *Esztétikai írások, 1930–1945*, 47.
35. Friedrich Engels, *Cola di Rienzi: Ein unbekannter dramatischer Entwurf*, ed. Michael Knieriem (Wuppertal: Peter Hammer Verlag, 1974).
36. Edward Bulwer-Lytton, *Rienzi, the Last of the Roman Tribunes* [1835] (London: G. Routledge and Sons, 1876).
37. Julius Mosen, *Cola Rienzi, der letzte Volkstribun der Römer* [1837] (Stuttgart: Cotta, 1842).
38. Richard Wagner, *Rienzi, der letzte der Tribuner*, written 1838–1840; first performed 1842.
39. Alex Ross, *Wagnerism: Art and Politics in the Shadow of Music* (New York: Ferrar, Straus and Giroux, 2020), 428–29.
40. Ibid., 560.
41. Edward Braun, *Meyerhold: A Revolution in Theatre* (London: Methuen Drama, 1998), 169.
42. Valentine and Jean-Claude Marcadé, "Des lumières du soleil aux lumières du théâtre: Georges Yakoulov," *Cahiers du Monde Russe et Soviétique* 13/1 (1972): 19.
43. Huntley Carter, *The New Theatre and Cinema of Soviet Russia* (New York: International Publishers, 1925), 144.

44. Galin Tihanov, "Viktor Shklovskii and Georg Lukács in the 1930s," *The Slavonic and East European Review* 78/1 (2000): 45.
45. Fredric Jameson, "Introduction" to *The Historical Novel*, 1.
46. See also my discussion in Chapter 10 of Lukács's essay on Georg Büchner's play *Danton's Death* in connection to the Moscow trials.
47. Agnes Heller, "Lukács' Late Philosophy," in *Lukács Reappraised*, 190.
48. Hegel, *Phenomenology of Spirit*, 444.
49. My chapter heading above alludes to István Mészáros's chapter "The Tragedy of Lukács and the Question of Alternatives" in Mészáros, *Beyond Capital* (London: Merlin Press, 1995), 282–303. Mészáros picks up on Lukács's consistent connection of dramatic forms with biographical life-forms, in both his pre-Marxist and Marxist writings, and applies this connection to Lukács himself.

Chapter 4

The Non-Contemporaneity of Lukács and Lukács: Cold War Contradictions and the Aesthetics of Visual Art

There is something paradoxical in speaking about Lukács's visual aesthetic, insofar as Lukács was strongly rooted in literary culture and in fact had relatively little to say explicitly about visual art or, for that matter, any of the other arts. It is indicative that in his early project for a comprehensive aesthetics, he intended to engage Bloch to write the section on music, recognizing his own very limited knowledge. While in his late aesthetics he considers the separate genesis of the different arts and thus discusses other arts such as music and architecture, his own library reflects the overwhelming attention he gave to literature, represented by shelf after shelf of complete works by classic authors in their original language, on the one hand, and on the other, rather meager shelves of books on other arts to which he dutifully made recourse.

As a commentator on visual art, especially today, Lukács seems "non-contemporary": profoundly out of step with contemporary art and aesthetics. His aesthetic theory, justifying a canon of works opposed even to the mainstream of twentieth-century modernism, was deployed in the service of a now historically obsolete, discredited cultural politics of East Bloc socialism. Lukács is non-contemporaneous in a more profound sense as well, through the dispersed reception of his work, particularly across the former East–West divide, in which different moments of Lukács's oeuvre were picked up and developed in divergent ways. In a sense, given these multiple contexts of reception, "György/Georg Lukács" could never be wholly contemporary with himself, but always signified a variable complex of current writing along with reiterations of earlier phases of his work in new contexts. Finally, I also allude to an additional sense of "non-contemporaneity" associated especially with Bloch, for whom being non-identical with one's time implied a reserve of potentiality unrealized but latent within the inheritance of culture. In this case, I circle back to our contemporary moment, in which the "non-contemporaneity" of the unfashionable Lukács may yet have something to offer.

Modern Art and the Problematic

Though still relatively sparse, writings and observations on visual art are more prevalent in the work of the young Lukács than in his mature works, and it is with a few key early points of reference that I will begin. I leave aside the fascinating article that Lukács published in September of 1913 in the *Frankfurter Zeitung* concerning the aesthetics of cinema, because in fact his interest in film derives less from the point of view of cinema as a medium of "visual culture" than from the relationship of film to drama as representational and narrative media that Lukács wants fundamentally to distinguish from one another. It is, however, of interest to note that while Lukács did not separately treat painting in his mature systematic aesthetics, *Die Eigenart des Ästhetischen* (The Specificity of the Aesthetic, 1963), in the second volume of this work he devoted a lengthy discussion to the aesthetics of film, in his chapter on "boundary-questions of mimesis" in media including music, architecture, applied arts, gardens, and film.[1]

Lukács, as J. Hoberman points out, had explicitly come to see film in 1960s Hungary in the role of the avant-garde, which in this rare case was not a pejorative designation for him. In connection with Lukács's positive response to Miklós Jansco's 1965 film *The Round-Up*, for example, Hoberman notes the apparent contradiction—or at least an unusual moment of openness—in Lukács's judgment of the film: "*The Round-Up* synthesized all that Lukács repressed. One could find here the 'decadent modernism' of Franz Kafka, Samuel Beckett, Eugène Ionesco, and Michelangelo Antonioni—but even more intriguingly, an imaginative representation of the circumstances under which the philosopher had led his life."[2] A less restrictive stance towards modernist techniques is also at least suggested by Lukács's comment on modern drama in his late interviews with Eörsi: "In modern drama there are undoubtedly traces of an incipient revival of the tragic. I have watched these developments with great care, because in my opinion it is important to point out that these things still exist today. [Mikhail] Lifshitz entirely rejected such phenomena."[3] It is likely, again, that Lukács viewed film as closer to drama than to visual arts, and hence his openness to new developments in drama may have extended to his reception of new Hungarian cinema.

The interview continues, however, to explicitly raise the question of visual arts as well, in connection to Lifshitz, Lukács's friend and former collaborator in Moscow:

> *Int.*: Were there also disagreements between Lifshitz and yourself on the plastic arts?
> *G.L.*: We disagreed to the extent that I regarded Cézanne and Van Gogh as pinnacles of modern art, whereas he placed the high points much further back in the past. (88)

A few years before Lukács's interview, Lifshitz had published his anti-modernist screed *The Crisis of Ugliness*, in which he damned all modern art and literature in a single judgment: "To me, modernism is the greatest possible treachery of those who serve the department of spiritual affairs."[4] Even for the aesthetically conservative Lukács, this was a sign that his friend had lost any compass in the actual life of the arts. Lifshitz's thought, Lukács believed, had stalled out at the crossroads of an academicized past and bureaucratized present in the Soviet Union. Lukács lamented: "Poor old Lifshitz stayed behind in Russia. I don't mean that as a criticism, but after all, what could he achieve in Russia? His ideas became conservative through and through. I will not say that this put an end to our friendship, but the fact is that Lifshitz is still brooding over ideas that I have long since left behind" (*Record of a Life*, 87).[5]

The key points of reference to the visual arts in Lukács's early writings include his essay on Gauguin, which appeared in *Huszadik Század* (Twentieth Century) in June 1907; his essay "The Parting of the Ways"; his essay "Aesthetic Culture"; and lastly, his "Lecture on Painting" (*Formproblemen in der Malerei*) dating from his doctoral studies in Heidelberg. What the first three of these essays have in common—and this would remain fundamental to Lukács's understanding of art throughout his long career—is his analysis of modern art as a *problematic* phenomenon with an increasingly uncertain place in the broader culture and society of his time. Art's problematic status in modernity derives, in the early Lukács's view, from the disintegration of culture as a unifying, binding force that incorporates art into the spaces of daily practice, ritual, and belief, thus also guaranteeing that the artist can draw upon a stable set of themes and topoi that will be communicable to and comprehensible by a determinate public. As culture disintegrates under the corrosive pressures of modernity, art is increasingly emancipated from its functional and symbolic roles in everyday life, and develops as a specialized practice whose significance is staked on its technical liberation from convention on the one hand and its functional liberation as autonomous aesthetic experience. However, this emancipation from convention and function comes at a considerable cost: the increasingly difficulty of discovering and legitimating artistic form, the increasing isolation and sense of uselessness of the artist as a social agent, and the evaporation of art's ethically formative power. Moreover, as Lukács already suggests in his early essay on Gauguin, the loss of socially conventional, readymade themes places a heavy intellectual burden on the artist to reflexively generate the worldview within which his or her artistic creation could be meaningful:

> Good painters were seldom original thinkers. Because creating ideas is hardly their role and ideas were no longer given them readymade as earlier, the subject matter (*tema*) came to lose all significance in painting. For the medieval painter, the Madonna was not a conceptual problem for she was already conceptualized and therefore presented only an artistic problem. But any artist who wanted to paint the Madonna today would have to conceptualize—for himself—his own relationship with the Bible; and this relationship would constitute the substance of his artistic process.[6]

It was typical of Lukács's early work—most notably, *Theory of the Novel*—to posit an earlier period of "integral civilization" when the artist or writer spontaneously drew from a cultural background and gave representative, "epic" voice to its values in a clarified, shapely, and communally understandable form. In the early works of Lukács's career, such as in his "Aesthetic Culture" essay, the medieval unity of Giotto's paintings or Dante's poetry with the theological worldview and Christian society modeled this epic spontaneity. Yet even as late as 1948, in an opening speech for the "Hungarian Reality" exhibition at the Fővárosi Képtár (Capital Gallery), the communist cultural pundit Lukács still appealed to such spontaneously communicable, unified cultural complexes, now situated by him in the masterpieces of early modern painting and implicitly available, at least as ideal and aspiration, to the coming age of popular-democratic and socialist culture. It is remarkable how closely in this speech he still echoes his thinking about the problematization of "subject matter" (*tema*) that forty years earlier he had advanced in relation to Gauguin. Lukács stated:

> As for Leonardo, Michelangelo, or Rembrandt, the spiritual, moral, social, even philosophical depiction of the world by painterly or sculpture means was not a "thematic" question, a question of "content." In their eyes the visible world still signified that the highest manifestations of spirituality and morality so to speak immediately and out of themselves were transformed into immediately sensual—painterly, sculptural—problems and purely artistic solutions to these.[7]

In another important programmatic essay from the People's Democracy period—his April 1947 essay "Free or Directed Art?"—Lukács provided yet another view of this question of "theme," again drawing on earlier examples in which the problematic modern division of form and content had not yet occurred. "Theme" implied an indivisible complex that was at once form-governing and rich with social and conceptual content:

> A superficial view might incline one to conceive of thematic constraints as merely related to content, yet in so far as no theme is simply raw material, but may become fully thematic in the first place only in relation to a determinate world-view, the possibilities grasped in this transformation of the theme are dialectically turned into forces that govern the most profound questions of formation and structure. (The Orestes theme; the Last Supper in Giotto, Leonardo, Tintoretto, and such like.)[8]

Lukács's diagnosis of art's predicament in modernity thus preceded his Marxist aesthetics, in which, however, he refashioned his earlier analysis through historical materialist categories.

As his critique of impressionism in "The Parting of the Ways" indicates, Lukács was in search of an ethical teleology for art well before Marxism provided it for him and before later forms of artistic modernism—such as surrealism and abstract art—would come to fill the negative role that impressionism played early on in his thinking:

> Impressionism always stopped at the discovery of possibilities of expression; it always realized its directions in the discovery and disappearance of new means of expression, which constantly rigidified them into mannerisms. Impressionism always merely provided points of view, which would help it to get somewhere. But it didn't want to get anywhere.... The new art is the art of creating the whole, that of going the whole way, of profundity.[9]

We have here a set of elements that would also characterize Lukács's later critical thought, though he would give it a very different conceptual underpinning. He insists on the importance of the artist's worldview as embodied in the artwork; he evokes "totality" ("the creation of the whole") and penetration beyond immediacy ("profundity"); and he connects aesthetics to the sphere of ethics ("tasks and duties"). Socialism, among other things it provided Lukács, also offered him a solution to the problems he perceived—and regretted—in modern art. The socialist worldview and ideal allowed him to believe that modern art's problematic status might be transcended if a unified socialist culture were established and a new role for art as an ethically formative element of that new culture emerged.

Lukács developed these ideas essayistically, and his interest is less specifically in modern painting as an aesthetic medium and mode than in its status as a symptom of what, following the example of Simmel, he would define as the "tragedy of modern life," traced out in the metaphysical conflict of "soul" (or "life") and "form." However, as I have previously discussed, we know that during Lukács's study in Heidelberg during World War I, he attempted and abandoned a systematic philosophy of art, only rediscovered after his death. Because here he was engaging with the most important formalist aesthetic philosophies of the time, especially the work of Konrad Fiedler, Adolf Hildebrand, Gottfried Semper, and Alois Riegl, painting served as something more than just an example for essayistic treatment. Anticipating later formalist modern critics such as Roger Fry, Clive Bell, Clement Greenberg, and Michael Fried, Fiedler in particular argued against the primacy of language and literary "subject matter" in favor of a notion of pure visuality that was, he claimed, at the basis of the aesthetic experience of visual art. He also argued that the "content" of works referred back to the creative process of the artist, and that the reception process was a matter of the spectator retracing in his or her mind the feelings and technical dispositions the artist experienced in creating the work. Throughout his Heidelberg aesthetic writings, Lukács firmly rejects any appeal to a special, "creative" psychology of the artist or the idea of artistic reception as involving access, reconstructively or projectively, to the inner experiences of the artist. Instead, he emphasizes the problem of artistic form, which ensures the autonomy of the artwork's communicative content, distinct from either the artist's inner experience or the spectator's. Artworks, in Lukács's view, initiate artistic communication as what we might now call a performative speech act, which depends on the work's formedness. But form, for Lukács, does not speak, as in Fiedler, only about the creative process by which the work came into being. It also expresses the work's intrinsic intentional relation towards meaningful objects, actions, bodies, and ideas in the world. In other words, form points beyond itself, towards a meaningful world, and the formed work is thus necessarily "about"—intentional of—worldly states of affairs.

Lukács attempted to develop this general aesthetic theory into a specific treatment of the categories of painting, in a lecture he wrote probably around 1916. Influenced by neo-Kantian philosophies, he sought to establish correlations between particular cognitive-emotional states of the subject and generic form-content complexes of works of painting. The subjective dispositions were, so to speak, a priori structures within which the objects of painting were constituted, and those transcendental conditions of constitution lent the empirical genres of painting their phenomenological underpinnings. Accordingly, Lukács distinguishes between three states of the subject: "mood" (*Gemüt*) "soul" (*Seele*), and "spirit" (*Geist*). Mood, in Lukács's view, involved withdrawal from the outer world in order to give free rein, by means of this initial withdrawal, to a pure curiosity that yields a colorful world of feelings, sensations, and intensities. Soul, in contrast, is a deepening of this withdrawal into an interiority in which the object has no self-subsistence, but rather serves only as a mirror for deep subjective states. Lastly, spirit, for Lukács, implies a return to objectivity, but an objectivity enriched and redeemed by its intensive incorporation into the form-world of the painted work. "The world [of spirit] may only be the fully redeemed world," Lukács writes, "that is, things no longer remain in their ordinary thingliness with only the subjectivity of life woven around them, but also as things they develop to the absolutely highest degree possible and as such, without contradiction and dissonance, find their place in a new, appropriate world, the world of the artwork."[10] Although this lecture precedes his Marxist analysis of "reification," already in these early aesthetic writings Lukács is claiming, as he would in his late aesthetics, that the work of art breaks through reification and fetishism in order to reveal—with deep "realism"—the true objectivity of things and actions.

Lukács goes on to map these dispositions onto genres of painting. Mood, he argues, corresponds to the "still life," and he argues, in line with his early essayistic critique of impressionism, that the better part of impressionist art can be understood to have this underlying phenomenological structure of "still life." To soul, in contrast, Lukács connects the genre of portrait and especially the self-portrait. Spirit, he suggests, relates to two possible genres: the landscape, which exposes space and the object of nature in the light of a philosophy of nature that lets their essences appear, and "composition," or the "heroic composition." By composition, he means the composition of movements of human bodies in their tensions and relations to one another, as in the paintings of Rubens or Caravaggio, "such that a world comes into existence in which humanity striving intensively and expressively to the highest degree becomes perfectly calm and harmonious" (241).

Lukács and Visual Art in the "People's Democracy"

Lukács would abandon his aspirations to write a systematic aesthetic at this time, yet as already noted, a trace of his earlier thinking comes back in his occasional speech for the "Hungarian Reality" exhibition in 1948. There, expressing his typical disapproval of autonomous form-problems, he sketches a development in which the representational genres lose their connection to a priori form-content complexes and tend towards the reified, superficial play of forms, colors, and sensations that Lukács saw as characteristic of still life. We should furthermore note that "still life" remained one of his favored metaphors for discussing, in a wide variety of contexts, the immediate appearance of the reified world:

> On the other hand so-called "pure" art came into being, first necessarily and spontaneously, later with programmatic intention: an art without subject-matter. In this light—artistically as well—painting and sculpture was impoverished. Contentless composition became ever poorer and self-centered, it more and more lacked within itself the self-evident, calm necessity of earlier great art; the more that portraits, landscapes, etc., turned into pure formal problems, the further they developed in the direction of a sort of deadened still-lifeness. ("Művészet és valóság," 184)

For nearly three decades, following his early writings on visual arts, however, Lukács would occupy himself primarily with literary and philosophical study, along with practical political activity. Although in the late twenties and thirties he might, for example, in arguing against "tendency literature," have taken up questions of visual and cinematic documentary culture, or photomontage, which were hotly debated in the 1930s, he really concentrated only on the "*literature* of facts." Similarly, though his writings on realism during the 1930s can be understood as participating in a climate of debate in the Soviet Union around notions of typicality in artistic representation that also extended to visual arts, again Lukács's focus was almost exclusively on narrative fiction and drama. Some of his most important literary study dates from his exile years in the Soviet Union, including his writings on the historical novel, his studies of nineteenth-century German literature, and his reconstruction with Mikhail Lifshitz of Marx's and Engels's writings on literature. He also researched and composed the work that would be published after World War II as *The Destruction of Reason*, a Marxist critique of the decadence of German philosophy that would strongly inflect Lukács's rejection of the irrationalistic worldviews he discerned in modernist literature and art and especially in criticism—like Adorno's—that sought to justify modernist art forms and practices. But there is little evidence that Lukács engaged in any significant way with the visual art of either the Soviet Union or the West during the 1930s, which, we should recall, saw the imposition of an official socialist realist aesthetic in visual as well as literary arts, the flourishing of mural art in Mexico, the state support of documentary and public art in the United States, the dissemination of surrealist ideas and practices in visual art, the engagement of left artists in the anti-fascist struggle in Spain, the establishment of fascist and Stalinist neoclassical styles of monuments and architecture, and many other developments to which a more visually attuned philosopher and critic might have paid attention. Lukács seems literally to have kept his head down during this period in the USSR, in books, and given little heed to the rapidly transforming iconosphere around him.

When Lukács returned from Moscow to Budapest after 1945, however, he suddenly found himself Hungary's most famous left-wing intellectual, and he was drawn actively into public life as a university professor, literary authority, public speaker, and publisher of an astonishing number of books, including several that dated back to work in the Soviet Union and others, like *Literature and Democracy*,[11] that collect commentaries on various current cultural tendencies and occasions. In the fluid situation between 1945 and 1948, with the Communist Party tightening its grip on political and cultural institutions, but with the possibility that the Soviet Army, per diplomatic agreement, would pull out of occupied East–Central Europe, Lukács counted on a long road to socialism with political pluralism lasting perhaps for decades. In that context, he sought to think through what he believed should be the orientations in culture most likely to resist the restoration of fascism and to encourage populist democracy and eventually the transition to socialism. Once again, his writings of this time are overwhelmingly concerned with literature and literary history, which he saw as the most efficacious means of cultivating progressive attitudes and worldviews. Yet his broad public activities also included exceptional interventions into the visual arts, such as his opening speeches at an exhibition of Noémi Ferenczy in 1947 (published in *Forum*) and the 1948 "Hungarian Reality" exhibition, the text of which was published in the May issue of the journal edited by the ex-avant-gardist Sándor Bortnyik, *Szabad Művészet* (Free Art). He also served on a committee in 1947 to select the winner of a competition for a new sculpture of the leftist poet Attila József, probably because of its clear literary content. By far, however, his most extended and influential text on visual arts was his polemic against "Hungarian Theories of Abstract Art," published in *Forum* in 1947, which focused on recent texts by Ernő Kállai (*Nature's Hidden Face*) and Béla Hamvas and Katalin Kemény (*Revolution in the Arts*),[12] which paralleled the formation of two post–World War II artist groups, the surrealist-influenced "European School" and the "Abstract Art Group."

The indirection of Lukács's attack on abstract art is revealing: he chooses not to discuss a single actual work of surrealist or abstract art, but rather what he saw as the theoretical discourse that served to legitimate abstractionist and surrealist practice and that supplied, in his view, the dangerous worldview of this art's seemingly incommunicable, ultraformalistic, or vacuous subject matter. Though one can regret Lukács's implicit dismissal (and role in the eventual suppression) of some of the most important Hungarian painting of his time, it must be said that he saw at least one question at stake in abstract art with surprising acuteness. Just as Charles Harrison, a critic close to the Art and Language group, would argue in his 1980 essay "The Ratification of Abstract Art" that abstract art was parasitic on language for its meaning and that linguistic interpretations of abstract art were institutionally posited,[13] Lukács already in 1947 argued along analogous lines that abstract art depended on a discursive supplement furnished by questionable philosophies such as Kállai's eclectic "bioromantic" appropriation of scientific concepts or Hamvas's new-age pastiche of non-Euclidian geometry, relativistic physics, theories of the unconscious, and myth theory:

> If we are here considering the theoretical works of Ernő Kállai and Béla Hamvas, it is in order to seek the principles that motivate and justify abstract art philosophically. . . . This, however, is far from deciding the following question: whether there is an essential relation between such theoretical argumentation and abstract art's artistic principles and practice. For the antagonism with several centuries of European artistic tradition which is manifested in the artistic practice of abstract art, it requires a completely different theoretical legitimation from normal style-changes in the different traditions. In order to see the justification of abstract art, we would have to re-evaluate all the basic concepts of previous aesthetics. Indeed—in so far as genuine aesthetics stand in the closest relation with a number of problems in our world-views—all the questions of world-view would have to be re-examined as well. It is the value of these books by Kállai and by Hamvas and Katalin Kemény that they attempt this re-evaluation. . . . If these theories—quite divergent from each other—do not cover precisely and at every point the practice of abstract art and the convictions of some of its adherents, there is, nonetheless, something indicative and symptomatic in the fact that they attempt to justify abstract art theoretically, today, in 1947, in this way.[14]

Lukács's diagnosis of this "symptomatic" justification measures it against the social tendencies of "progress" that he sees in the present moment in Hungary. In this diagnosis, he draws strongly upon his philosophical critique of irrationalism, which he would also deploy in other topical cultural debates, including in his criticisms of the political psychology of the liberal theorist István Bibó, his opposition to existentialist tendencies, and his arguments for realist literature in reconstruction Hungary. Dogmatically persuaded by his own study that any compromise with irrationalistic worldviews would contribute to the restoration of fascism—or at least discourage the intelligentsia from resisting this restoration—Lukács waged a many-sided polemical battle, of which his argument against theories of abstract art was, seen at our historical distance, little more than a minor and occasional skirmish.

Indeed, although he openly declares his desire to influence "some artists [to] reject these theories, if they consider what, thought through to their conclusions, they entail and where they lead" (225), Lukács probably did not anticipate how successful this essay would be in torpedoing emergent abstract tendencies nor the repressive means by which their marginalization would take place. Pataki and György note the influence of Lukács's essay: "György Lukács's article was taken [by the modernistic painters] to be a declarative pronouncement of cultural politics, and it was felt from reading it that new times were coming, rendering their activity impossible and not just in an aesthetic sense."[15] Elsewhere, Pataki summarizes this sense of a decisive turn following the publication of Lukács's article, which was, of course, not so much the "cause" of abstract art's suppression as rather the willing instrument in the larger political, ideological, institutional, and geopolitical changes that were in train, driven by a Communist Party leadership that sought the full-scale Sovietization of Hungary like the rest of occupied East–Central Europe. Pataki usefully surveys the variable rhythm of these events in Hungary, Poland, Czechoslovakia, Bulgaria, and Romania, and notes with regard to Hungary that the imposition of socialist realism took place gradually, with tactical alliances between communist cultural politics and prestigious artistic leftists of an earlier generation, including Aurél Bernáth, Róbert Berény, and Bertalan Pór. But from the beginning of 1948, Pataki argues, to the end of the year, there was a decisive change: "already only those efforts judged useful to the public and society could make it through the [narrowing path], and beneath the articulations of the different groups themselves, in case of divergences of view, a crushing, unitary, centrally directed artistic consciousness."[16]

Lukács's article was not singularly responsible for this development, but it provided effective theoretical ammunition against the tendencies that the Hungarian Communist Party's cultural leadership wanted to sideline and surpress. Pataki and György note affirmative reference to Lukács's article in Márton Horváth's essay "An Evaluation of the Literary Life in the Hungarian Democracy," published in *Csillag* in March of 1948. Already a year earlier, in an article in *Magyarok*, Máriusz Rabinovszky deployed Lukács's language of social decay to characterize abstract and other modernist manifestation in the visual arts: "Insofar as today we are building a new society and a reality worth living in, the turn in the arts that were still legitimate in the recent past are today already obsolete, reactionary orientations. From now on every honorable can breathe a sigh of relief: relief from modern society having to occupy itself further with these manifestations smelling of decay."[17] A forum on abstract art in the October 1947 *Szabad Művészet* that included contributions by Iván Hevesy, Gábor O. Pogány, Máriusz Rabinovszky, and Balázs Vargha was followed by a note that refers their readers to Lukács's essay, which "condemns this style's theoretical foundations" (186). In this subsequent feeding frenzy of communist culture-sharks, Lukács's essay may stand out for a higher degree of intellectual seriousness and for its consistency with his other long-established theoretical and historical analyses, which makes it more, I believe, than just a cynical tactical document positioning cultural life in Hungary for full Sovietization. All the more fatal was it, then, that this respected scholar drew the first blood in the debate around abstract art, which, unbiased historical and theoretical reflection suggests, is anything but intrinsically hostile to socialism.

Lukács vs. Lukács: Cold War Divergences

I now turn from this historical account of Lukács's engagements with visual arts to reflect further on his significance for artistic developments beyond his limited direct contacts and yet of greater pertinence for understanding Lukács's place, if any, in theories and practices of contemporary art. First, in light of the theme of Cold War non-contemporaneity, I would observe a paradox of Lukács's "eastern" and "western" reception. This is a complicated issue, especially when one looks at Lukács's role in Germany and Italy, and in the New Left in Great Britain and the United States. But simplifying, we can note that throughout the later 1950s and 1960s, while Lukács was ever more doggedly advocating "great realism" and rejecting nearly the whole of twentieth-century modernist and avant-garde art and literature, his early writings, especially his theory of "reification" and action in his 1923 work *History and Class Consciousness*, were being taken up by the German- and English-speaking New Left and influencing artistic as well as political activism.[18] Through a reading of Lukács, or through an absorption of his critique of reification secondhand through the work of Lukács-influenced Frankfurt School thinkers such as Benjamin, Adorno, and Marcuse, it became possible for artists and critics to challenge the status of the artwork as fixed object and to refocus art on "art-work" (labor) and action (process). For example, Marcuse, whose critique of one-dimensional experience is essentially an application of Lukács's conception of reification to the post-war Fordist, consumerist society of the United States, took up the question of realist and anti-realist art in his now largely forgotten book on *Soviet Marxism* from 1959 (a book which, however, the German radical student leader Rudi Dutschke notes was important for youth like him growing up in East Germany in developing a revolutionary outlook independent of official communism). If at this time Lukács was looking for more breathing room for the arts in the tradition of great nineteenth-century realism, which he contrasted to the shallow schematism of official socialist realism, Marcuse in his chapter on socialist art argued for an art that imaginatively transgressed the bounds of representing actually existing society. He thus praised the modernist innovations of abstract and surrealist art, because they offered resources of critical negativity and free subjectivity in the one-dimensional administered societies of the Soviet bloc, but in different ways also exerted pressure on the consolidating one-dimensional Western societies of affluence. Yet where Marcuse and Lukács agree—opposing what we might see as the defining element of many avant-garde and neo-avant-garde artistic tendencies—is that the principle of form is definitive of art, and any challenge to the centrality of form to art is a negation of art itself, to the detriment of art's positive social and ethical effects.

I have written in my book on *Modernism and the Frankfurt School* about the irony of Marcuse's role during the 1960s in providing philosophical legitimation to avant-garde practices such as happening, early performance art, and Living Theatre, when he himself, whose aesthetic tastes ranged more towards Goethe and Beethoven than Carolee Schneemann and John Cage, explicitly repudiated these artistic tendencies.[19] For example, in *An Essay on Liberation*, Marcuse's most utopian book of the 1960s, he defends the autonomy of art against neo-avant-garde experimentation:

> Transforming the intent of art is self-defeating—a self-defeat built into the very structure of art. . . . The very Form of art contradicts the effort to do away with the segregation of art to a "second reality," to translate the truth of the productive imagination into the first reality.[20]

Art, for Marcuse, is defined by its separation from life—its ontological status as "appearance" and "illusion" (*Schein*), which Lukács's analyses suggest give art a certain affinity with or even necessary entanglement in socioeconomic processes of reification. Yet he did not advocate an avant-garde breaking out of this space of aesthetic illusion through actionism, but rather the intensification of the imaginative difference that the *Schein-Welt* of art preserved. Art, for Marcuse, has sufficient means in itself for the critique of its own limits, and any attempt to exit the circle of art would make for both bad politics and the negation of art. Radical artists and New Left thinkers, however, drew different conclusions. They believed that the arts could and should aspire to bring about Marcuse's "new sensibility" more directly, in intentionally designed situations, spaces, and happenings—thus adumbrating a world of heightened sensual intensity, bodily enjoyment, and personal freedom. Lukács would have certainly rejected being put in the same bed with Marcuse, whom he considered little more than Western culture's most fashionable romantic anti-capitalist; and he would have been utterly horrified to know that his Marxist theories might be contributing to such decadent, avant-garde artistic phenomena as Andy Warhol's multimedia Factory, Robert Morris's and Carolee Schneemann's performance *Site* (which meditates on the relations of construction labor, the artwork, and gender), or Vienna Actionist rituals and actions. But it happened that the critical armature of his critique of reification offered powerful legitimation and even political motivation for a range of conceptual, process-oriented, and performance-based art practices that shared a common aim of dissolving the reified object-nature of the artwork and exposing art's roots in the exertions and passions of human actors.

Second, during the thaw leading up to the 1956 uprising in Hungary, Lukács's arguments for realism underwent a subtle shift. He argued, as I have discussed, that in the new context opened by the death of Stalin and the relative liberalization that he anticipated under Khrushchev, the primary contradiction in the world context was no longer the political struggle for socialism against capitalism, but rather the struggle, through democratic popular action, for peace. Realism in this context now meant for Lukács the representational basis for a shared vision of a civic activism—the ability of human beings to change their world through conscious action—bridging the differences between the socialist and capitalist world in the interest of "peaceful coexistence," as the rather over-optimistic slogan of the day would have it. As he writes: "Nobody can work effectively for peace unless he is firmly convinced that society is amenable to the processes of reason and that human effort—in terms of individual, as well as mass action—*can* influence historical events."[21] But as Heller has argued in relation to Lukács's late aesthetics,[22] the more Lukács detached the need for realism from a specific pathway to socialism, the less persuasive his dogmatic insistence on realist style and ressentiment against artistic modernism appeared. It seems entirely possible to believe that art can help cultivate, through both negative-critical and positive-educative modes, various progressive social and ethical values, without believing that good and bad ethics or peace and war align with realist and modernist artistic outlooks. Even if we accept the argument of Lukács's late aesthetics that art heightens our experience of objectivity by "de-anthropomorphizing" it through form and by peeling away the encrustations of social mystification, there is no reason to believe that these effects are the monopoly of a small set of nineteenth-century forms, genres, and media.

To take this argument a little further into speculative territory, I would like to refer briefly to a provocative set of works by the conceptual art group Art and Language from the late 1970s and early 1980s that challenged the idea that abstract-nonrepresentational and realist-representational styles were fundamentally distinct. These styles were rather, Art and Language implied in their Wittgenstein-influenced visual analyses, more a question of duck/rabbit-like "aspectual" modalities, a function of "seeing-as" by particular viewers with particular perspectives and competences. Their project started, as they have noted, as a joke, which appealed to them precisely because of what seemed to them its impossibility: to execute a socialist-realist-style painting in the abstract, all-over, dripped style of Jackson Pollock.[23] This artistic jape, however, gave rise to serious studies and works such as the various instantiations of *Portrait of V.I. Lenin in the Style of Jackson Pollock*, *Portrait of V.I. Lenin in July 1917 Disguised by a Wig and Working Man's Clothes in the Style of Jackson Pollock*, and *Joseph Stalin Gazing Enigmatically at the Body of V.I. Lenin as It Lies in State in Moscow in the Style of Jackson Pollock*. These works are rich studies in Cold War critical and art-ideological oppositions; but they took on special resonance in the wake of scholarship in the 1970s and early 1980s from Max Kozloff to Serge Guilbaut and others who traced how abstract expressionism and the canonizing critical discourse surrounding it, especially Greenberg's formalism, were supported by the CIA and US State Department as a soft-power cultural weapon of the Cold War.[24] The deconstructive efforts of Art and Language suggest how much these apparently intuitive stylistic oppositions were discursively and institutionally imposed on the corpus of images, rather than being an essential feature of so-called realist or abstract styles. However, if this is true, the same critical arguments can be turned upon the "realist" side of the argument, such as the alignment by Lukács of realism with the outlook of human progress and modernism with fatalism, pessimism, and acquiescence in barbarism. Art and Language's point in the Lenin/Pollock works is not to advocate for either side, but to understand the opposition as a structural pivot of a whole system of twentieth-century art ideologies and critical discourses, with the implicit view that a genuinely critical art might involve contextually sensitive, singular constellations of abstract and realist elements that resist the large-scale binaries derived from Cold War ideologies and geopolitical divisions.

My George Lukács-Book: László Lakner

I conclude with a return to Hungary and more direct reference to Lukács, with a set of works by the artist László Lakner. Since I have discussed at length Lukács's early aesthetics, I begin with a work by Lakner that quotes—or visually presents a quote—from Lukács's early essay "Aesthetic Culture," the "Citation Piece."[25] The quote reads: "Form: the maximum expression of potential forces in a given situation." Two things are notable about Lakner's work. First is its engagement, typical of conceptual art, with language and the interplay between viewing and reading, between words as bearers of meaning and as desemanticized visual material in a painting or other visual genre. With Lakner, however, I would suggest, this general conceptualist interest is overdetermined by a specific contextual and thematic reference to the quotation's source: to the overwhelming dominance of literature and textuality in the aesthetics of Lukács specifically, and one might even say, in the broader media ecology within socialism that Lukács's authoritative writings helped to erect and support. Furthermore, Lakner's quotation ends on an incomplete note, with a semi-colon. Lukács's text continues: "this constitutes the true ethic of forms. The form sets the outward boundary, and inwardly it creates infinity" ("Aesthetic Culture," 156). Lakner performatively stages the failure to give his work intensive, closed form of the sort that Lukács advocated, choosing the quotation mark as a kind of arbitrary, conventionalized boundary. Lakner deconstructs the essential difference between language and visuality as formative principles, seeing both as governed by both convention and the constrained but still not unsubstantial freedom of the artist's choice.

Lakner takes this work further with a series of book-objects of which the paradigmatic instance was his *My George Lukács-Book* of 1970 (Figure 4.1). As he tells it, this work originated in his acquisition in the 1950s of a copy of the philosopher's book *A polgári filozófia válsága* (The Crisis of Bourgeois Philosophy), signed by Lukács. When Lakner got around to reading it, he says, he found it disappointing and tied it up with string and hung it up on the wall of his Kmetty Street studio. While that "original" was lost during a move in 1961, Lakner took up the tied-up book idea again with another Lukács work, *The Specificity of the Aesthetic*, Lukács's late aesthetics.

According to Tünde Topor, this work was accompanied by a renewed interest on Lakner's part in reading Lukács's work, especially his early writings, from which, for example, the Lukács quote from the "Aesthetic Culture" essay can be situated.[26] There are several layers of meaning that

Lukács and Visual Arts 97

Figure 4.1 László Lakner, *My George Lukács-Book/Mein Georg-Lukács-Buch*, 1970. Foto/Siebdruck, 70 × 50. László Lakner. Permission for use by Creative Commons Attribution Share-Alike 3.0 License.

this work engages. David Fehér calls attention to the thematic subtleties of Lakner's choice of Lukács's late aesthetics for his book-work:

> Lakner fetishizes and alienates Lukács's aesthetics at the same time; it is presented as a monument for art theory, but on the other hand, it is made unreadable, bound and corrupted. ... Lakner's photorealistic approach is generally different from the aesthetics of Lukács, which on the one hand finds realism a central question of Marxist aesthetics, but harshly criticizes every sort of naturalism. ... Lakner reproduces his bound Lukács book in a silkscreen, and also paints it in the style of the classical *trompe l'oeil* in an eminently naturalistic way.[27]

As with the "Citation Work," we experience the paradox of a book that has been closed and rendered unable to communicate by its intended means—words—but which has, at the same time and as a function of its illegibility, become an autonomous visual object. However, this visual object is not simply mute or meaningless. It has its own means of communicating, especially connotatively and indexically, about censorship, control of ideas, and the silencing of radical voices. It may also refer to Lukács's own biographical double binds, in which he played a role in keeping the power of his own ideas under wraps. Implicitly, with the striking metonymic image of Lukács's bound book, Lakner poignantly figures what Habermas would call "systematically distorted communication." Lakner at once acknowledges Lukács's role as one of Hungary's outstanding philosophical and literary thinkers, yet also his compromised relation to Stalinism and the imposition of the dictatorship, his official marginalization in the Lukács debate of 1949 and again after 1956, and his final ambiguous role in the 1960s as the elder statesman of Hungarian Marxism, who wavered between critique of actually existing socialism and professions of loyalty to the socialism putatively embodied by the regime.

I think there is another connotation of Lakner's work, however, that makes his artistic interpretation of Lukács deeper and, in its subtle intertwining of homage and critique, more moving. In his discussions of Tolstoy, Lukács argued that Tolstoy's realism lay not in his mimetic representation of events but rather in his evocation of possibilities, which one after another are explored by Tolstoy but which he then presents his characters as *failing* to realize. For Lukács, history had delivered any number of missed opportunities, failed attempts, disappointing half measures, and long-deferred realizations. For most of his career—the revolutionary period after the Bolshevik revolution and perhaps the early years of the 1930s excepted—Lukács believed the achievement of socialism would take a long time, perhaps many decades. In his last, unpublished major theoretical analysis written in response to the Soviet invasion of Czechoslovakia in 1968, Lukács noted that "the process of building a socialist democracy is an undertaking of long duration."[28] Referring to Marx's famous Latin citation "Hic Rhodus, hic salta" (Here is Rhodes, leap here), which Marx used in the *Eighteenth Brumaire* to indicate that socialism had to prove itself in the struggles of the situations of the present, Lukács concedes: "Today, Rhodus still lies in a distant future" (170).

Realism, I would argue, meant for Lukács understanding and accepting historical life as a rhythm of defeats, retreats, and disappointments in which one does not resign oneself to passivity but learns an active waiting. In his beloved Tolstoy, he had already diagnosed a realism that might be called a *realism of paralyzed action*:

> The world Tolstoy sees and depicts is to an increasing degree a world in which decent people can no longer find any opportunity for action.... When together with the strong and hopeful features of the approaching peasant

revolt he also gives poetic expression to the half-heartedness, its backwardness, its hesitations and lack of courage, he leaves his characters no other possibility save the old dilemma of capitulation or flight.[29]

He expressed this most poignantly in his writings on another Russian writer, Alexander Solzhenitsyn, in whose writings Lukács detected the signs of a "radical transformation [that] has been going on for decades in men's inner lives." "In the art of today," Lukács writes,

> the accent falls on man's inward life and conscience, on his moral decisions, which cannot be expressed, it may be, in any external act. . . . [T]here may be a long chain of crises of conscience, most of which cannot, as things are, or can only in exceptional circumstances, crystallize into outward action, although the ways in which they disclose themselves may be dramatic, often bordering on the tragic.[30]

Or as his friend Bloch once aphorized: "The hindering element is also in the possible."[31]

I would like to end with Lakner's 1994 collaborative installation with the Fluxus artist Emmett Williams, *Aesthetics*, based on Lakner's 1971 plan. It consists of a wall full of bound and hung books, including Lukács's *Eigenart des Ästhetischen*. I would suggest we view this installation not merely pessimistically, as a monotonous tableau of censorship, a mass incarceration of radical thinkers in their individual, book-like prison cells. Rather, I want to suggest that Lakner is also presenting in this work a Tolstoy-like tableau of unrealized possibilities, what Jameson would call "seeds of time,"[32] that await a later moment of unbinding. In *The Process of Democratization*, drafted while he was already dying of cancer, Lukács evoked a posterity for socialism that resided, at present, solely in books, perhaps in a few of his own among them. In his evocation of a retreat to theory, after the closure of practice that the Soviet suppression of the Prague Spring once again forced him to confront, he came closer to Adorno than perhaps ever before in his long career: "The present task of Marxism, the revival of Marxism after its long petrification under Stalin, cannot be directly connected to any existing societal movement. . . . On the contrary, the attempt at renewal must be initiated on the basis of theory" (*Democratization*, 158–59). Yet perhaps, after their long suspension, the time has come to cut Lukács down from the wall and open his books again. And reading him again in a new light and in new times, we may finally also be able to reopen Lukács's closed canon of great realists—Tolstoyian realists of unrealized possibilities—to include, among others, László Lakner there.

Notes

1. See Georg Lukács, *Die Eigenart des Ästhetischen*, Volume 2 (Neuwied am Rhein: Luchterhand, 1963), 489–521.
2. J. Hoberman, *The Red Atlantis: Communist Culture in the Absence of Communism* (Philadelphia: Temple University Press, 1998), 48–49.
3. Georg Lukács, *Record of a Life: An Autobiographical Sketch*, ed. István Eörsi, trans. Rodney Livingstone (London: Verso, 1983), 87.
4. Mikhail Lifshitz, *The Crisis of Ugliness: From Cubism to Pop-Art*, trans. David Riff (Chicago: Haymarket Books, 2018), 135.
5. For further on Lifshitz, see Stanley Mitchell, "Mikhail Lifshits: A Marxist Conservative," in *Marxism and the History of Art: From William Morris to the New Left*, ed. Andrew Hemingway (London: Pluto Press, 2006), 28–44.
6. Georg Lukács, "Paul Gauguin," in *The Lukács Reader*, ed. Arpad Kardarkay (Oxford: Blackwell, 1995), 161.
7. György Lukács, "Művészet és valóság," *Szabad Művészet* 5 (May 1948): 184.
8. György Lukács, "Free or Directed Art?" in *The Culture of People's Democracy: Hungarian Essays on Literature, Art, and Democratic Transition, 1945–1948*, ed. and trans. Tyrus Miller (Amsterdam: Brill, 2013), 138.
9. I have translated this from György Lukács, "Az Utak Elváltak," in *Ifjúkori Művek (1902–1918)*, ed. Árpád Tímar (Budapest: Magvető Kiadó, 1977), 285. The English translation in *The Lukács Reader*, ed. Arpad Kadarkay (Oxford: Blackwell, 1995), completely garbles the sense of the passage.
10. Georg Lukács, "Das Formproblem der Malerei," in *Heidelberger Ästhetik (1916–1918)*, eds. György Márkus and Frank Benseler (Darmstadt and Neuwied: Luchterhand, 1974), 236.
11. English translation in Lukács, *The Culture of People's Democracy*.
12. Ernő Kállai, *A természet rejtett arca* (Budapest: Misztótfalusi, 1947); and Béla Hamvas and Katalin Kemény, *Forradalom a művészetben* (Budapest: Misztótfalusi, 1946).
13. Charles Harrison, "The Ratification of Abstract Art," in *Towards a New Art: Essays on the Background to Abstract Art 1910–20* (London: Tate Gallery, 1980), 146–55.
14. György Lukács, "Hungarian Theories of Abstract Art," in *The Culture of People's Democracy*, 225.
15. Péter György and Gábor Pataki, *Az Európai Iskola és az elvont művészek csoportja* (Budapest: Corvina, 1990), 39.
16. Gábor Pataki, "'Van Alkonyat, Mely Olyan, Mint a Hajnal': Képzőművészeti Viták, 1948–1949", in *A fordulat évei, 1947–1949* (Budapest: 1956-os Intézet, 1998), 217.
17. Máriusz Rabinovszky, "Az absztrakt művészet körul," *Magyarok* 1947/4: 317.
18. For the German reception, see the discussions of *History and Class Consciousness* between Hans-Jürgen Krahl, Furio Cerruti, Detlev Claussen, Oskar Negt, and Alfred Schmidt in *Geschichte und Klassenbewusstsein*

Heute (Amsterdam: Verlag de Munter, 1971), online text at: http://www.krahl-briefe.de/ (accessed December 31, 2021); and Rüdiger Dannemann's collection of texts and interviews, *Georg Lukács und 1968: Ein Spurensuche* (Bielefeld: Aisthesis Verlag, 2009).
19. Tyrus Miller, *Modernism and the Frankfurt School* (Edinburgh: Edinburgh University Press, 2014), 114–46.
20. Herbert Marcuse, *An Essay on Liberation* (Boston: Beacon Press, 1969), 142.
21. Georg Lukács, *The Meaning of Contemporary Realism* (London: Merlin Press, 1963), 15.
22. Agnes Heller, "Lukács' Later Philosophy," in *Lukács Reappraised*, ed. Agnes Heller (New York: Columbia University Press, 1983), 177–90.
23. See Charles Harrison, "On 'A Portrait of V.I. Lenin in the Style of Jackson Pollock'," in Harrison, *Essays on Art and Language* (Oxford: Basil Blackwell, 1991), 129–49.
24. See Max Kozloff, "American Painting during the Cold War," *Artforum* 11 (May 1973): 43–54; Eva Cockcroft, "Abstract Expressionism: Weapon of the Cold War," *Artforum* (June 1974): 39–41; John Tagg, "American Power and American Painting: The Development of Vanguard Painting in the United States since 1945," *Praxis* 1/2 (1976): 59–79; David and Cecile Shapiro, "Abstract Expressionism: The Politics of Apolitical Painting," *Prospects* 3 (1977): 175–214; Serge Guilbault, *How New York Stole the Idea of Modern Art: Abstract Expressionism, Freedom, and the Cold War* (Chicago: University of Chicago Press, 1983).
25. The work is reproduced in David Féher, "*Consonants of Karl Marx*: Left versus Left in the Hungarian Neo-Avant-Garde: The Case of László Lakner," *Acta Historiae Artium 56* (2015): 346, Fig. 4.
26. Tünde Topor, "Lakner László," *Artmagazin 5* (2004): 28–31, http://www.artmagazin.hu/artmagazin_hirek/lakner_laszlo.144.html (accessed December 31, 2021).
27. Féher, "*Consonants of Karl Marx*," 347–48.
28. Georg Lukács, *The Process of Democratization*, trans. Susanne Bernhardt and Norman Levine (Albany: State University of New York Press, 1991), 159.
29. Georg Lukács, *Studies in European Realism* (New York: The Universal Library, 1964), 166–67.
30. Georg Lukács, "Solzhenitsyn and the New Realism," in *Marxism and Human Liberation*, ed. E. San Juan, Jr. (New York: Delta Books, 1973), 222–23.
31. "Something's Missing: A Discussion between Ernst Bloch and Theodor W. Adorno on the Contradictions of Utopian Longing," in Ernst Bloch, *The Utopian Function of Art and Literature: Selected Essays*, trans. Jack Zipes and Frank Mecklenburg (Cambridge, MA: The MIT Press, 1988), 17.
32. Fredric Jameson, *The Seeds of Time* (New York: Columbia University Press, 1996).

Part II

Theodor W. Adorno

Chapter 5

Adorno and/or Avant-Garde: Looking Back at Surrealism

In his *Aesthetic Theory*, the culmination of decades of critical writing on music, art, and literature, Adorno delineates several key developmental tendencies of modern art: its accelerated disintegration of artistic conventions, styles, and genres; its intensified reflexivity of artistic form; its extreme individualization of form and idiom at the cost of the communicability of experience; its diremption between raw materiality and extreme intellectualization; and its encompassing of artworks with few or no evident aesthetic qualities traditionally understood. Besides referring throughout the book to the aesthetic writings of Kant, Hegel, Schelling, Schiller, Nietzsche, Benjamin, and Lukács, Adorno also illustrates his arguments with allusions to a wide range of modern artists, writers, and musicians, including especially Baudelaire, Beckett, Brecht, Klee, Picasso, Schoenberg, Valéry, and Wagner. Not represented, in contrast, and somewhat surprisingly given Adorno's arguments about the disenchantment and deaestheticization of the artwork, are many key figures, tendencies, and media of the European and Anglo-American avant-gardes. Notably absent, for example, are major futurists such as Marinetti, Severini, Boccioni, Lewis, Larionov, Mayakovsky, and Kruchenykh; expressionists such as Stramm, Lasker-Schüler, Goll, Meidner, Marc, Kirchner, and Dix; dadaists such as Ball, Tzara, Janco, Grosz, Schwitters, Hoch, and Heartfield; abstract artists such as Malevich, Tatlin, Van Doesburg, Tauber-Arp, Albers, Pollock, Newman, Hantaï, Vasarely, or Stella; sculptors such as Brancusi, Gabo, Arp, Kobro, Giacometti, Moore, Arman, Tinguely, Schöffer, Beuys, Judd, and Morris; photographers such as Stieglitz, Ray, Rodchenko, Moholy-Nagy, Krull, Brassaï, and Abbott; filmmakers including Eisenstein, Epstein, Ivens, Richter, Buñuel, Antonioni, Bergman, Warhol, and Godard; non-serialist musicians such as Satie, Varèse, Bartok, Ives, Weill, Messiaen, Xenakis, or Ligeti; neo-avant-garde groups such as COBRA, Vienna Actionism, the Independent Group, Gruppo 63, the Zero Group, the Living Theatre, or Fluxus;

architectural modernists including Gaudi, Wright, Taut, Sant'Elia, Gropius, Mies van der Rohe, El Lissitzky, Corbusier, the Smithsons, and Friedman; and the list could go on. John Cage and Marcel Duchamp, arguably the two most influential figures in twentieth-century art, are respectively represented by one sentence referring to one work of Cage and of Duchamp nothing at all.

To be sure, in a work of aesthetic theory, even one so resolutely oriented towards the historicity of modern art as Adorno's, one need not expect comprehensive reference to the history of twentieth-century art, or to the histories of modern music and literature; more selective mention of key examples supporting the conceptual argumentation is no doubt a legitimate way to proceed. Nor is my point to cast aspersions upon Adorno's unquestionably rich knowledge of and refined taste in the modern and contemporary arts. Still, my far from exhaustive enumeration of notable absences from *Aesthetic Theory* does highlight how selective a swathe of the rich landscape of twentieth-century European and Anglo-American arts is actually in view in Adorno's theory. It also suggests, in turn, how problematic its critical diagnostic may be when applied to the empirical history of the arts of his age, and how much more so for the globalized art world fifty years hence.

The intensity of Adorno's critical focus was bought, I would suggest, at the price of a set of exclusions that, for all their evident differences, appear as restrictive and defensive as those of Lukács in his anti-modernist advocacy of "critical realism." By way of Adorno's exclusion of numerous important avant-garde figures, movements, tendencies, and media/genres—consigned to a penumbra of failed or non-art—Adorno sought to legitimate modern art's de-aestheticization and polemical negativity philosophically, while yet defending the autonomous work against the more disruptive effects of the avant-garde on the work-concept of art and, accordingly, on the developmental teleology of artistic progress. On this point Adorno was explicit. Artworks are the preserve of an "entelechy" embedded in their bounded singularity as objects-events, "monads": "It is possible that the more problematic the concept of teleology becomes in organic nature the more intensively it condensed itself in artworks."[1] The normative idea of art's monadic "windowlessness"—the artwork's internalization of historical, political, and discursive contexts as immanent formal tensions of singular works—is the foundational condition of the aesthetic theory Adorno proposes. He stretches his delicate dialectical tightrope tautly over the gap between "progressive" or "regressive" artworks, according to Adorno's canonizing judgments. Such judgments, however, I would suggest, depend on prior, mostly unthematized acts of exclusion—exclusions that touch as much upon the art of the Euro-

American avant-gardes as on Adorno's various instances of moderate modernisms, *rappels à l'ordre*, neo-traditionalisms, Culture Industry, and kitsch—embedded in the conceptual underpinnings of Adorno's aesthetic theory. Specifically with respect to surrealism, thus, Adorno could be as adamant about its supposedly regressive nature as was Lukács himself.[2]

These underpinnings not only preserve (however paradoxically and tenuously) an autonomous artistic work-concept in the midst of an increasingly extreme modernism. They also allow Adorno to continue to employ, appropriately dialecticized and de-positivized, much of the conceptual apparatus of classical German philosophy. Unlike other theorists—most prominently Benjamin and Georges Bataille—who derived critical models and methodological implications from the avant-garde arts for use in historical, theoretical, and ethnographic study, thus also disrupting the idiom and critical-conceptual repertoire of these investigations, Adorno remains firmly with the lexicon and conceptual framework of traditional philosophy. However problematic a stark opposition between Benjamin and Adorno might be in general, in his 1979 essay "Adorno, Benjamin und die Ästhetik," Helmut Heißenbüttel in my view correctly suggests that Adorno's early rejection of Benjamin's theoretical appropriation of surrealism decisively conditioned Adorno's aesthetic theory:

> Rather, the opposition of Adorno to Benjamin already in the response of the 1930s to Benjamin's drafts, now read from the perspective of *Negative Dialectics* and *Aesthetic Theory*, is recognizable as the expression of a conception of philosophy which, vis-à-vis Benjamin, still remains in the framework of traditional philosophy; or at least, cautiously put, always strove to make the argumentation of Kant and Hegel its own, rather than that of surrealism, to which Benjamin ascribed a key role in the matter of theory.[3]

Furthermore and analogously, I concur with Peter Bürger's general characterization of Adorno's aesthetics as "anti-avantgardist"— both in the art-historical sense and in Heißenbüttel's deeper epistemological-methodological sense—and seek to explore some of the implications of that stance for *Aesthetic Theory*.[4] More specifically, I will take Adorno's general lack of consideration of a wide range of avant-garde activity as relevant context for a more focused look at Adorno's blind spot around *surrealism*, which is highlighted by both Heißenbüttel and Bürger, who follow Benjamin in his controversies with Adorno about artistic autonomy, artistic function, and the methods of critique.

Surrealism, I argue, is particularly notable as an instance of Adorno's more general anti-avant-gardism, given its early significance in

Adorno's formative arguments with Benjamin; its return in Adorno's "Rückblick" of the 1950s as an instance of avant-garde "aging" and neutralization; and its subsequent importance for younger literary critics and theorists such as Bürger and Elisabeth Lenk, who sought to renew the utopian spark between surrealism and critical theory after its post-war eclipse under Adorno's theoretical shadow. By the time Adorno's posthumous *Aesthetic Theory* had appeared in 1970, the student movement's surrealist-influenced calls to put the imagination in power had, as Bürger notes, consigned Adorno's criticisms to inactuality—at least for some years. In my conclusion, however, I will consider Bürger's own return to the problem of surrealism after the waning of the aesthetico-political vanguardism of the 1960s and 1970s, in his revisionary "Gespräch" of 2004 entitled "Surrealism in the Thought of the Postmodern."[5] There, though he continues to value the intransigence of the avant-garde spirit, it is now put in the service of a radical pessimism, which, while not leaving Benjamin's surrealism interpretation behind, may be seen to offer closer rapprochement with the late Adorno than Bürger might have imagined in the wake of the student movement.

Surrealism received at least cursory discussion in *Aesthetic Theory* and elsewhere in Adorno's critical writings on music and literature. However, Adorno's specific relation to surrealism has garnered only limited attention in the otherwise voluminous criticism of his writings, in part because it would mean focusing more on lacunae in his critical corpus rather than positive content.[6] One of the first and few critics to discuss this relationship was the writer Roberto Calasso, who, in his 1961 essay "Th. W. Adorno, il surrealismo e il 'mana'," connects Adorno and Horkheimer's analysis of mana and magic in *Dialectic of Enlightenment* to the surrealists' attempt to reenchant everyday life through the mobilization of the unconscious and the poetic advent of the marvelous.[7] Though Calasso was only able to draw upon a certain number of Adorno's essays (along with an impressive array of French theorists including Bataille, Leiris, Lévi-Strauss, Butor, Caillois, Sartre, Barthes, and Rosolato), he adumbrates with remarkable prescience Adorno's ambivalent conception of the avant-garde as it would emerge in the *Aesthetic Theory*, including his view of surrealism specifically. Most prominent in Calasso's diagnosis, as in Adorno's, are the motifs of the progressive neutralization of the scandal of the avant-garde as it is converted into culture; the dialectical seeds of demise in the surrealist movement's founding precepts; and the self-defeating antinomies of abstract subjective freedom that are embodied in surrealist techniques for the imaginative production of the marvelous:

> Paraphrasing the Adornian axiom about culture, one could say that to speak for surrealism means to speak against surrealism. Registering it with academic benevolence among the twentieth-century avant-gardes, tallying its pros and cons, would mean carrying to term that work of neutralization that the market has advanced for thirty years and that was already implicit in the premises of the movement along with its hatred of the market itself. (9)

As his correspondence with Lenk reveals, Adorno was himself aware of Calasso's text and mentions it to her as proof of his self-evident interest in surrealism as her dissertation topic. He also confesses, however, somewhat awkwardly, that he hasn't been able to read it, because it is in Italian. Lenk responds that an Italian friend is sending it to her and that she will be able "to find my way through it, more or less" (Adorno and Lenk, 71 and 125–27). But whether or not they eventually spoke further about Calasso's specific interpretation, there is a nuanced and telling exchange between Adorno and Lenk on the aging of surrealism and the putative obsolescence of the avant-garde—which is Calasso's interpretive crux as well in his discussion of Adorno and surrealism.

In 1969, Lenk published an afterword to the German translation of Louis Aragon's *Paris Peasant*, the work that had so excited Benjamin and that had inspired his historical investigations of the Paris arcades. In it, she concludes—echoing Aragon himself, in his essay "Introduction to 1930," published in the December 1929 issue of *La Révolution Surréaliste*[8]—with an argument about the waning of modernism's provocation and excitement. She writes: "The surprise effect of headlines, of 'readymade' and splendidly meaningless advertising slogans, is worn out. Things that were once expressions of protest are now savored as modern art by a public whose senses have become dulled" (Adorno and Lenk, 196). In his response to Lenk, in a letter of July 18, 1969, Adorno defends art and modernity against Aragon's (and, with a situationist-influenced inflection, Lenk's) attack, and at the same time suggests that the aging of surrealism must be sought in bases more particular to surrealism and not in modern art more generally:

> If I had anything critical to say, it would have to do with the somewhat dogmatic adoption of the theses about the obsolescence of modernity and, implicitly, of art itself. These things will be the subject of a whole chapter of my *work of progress* [*Aesthetic Theory*], whose second draft is now complete. . . . Perhaps a couple of sentences could be added in which the reason for the aging of surrealism itself is identified somewhat less summarily, and above all more sharply delineated from Aragon's own apologetic conversion to the Communist Party. I must confess to you that I am as little persuaded of the decline of the arts today as I was during the surrealist heyday. (Adorno and Lenk, 183)

Adorno, likely unfamiliar with Aragon's 1929 text, mistakenly conflates the position Aragon takes in this essay, solidly within the framework of surrealism, with his later apostasy and allegiance to socialist realism. "Introduction to 1930" was published in the movement's main journal (*La Révolution Surréaliste*) and is concurrent with the Second Manifesto of Surrealism (1930), of which Aragon is a signatory. In a draft response cut short by Adorno's death and never sent, Lenk answers to Adorno accordingly:

> By no means do I have a new manifesto to add to the already stereotypical ones on the decline of art; instead I wanted to defend the "obsolete" Aragon against the Communist one. Politics is not meant to be presented as the inheritor of art. What we have, rather, is a parallel, that corresponding to Aragon's surrealist phase there was an instinctive anarchism: the rejection of every police state, including the socialist one. . . . Moreover, in the new phase in which he sacrificed art to politics, in politics a rigid conservatism also makes itself felt. (Lenk to Adorno, undated draft from July–August 1969, in Adorno and Lenk, 184)

Both Lenk and Adorno seek to weave a fine dialectical line through the historical process ("aging," loss of tension) that affected surrealism following its first, noisy advent. Lenk, however, had experienced direct contact with Breton and the surrealist group in the 1960s, as well as *Internationale Situationniste* (she promised to send Adorno a copy: Adorno and Lenk, 128), the student movement (as an SDS activist), and the anti-psychiatric movement (she recounts a visit to the commune of Félix Guattari's FGÉRI: Adorno and Lenk, 172–75). She was thus more attuned to the possibility of neo-avant-garde retrieval and reanimation of avant-garde energies, including, in the case of surrealist currents, their radical reenvisioning of eroticism and sensual life. Adorno's context for understanding the neo-avant-garde afterlife of the original surrealist movement was, in contrast, strictly retrospective and museal. Although there is no reason to doubt his sincere interest and support of Lenk's work (he energetically sought to find her publication and other professional opportunities), his experience is limited to books and the occasional exhibition. In his correspondence with Lenk in 1964, Adorno mentions his work on a short essay on the "defense of Isms" (which was incorporated into *Aesthetic Theory*). He goes on in the same letter to reflect on the aging and reification of the avant-gardes by referring to his experience of a surrealism exhibit he saw in Vienna in 1962: "[T]he danger that the avant-garde will become rigid cannot be overlooked either—I became extremely conscious of it two years ago at the surrealist exhibition in Vienna. Everything depends on holding fast to the intent and not allowing it to be marketed, yet not becoming immured within it but instead really moving it forward" (Adorno and Lenk, 88).⁹ The convolutions of Adorno's *Aesthetic Theory* derive at least in part from the paradoxical imperative to hold to the intent of the avant-garde and drive it forward, without "becoming immured in it," as apparently surrealism and its successors had done.

Looking Back on Surrealism in Adorno's Aesthetics

As already noted, explicit references to surrealism in *Aesthetic Theory* are sparse, though not entirely absent. The first occurs in the "Art Beauty" chapter, in the passages on spiritualization and the chaotic, in which Adorno posits a continuity between Stéphane Mallarmé's symbolist constellations and the "dream-chaos of surrealism" of the early Breton (*Aesthetic Theory*, 94), and between Stefan George and the expressionists. Both these avant-garde manifestations and their symbolist precursors have in common, Adorno asserts, that each set their spiritualized, artificially constituted chaos against a spuriously ordered second nature. However, this trajectory is also a radicalization of the chaotic, which turns against art's semblance and thus "works against art" (94). The surrealist avant-garde, like the expressionist, is implicitly presented as a crisis-manifestation, unstably poised between artistic creation and the self-abolition of art. Yet in this respect surrealism is only an instance of the more general developmental trajectory of art in the twentieth century. Adorno focuses his more specific critique of surrealism on three additional interrelated motifs: *historical regression* in the selection and handling of its materials; the *aging and mortification* of its shock-effects; and the *formal insufficiency* of its montage to resist capitulating to a reified reality.

Adorno's articulation of this critique consistently takes Max Ernst's collages as its key example,[10] and through reference to Ernst sets surrealism and neoclassicism in relation to one another. Adorno centers his reading of both tendencies upon the theme of their regression to historically obsolete materials, their mobilization of what we might call a "bourgeois antiquity":

> Valéry so honed the concept of classicality that ... he dubbed the successful romantic artwork classical. This strains the idea of classicality to the breaking point.... It is only in its relation to this, as to a disaster, that neoclassicism can be adequately understood. It is directly evident in surrealism. It toppled the images of antiquity from their Platonic heaven. In the paintings of Max Ernst they roam about as phantoms among the burghers of the late nineteenth century, for whom they have been neutralized as mere cultural goods and

truly transformed into specters.... Antiquity's embodied epiphany in prosaic everyday life, which has a long prehistory, disenchants it. Formerly presented as an atemporal norm, antiquity now acquires a historical status, that of the bourgeois idea reduced to its bare contours and rendered powerless. Its form is deformation. (*Aesthetic Theory*, 298)

The roots of this analysis go all the way back to Adorno's musicological writings of the 1930s, in particular his 1932 essay "On the Social Situation of Music," in which he connects surrealism with the montage methods of Stravinsky and Weill, the latter of which he refers to as "the major representative of musical surrealism."[11] He writes:

It is not without meaning that the style of Weill's *Three Penny Opera* and *Mahagonny* stand in greater proximity to *L'Histoire du Soldat* than does Hindemith; it is a style based upon montage, which abrogates the "organic" structure of neo-classicism and moves together rubble and fragment or constructs actual compositions out of falsehood and illusion, as which the harmony of the nineteenth century has today been revealed, through addition of intentionally false notes. The shock with which Weill's compositional practices overexposes common composition means [unmasks] them as ghosts. (409)

In his 1949 book *Philosophy of New Music* he redeployed this basic critical motif, in which through its montage of desemanticized fragments of the past, surrealism appeared as a relevant corollary to Stravinsky's montages of historical idioms in his neoclassical compositions of the 1920s and 1930s. Adorno writes:

The final perversity of style is universal necrophilia.... Just as in Max Ernst's graphic montages, the image world of the parents—plush, buffets, and balloons—is meant to spark panic by seeming to belong already to the remote past, so Stravinsky's shock technique seizes upon the musical image world of the recent past.[12]

So too, in his 1956 essay "Looking Back on Surrealism," alluding here as well to Ernst's graphic collages, Adorno puts his accent on the backward-turned gaze of surrealism, fascinated by the aging image-stock of the recent past, rather than (in contrast to, for instance, Benjamin) surrealism's convulsive hermeneutic of desire and chance or its future-oriented, emancipatory aspirations to "transform life." Adorno suggests that surrealism exploded the objects of the precedent generation ("the world of the parents of Max Ernst's generation") in order to recover an original shock of childhood experience:

What Surrealism adds to illustrations of the world of objects is the element of childhood we lost; when we were children, those illustrated papers, already obsolete even then, must have leaped out at us the way Surrealist images do now. The subjective aspect in this lies in the action of the montage, which attempts—perhaps in vain, but the intention is unmistakable—to produce perceptions as they must have been then.[13]

He adds in emphasis: "Obsoleteness contributes to this effect."

Adorno reiterates yet again this same critical motif of a dream-like explosion of obsolete fragments, with reference to Ernst's collages, in his 1962 essay on Stravinsky. There, he writes that in neoclassicism the classical ideal—

> appeared as if in dreams, not as a whole genre, but in the form of plaster busts on wardrobes in the houses of the older generation, individual pieces of bric-à-brac and remaindered goods. In this process of individualizing a whole style into a set of monstrosities, the style was destroyed. It was damaged and rendered impotent by dreams hastily cobbled together and arranged. The basic stratum of neo-Classicism is not far removed from Surrealism. Stravinsky's Baroque revenants duplicate the statues in Max Ernst's *Femme 100 Têtes* which tumble among the living beings and whose faces are frequently missing as if they had been erased by the dream censorship.[14]

In this respect, then, Adorno's judgment of surrealism, narrowly exemplified by the graphic works of Max Ernst and viewed through the lens of Stravinsky, of whom Adorno was deeply critical, was sustained for decades up to his final work with unwavering consistency. Both neoclassicism and surrealism, in Adorno's view, register the denaturing of tradition in a bourgeois society increasingly incapable of confronting its own historicity and eagerly consuming reified fetishes that conceal its obsolescence.

While his references to surrealism in these passages are highly selective—outside of Ernst and the early De Chirico, Adorno's characterizations are hardly applicable to most surrealist works—the importance of this conceptual constellation for Adorno's aesthetics should not be underestimated. It represents, first of all, Adorno's displacement of Benjamin's surrealist-influenced notion that advanced modernity cites archaic prehistory in ephemeral dialectical images that bear an explosive potential for illumination and collective awakening. In his interpretation of surrealism—driven especially by his tendentious reading of Ernst's collages in analogy to Stravinsky's neoclassical compositions—Adorno inverts the Benjaminian relation of modernity and antiquity. Instead of inviting an innervating spark between historical extremes, as did Benjamin, Adorno places primacy on the conjunction's anesthetizing power, which helps to preserve undisturbed the illusion of a substantive connection between the prosaic present and the classical past, hence too ideologically conjuring a present that would be founded on something more solid than the effervescence of business and media cycles.

Adorno's understanding of Ernst's collages, as works that cobble together the debris of bourgeois interiors to recapitulate the recent past in its spleen-inducing deadness (or, as in his 1956 "Rückblick," to recapture childhood experience deformed by historical distance), also deflates the moment of insurrectionary reversal that Ernst himself, as well as other champions of surrealism like Benjamin, believed were being prepared in these scenes. In an essay from 1934 entitled "Max Ernst and His Reversible Images," the poet Tristan Tzara wrote the following about Ernst's collages, like those from *Une Semaine de Bonté*:

> Ernst, in the glacial silence of a rigorous introspection, whether at the inert point or at the static point of dreaming or waking, has most vividly illustrated that poetic activity which is defined, from the viewpoint of knowledge, as an unsystematized delirium of interpretation or as a continuous relation between psychic simulation and mimetism on the one hand, and the obsessional and irrational personality the residue of which is to be decanted. This activity, when it is limited to reversible meanings, finds in their very mobility inventive resources sufficient to identify them as powerful means of subversion and sabotage towards the actual world and towards its reality.[15]

As Benjamin's analogous reading of surrealism suggests, surrealist concatenations of images are only in a *preparatory* way a backward-turned mirror returning an image of the recent past distorted by reification and decay, as Adorno's critique would suggest. More important is their moment of exteriorization and shock, in which they mobilize the static elements of the city's spaces—dwelling places, shops, factories, markets, objects, and infrastructures—and project them outward as *images* charged with virulent energies to disrupt the present:

> No one before these visionaries and augurs perceived how destitution—not only social, but architectonic, the poverty of interiors, enslaved and enslaving objects—can be suddenly transformed into revolutionary nihilism. ... They bring the immense forces of "atmosphere" concealed in these things to the point of explosion.[16]

In the late 1920s and 1930s, Laurent Jenny has suggested, there was a shift of emphasis in the surrealist movement from the expressive, "passive" automatism of Breton's First Manifesto to the intentional production of provocative symbolic objects that might precipitate collective response, an "active" practice of automatism more closely associated with Dalí, Giacometti, Buñuel, Bataille, and Caillois.[17] This shift also coincided with the increasing politicization of the surrealist movement and its offshoots, leading various adherents towards the Communist Party, Trotskyism, aesthetico-political groupings such as Contre-Attaque and Acéphale, and the constitution of the Collège de

Sociologie by Bataille and his circle, with which both Benjamin and Adorno had contact.[18] Tzara and Benjamin are consistent with this surrealist avant-garde's emphasis on the actualization of art's potential for contagious propagation of shock and collective effect, bursting the artwork out of the containment of its autonomous form and function. Adorno's reading, in contrast, depends on heightening the perspective of obsolescence and depotentiation of surrealist shock, such that what once had seemed a ticking time bomb later proved to be nothing but a harmless, broken toy.

This argument leads directly to a second key topic of Adorno's presentation of surrealism in the *Aesthetic Theory*: as an exemplary case of the "aging" of the avant-garde and the reabsorption of its anti-art negativity back into the styles and techniques of art. Indeed, he had already identified this danger in connection to Kurt Weill's "musical surrealism" back in 1932. The negativity of surrealist montage, dependent on the shock value of its assemblage of reified fragments, is fleeting; in its paradoxical endurance as an artwork, however, it is prone to settle back into the conventions that it once disrupted or to normalize a new set of artistic conventions, a style:

> It is beyond question that Weill's music is today the only music of genuine social-polemic impact, which it will remain as long as it resides at the height of its negativity; furthermore, this music has recognized itself as such and has taken its position accordingly. Its problem is the impossibility of remaining at this height; as a musician, Weill must try to escape the responsibilities of a work method which, from the perspective of music, necessarily seems "literary," similar, in its way, to the pictures of the surrealists. ("On the Social Situation of Music," 409)

So too in *Aesthetic Theory*, Adorno notes that in its persistence beyond its brief flourishing as an avant-garde movement, surrealism reincorporated its anti-art and socially polemical negativity as technical features of artistic style:

> [I]mportant surrealists such as Max Ernst and André Masson, who refused to collude with the market and initially protested against the sphere of art itself, gradually turned towards formal principles, and Masson largely abandoned representation, as the idea of shock, which dissipates quickly in the thematic material, was transformed into a technique of painting. (*Aesthetic Theory*, 256)

Lastly, as has already been indicated in the discussion above, Adorno's critical posture towards surrealism is connected with his doubts about montage as a method of artistic construction, a position that puts him at odds with a broad range of artistic manifestations of the avant-garde, including surrealism, which he saw to be governed by the principle of montage. Thus, in his important discussion of montage in the section on "Coherence and Meaning," while Adorno does not explicitly mention surrealism, his judgment encompasses it along with constructivism. Indeed, we can hear echoes of Adorno's critique of Benjamin's surrealist-influenced montage method in the construction of the *Arcades Project* in this characterization of artistic montage in *Aesthetic Theory*:

> Montage is the inner-aesthetic capitulation of art to what stands heterogeneously opposed to it. The negation of synthesis becomes a principle of form. . . . The artwork wants to make the facts eloquent by letting them speak for themselves. Art thereby begins the process of destroying the artwork as a nexus of meaning. (155)

For Adorno, there are two problems with montage-construction that follow. First, in montage-practice, the semblance of meaning tends to be reimposed through an abstract structure that suppresses the particularity of the unprocessed material details: "Whatever is unintegrated is compressed by the subordinating authority of the whole so that the totality compels the failing coherence of the parts and thus however once again asserts the semblance of meaning" (155). And second, following from this, the shock value of the montage-construction's lack of unity of its elements is quickly dissipated, as the work falls apart into an abstract idea of its totality and the raw materiality of its components:

> The principle of montage was conceived as an act against a surreptitiously achieved organic unity; it was meant to shock. Once this shock is neutralized, the assemblage once more becomes merely indifferent material; the technique no longer suffices to trigger communication between the aesthetic and the extra-aesthetic, and its interest dwindles into a cultural-historical curiosity. (155–56)

Adorno's concluding phrase sums up his damning judgment of the historical avant-gardes. The ability of the avant-garde to shock, he suggests, has dissipated, leaving behind a litter of radical attempts but little of genuine artistic worth—except, paradoxically, when previously avant-garde artists abjured their avant-garde principles and reincorporated anti-artistic comportments as the basis of new formal styles.

Surrealism after Adorno: Lenk and Bürger

In conclusion I would like to discuss briefly the presentation of surrealism, more or less concurrent, by two successors of Adorno: Lenk, whose correspondence with Adorno I have already referred to extensively; and

Bürger, whose work has sparked renewed attention to the historical avant-gardes and neo-avant-gardes since his influential *Theory of the Avant-Garde* appeared in German in 1974 and in English ten years later.

Both Lenk and Bürger published studies of surrealism at the beginning of the 1970s that took up the theoretical mantle of Frankfurt School critical theory but broke with the limited and ultimately dismissive interpretation of Adorno. Partly this was a matter of a deeper immersion in the original sources and theories of surrealism and its successors; partly too it involved renewed attention to Benjamin's theoretically productive engagement with surrealism. But a decisive factor for both was also the political context of the French and German student uprisings, which charged their studies of surrealism—with its critique of work, its refusal of the division of labor, and its striving to transform everyday life and liberate desire—with a fresh sense of topical urgency.[19] Bürger is explicit about the extra-literary horizon of his scholarly engagement with surrealism:

> With the May '68 events at the latest, the topicality of surrealism becomes evident. Not because at this time slogans of surrealism stood on the walls of public buildings, but rather because here aspirations declared by surrealism since the 1920s found mass expression.... [T]he May events throw a new light on Surrealism, whose political implications have only now become fully visible; on the other hand, the study of surrealism should contribute to a better grasp of the aspirations and aporias of the May movement as an element in the unresolved present. (*Die französische Surrealismus*, 7)

Lenk had the experience of an extended residence in Paris and direct contact with Breton and other surrealists, as well as political involvement with the German SDS, French Trotskyism, and the writings and activities of the situationists. She too notes the connection she made between her study of surrealism, her adherence to the Frankfurt School theoretical project, and the May student rebellion: "My book on André Breton was written under the fresh impressions of the events of May 1968, and while writing it I always envisioned Adorno as the ideal reader. At that time, the two movements seemed to be of great contemporary relevance. Was it not they, ultimately, that unleashed the May events?" (Adorno and Lenk, 37).

Adorno, as Todd Cronan points out in an insightful review of *The Challenge of Surrealism*, set as a standard for surrealism's success the normative criterion of proper mediation "between individual fantasy and social whole" and had, of course, found the surrealists wanting. "Lenk," Cronan writes, "offers alternate criteria for surrealist success," rooted in Fourier, Sade, and surrealists: the liberation of the passions of the body and the unleashing of radical difference.[20] (I explore this liberationist tradition in greater depth in Chapter 8.) Lenk, Cronan concludes, interprets the Frankfurt School's project as "a renovation of the senses, an experiential model. It provided an 'alternative to politics' rather than a form of it." (52). This characterization of Lenk's revisionary stance resonates with her own statement of the conjunction of Frankfurt School theory and surrealism in her formation and subsequent thought:

> What links the Frankfurt School and surrealism is the protest against specialization, which, at the same time, is being played out at the highest level of the various specialized fields. They set the arts, disciplinary languages, and professional knowledge from the most diverse realms on a collision course, in order to force them, through the resulting shock, to set free a new way of thinking. . . . For their part, the surrealists . . . laid claim to a similarly broad social engagement as surreal practice. This they did with a vehemence that anticipated, in a nutshell, all the protest movements of the 1960s: antipsychiatry, prisoners' movement, antimilitarism, critique of fossilized university; however, the impulse was soon abandoned in favor of surrealism in the service of the Marxist revolution. (Adorno and Lenk, 49)

Lenk stresses, as Benjamin had decades earlier, the anarchist aspects of surrealism, but unlike her predecessor does not counter these with "methodical and disciplined preparation for revolution" (Benjamin, "Surrealism," 216). Rather, she sees surrealism's failure as that of having not sufficiently persisted in its all-sided insurrection against the paucity of reality, its too-rapid capitulation to a politics thought to be the necessary successor of its lyrical and eroticized demands for total freedom.

Bürger, by comparison to Lenk, is more sober in his assessment of the surrealist program. In many respects, he cleaves closely to Benjamin, both in his positive and his critical evaluation of the movement. On the one hand, surrealism is for him exemplary in its avant-garde attempt to destroy the autonomy of art and overcome its separation from life as a specialized activity. On the other hand, given the radicality with which it disrupted representation in language and image, it struggled with its own paradoxical demands for revolutionary efficacy, which depends on communication. In *Theory of the Avant-Garde,* Bürger summarizes (in very Benjaminian terms) surrealism's dilemma: "There is a danger here to which surrealism at least partly succumbed, and that is solipsism, the retreat to problems of the isolated subject. Breton himself saw this danger and envisaged different ways of dealing with it. One of them was the glorification of the spontaneity of the erotic relationship. Perhaps the strict group discipline was also an attempt to exorcise the danger of solipsism that surrealism harbors."[21] If Lenk envisions a redemptive retrieval of an original surrealism lent new social relevance by the experimental forms of life unleashed by the May events, Bürger remains more ambivalent, understanding the same tensions that animated surrealism in the 1920s and 1930s to have recurred in the life- and political forms thrown up by the rebellions of the 1960s and remaining to work through in the early 1970s.

Of greatest interest in Bürger's surrealism book for our concerns, however, are the methodological conclusions that he draws from the study of surrealism for a sociological theory of modernist literature. He explicitly situates his work at a dialectical juncture of Lukács's and Adorno's aesthetics, which, as we know, they themselves set in polemical confrontation. Bürger's own research into surrealism, he argues, helped set in relief the complementary limitations of both Lukács's and Adorno's theories of artistic modernism and to disclose the larger stakes of their critical debate:

> Neither of the two theories of the avant-garde sketched here is adequate to grasp the phenomenon in its contradictoriness. ... As the outcome of the preceding analysis, we can formulate that avant-garde literature, as we have investigated in the case of surrealism, should neither be seen as the sole possible form of protest against the existing social relations, nor rejected as decadent, but rather is to be understood as the most radical form of bourgeois protest against bourgeois society. (*Die französische Surrealismus*, 186)

In his essay for Dannemann's *Lukács und 68* volume, Bürger retrospectively sums this dialectical conclusion up with allusion to Adorno's own debates of the 1930s with Benjamin. Bürger writes that in his surrealism book, "I took up a constellation ... that over two decades constituted a focus of my reflections on aesthetics. At its foundation was the intuition that Adorno's aesthetic theory and Lukács's theory of realism were two halves, torn from one another, of a concept of aesthetic modernity."[22]

I will close by mentioning a fascinating short text that Bürger published much later, in 2004, which once more takes up, from a retrospective horizon, the question of surrealism's relevance for the present: "Surrealism in the Thinking of the Postmodern." Confronted by a younger interlocutor about the historical reversal of the avant-garde from virulent challenge to harmless object of museum collection and academic study, Bürger reflects on how his perspective has shifted towards a more pessimistic view of the avant-garde. But in a surprising dialectical turn, he also suggests how precisely this reevaluation helped him to reappropriate a motif that also originally animated surrealism— its dark nihilism, or as Benjamin put it, following the formulation of Pierre Naville, its "organization of pessimism."[23] Bürger writes that he explained to his friend how in the 1990s, working towards a new edition of his surrealism book, he had returned to the original sources and reread them with new eyes. He "discovered another surrealism than that which he had seen around 1970: a dark surrealism that circled around the motifs of despair, violence, and suicide and that contained almost nothing more of the overwhelming trust in a world of unlimited possibility that characterized the First Manifesto" ("Der Surrealismus im Denken der Postmoderne," 59–60).

Bürger goes on to expound how this retrospective look from a period shaped by the disappointment of the revolutionary hopes of his original engagement with the surrealists gave him insight into the resonances of this "dark" surrealism with the paradigm of postmodern theory, represented for Bürger by Bataille, Lacan, Derrida, and Foucault. This constellation, he argues, offers ways of approaching what is repressed and unthought within the present, of understanding how we are determined by the past not only through what has occurred, but also of what has failed to occur, what has gotten lost along the way. At this point, Bürger comes around to the analogous pessimism he sees in Adorno, who sought to come to terms with art and philosophy that persists beyond the moment of its projected overcoming, continuing in the wake of catastrophe. It is in this shadow tradition of radical pessimism, running from the surrealists to the postmodern, and theoretically articulated by thinkers ranging from Naville, Benjamin, Bataille, Lacan, and Adorno through Foucault, Derrida, and Bürger himself, that we may find the enduring actuality of the avant-garde, which can lend fresh impetus to our self-understanding and self-formation as heirs of the twentieth century. There is only one alternative, Bürger concludes, to the depressing implications of the avant-garde's failure to achieve its goals of transforming life, of its senescence and cooptation by the institutions of "culture" it rebelled against, its decline into, as Adorno put it, just another cultural-historical curiosity. That is "to rediscover the original impulse of the avant-garde: the energies of despair. . . . In the return to the avant-garde we commemorate a missed event, not in order retrospectively to realize it, rather to recognize in its absence that which determines our epoch like a fate" ("Der Surrealismus im Denken der Postmoderne," 67).

Notes

1. Theodor W. Adorno, *Aesthetic Theory*, eds. Greta Adorno and Rolf Tiedemann, trans. Robert Hullot-Kentor (Minneapolis: University of Minnesota Press, 1997), 179.

2. For an example of Lukács's position, see his 1947 essay "Hungarian Theories of Abstract Art," discussed in Chapter 4.
3. Helmut Heißenbüttel, "Adorno, Benjamin und die Ästhetik," in *Über Benjamin*, ed. Thomas Combrink (Frankfurt am Main: Suhrkamp Verlag), 143. In 1967, Heißenbüttel touched off a firestorm in a notorious polemic, "Vom Zeugnis des Fortlebens in Briefen," *Merkur* 21/3 (1967): 232–44, in which he accused the editors of Benjamin's work of distorting the materialist and militant aspects of Benjamin's conception of art. In his correspondence with his then-dissertation student Elisabeth Lenk, Adorno focused on Heißenbüttel's statements about Benjamin and surrealism: "That meanwhile in the *Merkur* there was an essay by Heissenbüttel on Benjamin that contained foolish things about him and me and above all about my relationship to surrealism, you are probably aware." See letter from Adorno to Lenk, March 10, 1967, in Theodor W. Adorno and Elisabeth Lenk, *The Challenge of Surrealism: The Correspondence of Theodor W. Adorno and Elisabeth Lenk*, ed. and trans. Susan H. Gillespie (Minneapolis: University of Minnesota Press, 2015), 133.
4. Peter Bürger, "Adorno's Anti-Avant-Gardism," *Telos* 86 (1990); Bürger, "Der Anti-Avantgardismus in der Ästhetik Adornos," in *Das Altern der Moderne: Schriften zur bildenden Kunst* (Frankfurt am Main: Suhrkamp, 2001), 31–47.
5. Peter Bürger, "Der Surrealismus im Denken der Postmoderne," in *Nach der Avantgarde* (Weilerswist: Velbrück Wissenschaft, 2014), 55–67.
6. Among the limited bibliography in English are: Richard Wolin, "Benjamin, Adorno, Surrealism," in *The Semblance of Subjectivity: Essays in Adorno's Aesthetic Theory*, eds. Tom Huhn and Lambert Zuidervaart (Cambridge, MA: The MIT Press, 1997), 93–122, which suggests a far more affirmative view of surrealism on Adorno's part than I think is tenable; Darren Jorgensen, "Uses of the Dialectical Image: Adorno, Surrealism, Breton, Benjamin," *Continuum: Journal of Media and Cultural Studies* 28/6 (2014): 876–84, which focuses on Adorno's critique of Benjamin's surrealist-influenced methodology in the *Arcades Project*; and the essays by Rita Bischof and Elisabeth Lenk in Adorno and Lenk, *The Challenge of Surrealism*.
7. Roberto Calasso, "Th. W. Adorno, il surrealismo e il 'mana'," *Paragone* 12/138 (1961): 9–24. My thanks to Stefano Marino for help in procuring this article.
8. Louis Aragon, "Introduction à 1930," *La Révolution Surréaliste* 12 (1929): 57–64.
9. The exhibition in question was the "Surrealismus, phantastische Malerei der Gegenwart" show at Vienna's Künstlerhaus, May 30–July 8 1962. It displayed 156 works, especially by artists of the Austrian school of "fantastic realism" and related neo-surrealist tendencies, such as Ernst Fuchs, Maria Lassnig, Rudolf Hausner, and Arnulf Rainer.
10. Adorno's familiarity with the breadth of surrealism's diverse artists, theories, and works appears to have been fairly limited. Max Ernst's work *The Lion of Belfort*, the first chapter of his 1934 collage-novel *Une Semaine de Bonté*, was in Adorno's possession, as Elisabeth Lenk reports.
11. Theodor W. Adorno, "On the Social Situation of Music," in *Essays on*

Music, ed. Richard Leppert, trans. Susan H. Gillespie (Berkeley and Los Angeles: University of California Press, 2002), 409. Notably, too, a biographical detail links Weill and Max Ernst, through Lotte Lenya, who had a brief affair with Ernst in the mid-1930s, then returned to Weill. In a letter to Adorno of May 31, 1935, Benjamin asks Adorno to arrange a meeting with Ernst and Lenya, whom, he says, "he would very much like to see" See Walter Benjamin, *Selected Writings, Volume 3: 1935–1938*, trans. Edmund Jephcott, Howard Eiland et al., eds. Howard Eiland and Michael W. Jennings (Cambridge, MA: The Belknap Press of Harvard University Press, 2002), 53. This suggests Adorno had personal acquaintance not only with Lenya, which is well known, but also perhaps with Ernst.

12. Theodor W. Adorno, *Philosophy of New Music*, ed. and trans. Robert Hullot-Kentor (Minneapolis: University of Minnesota Press, 2006), 149.
13. Theodor W. Adorno, "Looking Back on Surrealism," in *Notes on Literature, Volume 1*, ed. Rolf Tiedemann, trans. Shierry Weber Nicholsen (New York: Columbia University Press, 1991), 88.
14. Theodor W. Adorno, "Stravinsky: A Dialectical Portrait," in *Quasi Una Fantasia: Essays on Modern Music*, trans. Rodney Livingstone (London: Verso), 156.
15. Tristan Tzara, "Max Ernst and His Reversible Images," in Max Ernst, *Beyond Painting* (New York: Wittenborn, Schultz, Inc., 1948), 189.
16. Walter Benjamin, "Surrealism, the Last Snapshot of the European Intelligentsia," in *Selected Writings, Volume 2: 1927–1934*, eds. Michael W. Jennings, Howard Eiland, and Gary Smith, trans. Rodney Livingstone et al. (Cambridge, MA: The Belknap Press of Harvard University Press, 1999), 210.
17. Laurent Jenny, "From Breton to Dali: The Adventures of Automatism," trans. Thomas Tresize, *October* 51 (1989): 105–14.
18. Georges Bataille and André Breton, *Contre-Attaque: Union de lute des intellectuels révolutionnaires, 1935–1936* (Paris: Ypsilon Éditeur, 2013); *Acéphale: Religion, sociologie, philosophie* (Paris: Jean-Michel Placé, 1980); *The College of Sociology (1937–39)*, ed. Denis Hollier (Minneapolis: University of Minnesota Press, 1988).
19. This connection of Benjamin, surrealism, and the student movement was evident to Jürgen Habermas in his 1972 essay "Walter Benjamin: Consciousness Raising or Rescuing Critique," in *Philosophical-Political Profiles*, trans. Frederick G. Lawrence (Cambridge, MA: The MIT Press, 1983), 132: "Benjamin's proximity to surrealism has again been brought to our attention with the second wave of Benjamin reception that took its impetus from the student revolt." Along with Karl Heinz Bohrer, *Die gefährdete Phantasie oder Surrealismus und Terror* (Munich: Carl Hanser Verlag, 1970), Habermas refers to Elisabeth Lenk, *Der springende Narziß: André Breton's poetischer Materialismus* (Munich: Rogner & Bernhard, 1971), and Peter Bürger, *Die Französiche Surrealismus: Studien zum Problem der avantgardistichen Literatur* (Frankfurt am Main: Athenäum 1971).
20. Todd Cronan, "Operation Adorno," *Radical Philosophy* 194 (2015): 51.
21. Peter Bürger, *Theory of the Avant-Garde*, trans. Michael Shaw (Minneapolis: University of Minnesota Press, 1984), 53.

22. Peter Bürger, "Lukács-Lektüren: Autobiographische Fragmente," in *Georg Lukács und 1968: Eine Spurensuche*, ed. Rüdiger Dannemann (Bielefeld: Aisthesis Verlag, 2009), 20.
23. Pierre Naville, *La Revolution et les intellectuels* (Paris: Gallimard, 1975), 116–17.

Chapter 6

Avant-Garde *and* Kitsch, or, Teddy the Musical!

"And what about the musical theatre?"
—Reporter to People's Commissar Lukács, 1919

Do you remember the night I held you so tight
As we danced to the Wiener Schnitzel Waltz?
—Tom Lehrer, 1953

Avant-Garde *and* Kitsch?

Adorno is often characterized as one of the most adamant Western advocates of an elitist high culture modernism and as a powerful opponent of industrially produced, commodified mass art. He trained as a composer under the tutelage of Berg and remained a fierce critical advocate of the atonal music of Schoenberg and his circle, including Berg and Webern as well as younger contemporaries such as Ernst Křenek and Hanns Eisler. Adorno was also an important theoretical and critical contributor to the discussions that shaped post–World War II European "New Music" at Darmstadt and elsewhere, which encompassed a range of new compositional techniques from the further radicalization of serial composition to electronic music and the *musique informelle* influenced by John Cage. Adorno stood for an uncompromising commitment to musical progress, as he conceived it, which meant for him above all exploring the dissonant expressivity of new music through the relentless pursuit of advanced compositional techniques. In his studies of contemporary popular culture and in his collaborative work with Horkheimer on the standardization of culture within an ever more consolidated Culture Industry, in contrast, Adorno identified much of the music hearable on the airwaves, on record players, and in performance as a kind of degraded, stereotypical trash. Along with Horkheimer, he believed that the Culture Industry functioned to close the productive gap of thought, imagination, and experience between the artwork and the listener and to reduce both to a common industrial measure: standardized, schematic, unproblematic works produced for compliant, standardized consumers, themselves "mass-produced" to the measure of the goods they were being advertised and sold.

All this, certainly, could prepare us for a highly polarized and hierarchical view of the musical arts in Adorno's aesthetics, with singular works of technically advanced, serious, difficult, elitist, modernist art thoroughly segregated from popular, light, low-genre works that are nothing but shoddy products of a homogeneous Culture Industry. A very substantial part of the reception of Adorno's work has in fact accepted this dichotomous view, whether to advocate alongside Adorno for challenging works of new music, or, as is perhaps more common now, to argue against him in defense of jazz, rock, hip-hop, disco, electronica, or other popular musical forms.

While this dichotomizing view is not without evident ground in Adorno's texts, it nevertheless ignores subtler aspects of his musical aesthetics that blur and shade the gap between technically innovative experimental music and popular, including commercial, musical forms. In his concrete critical engagements with musical works, Adorno himself often complicates his own apparently binary schema with a more nuanced dialectic between popular and elite art forms. Over the span of his musical writings, from his early music criticism of the late 1920s and early 1930s, to his sociological studies of his American exile, to his mature writings from post-war Germany until his death in the late 1960s, though there are consistencies in his arguments and positions, there are also shifting accents and even on occasion significant revisions of earlier, more intransigent views of popular music.

Moreover, while Adorno emphatically canonized a short list of composers whose works advanced the technical development of the musical material and therefore, in his view, marshaled the weak critical forces of art against an increasingly inhuman society, his judgments of even these favored artists were rarely unequivocal. Typically, Adorno viewed the progressive achievements of individual artists or artworks within a force field of dialectical tensions, including between the extremes of the polarities made famous by Clement Greenberg, avant-garde and kitsch.[1] Like Greenberg, Adorno saw these artistic polarities as historically intertwined and even mutually constituted. But in at least some of his early music criticism around 1930, and tendentially even in his mature writings, Adorno went beyond suggesting, like Greenberg, that the avant-garde took dialectical impetus from defending contemporary art against the incursions of kitsch from the broader context of mass society. Adorno also understood kitsch as a complementary if distorting mirror for the avant-garde, and hence likewise viewed it as a possible resource or improbable ally in the avant-garde's search for new formal and functional characteristics of art. Not avant-garde and kitsch as exclusive opposites, then, but rather: avant-garde *and* kitsch as a social-aesthetic force field from which new, individuated, progressive artworks might spring up.

Adorno's greatest concern with the Culture Industry was not, I would argue, the danger of kitsch invading art, but rather that the tension that exists between avant-garde and kitsch would be washed away in the standardization of a *middling*, middlebrow culture.[2] Already in his 1928 exposé for the Vienna-based music journal *Der Anbruch*, Adorno sought a *tertium datur* between the snobbish dismissal of kitsch in the name of culture "values" and pseudo-populist celebration of it: "Against everything that is merely elevated mediocre art, against the now rotten ideals of personality, culture, etc., kitsch must be played out and defended. But . . . one must not fall prey to the flat-out glorification of kitsch . . . as the true art of our times, because of its popularity."[3] Years later, in "The Schema of Mass Culture," an unpublished essay intended to be the sequel of the Culture Industry chapter in *Dialectic of Enlightenment*, Adorno would lament the disappearance of *both* avant-garde and kitsch, making his abiding fear of a neutralized sphere of *pseudo*-art explicit:

> There is no longer either kitsch or intransigent modernism in art. Advertising has absorbed surrealism and the champions of this movement have given their blessing to this commercialization of their own murderous attacks on culture in the name of hostility to the same. Kitsch fares no better as hatred towards it becomes its very element. Sentimentality is robbed of its implausible character, of that touching but impotent Utopian moment which for an instant might soften the hearts of those who have been hardened and take them beyond the reach of their even harder masters.[4]

Dialectics of Kitsch

In the early 1930s, a period in which Adorno was especially engaged with the compositions and performances of his contemporaries, he developed a nuanced conception of kitsch and its function within the current music scene. Though remarks on kitsch are scattered throughout his writings, with different accents, we find a concentrated attempt to situate kitsch within his musical aesthetics in a short unpublished text entitled "Kitsch" dating from around 1932. Notably, Adorno defines kitsch as something other than just bad or tasteless or deficient art—and hence, something potentially justifiable and redeemable. He argues that kitsch is not a matter of the subjective shortcomings of the artist, whether in conception or execution, nor is it just a predilection of tasteless consumers; rather, it designates something *objective* in relation to the artwork and its forms. In his *Aesthetic Theory*, Adorno would recall this dialectical conception of kitsch first formulated thirty years earlier:

> Kitsch is not ... the mere refuse of art, originating in disloyal accommodation to the enemy; rather, it lurks in art, awaiting ever recurring opportunities to spring forth. Although kitsch escapes, implike, from even a historical definition, one of its most tenacious characteristics is the prevarication of feelings, fictional feelings in which no one is actually participating, and thus the neutralization of these feelings. Kitsch parodies catharsis. Ambitious art, however, produces the same fiction of feelings; indeed, this was essential to it. ... It is in vain to try to draw the boundaries abstractly between aesthetic fiction and kitsch's emotional plunder.[5]

Adorno was quite aware that the artistic intensities of Wagner's musical drama could end up in the kitschified Wagner cult ironized by Thomas Mann in his short stories "Tristan" (1903) and "The Blood of the Walsungs" (written 1905, published 1921) and even more savagely parodied by Georg Grosz in his Wagner *Gedenkblatt* from his 1922 album *Ecce Homo*, in which he depicts a corpulent, mostly nude German family engaging in Wagnerian cosplay. Similarly, the expressionist shriek rapidly settled into a mawkish "O Mensch!" note as its once radical gestures became conventional. The line between kitsch and avant-garde, between a poison that sickens and a poison that cures, is not a distinction between two essentially different sorts of artistic materials, but rather a bifurcation in the developmental tendencies of the artistic materials themselves as they unfold in new historical contexts.

Rather than existing in a "free-floating aesthetic" way, Adorno argues, kitsch takes shape historically and socially, as earlier artistic forms become, under the pressure of contemporary forces, reified and obsolete. Noting that one possible etymology of the word "kitsch" traces it to the English "sketch,"[6] Adorno observes:

> In music, at any rate, all real kitsch has the character of a model. It offers the outline and draft of objectively compelling, pre-established forms that have lost their content in history, and for which the unfettered artist, cast adrift, is not able to fashion the content on his own. Hence the illusory character of kitsch cannot be unambiguously traced to the individual inadequacy of the artist, but, instead, has its own objective origin in the downfall of forms and materials in history. Kitsch is the precipitate of devalued forms and empty ornaments in a formal world that has become remote from its immediate context.[7]

In turn, as an expression of reification, kitsch functions ideologically to conceal the current social situation of its consumers, by conjuring obsolescent forms of experience. However, Adorno also sees kitsch as having a contemporary justification in being a remembrance of a form-world that had a stronger objectivity than is now presently possible as artistic conventions disintegrate and artworks become ever more contingent and singular. Lastly, the concept of kitsch itself evolves historically. In this latter function of remembrance, kitsch becomes an unexpected partner of the avant-garde in exposing the compromises of the middling, moderate forms of the "juste milieu," which can claim neither the objectivity of past forms nor the radicalized invention of new forms. In the current moment, then, kitsch's sentimental remembrance of long-reified conventions may be in league with the aggressive anti-conventionality of the avant-garde, while the tasteful dismissal of kitsch may serve only to delude middlebrow cultural producers and consumers that the canonized forms they take for granted are still intact. Paradoxically, opposition to kitsch becomes, as the disavowal of the historical disintegration of artistic forms, a self-deluding, sublimated manifestation of kitsch itself. As Adorno archly puts it, "Thus the talk about kitsch itself begins to be kitschy, as it succumbs to the very historical dialectic from which its object emerged" ("Kitsch," 504).

This dialectical valuation of the low as the enemy of the middling informs other instances in which Adorno affirms the function of kitsch in the social field of art. In his 1960 monograph on Gustav Mahler, for example, Adorno positively evaluates Mahler's incorporation of low-culture, popular elements as a way of perspectivizing and invigorating the refined idioms of German nineteenth-century music:

> The unrisen lower is stirred as yeast into high music. The rude vigor and immediacy of a musical entity that can neither be replaced nor forgotten: the power of naming is often better protected in kitsch and vulgar music than in a high music that even before the age of radical construction had sacrificed all to the principle of stylization. This power is mobilized by Mahler. Free as only one can be who has not himself been entirely swallowed by culture, in his musical vagrancy he picks up the broken glass by the roadside and holds it up to the sun so that all the colors are refracted.[8]

He goes on to make the even starker claim that the aesthetic success of Mahler's work is inseparable from its intimacy with kitsch: "Not despite the kitsch to which it is drawn is Mahler's music great, but because its construction unties the tongue of kitsch, unfetters the longing that is merely exploited by the commerce that the kitsch serves" (39).[9] Yet in this recognition of kitsch as an expressive resource despite—or even because of—its degraded status, Adorno reprises more directly avant-garde views that he had first articulated in the late twenties and early thirties when confronting new works by young composers such as Weill, Křenek, Hindemith, and Eisler, who embraced elements of popular culture and metropolitan life to challenge social hierarchies embedded in received musical forms and functions. Not accidentally, in his 1930 review of Weill's *The Rise and Fall of the City of Mahagonny*, Adorno identifies the ghost of Mahler wandering among Weill's designedly skeletal popular forms: "One hears a peculiar strain of Mahler throughout the opera, in its marches, its ostinato, its dulled major and minor chords. Like Mahler, it uses the explosive force of 'low' elements to break through the middle and partake of the highest."[10]

In fact, Adorno saw the nearly unbridgeable divide between high and low, "serious" and "light," elite and popular music not as a historical constant nor as the logical derivation of a transcendental structure of taste, but rather as a regrettable product of the development of class society, and at its exasperated extreme, as a characteristic expression of contemporary late capitalist modernity. Adorno did not believe that, having historically emerged, this divide could or should be nostalgically disavowed, as if it did not constitute an objective condition within which any composer, whether artistic or commercial, had to work, or as if it could be merely formally subsumed in a hybrid work of, for example, symphonic jazz or popularized classical music. But it could be registered, reflected on aesthetically, and critically displaced, through the experience and working through of formal tensions and stylistic dissonances within artistic works.

As the example of Mahler suggests, one of the ways in which this indexing of social contradictions might take place is by incorporating high–low formal and material tensions into the work itself. Adorno was critically allergic to composers and works in which he detected a will to what he called in his debate with Lukács an "extorted reconciliation" of these contradictions: examples include, for him, Stravinsky and Hindemith at the top of a list of far less distinguished figures. But as a corollary to his criticism of these composers, he positively evaluated composers who preserved within musical forms the internal contradictions of both elite and popular musical materials, acknowledging the potential social isolation and loss of communicability of the former, and the potential routinization and regression of artistic communication in the latter. Or as Adorno concluded in another context:

> Though attempts to define kitsch usually fail, still not the worst definition would be one that made the criterion of kitsch whether an art product gives form to consciousness of contradiction—even if it does so by stressing its opposition to reality—or dissembles it. . . . As something that has escaped

from reality and is nevertheless permeated with it, art vibrates between this seriousness and light-heartedness. It is this tension that constitutes art.[11]

Adorno was also able to perceive a critical value to amateur or otherwise artistically impoverished performances of musical works, insofar as such performances, in contrast to virtuosic ones, lay bare the contradictions that expert performances cover with a layer of aesthetic semblance, keeping them from rising to consciousness. As he writes in a note from 1954 following a lecture by Rudolf Kolisch at Darmstadt:

> Lively music-making, by children, amateurs, entertainers and such like, supplies the theory [of musical reproduction] with the most important exemplary material. First, because here the music appears with all its cracks and holes, so to speak, deconstructed into the elements of every dimension of which it is constituted, and through it one can observe, as with broken toys, how it "works." The tears are so many windows onto the problems of interpretation that proficient execution normally conceals, but then one can see in the approaches of those subjects all those things that also inspire bad *official* music-making, but which are covered up there by good manners, by the "good musician"; the normal musical education is nothing other than the history of such concealment. One should understand and deduce Toscanini from the perspective of the Frankfurt Palmengarten orchestra, and Bruno Walter from the salon trio of the Hotel Waldhaus in Sils-Maria.[12]

Adorno here presents tasteless performance as the secret sharer of the deceptively "fine" performance of the guardians of musical good taste. This dialectic would inform Adorno's affirmation of the raw and ugly sonorities that Křenek and Weill availed themselves of in their music of the 1920s. Yet Adorno's suggestion goes deeper, to the structural contradictions of musical works themselves and the role of performance in repressing them or allowing them to come to awareness in the listener. He implies that works of music, even the most elevated, have the capacity to become kitsch if, in their performative realization, constitutive tensions are dissembled rather than made perceptible. Ironically, then, one form of bad art becomes the counterpoison to a far more dangerous form. The amateur's scuffing of the aesthetic polish of the well-executed work protects it from its own potential to become high-culture kitsch; through its debasement, its truth-value may be renewed.

But Stay, Weill—You're Quite Good Looking!

I now turn in greater detail to a key example for Adorno of this artistic negotiation of high-elite and low-popular forms, or formulated more abstractly, of art's serious and lighthearted aspects: Kurt Weill. Adorno found a thought-provoking example in the early musical theatre works of Weill, for whom he had an ambivalent admiration and, during their shared exile in the United States in flight from fascism, an on-again, off-again friendship. Adorno dedicated a number of short reviews and essays to Weill's work, spanning a period of nearly thirty years and extending beyond the death of Weill in 1950. During the 1930s, still himself a practicing composer, Adorno even attempted to write a Weill-influenced musical theatre piece—or "*Singspiel*," as Adorno characterized it—based on the popular Huckleberry Finn and Tom Sawyer characters of the American novelist Mark Twain, entitled *Der Schatz des Indianer-Joe*.[13] Though he ultimately abandoned the project, leaving only a libretto behind, it formed the basis of a tense exchange of letters between Adorno and Benjamin, who was at the time at work on his cultural history of nineteenth-century Paris, the *Arcades Project*.[14]

When Adorno, Weill, and Brecht were all in exile from fascism in the United States in the 1940s, Adorno sought—unsuccessfully—to intercede with Weill on a new staging of Brecht and Weill's musical success of the late 1920s, the *Threepenny Opera*. As Adorno wrote from Los Angeles to Weill on March 31, 1942:

> Now as far as the performance itself is concerned, we are talking here about the founding of a Negro theatre on a national level, backed by Paul Robeson and the so-called Negro Lodges, therefore considerable moral backing, with financial consequences, if successful, which offer you and Brecht good prospects. The *Dreigroschenoper* should be the first work to be showcased on this stage by this group.[15]

Although Adorno was at least partly seeking to lend a practical hand to the impoverished exile Brecht, the nature of the proposed production was highly surprising if one accepts too easily the image of Adorno as uncompromisingly mandarin and anti-popular. The production—perhaps inspired by Virgil Thomson's successful 1934 staging of Gertrude Stein's *Four Saints in Three Acts*, George Gershwin's 1935 "folk opera" *Porgy and Bess*, and the recent formation of Negro Theatre Units in several cities under the Federal Theatre Project[16]—was to involve an all-Black cast and adapt Brecht and Weill's late Weimar social satire to the new context of midcentury US race and class relations, including treating Weill's original arrangements to a jazz adaptation. Notably, too, Adorno suggested that this California-launched initiative could prove strategic as a means of shaking up what he conceived to be the conservative, standardized musical theatre of Broadway. Though in a letter to Lotte Lenya, Weill implies that he gave Adorno a thorough tongue-lashing for sticking his nose where it didn't belong,[17] Weill's actual response to

Adorno was bluntly honest in rejecting his suggestions, yet in fact not uncordially or unsubstantively engaged with Adorno's arguments for the project. First, Weill completely rejects Adorno's dismissal of Broadway as narrow and artistically closed and offers a full-throated defense:

> What you say about the "Broadway Theatre" is, in my opinion, absolutely wrong. I have other people from over there [i.e. California] seen [sic] making the same mistake. They see a few shows on Broadway, they compare them with the best things they have seen in German and they pass a judgement on the entire American Theatre. ... I have made a thorough study of the American theatre and I have seen all the important shows in this country, on Broadway and outside of Broadway, in the last seven years, and I can assure you that they have done just as much "experimental" theatre of every type here as we have done in Germany. They had the expressionistic theatre, the epic theatre and the surrealist theatre. ... [N]ext to Russia, Broadway is today the most interesting theatre center in the world. You are entirely wrong when you say that any theatre experiment has to be done somewhere else and then forced on Broadway.[18]

And despite his unconcealed irritation with Brecht's failure to consult him at the outset of the project several months earlier, Weill also expresses his willingness to compromise, out of compassion for the Black actor Clarence Muse, who had collaborated on the script for the 1939 musical film *Way Down South* with Langston Hughes, later also to be Weill's librettist for the 1946 musical *Street Scene*, and to some extent even out of understanding for Brecht's worrisome financial precarity. Weill tells Adorno: "This poor fellow Clarence Muse wrote me a desperate letter. He is really in an awful position. I have therefore decided to put aside all my doubts and all my objections and have worked out a proposition which would allow them to go ahead with their production, but to show it in California only. I have to see it first and see if I want my music to be used or not" (Weill to Adorno, 5). Unfortunately, further discussions transpired and even thornier complications and conflicts between Weill and Brecht arose, to the point that Weill angrily pulled out altogether. The proposed staging was never realized.[19]

Musical Potpourri

Before turning to Adorno's writings on Weill, I would like first to briefly explore a generic term that Adorno likely took over from Křenek and in turn applied in his critical assessments of Weill's works such as *The Threepenny Opera* and *The Rise and Fall of the City of Mahagonny*, written in collaboration with Brecht. It appears in a number of different contexts in Adorno's music criticism, including in the writings on

Culture Industry of the 1940s, but has particular resonance in his critical writings of the late 1920s and early 1930s. That term is the musical "potpourri."

In this context, "potpourri" refers to the presentation of musical material, usually in light and popular forms such as operettas and revues, that is sequential and without thematic development or repetition. Though dating to the eighteenth century, it especially characterized light, comic forms of stage music in the nineteenth century; it thus has a close affinity with operetta and eventually the musical as well. Adorno employs it in this context, for example, in his 1928 essay on Schubert, in which he refers to the mediation of the biography and music of Schubert through sentimental Austrian kitsch cultural products such as Rudolf Hans Bartsch's popular novel *Schwammerl* (Mushrooms, 1912) and Heinrich Berté's operetta drawn from it and a pastiche of Schubert's music, *Das Dreimäderlhaus* (The House of Three Girls, 1916), which was also the source of enormously popular American Broadway and British adaptations (US: *Blossom Time*; UK: *Lilac Time*) and several film adaptations as well. Surprisingly, given his later hardening against such Culture Industry products, Adorno finds in such kitschy potpourri a hollowing out from within of the illusion of organic form developing from its own immanent forces, and the replacement of the living artwork with an ossified skeleton of motifs that the potpourri strings together. "No theme, once past, could bear such emphatic proximity to another," Adorno writes; "one senses a terrible rigor mortis in the opera potpourris of the nineteenth century."[20] Living form is replaced by a reified crystalline structure that reveals something essential about Schubert's music that is concealed by romantic ideology, the potential denaturing of its putatively organic unity, in short, its secret affinity to the broader reification of the public sphere:

> The cells that are layered in the potpourri must have been interwoven according to a different law than the unity of living entities. Even if one concedes that Schubert's music, relatively speaking, is one that grew rather than being fashioned: its growth, very much fragmented and never content with itself, is not herbaceous but, rather, crystalline. By reinforcing the original configurative separation of Schubert's traits, and thus the constitutively fragmentary nature of his music, the conserving transition to the potpourri illuminates the entire Schubertian landscape. One should not mistake it for a coincidence that, in the nineteenth century, the potpourri developed as a surrogate musical form at the same time as the miniature landscape became popular for bourgeois consumer items of all kinds, culminating in the postcard. ("Schubert," 28)

Here Adorno is less concerned with the poor quality and sentimentality of Berté's potpourri of Schubert than with the truth it unwittingly reveals about Schubert's music even as it condenses it into treacle: "At irregular intervals, like a seismograph, Schubert's music registered the message of humanity's qualitative change. The response, fittingly, is that of weeping—whether it is the weeping of the most impoverished sentimentality in *Das Dreimäderlhaus* or the weeping of a shaken body. . . . [W]hat it holds up to our fading, overflowing eyes . . . are the ciphers of an eventual reconciliation" ("Schubert," 45–46).

Another short essay on popular music that Adorno wrote in 1934, "Music in the Background," treats the experience of music performed in cafés and is highly relevant to his contemporary understanding of Křenek's and Weill's musical achievement. This essay, remarkably, in light of the stereotypical image of Adorno, ascribes a special authenticity to the awkward rearrangements and imperfect performances of outmoded music from the repertoire of nineteenth-century opera and romantic music. The potpourri is, for Adorno, responsible for the characteristic sound and experience of the café background. "Has anyone ever listened carefully to this sound?" he asks.[21] The music, he suggests, is stripped of its aesthetic trappings and blends with the environment in a way that almost hyperbolically submits to obsolete convention, thus becoming, compared to the experience of artistic concert music, refreshingly, even innovatively, stripped of aesthetic pretense:

> Nowhere has music become so wholly appearance as in the café. But in appearance, it is preserved. It must, or so it seems, be thus emancipated from all human seriousness and all genuineness of artistic form if it is still to be tolerated by human beings amidst their daily affairs without frightening them. But it is its appearance that lights up for them. No—that lights them up. They do not change in it, but their image. . . . Background music is an acoustic light source. ("Music in the Background," 508)

This musical function, that of illuminating the anomymous background of metropolitan modernity and allowing the human forms in it to appear in sharper, more distinct focus, is fulfilled by the potpourri's dissolved forms:

> Everything is in arrangements for the salon orchestra, which falsifies and alters it. It softens conceived passages into intimacy, blows up tender ones with tremolo and vibrato. The works dissolve in all this, and dissolved works, by those once-famous, then forgotten masters, are the right ones for background music. The question is only whether they stop at dissolution. In dissolution the works fall silent. Here they become audible again. (508)

In Adorno's exposition of the potpourri form, moreover, the emphasis falls not only on the mixed, miscellaneous quality of the potpourri, but also the reified *deadness* of its elements. Drawing upon the dual sense of potpourri, Adorno compares these arrangements as comparable to "bouquets of dead flowers" (508). Deadness, however, is not, for him, a solely negative aspect. It supports the very possibility of the efficacy of the potpourri to fulfill its social function of adaptation to the background to everyday life:

> The joints between the brittle sounds into which they are layered are not firmly bonded. Through them shimmers the mysterious allegorical appearance that arises whenever fragments of the past come together in an uncertain surface. What is true for the vertical sound is no less true horizontally, for the passage of time. The cafés are the site of potpourris. The latter are constructed out of the fragments of the work, its best-loved melodies. But they awaken the ruins to new, ghostly life. (508–9)

The potpourri's pastiche-like assembly of conventional elements and effects does not pretend to reanimate convention with new organic life. It rather illuminates the artificial, even uncanny tension between mechanical energy and enervation of the café environment, as these tunes jostle and jar across the isolated but aggregated conversations, encounters, conspiracies, and deals going on intermittently at the tables. It is this aspect of the potpourri too which, Adorno argues, Mahler turned into a rigorous compositional procedure of renewing disintegrated popular forms:

> What in the potpourri was the necessity of indiscriminately assembling hackneyed melodies becomes in him the virtue of a structure that sensitively thaws the frozen groupings of accepted formal types. ... It assists the decayed themes it accumulates to an afterlife in the second language of music. ... In his works the potpourri form, through the subterranean communication of its scattered elements, takes on a kind of instinctive, independent logic. (*Mahler*, 35)

The notion of potpourri took on new actuality in the 1920s with modernist composers such as Křenek and Weill, as they explored jazz, cabaret music, film music, and other popular forms as inspirations for the destructured, episodic montage-forms of the modernist *Zeitoper* and *Singspiel*. For example, Křenek composed a "Potpourri for Large Orchestra, op. 54" in 1927, contemporaneously with his most famous *Zeitoper, Jonny spielt auf*; it was especially marked by the influence of French neoclassicism but included a variety of incongruously juxtaposed musical styles.[22] A solo piano "Potpourri aus Jonny *spielt auf*, op. 45" in an arrangement by the young Hungarian composer Jenő Takács appeared the following year.[23] Even while modernist composers such as Schoenberg and Berg rejected potpourri, in their writings of the late 1920s they took note of its prevalence among younger contemporaries.

Thus, in a 1928 article entitled "The 'Problem of Opera'" in which he justifies his use in *Wozzeck* of larger-scale developmental forms more typical of symphonic music, Berg suggested that operas that appropriated the elements of popular culture in potpourri forms merely reflected contemporary modernity, but—artistically, as well as, implicitly, sociologically—lacked means to point beyond it into the future: "The use of 'contemporary' means—such as cinema, revue, loudspeakers, jazz—guarantees only that such a work is contemporary. But that cannot be called a real step forward; after all, this is the point we have reached, and we can't get further on simply by being here."[24] In a December 1929 letter to Schoenberg, he quipped that he had "to do my utmost to see that *Wozzeck* isn't staged as the 'Two-Penny Opera.'"[25]

For his part, Schoenberg wrote up a wittily biting send-up of his students and contemporaries—including Křenek and Adorno—in his 1929 "Glosses on the Theories of Others," responding to recent issues of the music journals *Der Anbruch* (which had Adorno among its major contributors) and *Melos*. Schoenberg offers the following hyperbolically mixed metaphor to define the potpourri:

> If music is frozen architecture, then the potpourri is frozen coffee-table gossip, instability caught in the act, a parody of all logical thinking. It is justified, to any degree at all, only as a harmless travesty; it behaves as people behave when they get together socially—jumping from one thing to another, so that an egg-recipe suggests Columbus, a match a risqué story, and the decline of the world a boxing match—all involuntary associations against which primitive brains are defenceless, to which they succumb, being able to link them only by the word "and": A and X. Potpourri is the art of adding apples to pears; its law applies without being able to divide, and it multiplies through non-repetition. It is an accumulation, a mass of things adding up to nothing. It has parts but no articulation, combination but no cohesion. A pen-knife is sewn on to a nose, and a town clock on to the knife, and a mood on to the lot.[26]

More seriously, with respect to Křenek, who according to Schoenberg characterizes his operas as being composed in this manner, Schoenberg suggests that this simply may be self-misrecognition on Křenek's part, his theory not capturing what is actually going on formally in his works. He suggests that the original creative act, which conceives an opera as a unity, is preserved even if the composer rearranges and interleaves the parts according to a constructive, montage-like logic: "the creator's potential could be sufficiently strong to ensure the work's adhering to its 'status nascendi' sufficiently long—the creative act's being sufficiently extended—for there still to be an awareness, when individual sections were interchanged, of the formal requirements resulting from previous and succeeding sections. In that case, even transpositions and new interpolations would satisfy the will to form, in accordance with the original conception" (314). In short, Schoenberg asserts that Křenek's operas do not in fact instantiate the arbitrariness of the potpourri. Potpourri is a false theoretical description for the loosened but still valid compositional forms that Křenek has invented and himself been bound by in realizing his works.

Adorno utilized the concept of "potpourri" to speak of Weill's work already in 1929, in his review of the *Threepenny Opera* and even more explicitly in a review of Weill's orchestral suite derived from the *Threepenny Opera* in the "Little Threepenny Music for Wind Ensemble." Adorno anticipates his own formulation of the potpourri as "acoustic lighting" in concluding his 1929 *Threepenny Opera* review. He writes:

> With none of the *Threepenny Opera*'s melodies can one perform reconstruction; their excavated simplicity is no less than classical. But ultimately they can nevertheless be played in bars, whose half-darkness they suddenly illuminate, as if sung in country fields. ... Successful interpretation of what is already past constitutes the signal of a future element that becomes visible because the aged has become interpretable.[27]

In his review of Weill's orchestral suite "Little Threepenny Music," Adorno from the outset makes the potpourri the conceptual lever of his reflections: the potpourri is the result of a historical process of disintegration of the opera and operetta, which in turn becomes a resource for compositional innovation on Weill's part. "The step from the opera to the potpourri," Adorno writes,

> is pre-indicated to a music that from the first beat on has to do with fragments of a sort that would otherwise constitute the potpourri; the potpourri changes them back into their true form that the merely apparent unity of the relationship of their surfaces had concealed. ... Memory-shards of the exploded essences of opera and operetta contract in [Weill's *Threepenny Opera*] to the density of dreams and alarm us as if they had risen from the realm of the past and with all the marks of their destruction.[28]

If Adorno emphasizes the contiguity of the *Threepenny Opera* to the potpourri form, Weill's "Little Threepenny Music" represents in his view a further radicalization of this relation, a further disintegration of the musical material and deployment of montage technique as compositional means:

> Now Weill has also derived from the *Threepenny Opera* the potpourri that was always hidden within it, already in the text, the cohesion of which so often explodes, as if an anonymous potpourrist had stridden around in it, with the modulations, which are themselves like the wreaths of our tone-master, and with all the themes, which are singable but not well rhymed, rather arrayed

in artificial arbitrariness. This has now thus truly been emancipated from the last semblance of a form-totality, one after the other, without anything in between. ("Kleine Dreigroschenmusik," 541–42)

In his 1930 notes to *The Rise and Fall of the City of Mahagonny*, Weill remarked his progress with this opera beyond the more episodic *Singspiel* form—a successor to the potpourri—and his use of more extensive musical construction connecting the narrative "situations": "The 'Song' form established in the Baden-Baden piece [the 1927 *Mahagonny Singspiel*], and carried on in such subsequent works as *The Threepenny Opera*, the *Berlin Requiem* and *Happy End*, was of course inadequate for a full-length opera; it needed to be supplemented by other, larger-scale forms."[29] In his 1930 review of *Mahagonny*, Adorno follows Weill's lead in presenting the opera as a dialectical overcoming of potpourri forms: "this music, cobbled together from triads and wrong notes, the nails hammered down with the strong beats of old music-hall songs that are not known but remembered as parts of the genetic makeup, and glued with the stinking adhesive of softened opera potpourris—this music, made from the ruins of past music, is entirely contemporary" ("Mahagonny," 197). As Adorno concludes, despite its disparate material, the opera is "through-composed, unfolding according to its own infernal standards" (198). The tension between disparateness and construction is integral to Weill's theatrical as well as musical intentions, though the musical logic is now primary. The music, Weill notes, "no longer furthers the plot"; rather, the sequence of its twenty-one "self-contained musical forms," as Weill notes, lend the individual narrative tableaux a "dramatic form only in the course of their musically dynamic succession."[30]

Vanguard of the Musical

Adorno's later reflections on Weill modulate these early formulations, especially in light of Weill's success in America in composing popular musicals and songs, but also retain this basic view of Weill's achievement as bound to his attempt to explore the tension between popular and avant-garde music.[31] In a controversial obituary for Weill in 1950, Adorno argued that in bringing a Brechtian epic-theatre demontage and remontage of materials to musical works, Weill demonstrated "an extraordinary and original sense for the function of music in theatre."[32] Adorno went on to suggest, provocatively, that Weill's greatest achievement may have been in recasting the role of contemporary composer as a "musical director [*Musikregisseur*]," in the sense of a theatre or even film director. He notes Weill's affinities, in the deep-seated dramatic and performative qualities of his music, to Stravinsky, and like Stravinsky, Weill is named as a key source of an ambiguous legacy in twentieth-century music. "It would hardly be an exaggeration to say," Adorno concludes, "that the rudimentarization of so much contemporary music, its retrogressive hostility to experiment, is inseparable from the conscious experiments of Weill" ("Kurt Weill," 546). Yet Adorno would continue to elaborate in more sympathetic ways this legacy of Weill as "musical director," for example, in his essay from 1955 entitled "After a Quarter Century," originally presented as program notes to the Düsseldorf premiere of Weill's Broadway musical *Street Scene*. In this essay, Adorno evaluates Weill's dramatic alienation of musical material as allowing a successful suspension of the divide between serious and light, avant-garde and popular idioms:

> The change of musical function with Weill had as its result that the musical director no longer acknowledged firm boundaries between serious and light music. The collective impulses that he obeyed were stronger than the artistic education, otherwise neo-classical and hostile to expression, that he had received from Busoni. . . . But his extraordinarily alert and aggressive literary sense had, in those of his works that count, likewise protected him from simply giving himself over to attractive popular music. A fruitful disturbing element intruded. He heard, spurred by Stravinsky, manifestations of light music to be already so false and perforated, as its inner substance is, and perceived the true monstrosity of the musical. This lent him his characteristic mobility, a music of rags and debris, as oblique to the demands of high art as to the kitsch of the serial production line.[33]

In this short essay Adorno is not uncritical of Weill, particularly his American-period popular works; yet he generally acknowledges the artistic accomplishment of Weill in negotiating an ambivalent, paradoxical role with regard to popular music and its public: "He partook of the paradox of a music that electrified the public and yet slapped in the face all the demands of the public that he himself fulfilled. By the force of this paradox the image of musical culture trembled like a wavering [*wacklige*] curtain. Between the two poles of a split musical consciousness this image ignited" ("Nach einem Vierteljahrhunderts," 551). In another essay originally published in 1957 and revised in 1966, "Questions of the Contemporary Opera-Theatre," in contrast, Adorno's judgment of Weill's American works is much harsher:

> [H]is extraordinary accomplishment as musical director [*Musikregisseur*], his instinct for the montage of musical scraps in the *Threepenny Opera* proved itself only so long as he rigorously renounced authentic composition. As soon

as he allowed himself to be steered by great musical forms, he failed and through the striving for higher things that he once had mocked fell under the spell of the mere theatre of amusement, the American musical.[34]

I will conclude by remarking a curious polemical exchange about Weill in the journal *Der Monat* in 1956, in which Adorno answered an essay by the critic Horst Koegler entitled "Vortrupp des Musicals" (Vanguard of the Musical) with his own essay entitled "Vortrupp und Avantgarde: Eine Replik" (Vanguard and Avant-Garde: A Reply). Remarking on the staging of Weill's *Street Scene* in Düsseldorf, Koegler had taken issue with the negative responses of German critics, in which he saw entrenched prejudice against popular music and especially the American musical. Taking a jocular swipe at Adorno, Koegler wrote that these critics propagated "a progressivism at any price . . . to which any true public success would already in advance be suspicious (incidentally, an excellent theme for Adorno: 'The Aging of the New Criticism')."[35] In terms that recall Weill's response to Adorno in their correspondence about Brecht's plan for a reprised *Threepenny Opera*, Koegler accuses the critics of ignorance and prejudice against the American musical theatre to which Weill had brought significant innovations:

> The view that Broadway's influence is soul-killing and corrupting for every artist is so widespread here that its cultural-political consequences cannot be ignored. In fact, the condemnation of Weill wavers according to the political standpoint of the critic (or their papers): pretty much everything can be encompassed from the infinite feeling of superiority of the tradition-conscious European who casually looks down on the fully automatic American mix-culture, to the regretful *mea culpa* that it was in the end we ourselves who exiled Weill to this wasteland of brimming fleshpots. (69)

Adorno himself clearly estimated the earlier, "Brechtian" Weill more highly than the later writer of American musicals and hit songs and on this point is unbending in his response to Koegler: "One need only play songs out of the old edition of *Mahagonny* and the *Threepenny Opera* and immediately afterward such as 'Lady in the Dark' and 'One Touch of Venus,' and one will hear all that which Weill had to sacrifice to the bad smoothness of popular music."[36] But he grants the form of the popular musical two points in balance. First, he argues that the relaxing form of the musical was a healthy antidote to the nationalistic bombast of "new German" musical drama, which in Adorno's view was both aesthetically unbearable and compromised by its relation to fascism. And he restates anew his argument that in his early works Weill managed to hold serious and light music in tension in a way that genuinely blurred their boundaries, shining a spotlight on the contingency of the social divide that exists between an elite avant-garde listenership and the mass public of popular music.

In defending his position against Koegler, Adorno suggests that the problem lies not with the popularity of the musical, but rather with its failure to develop its progressive, even populist potentials functionally and formally. Yet if this is the case, Adorno argues, critics such as Koegler do not help release these potentials by their affirmative posture towards popular music, but rather stand in league with the forces that standardize and deform it. To Koegler's tweaking about "the aging of the new criticism," Adorno offers a "counterproposal." Koegler, he writes,

> should compose an essay entitled "The Highbrow as Lowbrow." Since the break between advanced art and broader reception became radical, there have been intellectuals who have hoped to break out of their socially prescribed isolation by spasmodically and masochistically defecting to the other side. They have intended to save the fractured spirit through alliance with hostility to spirit. (803)

The onus, then, Adorno argues, "lies not with overreaching critics, but with musicals which, purged of such ferment [as that which Weill represented], declined into a kitsch, the seamlessly planned effects of which are not better but worse than that of old-fashioned kitsch, in which awkwardness and helplessness at the same time allowed unrestrained impulses to pass through" (803).

Notes

1. Clement Greenberg, "Avant-Garde and Kitsch," *Partisan Review* 6 (1939): 34–49.
2. For more on "middlebrow" culture, see Dwight McDonald, "Masscult and Midcult" (1960), in McDonald, *Masscult and Midcult: Essays against the American Grain* (New York: New York Review of Books, 2011), 3–72; Lawrence W. Levine, *Highbrow/Lowbrow: The Emergence of Cultural Hierarchy in America* (Cambridge, MA: Harvard University Press, 1988); Joan Shelley Rubin, *The Making of Middlebrow Culture* (Chapel Hill: University of North Carolina Press, 1992).
3. Theodor W. Adorno, "Zum *Anbruch*: Exposé," in *Gesammelte Schriften* 19, ed. Rolf Tiedemann (Frankfurt am Main: Suhrkamp Verlag, 1984), 602. For further discussion of this problematic of kitsch in Adorno's thinking of the late 1920s and early 1930s, see Levin, "For the Record," 27–28.
4. Theodor W. Adorno, "The Schema of Mass Culture," in *The Culture Industry: Selected Essays on Mass Culture*, ed. J.M. Bernstein (London and New York: Routledge, 1991), 68.
5. Theodor W. Adorno, *Aesthetic Theory*, eds. Greta Adorno and Rolf

Tiedemann, trans. Robert Hullot-Kentor (Minneapolis: University of Minnesota Press, 1997), 239.
6. A keyword entry from the University of Chicago's *Theories of Media* website contextualizes Adorno's etymological suggestion in a far more uncertain field of possible derivations: "Though its etymology is ambiguous, scholars generally agree that the word 'kitsch' entered the German language in the mid-nineteenth century. Often synonymous with 'trash' as a descriptive term, kitsch may derive from the German word *kitschen*, meaning *den Strassenschlamm zusammenscharren* (to collect rubbish from the street). The German verb *verkitschen* (to make cheap), is another likely source. Similarly, the Oxford English Dictionary defines kitsch in the verb form as 'to render worthless,' classifying kitsch objects as 'characterized by worthless pretentiousness.' Other potential sources also include a mispronunciation of the English word *sketch*, an inversion of the French word *chic*, or a derivation of the Russian *keetcheetsya* (to be haughty and puffed up)." See https://csmt.uchicago.edu/glossary2004/kitsch.htm#_ftn2 (accessed December 31, 2021).
7. Theodor W. Adorno, "Kitsch," in *Essays on Music*, ed. Richard Leppert, trans. Susan H. Gillespie (Berkeley and Los Angeles: University of California Press, 2002), 501.
8. Theodor W. Adorno, *Mahler: A Musical Physiognomy*, trans. Edmund Jephcott (Chicago: University of Chicago Press, 1992), 36.
9. For an insightful discussion of Adorno's complex views on kitsch and their connection to his interpretation of Mahler, see Richard Leppert, "Nature and Exile: Adorno, Mahler and the Appropriation of Kitsch," in Leppert, *Sound Judgment: Selected Essays* (Burlington, VT: Ashgate, 2007), 247–62.
10. Theodor W. Adorno, "Mahagonny," in *Night Music: Essays on Music, 1926–1962*, ed. Rolf Tiedemann, trans. Wielan Hoban (London: Seagull Books, 2009), 199.
11. Theodor W. Adorno, "Is Art Lighthearted?", in *Notes to Literature, Volume 2*, trans. Shierry Weber Nicholsen (New York: Columbia University Press, 1992), 249.
12. Theodor W. Adorno, *Towards a Theory of Musical Reproduction*, trans. Wieland Hoban, ed. Henri Lonitz (Cambridge: Polity Press, 2006), 127.
13. The libretto was first published in 1979 as Theodor W. Adorno, *Der Schatz des Indianer-Joe: Singspiel nach Mark Twain*, ed. Rolf Tiedemann (Frankfurt am Main: Surhkamp Verlag, 1979). Tiedemann's afterword appeared in English translation as "Adorno's *Tom Sawyer* Opera Singspiel," trans. Stefan Bird-Pollan, in *The Cambridge Companion to Adorno*, ed. Tom Huhn (Cambridge: Cambridge University Press, 2004), 376–94. Though much of the music was never composed, a recording of two songs from the incomplete *Singspiel* were recorded in 1988 in the Alten Oper Frankfurt; see Theodor W. Adorno, *Kompositionen*, CD, Wergo 6173-2, 1990.
14. See the letters of Benjamin to Wiesengrund-Adorno, January 29, 1934, and Wiesengrund-Adorno to Benjamin, March 4, 1934, in Theodor Adorno and Walter Benjamin, *The Complete Correspondence, 1928–1940*, ed. Henri Lonitz, trans. Nicholas Walker (Cambridge: Polity Press, 1999), 23–27.
15. Letter of Adorno to Weill, March 31, 1942, *Kurt Weill Newsletter* 21/2 (2003): 4.

16. See Ronald Ross, "The Role of Blacks in the Federal Theatre, 1935–1939," *The Journal of Negro History* 59/1 (1974): 38–50.
17. See letter of Weill to Lotte Leyna, April 8, 1942, in *Speak Low (When You Speak Love): The Letters of Kurt Weill and Lotte Lenya*, eds. Lys Symonette and Kim Kowalke (Berkeley and Los Angeles: University of California Press, 1996), 320.
18. Letter of Weill to Adorno, April 7, 1942, *Kurt Weill Newsletter* 21/2 (2003): 5.
19. For details of this failed staging, see Joy H. Calico, *Brecht at the Opera* (Berkeley and Los Angeles: University of California Press, 2008), 78–83.
20. Theodor W. Adorno, "Schubert," in *Night Music*, 26.
21. Theodor W. Adorno, "Music in the Background," in *Adorno on Music*, 507.
22. For more detail on *Potpourri*, op. 54, see Alexander Carpenter's 2017 preface to the score at: https://repertoire-explorer.musikmph.de/wp-content/uploads/vorworte_prefaces/3014.html (accessed December 31, 2021).
23. "Potpourri aus der Oper Jonny spielt auf von Ernst Křenek op. 45," Piano Solo (Vienna-Leipzig: Universal Edition, 1927).
24. Alban Berg, "The 'Problem of Opera'," in Willi Reich, *Alban Berg*, trans. Cornelius Cardew (New York: Harcourt, Brace & World, 1965), 63.
25. Letter of Alban Berg to Arnold Schoenberg, December 10, 1929, in *The Berg-Schoenberg Correspondence: Selected Letters*, ed. Juliane Brand, Christopher Hailey, and Donald Harris (New York: W.W. Norton and Company, 1987), 392–93.
26. Arnold Schoenberg, "Glosses on the Theories of Others," in *Style and Idea*, ed. Leonard Stein, trans. Leo Black (Berkeley and Los Angeles: University of California Press, 1975), 314–15.
27. Theodor W. Adorno, "Zur Dreigroschenoper," in *Gesammelte Schriften* 18, ed. Rolf Tiedemann (Frankfurt am Main: Suhrkamp Verlag, 1984), 540.
28. Theodor W. Adorno, "Kurt Weill: Kleine Dreigroschenmusik für Blasorchester," in *Gesammelte Schriften* 18, 541.
29. Kurt Weill, "Notes to My Opera *Mahagonny*," in Bertolt Brecht, *The Rise and Fall of the City of Mahagonny* and *The Seven Deadly Sins of the Petty Bourgeoisie*, eds. John Willett and Ralph Manheim, trans. W.H. Auden and Chester Kalman (New York: Arcade Publishing, 1996), 91.
30. Weill, "Notes to My Opera *Mahagonny*," 92.
31. For further consideration of Adorno's relation to Weill's European and American works, see also Lydia Goehr, "*Amerikamüde/Europamüde*: The Actuality of American Opera," in Goehr, *Elective Affinities: Musical Essays on the History of Aesthetic Theory* (New York: Columbia University Press, 2008), 257–306.
32. Theodor W. Adorno, "Kurt Weill," in *Gesammelte Schriften* 18, 544.
33. Theodor W. Adorno, "Nach einem Vierteljahrhunderts," in *Gesammelte Schriften* 18, 550.
34. Theodor W. Adorno, "Fragen des gegenwärtigen Operntheaters," in *Gesammelte Schriften* 19, 486.
35. Horst Koegler, "Der Vortrupp der Musicals," *Der Monat* 8/1 (1956): 69.
36. Theodor W. Adorno, "Vortrupp und Avantgarde: Eine Replik," in *Gesammelte Schriften* 18, 801.

Chapter 7

Remediating Opera: Media and Musical Drama in Adorno and Kluge

Throughout the decades-long span of his musicological criticism, Adorno took up problems of opera as indices of broader social changes in what we might call the musical public sphere: the spaces of public reception and critical discussion of musical works that organized the social experience of music and shaped its role in the cultural constitution and evolution of the European middle classes.[1] We can therefore, I would suggest, see opera as occupying an analogous position in Adorno's corpus of musical criticism to that of drama in Lukács's literary criticism: as a concentrated site where historical experience could be performatively mediated, rendering it graspable in terms of characters, their actions, and in the case of opera particularly, their desires and passions, in distilled, almost archetypal dramatic situations. For Adorno, however, the question of opera's changing public and hence its capacity to mediate historical experience was closely tied to problems of its *technical* mediation, including its evolving relations to mass media of production and reproduction from live performance in opera houses to its dissemination through radio, film, and sound recording. Adorno, moreover, also considers opera's mediations within the framework of what we could characterize, somewhat anachronistically, as an ecology of media, reflecting his underlying postulate that the differentiation of media is a dynamic and historically developing process and that individual media receive their significance not just immanently, through internal formal developments, but also relationally in their collisions and interactions with other media. Opera's constitutive musical, dramatic, and literary aspects—and the often-contradictory interactions between them—are brought into focus in his opera-critical writings, as are the artistic and social-institutional interactions of musical drama with media such as live theatre, the novel, radio, cinema, and television.

In the first part of this essay, I discuss Adorno's views on the technical remediation of opera, especially in its connection with the media of radio and of sound recording.[2] I utilize the term "remediation" here in the sense given by Jay Bolter and Richard Grusin: "Our culture conceives of each media or constellation of media as it responds to, redeploys, competes with, and reforms other media. . . . No medium, it seems, can now function independently and establish its own separate and purified space of cultural meaning."[3] I go on in the second half to consider Adorno's ascription to opera of a key anticipatory role in forming the Culture Industry that would only later be fully consolidated and intensified by the sound recording and film industry, as Adorno and Horkheimer expounded in *Dialectic of Enlightenment*. I concentrate here especially on the cinematic mediations of opera, highlighting Adorno's complex views on the various interactions of opera and film, in which he ambivalently identified progressive potentials. I conclude my discussion of Adorno by considering his more schematic and thoroughly negative judgment of television in the mediation of music, including the televisual presentation of opera. In a final section, I explore the rich intermedial work of Alexander Kluge, whose prolific writings, interviews, films, and television shows set the question of opera's mediations in a new light extending beyond the critical horizons set out by Adorno.

Adorno and the Mediations of Opera

Opera offered Adorno a particularly sensitive index of changes in the public sphere of music, precisely because by the 1920s and 1930s, when he was most actively engaged with opera listening and reviewing, the crisis of opera's public character was becoming ineluctable. Already in a 1930 essay entitled "New Opera and Public," Adorno noted that the opera represented the loneliest branch of new music, which at once registered a long-developing crisis in the nineteenth-century listening public and deepened it still further. If its isolation begins with modern forms and contents that disallow ready comprehension, the ultimate fate of contemporary opera nevertheless would be decided beyond the opera house, in the changing social relations threatening its traditional bourgeois public and offering tenuous hope for the formation of new publics, out of the working classes and white-collar workers. Yet the situation of the present was one of protracted uncertainty about opera's actual listener- and spectatorship. "The new opera," Adorno writes, "has up to now found its public even less than other new music."[4]

By the late 1950s and early 1960s, however, Adorno's prospect for opera to take on new public life had darkened. In his 1959 essay "Bourgeois Opera," he writes:

To focus our thoughts about contemporary theater on opera is certainly not justifiable in terms of opera's immediate relevance. Not only has the crisis of opera been well known and persistent in Germany for thirty years (that is, since the time of the great economic crisis), not only have opera's place and function become questionable in society today, but beyond this . . . opera has come to seem peripheral and a matter of indifference.[5]

In his lecture on opera within the 1961/62 radio series that became his *Introduction to the Sociology of Music*, Adorno raised opera to the level of a methodological problem in a sociology of culture that was based on hermeneutical readings of culture forms to gain insight into social functions and structures. Opera was a test-case for an artistic medium in which the relation between artistic form and social function had radically diverged, even disintegrated to the point of collapse, so that the presumption that an artwork bears a representational or figurative relation to social reality was being strained to its breaking point. Opera had become, in the terms of Lukács's early drama theory, "problematical" and "non-representative":

A kind of chasm has opened between opera itself and present-day society, including those members it delegates to serve as an opera audience. . . . But in this chasm opera has made itself at home. . . . It offers the paradigm of a form that is incessantly consumed, although it has not merely lost its intellectual topicality but, in all likelihood, can no longer be adequately understood at all.[6]

Adorno unsparingly presents opera as a zombie-like form of culture, uncannily living on beyond the decease of its public function:

The opera is one of the stopgaps in the world of resurrected culture, a filler of holes blasted by the mind. That operatic activities rattle on unchanged even though literally nothing in them fits any more, this fact is drastic testimony to the noncommittal, somehow accidental character assumed by the cultural superstructure. The official life of opera can teach us more about society than about a species of art that is outliving itself and will hardly survive the next blow. (83)

Opera, Adorno suggests, has ceased to bear any real aesthetic or social substance; precisely this vacancy makes it a poignant index of the social situation of art in contemporary society. Opera's unacknowledged posthumousness, its loss of any living correspondence with the real relations of society, is itself what demands social-critical interpretation. Richard Leppert thus summarizes Adorno's critical judgment about opera as "a broad polemic against the institutions of opera and opera music, as well as the consumption of opera, the last read through the actuality of audience antipathy to modern music (including opera) and its love affair with endlessly restaged warhorses comprising the standard repertory."[7]

Early in his career, in his performance reviews, his debate with Benjamin about technical reproducibility, and his studies of music and radio for the Princeton Radio Project during his exile in the United States, Adorno extensively considered how musical experience was affected by its dissemination in live-performed and technically mediated forms. A direct extension of his radio music research, in turn, was his subsequent collaboration with Eisler on a study of film music, which is decisively shaped in its composition, its orchestration and recording, and its projection and reception by cinema's industrial apparatus. So too, the critique of Culture Industry that Adorno and Horkheimer articulated in *Dialectic of Enlightenment* took Adorno's research into radio and cinema music, along with his theoretical investigations into the reification of listening, as crucial background. Following his return to Germany after the war, Adorno would continue to devote critical attention to the changing experience of music under the pressure of cultural administration, cultural industry, and technical media such as recording, radio, and television.

While Adorno's critical and theoretical attention was trained most forcefully on instrumental music, opera certainly constituted an important secondary focus of his musicological work and thought. In his early music criticism for *Der Anbruch*, *Die Musik*, and other music-critical forums in the late 1920s and early 1930s, he commented on performances of historic and contemporary operas such as Mozart's *The Magic Flute* and *Don Juan*, Beethoven's *Fidelio*, Meyerbeer's *The African Maid*, Verdi's *The Force of Destiny* and *Falstaff*, Wagner's *Lohengrin* and *Parsifal*, Humperdinck's *Hansel and Gretel*, Busoni's *Faust*, Puccini's *Madame Butterfly* and *Turandot*, Strauss's *Elektra* and *The Woman Without a Shadow*, Berg's *Wozzeck*, Sekles's *The Ten Kisses*, D'Albert's *The Golem*, Pfitzner's *Palestrina*, Křenek's *Johnny Plays Up*, Hindermith's *Cardillac* and *News of the Day*, Janáček's *The Macropulos Case*, Brand's *Machinist Hopkins*, Antheil's *Transatlantic*, and Weill's *Mahagonny*, among many others.[8] In his 1929 review "Berlin Opera Memorial," Adorno vividly describes an avant-garde multi-media event at the Kroll Opera House in which Zemlinsky and Klemperer traded off conducting *Tales from Hoffmann*, with light and images provided by the former Bauhaus master László Moholy-Nagy.[9] Beyond such occasional pieces and reviews, one of Adorno's most important works dedicated to opera was his 1952 book on Wagner, much of which dated back to Adorno's original composition of the study in the 1930s. While his other musical monographs on Schoenberg and Stravinsky, Mahler, and Berg do not extensively discuss opera (with the slight exception of his chapters on Berg's *Wozzeck* and *Lulu*), he nevertheless dedicated lengthy essays to Bizet's *Carmen*, to Schoenberg's *Moses und Aron*, to the contemporary legacies of Wagner and Strauss, and to sociological questions of opera and its public.

Still, in the formative experience of his work on the sociology of listening for the *Zeitschrift für Sozialforschung* and the Princeton Radio Project in the 1930s and 1940s, opera is not particularly foregrounded as a concern. In his important essay "On the Fetish Character in Music and the Regression in Listening," excepting incidental mention of Berlioz and Wagner, the only significant reference to opera is to Mozart's *Magic Flute*, in which, Adorno claims, the utopia of merging enlightenment with light comic opera is achieved for the first and last time.[10] Similarly, among the various writings from the Princeton Radio Project, which were reconstructed by Hullot-Kentor as *Current of Music*, references to opera are relatively sparse. These include, for example, Adorno's drily ironic remarks on the NBC's *Music Appreciation Hour*, in which he chastises the prudish language with which the program "summarized" the plot of *Tristan and Isolde* as a moralistic matter of the ill-starred lovers trying to avoid adultery:

> *The Music Appreciation Hour* evokes the idea that they simply suffer, because for reasons of conventional morality they cannot get together. As a matter of fact, they do get together, and adultery is the presupposition of the whole *Tristan* plot. If one is afraid to speak about adultery, one should not speak about *Tristan*. One had better not even play it. The assumption, however, that an adolescent would not suspect the true story when faced with the plot of *Tristan* is absurd.[11]

More revealing, however, than such shots of critical wit is Adorno's own exposé for a music education radio course, "What a Music Appreciation Hour Should Be." Notably, he argues that the course's engagement with opera should be limited, because unlike with chamber and symphonic works, it would be more difficult to offer listeners a grasp of an opera as a whole:

> The second element [of the course] is *opera*, for example as found in the works of Bizet, Verdi and perhaps Wagner. ... [H]owever, this material should not be foregrounded in the first course, primarily because here the educational aim would be in an understanding of opera as a unity, which can only be achieved in conjunction with real performances. For the moment we shall put the problem of opera on hold, but in certain cases fall back on operatic works that are characteristic in some other sense that is relevant to the course. (*Current*, 221)

Adorno alludes primarily to constraints of the radio medium for the music pedagogical purposes at issue: a short radio hour program would allow only perhaps a single act of an opera, or a set of excerpts, but not an analysis of a full work.[12]

It is remarkable that Adorno does not mention here the New York Metropolitan Opera's weekly radio broadcasts of full opera performances, to which he had access as a listener and investigator and which could have mitigated, within the radio medium, the temporal limits of his projected music appreciation program. The Metropolitan Opera had in fact already begun irregular partial broadcasts of operas in 1910, but began delivering the first full broadcast performances in 1931 with Humperdinck's *Hänsel und Gretel* and Wagner's *Das Rheingold*, and from 1933 onwards carried mostly full-length performances.[13] Adorno does remark this broadcast series, but implicitly only to dismiss it as irreparably compromised. Thus in notes on what he labels a "propaganda publication of NBC," he quotes without further comment the following passage from the publication about the Saturday opera broadcasts, presumably as an egregious instance of American kitsch sensibility: "Among the social events of Honolulu are the radio opera breakfasts. . . . Rangers and cow punchers gather on Saturday afternoons at the Cody Museum in Wyoming (dedicated to the memory of Buffalo Bill) to hear the broadcasts from the stage of the Metropolitan" (*Current*, 469). The image of cowboys raptly listening in the Buffalo Bill Museum to "*Vissi d'arte*" proved a bridge too far into the American cultural wilds for the recently emigrated Adorno.

We can also see, however, in Adorno's sidelining of opera in his radio music studies a reflection of his theoretical concern with the reification, regression, and "deconcentration" of listening, which disintegrates the experience of musical form from within. What for Adorno was most troubling about the radio symphony was its atomizing of the elements of the symphony's integral form into quotation or image-like bits that allude to the work rather than experientially enacting it, through a live immersive presentation of its temporality, spatiality, and dynamics. "[T]hrough radio," Adorno writes—

> the individual elements of symphony acquire the character of quotation. Radio symphony appears as a medley or potpourri in so far as the musical atoms it offers up acquire the touch of having picked up somewhere else and put together into a kind of montage. What is heard is not Beethoven's Fifth but merely musical information from and about Beethoven's Fifth.[14]

It is arguable, however, that in their navigation of narrative plot and their striving after dramatic effect—albeit often in hackneyed or absurd ways—operas rarely exhibit the degree of musical unity and developmental shape that more autonomous instrumental music might achieve.

Adorno would, of course, also argue that instrumental musical form had reached its most encompassing synthesis in Beethoven's symphonies and that Beethoven's "late style," manifested in the late piano concertos and the *Missa Solemnis*, already exhibited the growing dissolution that would culminate decades later in free atonality. In opera, however, such thoroughgoing integration was the much later and exceptional accomplishment of Wagner and, in Adorno's view even more so, of Alban Berg. Thus, he describes *Wozzeck* as having carried "the art of transition much further than Wagner ever conceived possible," "to the point of pervasive mediation."[15] *Wozzeck*'s composition—

> is as articulated, explicated, and variationally developed as only great music is, as are the instrumental movements of Brahms or Schoenberg. It gains its autonomy from its own inexhaustible, self-renewing development, while those opera scores that divorce themselves from the scenic action and go their own unrestrained way threaten for that very reason to become monotonous and boring. ... *Wozzeck* fulfills Wagner's demand that the orchestra follow the drama's every last ramification and thus become a symphony, and in so doing finally eliminates the illusion of formlessness in music drama. The second act is quite literally a symphony, with all the tension and all the closure of that form, and at the same time at every moment so completely an opera that the unaware listener would never even think of a symphony. (87)

In fulfilling and carrying further Wagner's aspirations for a musical drama that would exceed the conventional limitations of opera, *Wozzeck* rewards the sort of "structural listening" that Adorno directed towards Beethoven, Brahms, and Schoenberg. Yet Berg's is a late and singular accomplishment in musical-dramatic form, rising above and beyond the compositional flatlands of opera more generally.

Given Adorno's pedagogical aim to strengthen radio listeners' ability to listen with concentration and better apprehend music's formal development, then, the opera's long duration and less autonomous, looser form made it a problematic source of examples for his reformed musical appreciation program. Nor did the short-playing recording technology available in the 1930s support longer-duration structural listening. If anything, in Adorno's view, recordings reinforced the tendency towards fragmentation and reification of the excerpted part at the expense of the larger work. On short-playing records, operatic arias, duets, and overtures became more like hummable popular "hits" than synechdoches of larger musical structures. In the 1930s, Adorno saw no significant alternative or technical complement to live performances that might foster in the contemporary public a deeper musical understanding of opera.

As already noted, Adorno's perspectives on opera in his critical writings became increasing negative in the 1950s and 1960s. This makes all the more surprising his late essay published in *Der Spiegel* in 1969, "Die Oper überwintert auf der Langspielplatte" (Opera hibernates on the LP),[16] in which he more hopefully considered the technological remediation of opera by means of long-playing records, which allow experience of musical works that is distinct from that afforded by live performance in opera houses, radio or television broadcasts, or even the short-playing records of earlier years. In this connection, Adorno notes that there are two senses to the word *Technik* in relation to music. The first has to do with compositional *techniques*, while the latter involves the technical apparatus by which the music is brought to its public, which in the contemporary period is increasingly administrative, technological, and entangled with extra-artistic commercial and financial dynamics: "industrial processes that are applied to music for the purpose of its mass dissemination" ("Opera and the Long-Playing Record," 283). Though different, Adorno argues, the two aspects of musical *Technik* also interpenetrate and influence one another. A change in the technology through which opera is disseminated may thus affect the experiential content of existing works as well as influence the composition and presentation of new works. In this light, Adorno entertains the hypothesis that the long-playing record might remediate opera in a way that would renew or at least preserve the genre's living musical and dramatic content, countervailing the contemporary disintegration of the opera-listening public and the growing obsolescence of traditional forms of reception.

The key features of long-playing records that Adorno sees as nothing short of "revolutionary" are their capacity to register and reproduce long-duration works in full and their potential, hence, to constitute an archive or "museum" of integral works that can be accessed repeatedly and at will. These features help overcome the limitations of single live performances (with the fluctuations of listeners' attention and fallible memory as corollaries) and of mediated excerpts on radio, short-playing sound recordings, or film. "The entire musical literature," Adorno writes, "could now become available in quite-authentic form to listeners desirous of auditioning and studying such works at a time convenient to them" ("Opera and the Long-Playing Record," 283). He refers to his own essay on questions of museums and musealization in the writings of Paul Valéry and Marcel Proust, in which he compares Valéry's view that art is reified and neutralized as soon as its living context is relinquished to that of Proust, for whom everything begins with "the afterlife of the work of art," allowing him, as Adorno writes, "to perceive history as landscape."[17] Adorno's metaphor of "hibernation" clearly aligns him with Proust—and implicitly too with Benjamin's affirmation of collection and the reconstellation of historical materials—in perceiving museal recontextualization as a potentially positive process:

> Nor need they fear that the recorded works will be neutralized in the process, as they are in opera houses. Similar to the fate that Proust ascribed to paintings in museums, these recordings awaken to a second life in the wondrous dialogue with the lonely and perceptive listeners, hibernating for purposes unknown. ("Opera and the Long-Playing Record," 285)

Already in 1963, in fact, in his essay "On the Musical Use of the Radio," Adorno had suggested that radio broadcasts of music might be the occasion for constituting such recording archives, and he specifically refers to their impact on interpretation, because of the registration of multiple versions of a piece. "Boulez," he notes, "for a recording of *Wozzeck* to replace that of Mitropulos, which should never have been released, required seventy rehearsals. Such a practice . . . finally allowed the fundamental ill of the contemporary field of conducting to be eliminated, the fiction that through mere gesture, rhythmic technique, and skillful giving of cues, the work as conceived by the conductor can be translated to the orchestra and into sensuous phenomena."[18]

Besides this impact on interpretation by conductors and musicians, Adorno also foresees a reflexive impact of the long-duration recording back onto the forms of opera as created by composers and, through the mediation of appropriate reproduction, also then as experienced by well-prepared listeners. He argues that the long-playing recording is approaching the condition of a "compositional form" that will make clear the polarization of musical art into avant-garde and kitsch, a split obscured by the official forms of opera performance culture:

> The gramophone record becomes a form the moment it unintentionally approaches the requisite state of a compositional form. Looking back, it now seems as if the short-playing records of yesteryear . . . unconsciously also corresponded to their epoch: the desire for highbrow diversion, the salon pieces, favorite arias, and the Neapolitan semihits. . . . This sphere of music is finished: there is now only music of the highest standards and obvious kitsch, with nothing in between. The LP expresses this historical change rather precisely. ("Opera and the Long-Playing Record," 285)

His implication is that long-playing recordings hold out hope for the gradual constitution of a historically informed and aesthetically demanding listening public for opera (and for music more generally). In turn, rather than compromising out of professional necessity with the conservative tastes of the public, the composer will be challenged by listeners to explore new artistic materials and techniques.

Opera Mediation through Film and Television

While Adorno's comments on opera's relation to film are more limited than his radio-related writings, the topic recurs in several of his musicological writings, organized around a few key critical motifs. In the background of Adorno thinking about opera and film was a broader cultural discourse developing in the first few decades of the twentieth century that considered the two media as secret sharers, twins that possessed a common or parallel fate. As Lydia Goehr has pointed out, some participants in the debates about opera and film saw film as relieving opera from the drive towards technical integration and innovation—from the Wagnerian ambition to create a musical-dramatic *Gesamtkunstwerk*—thus allowing opera composers more modest, more bearable technical demands. Others, Schoenberg among them, saw film as forcing opera to abandon realism and find new dramatic means, since many of the old features of opera had been thoroughly outdone by film.[19] Adorno himself tended to see the relationship between opera and film as *prefigurative*: opera, as it developed during the nineteenth century, was the anticipation of features that would only be fully realized later in film. Most famously, he underscored Wagner's phantasmagoric anticipation of cinema, the "birth of film out of the spirit of music."[20] He quotes Houston Stewart Chamberlain's letter to Cosima Wagner in 1890, in which Chamberlain suggests playing Liszt's *Dante* symphony in a darkened room with moving pictures in the background. Adorno comments: "Few documents could demonstrate more tellingly how inaccurate it is to assert that mass culture was imposed on art from outside. The truth is, it was thanks to its own emancipation that art was transformed into its opposite" (107–8). Andreas Huyssen argues that not only did Adorno read Wagner through the Culture Industry concept he articulated in *Dialectic of Enlightenment*, but also that the Culture Industry analysis is already rooted in Adorno's first version of his Wagner book in the 1930s, despite its post-*Dialectic of Enlightenment* publication in the early 1950s. Huyssen writes that "the framework for his theory of the culture industry was already in place *before* his encounter with American mass culture in the United States. In the Wagner book the pivotal categories of fetishism and reification, ego-weakness, regression, and myth are already fully developed, waiting, as it were, to be articulated in terms of the American culture industry."[21]

Rather than a radical break between the two forms, in Adorno's view, there was a migration and metamorphosis of the opera-going public into a film-viewing public, while opera itself increasingly adapted to the expectations of cinema's entertainment- and attraction-hungry public. In "Bourgeois Opera," Adorno writes:

> Opera shares with film not just the suddenness of its invention but also many of its functions, among them the presentation to the masses of the body of inherited common knowledge, as well as the massiveness of the means, employed teleologically in the material of opera as in film, which lent opera ... a similarity to the modern Culture Industry.... It is ... astounding how early some of the worst abominations of today's Culture Industry announced themselves in opera, at the precise point where the naive person, in looking to the past, expects to find something like the pure autonomy of the genre. ... [O]pera as a consumer product is entangled in calculations regarding the public—in this sense, too, it is related to film. ("Bourgeois Opera," 20)

In his *Introduction to the Sociology of Music*, he further suggests that key features of opera which once secured its public have been taken up latterly and amplified by film:

> It was ... not just the evolution of music which so far outran the operatic stage and its audience with any contact.... The social conditions, and thus the style and content, of traditional opera were so far removed from the theatergoers' consciousness that there is every reason to doubt the continued existence of any such thing as an operatic experience. The aesthetic conventions it rests upon, perhaps even the measure of sublimation it presupposes, can hardly be expected of broad listening strata. But the charms which opera had for the masses in the nineteenth century and earlier, in the Venetian, Neapolitan, and Hamburg performances of the seventeenth—the decorous pomp, the imposing spectacle, the intoxicating color and sensuous allure—all this had long since wandered off to motion pictures. The film has materially outbid the opera, while intellectually underbidding it so far that nothing from its fund could keep it competitive. (80)

In their jointly authored study of film music, *Composing for the Films*, Adorno and Eisler likewise suggest that the emergence of cinema and the culmination of a long-developing crisis of opera coincided in the first decade of the twentieth century. Film, in their view, affects not only the external conditions of opera's reception but also those of its composition, for example, in works by audience-conscious composers such as Richard Strauss:

> [A]t the time when motion-picture music was in its rudimentary stage, the breach between the middle-class audiences and the really serious music which expressed the situation of the middle classes became unbridgeable. This breach can be traced as far as *Tristan*, a work that has probably never been understood and liked as much as *Aida*, *Carmen*, or even the *Meistersinger*. The operatic theatre became finally estranged from its audience between 1900 and 1910, with the production of *Salome* and *Electra*, the two advanced operas of Richard Strauss. The fact that after 1910, with the *Rosenkavalier*—it is no

accident that this opera has been made into a moving picture—he turned to a retrospective stylized way of writing reflects his awareness of that breach.²²

Adorno and Eisler refer glancingly here to the silent film version of *Der Rosenkavalier* by director Robert Wiene—better known for his expressionist masterpiece *The Cabinet of Dr. Caligari*—from 1926. Either might have seen it at its original release.²³ Rather than Strauss, however, who was somewhat cool about the project, the filming of *Rosenkavalier* was, in fact, more the initiative of its librettist Hugo von Hofmannstahl, who sought to ease his financial straits through a lucrative film version. Although initially enthusiastic, Hofmannstahl himself quickly soured on Wiene, who he complained had made the dullest and crassest of films from his plot, and eventually it was withdrawn from circulation so that Hofmannstahl could pursue another, sound film version in Hollywood with United Artists, which never came to fruition. The highly cultivated, sensitive Austrian playwright, Adorno would have found apt, viewed the low cultural niveau of the American public as precisely the promising reason why a Hollywood *Rosenkavalier* sound film might prove a success in the American market. "The magnitude of the opportunities lies particularly with the North American business," wrote Hofmannstahl. "One can hardly imagine the possibilities for circulation in this monstrously large, completely theatreless and theatre-hungry Land."²⁴

In his 1963 essay "On the Musical Use of the Radio," Adorno took a more positive stance towards the reproductive possibilities of film, comparing film favorably to the radio as a medium for the dissemination of music, at least when used intelligently and creatively. He saw film as the technically more progressive medium, insofar as production and reproduction come together before the spectator on the screen, unlike the static and distanced situation of the radio listener. The changing position of the camera, close-ups, and other techniques allow for a mobility in the situation of listening that can help overcome the distance from the listener and lead to a more appropriate reception of the work ("Über die musikalische Verwendung des Radios," 396). He notes with approval that Alban Berg had considered a film of *Wozzeck*, remarking that Berg "thought especially of the very polyphonic and complex street scene in the second action," and comments: "one could with a sound film recording through respective microphones select the thematic voices for dramaturgical impact" (397). He notes Berg's incorporation of film projection in the interlude in *Lulu*'s second act and ventures that Lulu's many-layered character would benefit from a similar microphonic technique as he had suggested in connection with *Wozzeck*.

In conclusion, it is notable that Adorno did not extend his more positive assessment of film's mediation of opera in his latter years to the medium of television. For the most part, he is quite dismissive. In his essay on opera and long-playing recording, for instance, in contrast to his optimistic view of the opera record album's potentials, he devotes a damning two sentences to televised opera even in comparison to the deeply compromised situation of live opera: "Television broadcasts of gala opera evenings do not make things any better. A million praline boxes are actually worse than one single one that still retains something of the childlike joy of blissful moments" ("Opera and the Long-Playing Record," 284). His judgment of televised music generally was communicated by a pointed quote from an interview with *Der Spiegel* in February 1968: "Musik im Fernsehen ist Brimborium" (Music on Television is Mumbo-Jumbo).

In this interview, Adorno first raises a (somewhat hackneyed) phenomenological point about the sensorial essences of television as an optical medium and music as an acoustic art form:

> Television, as an optical medium, stands in a somewhat foreign relation to music, which is essentially acoustic. In advance, there follows from televisual technology a certain displacement of attention, which is not favorable to music. In general, music is there for hearing and not seeing.[25]

Yet even if Adorno's point is granted concerning instrumental music, it is not clear how compelling it is in connection with opera, which, along with its musical basis, also has essential dramatic features that an "optical medium" might support even better than live performance. Adorno and the *Spiegel* interviewer, however, go on to discuss at length how current television broadcasts of operas are also riddled with Culture Industry traits and gross flaws of interpretation and performance. Among the objections Adorno raises to televised music broadcasts include: their emphasis on unessential aspects of the music to the detriment of attention to essential features of the composition; their tendency to overstress so-called main voices or melodies, tearing them "out of any relation to the music weave" ("Musik im Fernsehen," 561); their employment of kitsch settings and imagery to accompany the chestnuts of the "classical" repertory; and the "star" presentation of "telegenic" conductors like Herbert von Karajan as genius-magicians who gesturally conjure up music through the orchestra, thus becoming, as Adorno says, a TV "actor of their own artistic accomplishment" (566). Adorno argues that any possible positive use of television for musical or operatic purposes would require posing the question of a medium-specific music and musical procedure, if such false and inadequate phenomena are to be avoided. He acknowledges the nascent efforts of new-music composers such as Karlheinz Stockhausen, Mauricio Kagel, and György Ligeti to approach television seriously as a technical medium for musical production and reproduction.

In the end, however, he also concedes that in the face of the "dominant productions of the culture industry, this is like a drop on a hot stone" (563). Artistically advanced new-music operas thus offer only the faintest glimmer of light for a path forward in the televisual medium. With regard to the historical legacy of opera, the mass dissemination of "classic" operas through television offers only false hope for a way out of the genre's crisis, since it only deepens the loss of operatic works' ability to occasion authentic experience in its public. "The televised *Figaro* is no longer *Figaro*" (569), Adorno laments. Concert broadcasts and opera for television, he concludes, remain for the present nothing more than "a piece of empty culture business" (569).

Alexander Kluge: Operatic (Re-)Mediations

The writer, filmmaker, television director, and critical theorist Alexander Kluge began his direct engagement with the Frankfurt School as a student and subsequently as a lawyer for the Institut für Sozialforschung in Frankfurt. The legal profession, however, as Kluge has noted, "really bored me," and he considered both writing and film as ways to "escape jurisprudence."[26] Though Adorno in fact sought to discourage Kluge from pursuing either artistic career, he did eventually write to Fritz Lang to ask if he might take Kluge on as an assistant. As Kluge drily observed, Lang "did no such thing, but he did let me watch as an intern" on the set of the 1959 film *The Tiger of Eschnapur* (Kluge, *Difference and Orientation*, 151), which spurred Kluge's interest in film. Notably, a Lang-like figure and a production situation like that which plagued the filming of *The Tiger of Eschnapur* would later become the subject of Kluge's 1985 film *The Blind Director* (*Der Angriff der Gegenwart auf die übrige Zeit*). But Kluge notes that Adorno did not even esteem Lang's film work highly and largely avoided viewing films altogether; he mentions that Adorno probably saw only two of Kluge's own films and did not really care for them (Kluge, *Difference and Orientation*, 361). Kluge considered this failure to engage more deeply with cinema a missed opportunity that weakened Adorno's Culture Industry analysis:

> Had he not been so set against Hollywood, he could have developed an image theory based on the commodity fetish, i.e. the images and the exchangeability rooted in every commodity, as well as an exact method. This could have been

a consciousness industry chapter. Instead, he simply criticized Hollywood's distribution system as a propaganda machine that developed through advertising. (361)

As to film music, in reference to Adorno's coauthored book *Composing for the Films*, Kluge bluntly states that without Eisler, "He was dead" (362).

In his work reflecting on and interrogating opera, however, Kluge signals a profound indebtedness to Adorno, even as his multifaceted, experimental practice of remediating opera plots, descriptions of performances, performance spaces, and anecdotes also exceeds Adorno's critical exploration of opera mediations such as radio, recording, film, and television. In his film and accompanying books *Die Macht der Gefühle* (The Power of Feelings, 1983), in his montages of television programs such as *Das Kraftwerk der Gefühle* (The Powerplant of Feelings, 1998–2007) and *Finsterlinge Singen Bass* (The Sinister Ones Sing Bass, 1998–2007), as well as in his illustrated montage-book *Herzblut trifft Kunstblut: Erster Imaginärer Opernführer* (Heart's Blood Meets Fake Blood, 2001), Kluge analytically breaks down and reassembles opera culture to reveal its experiential contents—mummified, like the entombed lovers in Verdi's *Aida*, an opera Kluge returns to again and again, in increasingly obsolescent artistic forms.[27] Kluge's approach is motivated by a Benjamin-inspired archeological approach to opera and its media, which he allegorizes in his mini-narrative "An Archeologist of Opera," with a focal character who flies between his archeological work in Syria and various European opera performances. The archeologist notes:

> As for what is happening on the stage, I am interested in the details. It is not the *plot* revealing the signs that refer to the goings-on in the opera I would like to know about. The story is only the mask for it. The secret lies in the minor points of the action, in tiny fragments. When we excavate, we also rarely find the entire object from antiquity—just splinters and remnants that we fit together.[28]

His micrological, analytic orientation to the opera, giving preference to the detail and fragment over the whole, is wedded by Kluge to a second guiding idea, also indebted to Adorno: an unearthing of underlying abstract *formulae* of operatic narrative, related to concrete experiential needs, which motivated Adorno to suggest writing "imaginary guides to the opera," a suggestion that Kluge would literally take up.

The genre of the opera guide, Kluge notes, "harbors a literary form that has so far been insufficiently utilized. Nobody would confuse the text of the opera with the guide itself. The opera guide thus permits a perspectival foreshortening which—if one were to group diverse operas, as it were, in a long shot—could elucidate affinities among opera motifs."[29] Kluge also explored the possibilities of translating this foreshortening into film in short films such as *5 Stunden Parsifal* (1998), a condensation of the whole of Wagner's *Parsifal* into a single minute, and his forty-seven-minute television montage *Soprano gegen Bass* (1997–2006), which draws examples from *Nabucco*, *I Due Foscari*, *Macbeth*, *Luisa Miller*, *Il Trovatore*, *La Traviata*, *Les Vépres Siciliennes*, *La Forza Della Destino*, and *Don Carlos*, to analyze the operatic embodiment of seven narrative functions: "1. Women who fight for their men; 2. Destiny rages; 3. Fathers against their sons; 4: The sopranos; 5. Killed by the bass; 6. Murder night in Palermo; 7. Grand finales." Kluge comments: "What patron attending an opera notices immediately that the music of the Grand Inquisitor in *Don Carlos* is the same as the music of the assassin in *Rigoletto*? Does one realize (if one only attends one opera on one particular evening) how related and yet how extremely different the finales of Verdi's operas are? Thus 12 x Verdi in context. A special contribution to Xaver Holzmann's Imaginary Opera Guide."[30] So too in his televised interviews with the renowned German opera director and administrator August Everding, published in book form as *Der Mann der 1,000 Opern* (The Man of 1,000 Operas, 1998), Kluge emphasizes the experiential condensation that opera direction entails (mirrored also in his own remediation of Everding's work in print and on screen): "Naturally, August Everding has not directed 1,000 operas. But one cannot stage a single opera well if one does not know 1,000 operas. Operas are related to one another. They create an *opera world*."[31] Kluge likewise sees such an accumulation and condensation of experience paradigmatically in the figure of Elina Makropulos in Leoš Janáček's 1926 opera *The Makropulos Affair*: both the daughter of a Prague alchemist who gives her a formula for immortality and her contemporary reincarnation as the opera diva Emilia Marty three hundred years later. Thus, in a scene in the film *Die Macht der Gefühle*, Kluge notes of Elina/Emilia, "All her feelings are 300 years old. She has, so to speak, an overview of 28 wars."[32]

Whether mediated textually, as in the *First Imaginary Opera Guide*, or through the technical means of film and television, Kluge's analytic decomposition and montage of opera narrative aims at developing new, alternative versions of plots, remediations especially of the tragic fate to which operas typically bind their heroes, often thus affirming in an emotionally compelling register the ideological and social constraints of their time. As Kluge's avatar "Xaver Holzmann" states in a (fictitious) interview about his project for an imaginary opera guide:

—We know what an opera guide is, but what do you mean by "imaginary"?—
I'm asking: What are the operas that don't exist? The twentieth century
offers us operatic themes, just as every other century provides material
worthy of serious treatment, i.e. an opera, a "work," but operas exist for
certain themes and not for other ones. That was what interested me. On
that basis I'm developing a proposition or an algorithm. If opera history
contains around eighty thousand operas, why shouldn't we have the chance
to create about seven hundred missing operas that would be needed to
convey the substance of our contemporary experience? (Kluge, *Temples of
the Scapegoat*, 57)

Kluge holds the view that the experiential contents of operas are entombed in an outmoded, reified artistic form, addressed, as Adorno diagnosed, to a disintegrated or even no-longer-existent listening public. Yet at the same time, analytic remediation of opera motifs and elements can address gaps in our ability to give expression to and work through contemporary experience, while the emotional charge of operatic materials breathes new life into textual, dramatic, and cinematic art forms.

In 1970, the East German playwright Heiner Müller—one of Kluge's favorite interview conversation partners—published a short text, "Six Points about Opera," which followed his composition of the libretto for Paul Dessau's *Lanzelot*, which was first performed in 1969.[33] Müller expressed the view that the opera opened a wider field for "the increasing aestheticization of praxis, the *Aufhebung* of the contradiction of work and play, daily life and history, private existence and society in the unity of socialism and scientific-technological revolution," because it is "better equipped to present 'non-antagonistic contradictions' than the drama."[34] Echoing Wittgenstein's *Tractatus* with an artistic twist, he argued that opera extended the operative means of theatre in adding music and voice to gesture and language. Opera allowed a kind of communication with a not yet realized future, as Bloch had envisioned in *Spirit of Utopia* in 1918. As Müller writes, "What one cannot yet say, one can perhaps sing"; and, identifying opera and utopia explicitly, he concludes: "Every song contains a utopian moment, anticipating a better world" (161).

In "Anti-Oper," a videotaped and televised conversation with Kluge almost twenty-five years later, after the fall of the Berlin Wall, Müller looks back on his utopian hopes for the opera and revises his evaluation:

Müller: Today I would be more skeptical. Today I would say that when everything has been said, the voices become sweet, and then comes the opera ...
Kluge: And that's a kind of fraudulent undertaking?
Müller: Yes.[35]

Kluge follows up by remarking that in the nineteenth century, the great period of the construction of opera houses, these were corollary expressions of national pride to displays of military power such as fleets or parades of cavalry soldiers. But, he suggests, the times are dire for the opera:

> If now the operas must leave the opera houses and become partisans, just as soldiers must become partisans—if that is the case, there would be an anti-opera, a counter-movement. (394)

Kluge closes with an allusion to Adorno's well-known metaphor, in *Minima Moralia*, of "leaving behind messages in bottles on the flood of barbarism bursting on Europe," used originally in connection with Nietzsche.[36] Thinking of the opera version of Müller's *Die Hamletmaschine* by Wolfgang Rihm (1987), who also makes an appearance in this TV segment, perhaps as well of other post-Brechtian, politically radical new-music operas such as Luigi Nono's *Al Gran Sole Carico d'Amore* (To the Great Sun Burdened with Love, 1975) and Helmut Lachenmann's *Das Mädchen mit den Schwefelhölzern* (The Little Match-Girl, 1997),[37] Kluge asks the playwright: "Could there be opera in the form of a message in a bottle?" (394). We should note, however, that Kluge's "partisan" metaphor suggests the *detournement* of Adorno's bottled message into something more targeted and explosive in its relation to the future: a musical and dramatic Molotov cocktail tossed out into the streets, rather than a lonely last missive cast upon uncertain waters.

I will conclude by referring to just two additional short texts by Kluge—among the many hundreds I might choose from—that illustrate his awareness and interest in the complex interactions of opera and film, which date back to the early period of film history, when paradoxically operas offered ready material for adaptation to the silent film (see also my discussion of the *Rosenkavalier* film) and film projection was seen as an innovative means of refreshing the contemporary opera by composers such as Křenek (*Jonny spielt auf*, 1927), Darius Milhaud (*Christophe Columb*, 1930), and George Antheil (*Transatlantic*, 1930). The first of these Kluge texts is entitled "Why Cinema Was Unable, Due to Its Conditions of Production, to Become the OPERA OF THE TWENTIETH CENTURY." The title refers to an idea of Adorno's concerning the connection of opera and film, and Adorno figures directly in the text as well:

> Theodor W. Adorno once had occasion to call Fritz Lang—not without a certain affection in his tone—his "kitsch brother." The epithet was not meant disparagingly, Adorno responded when I asked him about it. Otherwise, he

added, he wouldn't have used the word *brother*. With this remark, he was referring to a certain audacity, brutality, or insouciance with which Fritz Lang—it was simply part of the film business—pruned material and opera-ready plots for use by the public and his direction. Lang had been applying this methodology—especially to films, which he considered by-products—since his early period. (*Temple of the Scapegoat*, 164)

Kluge goes on to explain that Adorno had referred specifically to Lang's 1919 film *Harakiri*, which stole its plot from Puccini's *Madama Butterfly*, while modifying it sufficiently to avoid having to pay copyright for its use. Kluge notes that Lang's changes "sacrificed much of the sense and many of the emotionally comprehensible situations," focusing instead on parallel montages of the plot's different elements, underscored for the viewer by dramatic tinting (Kluge, *Temple of the Scapegoat*, 164). He ends on an open-ended question, supposedly posed by Adorno (though, in fact, the whole story has the scent of a fictitious invention of Kluge, who is deeply immersed in cinema history, while Adorno was not): "Adorno asked: could music have saved Fritz Lang's 1919 film?" The irony in Adorno-Kluge's question lies in the tension between Lang's analytic approach to the Puccini opera as a source of materials to appropriate and deploy through montage versus Adorno's putative view that the formal logic of music might have lent Lang's film the articulation and integrity it lacked as film. We might even see here Kluge restaging the arguments about montage and technical reproducibility that Adorno carried out with Benjamin, with Kluge as the next-generation heir of both sides of the argument in new contexts and disposing over new technical means.

My final example derives from Kluge's imaginary opera guide, in a passage on the Marx Brothers and opera. If in his 1932 essay on the Marx Brothers (based on his viewing of *Animal Crackers* and *Monkey Business*), Antonin Artaud had been able to see in their films "a hymn to anarchy and total rebellion,"[38] Kluge takes up *A Night at the Opera* (1935) with a different political valence:

> It's a matter of a Verdi opera in the Marx Brothers' film. The arrogant singer-stars of the first rank dominate the stage. There are however two alternate singers, in love with one another, whose way to the ramp is blocked by the stars. Here the Marx Brothers know how to help out. They disrupt the opera's business and push the stars out of the way. The backup singers take their places.
>
> The Marx Brothers are innovative in the opera. To channel the little couple towards success, they create chaos. It is not very cruelly presented, but it signifies: the extermination of the old is allowed. If the process that was followed by the Marx Brothers were translated into the Russia of 1936, then the political stars there, the comrades of Lenin, would be transferred to the gulag

or shot. In this way the young reach the top spots. Happiness derives from cruelty, or it doesn't even become funny.[39]

In the unlikely affinities of the Marx Brothers with the Moscow trials (discussed at greater length in Chapter 10), Kluge unearths the communicating vessels connecting seemingly autonomous opera and film culture to the traumas of the historical moment in which they emerged. Indeed, at the beginning of the show trials, as Katerina Clark has pointed out, a new campaign was also launched against formalism in the arts, with theatre, opera, and dance in the crosshairs. The first salvo against the "leftist" aesthetic deviationists was, in fact, launched against an opera: Dmitri Shostakovich's *Lady Macbeth of Mtsensk*, which a January 1936 article in *Pravda* characterized as petty-bourgeois, formalist, vulgar, and neurotic.[40] It is only in retrospect, Kluge implies in his story, in the hidden traces preserved in the artifacts disinterred through his media-archeologist's labor, that the catastrophic events of the 1930s can at last be given expression and worked through for contemporary experience.

Notes

1. On the formation of European musical publics in the nineteenth century, see William Weber, *Music and the Middle Class: The Social Structure of Concert Life in London, Paris, and Vienna between 1830 and 1848* (London and New York: Routledge, 1975, 2004); Antje Pieper, *Music and the Making of Middle-Class Culture: A Comparative History of Nineteenth-Century Leipzig and Birmingham* (New York: Palgrave Macmillan, 2008).
2. See also Thomas Y. Levin, "For the Record: Adorno on Music in the Age of Its Technical Reproducibility," *October* 55 (1990): 23–47.
3. Jay David Bolter and Richard Grusin, *Remediation: Understanding New Media* (Cambridge, MA: The MIT Press, 1999), 55.
4. Theodor W. Adorno, "Neue Oper und Publikum," in Adorno, *Gesammelte Schriften* 19, ed. Rolf Tiedemann (Frankfurt am Main: Suhrkamp Verlag, 1984), 476.
5. Theodor W. Adorno, "Bourgeois Opera," in Adorno, *Sound Figures*, trans. Rodney Livingstone (Stanford: Stanford University Press, 1999), 15.
6. Theodor W. Adorno, *Introduction to the Sociology of Music*, trans. E.B. Ashton (New York: Continuum, 1976), 81.
7. Richard Leppert, "Adorno and Opera," in *A Companion to Adorno*, eds. Peter E. Gordon, Espen Hammer, and Max Pensky (Hoboken, NJ: Wiley Blackwell, 2020), 445.
8. These reviews can be found in the lengthy selection of Frankfurt Opera and Concert reviews, spanning from 1922 to 1934, in Adorno, *Gesammelte Schriften* 19, 9–255.
9. Theodor W. Adorno, "Berliner Opernmemorial," in *Gesammelte Schriften* 19, 267–75.

10. Theodor W. Adorno, "On the Fetish Character in Music and the Regression in Listening," in *The Culture Industry: Selected Essays on Mass Culture*, ed. J.M. Bernstein (London: Routledge, 1991), 32.
11. Theodor W. Adorno, *Current of Music: Elements of a Radio Theory*, ed. Robert Hullot-Kentor (Cambridge: Polity, 2009), 184.
12. Adorno notes that the NBC's *Music Appreciation Hour* offered the full second act of Verdi's *Aida* in one of its programs, "certainly a good selection for presentation." (*Current of Music*, 190).
13. For historical information about the Met's opera broadcasts, see Paul Jackson, *Saturday Afternoons at the Old Met: The Metropolitan Opera Broadcasts, 1931–1950* (Portland, OR: Amadeus Press, 1992).
14. Theodor W. Adorno, "The Radio Symphony," in *Essays on Music*, ed. Richard Leppert, trans. Susan H. Gillespie (Berkeley and Los Angeles: University of California Press, 2002), 262.
15. Theodor W. Adorno, *Alban Berg: Master of the Smallest Link*, trans. Juliane Brand and Christopher Haley (Cambridge: Cambridge University Press, 1991), 85.
16. Theodor W. Adorno, "'Die Oper überwintert auf der Langspielplatte," *Der Spiegel* 23/13 (March 23, 1969), https://www.spiegel.de/kultur/die-oper-ue berwintert-auf-der-langspielplatte-a-7a5d1cef-0002-0001-0000-00004570 2462 (accessed December 31, 2021). English translation as "Opera and the Long-Playing Record," trans. Thomas Y. Levin, in Adorno, *Essays on Music*, 283–87. For a very early consideration of the gramophone record, published in *Der Anbruch* in 1928, see Adorno, "Nagelkurven," in *Gesammelte Schriften* 19, 525–29, and his 1934 essay, "Die Form der Schallplatte," in ibid., 530–34.
17. Theodor W. Adorno, "Valéry Proust Museum," in Adorno, *Prisms*, trans. Samuel and Shierry Weber (Cambridge, MA: The MIT Press, 1981), 180–81.
18. Theodor W. Adorno, "Über die musikalische Verwendung des Radios," in Adorno, *Gesammelte Schriften* 15, ed. Rolf Tiedemann (Frankfurt am Main: Suhrkamp Verlag, 1976), 391.
19. Lydia Goehr, "Film as Visual Music," in Goehr, *Elective Affinities: Musical Essays on the History of Aesthetic Theory* (New York: Columbia University Press, 2008), 222–23.
20. Theodor W. Adorno, *In Search of Wagner*, trans. Rodney Livingstone (London: Verso, 1981), 107.
21. Andreas Huyssen, "Adorno in Reverse: From Hollywood to Richard Wagner," in *After the Great Divide: Modernism, Mass Culture, Postmodernism* (Bloomington: Indiana University Press, 1986), 42. Cf. Karin Bauer, who argues that Adorno connects Wagner's *Gesamtkunstwerk* to the technological conquest of the aesthetic and a foreshadowing of the productions of the culture industry. See Bauer, "Adorno's Wagner: History and the Potential of the Artwork," *Cultural Critique* 60 (2005): 78.
22. Theodor Adorno and Hanns Eisler, *Composing for the Films* (London: Continuum, 1994), 38. Adorno elaborated his view of Strauss in his tartly critical early essay on the composer, "Richard Strauss: Zum 60. Geburtstage: 11 June 1924," in *Gesammelte Schriften* 18, ed. Rolf Tiedemann (Frankfurt am Main: Suhrkamp Verlag, 1984), 254–62; English translation: "Richard

Strauss. Born June 11, 1864," Pt. 1, trans. Samuel Weber and Shierry Weber, *Perspectives of New Music* 4/1 (1965): 14–32 and Pt. 2, trans. Weber and Weber, *Perspectives of New Music* 4/2 (1966): 113–29.
23. This can now be seen in a restored 2007 DVD version from Das Filmarchiv Austria: *Der Rosenkavalier* (1925, dir. Robert Wiene), accompanied by a book of documents and essays: *"Ein sonderbarer Ding": Essays und Materialien zum Stummfilm DER ROSENKAVALIER*, ed. Günter Krenn (Vienna: Verlag Filmarchiv Austria, 2007).
24. Hugo von Hofmannstahl to Johannes Oertel, June 20, 1929, in *"Ein sonderbarer Ding,"* 209.
25. Adorno, "'Musik im Fernsehen ist Brimborium'," in *Gesammelte Schriften* 19, 559.
26. Alexander Kluge, *Difference and Orientation: An Alexander Kluge Reader*, ed. Richard Langston (Ithaca, NY: Cornell University Press, 2019), 151.
27. For critical discussion of Adorno's and Kluge's views of *Aida*, see Lydia Goehr, "*Aida* and the Empire of Emotions (Theodor W. Adorno, Edward Said, and Alexander Kluge)," *Current Musicology* 87 (2009): 133–59.
28. Alexander Kluge, *Temple of the Scapegoat: Opera Stories*, trans. Isabel Fargo Cole, Donna Stonecipher et al. (New York: New Directions, 2018), 167.
29. Alexander Kluge, "On Opera, Film, and Feelings," *New German Critique* 49 (1990): 137.
30. Alexander Kluge, Supplementary text to *Finsterlinge singen Bass*, DVD (Munich: Edition Filmmuseum, 2008), n.p.
31. Alexander Kluge and August Everding, *Der Mann der 1000 Opern: Gespräche und Bilder* (Hamburg: Rotbuch Verlag, 1998), 9–10.
32. Alexander Kluge, *Die Macht der Gefühle* (Frankfurt am Main: Zweitausendeins, 1984), 138.
33. Müller's libretto is published as "Drachenoper" in Müller, *Werke* 3, ed. Frank Hörnigk (Frankfurt am Main: Suhrkamp Verlag, 2000), 411–47.
34. Heiner Müller, "Sechs Punkte zur Oper," in Müller, *Werke* 8, ed. Frank Hörnigk (Frankfurt am Main: Suhrkamp Verlag, 2005), 161.
35. Heiner Müller, with Alexander Kluge, "Anti-Oper, Materialschlachten von 1914, Flug über Siberien," in Müller, *Werke* 12 (Frankfurt am Main: Suhrkamp Verlag, 2008), 393.
36. Theodor W. Adorno, *Minima Moralia: Reflections from Damaged Life*, trans. E.F.N. Jephcott (London: Verso, 1974), 209.
37. These operas, along with Wolfgang Rihm's *Die Eroberung von Mexico* (The Conquest of Mexico, 1992) feature prominently in Kluge's epic-montage compilation films such as *Nachrichten aus der ideologischen Antike: Marx/Eisenstein/Das Kapital* (2008), *Früchte des Vertrauens* (2009), and *Wer sich traut, reißt die Kälte vom Pferde* (2010).
38. Antonin Artaud, "The Marx Brothers," in Artaud, *Selected Writings*, ed. Susan Sontag, trans. Helen Weaver (Los Angeles and Berkeley: University of California Press, 1976), 241.
39. Alexander Kluge, "Die Marx Brothers in der Oper," *Herzblut trifft Kunstblut*, 20. Kluge also notes the use of the Marx Brothers iconography by the student movement, animated by an analogous spirit of generational revolt taking on political dimensions.

40. Katerina Clark, *Moscow, the Fourth Rome: Stalinism, Cosmopolitanism, and the Evolution of Soviet Culture, 1931–1941* (Cambridge, MA: Harvard University Press, 2011), 211. For the attack on *Lady Macbeth of Mtsensk* see: "Sumbor vmestro muzyki," *Pravda* (January 28, 1936), 3; English translation online at https://web.archive.org/web/20110127123117/http://www.arnoldschalks.nl/tlte1sub1.html (accessed December 31, 2021).

Part III

Critical Theory

Chapter 8

Perversion and Utopia: Sade, Fourier, and Critical Theory

In the introduction to his most notorious work, *The 120 Days of Sodom*, the Marquis de Sade provides a descriptive catalogue of the "dramatis personae" of his opus and the "statutes" they agree to adhere to, along with a description of the place in which their orgies will transpire and authorial instructions to the reader about how to consume the work. He addresses the reader with an offer to deny them any sort of conventional, "natural" pleasure in favor of the pleasures to be found in the perverse and criminal:

> And now, friend-reader, you must prepare your heart and your mind for the most impure tale that has ever been told since our world began, a book the likes of which are met with neither amongst the ancients nor amongst us modern. Fancy, now, that all pleasure-taking either sanctioned by good manners or enjoined by that fool you speak of incessantly, of whom you know nothing and whom you call Nature; fancy, I say, that all these modes of taking pleasure will be expressly excluded from this anthology, or that whenever peradventure you do indeed encounter them here, they will always be accompanied by some crime or colored by some infamy.[1]

Sade occupies an ambivalent place in the canon of critical theory. On the one hand, he has been taken as an extreme avatar of the reification Lukács identified with modern capitalism's calculative rationality and that Horkheimer and Adorno discerned in the long trajectory of humankind's domination of nature. For the latter, Sade's geometrically varied and exhaustively catalogued tortures anticipate the horrors of Auschwitz, that exceptional "zero-degree sociality" of industrial mass murder which Horkheimer and Adorno's successor Axel Honneth likewise points to as the ultimate example of reified humanity.[2] On the other hand, however, since Sade does not merely represent the perverse pursuit of pleasure, but also generalizes it as a maxim, doctrine, or ideology, he evokes the possibility of an expanded conception of communal happiness, a paradoxical utopia of perversion.[3]

I will begin by considering some of the reflections of Sade on these issues, as instanced in the introduction to the *120 Days of Sodom*. Here I follow the lead of Dalia Judovitz, who highlights that for Sade the sexual dimension of perversion is the vehicle of a more radical, destructive attack on "the premises of rational thought."[4] Hence, I do not discuss in detail the admittedly important issues of sexuality within the problematic of perversion, nor the rich conceptual legacy of psychoanalytic thought seeking to explicate perversion's genesis and psychic functioning. Rather I pursue the derivative question of perversion's relation to rationality and its potential for a critique of rationality's existing forms and institutional embodiments. I thus focus my discussion on two partially intersecting groups of thinkers—the Frankfurt School and Georges Bataille's circle—who, in their critiques of modern rationality, were strongly influenced by the early twentieth-century rediscovery of Sade (along with his utopian contemporary and complement, Charles Fourier). Considering a variety of examples from Marcuse, Horkheimer and Adorno, and Benjamin, as well as from Bataille and Pierre Klossowski, I attend especially to how their various interpretations of Sade, often juxtaposed to Fourier, treat the communication and communalization of perversion *as a potential dimension of utopia*. I trace a trajectory of mid-twentieth-century debate from positions that treat affirmatively the utopian potentials of Sade's perverse texts, but also that sublimate or otherwise redeem perversion from the destructive implications of Sade's vision, to positions that are more skeptical about Sade's putatively utopian traits. Klossowki's evolution is, I argue, exemplary, as it shifts from affirmative explications of Sade to increasingly critical treatment in the name of a Fourierian utopia of liberated perversion.

Lastly, extrapolating beyond the immediate theoretical examples I examine, I view these thinkers as grappling with the definition of the perverse/utopian text and the relation it establishes with the pleasure of its readers. How, they ask, through an encounter with textual images and narratives of perversion, might readers be hailed into a not yet assembled utopian community of pleasure? In their initial encounters with Sade's text, Bataille's circle in particular, but also Benjamin, glimpsed an alternative to rationalistic conceptions of the theory–practice relationship. In the shock of Sade's text—in ways akin to Artaud's directly affecting "theatre of cruelty"—an immediate translation of words to action became visible to them, suggesting a directly embodied, emotively compelling, and imagistically mediated path from revolutionary ideas into insurrectionary social practice.

Sade's Perversions

Late in the introduction to the *120 Days*, Sade enters upon a lengthy description of Durcet's château, Silling, where four principal libertines have agreed to conduct their orgies. From the outset of the description, Sade's emphasis falls on Silling's extreme isolation and inaccessibility; it is hyperbolically constituted as a place of silence and solitude, a "locus solus." Sade notes that the castle is accessible only by a bridge over a precipice over a thousand feet deep. When the last of their crew has arrived, "the bridge ... was destroyed immediately ... and from this moment on, all possibility of communicating with the Château of Silling ceased.... [T]he bridge removed or destroyed, there is not on this entire earth a single being, of no matter what species you may imagine, capable of gaining this small plot of level land" (Sade, *120 Days*, 236). Sade goes on to describe its internal rooms and furnishings in lavish detail, but hesitates before the innermost cell of terror and voluptuousness, the dungeon, which is a place of absolute solitude within a place of near-absolute solitude, and symbolically in excess of its literal function as a place of burial, disintegration, disappearance, and death, for both the libertine tormentor and his victim:

> A fatal stone there was which, cunningly made, could be raised from below the step of the gallery; beneath that stone one beheld a spiral stairway, very narrow and very steep, whose three hundred steps could convey you down into the bowels of the earth, to a kind of vaulted dungeon, closed by triple doors of iron, and in which was displayed everything the cruelest art and the most refined barbarity could invent of the most atrocious, *as much for gripping one with terror as for proceeding to horrors.* (239; emphasis mine)

Sade, however, does not merely describe this place; he also, in elliptical form, *narrates* its description to one of the libertines, the Duc. Implicitly, the Duc's reception is a hint to the reader to how to respond to the passage she has just finished reading: "I know not what will transpire in that nether place, but this I may say without doing our tale a disservice, that when a description of the dungeon was given the Duc, he reacted by discharging three times in succession" (239). For Sade, thus, it is the *topos*, or better, the utopian *ou-topos*, the solitary "nowhere," the displacement of the self in the imagination of absolute incommunicability, that becomes the "good place" (*eu-topos*) of voluptuous, perverse pleasure.

If the logic of fetishism displaces erotic desire onto an adjacent object, a metonymy of the living body, here the abstraction and isolation of the space itself, evoked to the imagination by description, even more than any described implement in it, provokes the orgasm of the Duc (and if Sade has his way, also that of the reader). Other of Sade's descriptions of spaces, apparently quite different in manifest content, nevertheless reinforce this eroticizing of spatial *displacement* or *disintegration*, as in this scene from *Philosophy in the Bedroom*, in which Madame de Saint-Ange explains the function of mirrors in heightening the pleasures of the sexual act she will perform with Eugenie, both for themselves and for Dolmance, whom Madame de Saint-Ange will "frig" as he watches them:

> MADAME DE SAINT-ANGE— . . . Onto the couch, my sweet.
> EUGENIE—Oh dear God! the delicious niche! But why all these mirrors?
> MADAME DE SAINT-ANGE—By repeating our attitudes and postures in a thousand different ways, they infinitely multiply those same pleasures for the persons seated here upon this ottoman. Thus everything is visible . . . everything must be seen; these images are so many groups disposed around those enchained by love, so many delicious tableaux wherewith lewdness waxes drunk and which soon drive it to climax.[5]

In the multiplication of the bodies' figures, all three are absorbed into a disintegrated and placeless space of reflection that excites pleasure more than the physical interaction of the flesh. The shattering of bodily unity in the mirrors' reflections already presages the shattering of identity in the trio's intermingled convulsions of orgasm, forming a "community" of perverts. It is only a quick step from this eroticized abstraction of voluptuous bodies to the eroticizing of abstract space itself, the "nowhere," solitary, closed, and void. Moreover, as Judovitz points out, there is a further "reflexivity" that relates the mirrors' multiplication and displacement of sexual pleasure of the body to the proliferating representations of sexual perversion in Sade's own text. Sade's "mirror" images of the body, she writes, "redefine pleasure as a perverse excess generated through representation. . . . Perversion in this context no longer functions as the expression of particular forms of deviation, but emerges as a general attitude toward representation" (Judovitz, 157). The most important mirror apparatus for generating such deviant representations is Sade's own literary text itself, with its ironizing layers of "mirror authors" who multiply and scatter authorial subjectivity throughout the work (Judovitz, 150).

Complementary to Sade's hint that his reader should seek in the described spaces of the text the source of a heightened voluptuary pleasure is the displacement into solitude they afford. Sade also explicitly instructs readers about how to use this text to expose and illuminate whatever passion might animate the individual reading in isolation. Sade's guidance follows the centrifugal and centripetal spatial displacements I have already discussed in connection with the mirrored niche and the subterranean dungeon: the isolation of bodies in havens of solitude, the multiplication and dissemination of bodies through representations. Sade multiplies in number and detail the perversities put on display before the reader, exploding the imaginable perspectives on sex into a profusion of shards; yet he also conjures a selectivity and singular focus that the reader's own hidden and perhaps unavowed passion must supply. Somewhere in this monstrous enumeration of perverse acts, Sade suggests, a reader will find something singularly his or her own:

> Many of the extravagances you are about to see illustrated will doubtless displease you . . . but there are amongst them a few which will warm you to the point of costing you some fuck, and that, reader, is all we ask of you. . . . It is up to you to take what you please and leave the rest alone, another reader will do the same, and little by little, everyone will find himself satisfied. It is the story of the magnificent banquet: six hundred plates offer themselves to your appetite; are you going to eat them all? No, surely not, but this prodigious variety enlarges the bounds of your choice. . . . [C]hoose and let lie the rest without declaiming against that rest simply because it does not have the power to please you. Consider that it will enchant someone else, and be a philosopher. (Sade, *120 Days*, 253)

Through close attention to the fine-grained differences spanning the analogies, the reader will come more definitively to identify the uniqueness of his or her own solitary passion. "As for the diversity," Sade writes:

> it is authentic, you may be sure of it; study closely that passion which to your first consideration seems perfectly to resemble another, and you will see that a difference does exist and that, however slight it may be, it possesses precisely that refinement, that touch which distinguishes and characterizes the kind of libertinage wherewith we are here involved. (253)

Sade suggests here a kind of parodic version, or perversion, of a Catholic spiritual exercise, intended to aid the imagination in envisioning the suffering of Christ and intensify the meditator's empathy by dwelling on the details of his wounded body. In his brilliant conjunction of Sade and Loyola (and beyond, Fourier), Barthes discovered an analogous "tradition" of Sadean *écriture* across historical periods and creeds: "the same writing: the same sensual pleasure in classification, the same mania for cutting up (the body of Christ, the body of the victim, the human soul), the same enumerative obsession (accounting for sins, tortures, passions, and even for accounting errors), the same image practice (imitation, tableau, séance), the same erotic, fantasmatic fashioning of the social system."[6]

Sade accounts for the attentional economy of his reader according to the same centrifugal/centripetal scheme, which pulls reading towards the extremes and excises the center where an imputed "normal" reader of novelistic narrative might dwell. Noting, for example, that his descriptions of his four principal libertines are done "not in a manner that would seduce or captivate a reader" (Sade, *120 Days*, 197), he nevertheless urges the reader to imagine the four attentively as he moves through his catalogue of outrages and tortures over months of narrated time:

> And such, dear reader, are the four villains in whose company I am going to have you pass a few months. I have done my best to describe them; if, as I have wished, I have made you familiar with even their most secret depths, nothing in the tale of their various follies will astonish you. I have not been able to enter into minute detail with what regards their tastes. . . . But as we move progressively along, you will have but to keep an attentive eye upon our heroes, and you'll have no trouble discerning their characteristic peccadillos and the particular type of voluptuous mania which best suits each of them. (210)

Yet as Sade indicates in another passage, his torrent of expository information about the libertines, the statutes of their contract, the location of their orgies, and their various accomplices and victims is not to be taken as the primary matter of interest at all. Rather, it is intended to prepare his reader's mind for an uncommitted attention in which, Sade has advised, she will become receptive to the sudden onrush of perverse passion when "the particular type of voluptuous passion" described corresponds with her own; and in which, as the proffered items correspond or not to her taste, the analogy of pleasure and community of singular perverts may be "philosophically" apprehended. "[A]fter the exact description we have given him of everything," Sade writes, his reader "will now have no more to do than follow the story, *lightly and voluptuously*, his mind impeded by nothing, his memory embarrassed by no unexpected intrusions" (240). Just as Sade's introductory descriptions, spatially, have led us down into Silling's dungeon, so too they lead the reader psychologically to an empty place of imagination in which, vigilant for any perverse passion that might arise, she need fear no obstacles, intrusions, or embarrassments to voluptuary expression.

Sade's text merely "displays" the array of perversions in which any given reader might find possible pleasure; it is the appropriate mindset and affectivity of the reader, however, in complicity with Sade as author, that provides the machinery by which the actualization of perverse pleasure might be carried to consummation. Through those descriptions that resonate with a reader's singular passion, Sade offers a direct, spasmodic pleasure from reading. For those descriptions that do not so move the reader, Sade offers the compensatory analogue of pleasure, an intellectual apprehension that other readers, though not moved by the same descriptions to orgasm, will have been analogously stimulated by some other act included somewhere in the "anthology" of perversions. Through this analogy, in turn, Sade also seems to imply the potential coming-into-being of an impossible *community* of readers, who possess in common exclusively their own singular desires and the analogical distribution of fine differences among them. (Anticipating my later discussion of Fourier, Sade's appeal to analogy is a point of intersection with the utopian socialist. Fourier establishes an analogical system of "harmonies" as the basis of his utopia.)

Ironically or not, Sade recruits these readers as the citizens of a new republic of perversion, bearers of specifically *utopian* longings.[7] As Élisabeth Roudinesco puts it, "Sade is, in a sense, outlining a social model based upon the generalization of perversion."[8] Only by projecting Sade's thought into a utopian "nowhere" may we thus reconcile the asociality of his solitary desires with the incessant loquaciousness of his libertines and their creator's compulsive drive to exhaustively enumerate their crimes in writing. As Simone de Beauvoir correctly noted, "Sade's sexuality is not a biological matter. It is a social fact."[9] She might have added: the society in which Sade's sexuality could be actual finds place only in a utopian "nowhere."

Marcuse: Polymorphous Perversity as Aesthetic Utopia

In his influential "philosophical inquiry into Freud" *Eros and Civilization*, Marcuse dedicated a full chapter to the "aesthetic dimension."[10] It explores the elevation of human sensuousness to high culture in art, with reference to foundational texts of aesthetics by Baumgarten, Kant, and Schiller; but it also hints at aesthetic prospects that might open up beyond the limited forms and genres of art. Starting from art and extrapolating from it a holistic expansion of aesthetic experience, Marcuse suggests that a fully actualized aesthetic might felicitously reconcile even the lowest bodily instincts and sensations with symbolization, material organization, and play, thus ultimately diffusing the free governance of an "aesthetic state" over the whole of human life. Consistent with his focus on Freud, Marcuse connects sexuality and the aggressive and masochistic instincts with this liberation of sensuousness in an all-sided, free order of the aesthetic. Inevitably, then, Marcuse must deal with the problem of those destructive "passions," which appear under the sign of "perversion," in his redeemed society.[11]

Marcuse faces this challenge head-on, stressing the loose "polymorphous-perverse" nature of sexuality at its origin, and understanding the nomination of certain impulses and practices as "perversions" as a result of imposing social organization on essentially asocial drives: "The societal organization of the sex instinct taboos as perversions practically all its manifestations which do not serve or prepare for the procreative function" (*Eros and Civilization*, 49). But the repressed ineluctably returns in the form of perverse practices and representations, which "express rebellion against the subjugation of sexuality under the order of procreation, and against the institutions which guarantee this order" (49). Marcuse goes on to find in the perversions an insurrectionary symbol, revolting against the institutions of society and even against human nature itself. The perversions, in their symbolic nature, foreshadow the emergence of "the new man" of utopian fantasy:

> Against a society which employs sexuality as a means to a useful end, the perversions uphold sexuality as an end in itself. . . . They establish libidinal relationships which society must ostracize because they threaten to reverse the process of civilization which turned the organism into an instrument of work. They are a symbol of what had to be suppressed so that suppression could prevail and organize the ever more efficient domination of man and nature—a symbol of the destructive identity between freedom and happiness. (50–51)

Marcuse revisits the question of perversion later in the book, noting the role of civilized morality in tabooing the body as an object of pleasure, especially insofar as it enters into social relations of exchange and reciprocity. Up to now, Marcuse ironizes, this has been "the ill-reputed privilege of whores, degenerates, and perverts" (*Eros and Civilization*, 201). This morality reflects the social division between social and private spheres, in which reified exchange relations predominate in the former and idealized moral relations rule the latter. How then to understand what it would mean to overturn this order, extending the "privilege" of bodily reification—the treatment of the body as an object or implement of pleasure—from the social underworld to society as a whole?

Marcuse suggests that the reduction of reified relations in the social sphere (a coded way of speaking about the overcoming of capitalist exchange relations and the institution of some form of socialism) would allow the psycho-sexual taboos on the uses of the body to be mitigated. The body would be released into an expanded realm of pleasures:

> No longer used as a full-time instrument of labor, the body would be resexualized. The regression involved in this spread of the libido would first manifest itself in a reactivation of all erotogenic zones and, consequently, in a resurgence of pregenital polymorphous sexuality. . . . The body in its entirety

would become an object of cathexis, a thing to be enjoyed—an instrument of pleasure. This change in the value and scope of libidinal relations would lead to a disintegration of the institutions in which the private interpersonal relations have been organized, particularly the monogamic and patriarchal family. (201)

What Marcuse originally viewed as insurrectional in the perversions can now be incorporated into an evolutionary and transformational process, which defuses the destructive energies latent in the perversions. This liberation of the body under new institutional conditions must not, he underscores, be mistaken for "the release of constrained sexuality *within* the dominion of [existing] institutions" (*Eros and Civilization*, 202). The latter may at best be an insurrectional release of frustrations, in which "the libido continues to bear the mark of suppression and manifests itself in the hideous forms so well known in the history of civilization; in the sadistic and masochistic orgies of desperate masses, of 'society elites,' of starved bands of mercenaries, of prison and concentration camp guards" (202).

Marcuse's conceptual trajectory leads from rebellious perversion, subjugating all social and human reproduction to a singular sexual aim, into "a rationality of gratification in which reason and happiness converge" (224) and "a libidinal morality" (228): new forms of social and human reproduction no longer in contradiction with the experience of happiness and pleasure. In good Hegelian fashion, Marcuse has raised perversion to a new universality, but at the cost of dissolving its particular, provocative content and conditioning—and hence, in essence, canceling the category of "perversion" as such. For as Laplanche and Pontalis succinctly note in their entry on perversion in *The Language of Psychoanalysis*, "It is difficult to comprehend the idea of perversion otherwise than by reference to a norm,"[12] and it thus hardly makes sense to speak of perversion when its substantive content has been sublimated and rendered "normal" or even normative (as an element of Marcuse's new "libidinal morality," for instance). Moreover, as they note, "In psychoanalysis, the word 'perversion' is used exclusively in relation to sexuality," not, for example, in relation to deviant forms of non-sexual instincts such as self-preservation (307). In its universalization as envisioned by Marcuse, however, perversion, a sexualized manifestation of revolt under the conditions of repression, is redeemed as a higher form of reason and morality from which the specifically *sexual* aspect of pleasure has been dispersed across a spectrum of social spaces, practices, and objects. Perversion becomes, instead, a form of negativity in relation to deficiencies in the modern form of social rationality and, as a figure of utopia, a "not-yet" potential for the future.

Marcuse offers a comprehensive and compelling case for a "eudaemonistic" view of the perversions. By incorporating perversion into a generalized aesthetic, Marcuse revalues what in current society appear as singular, often destructive, and exclusively sexual acts, and reinterprets them as ethically justifiable precursors of—and eventually, contributors to—humankind's *collective*, sensuous happiness. Yet in what follows, I explore alternative views of perversion by thinkers who deploy it, as did Marcuse, for a critique of rationality, but unlike him, do not dissolve it into an ethical generality, thus dispossessing it of transgressive, singular, and insurrectionary characteristics. These thinkers—including Adorno and Horkheimer, Benjamin, Bataille, and Klossowski—tarry with perversion's negativity *as such*, observing, with differing degrees of approbation, the limits to its sublimation or mitigation. Their evaluation of perversion—and its implications for literary and other aesthetic forms it invests, for the potential forms of aesthetic pleasure these occasion—is marked by the persistence of the perverse: its stubborn demand to be treated on its own singular terms.

The Dark Side of Enlightenment: Horkheimer and Adorno

In the background of Marcuse's account, by necessity, stand two key historical reference points: Sade, whom Marcuse surprisingly mentions only under the mask of "sadism" or "sadomasochism," and the utopian socialist Fourier, to whom Marcuse devotes some explicit discussion in *Eros and Civilization*. Fourier, Marcuse suggests, is the most important modern thinker to have conceived of a social reorganization around the gratification of the passions, and in particular, through the idea of libidinally gratifying work. "The transformation of labor into pleasure is the central idea in Fourier's giant socialist utopia," Marcuse writes (*Eros and Civilization*, 217). Hence, "Fourier comes closer than any other utopian socialist to elucidating the dependence of freedom on non-repressive sublimation" (218). In his attempt to realize this aim through a complex, highly regulated system of subdivisions and correspondences, however, Fourier's utopia ultimately exemplifies for Marcuse a vision of rigidly administered passions rather than liberated ones. With a provocative reference to the Nazi mass organization of leisure—*Kraft durch Freude*[13]—Marcuse concludes: "The working communities of the *phalanstère* anticipate 'strength through joy' rather than freedom" (218). If Fourier can be viewed as a predecessor who was on the right path but went astray, Sade himself finds no place at all in Marcuse's libidinal republic and aesthetic state. The destructive instincts that now express themselves as sadism may, when sublimated, provide the necessary dose of negativity to modify the object of playful work, but will no longer be allowed to leap to extremes of cruelty, frenzy, and destruction, as in the oeuvre of Sade himself.

It is notable that Marcuse simply elides Sade from consideration, given the serious attention to Sade paid by his colleagues Adorno and Horkheimer in *Dialectic of Enlightenment* and by Benjamin in his investigations of nineteenth-century Paris. In their "excursus" entitled "Juliette or Enlightenment and Morality," Horkheimer and Adorno treat Sade as Kant's evil twin, whose work betrays the self-consuming, destructive dynamic of Enlightenment rationality. Sade's wicked initiate Juliette, in their account, is a perfect avatar of Sade; she:

> embodies [in psychological terms] neither unsublimated nor regressive libido but intellectual pleasure in regression—*amor intellectualis diaboli*, the joy of defeating civilization with its own weapons. She loves systems and logic. She wields the instrument of rational thought with consummate skill.[14]

They present Juliette as an authentic *perversion* of Enlightenment: inseparable from the intellectual methods, themes, and concerns of Enlightment thought, she turns them towards deviant ends of cruelty and pleasure. Almost concurrently with Horkheimer and Adorno, Maurice Blanchot, in his *Lautréamont and Sade*, likewise foregrounded Sade's intimate entanglement of rationality and irrationality, his proliferating *logic* of perversion. "This is Sade's primary and main peculiarity," Blanchot writes:

> that at every moment, his theoretical ideas release the irrational forces that are bound up with them. These forces at once animate and frustrate his ideas, doing so with such impetus that his ideas resist these forces, and then yield to them, seeking to master this impetus, which effectively they do, but only while simultaneously releasing other obscure forces, which will lead, twist, and pervert them anew. The result is that everything said is clear, but seems at the mercy of something unsaid, which a bit later is revealed and is again incorporated by the logic, but, in turn, it obeys the movement of a still hidden force. In the end, everything is brought to light, everything comes to be said, but this everything is also again buried within the obscurity of unreflective thought and unformulatable moments.[15]

For Horkheimer and Adorno, this return of an obscure, repressed affectivity within the critical movement of rational thought is first and foremost a *social* dialectic, the unfolding of the unresolved relation between enlightenment and domination. In the microcosm of his châteaux, through the alternating narratives and destructive orgies of his libertines, Sade gives a terrifying exposition of its logic.

With reference to Roger Caillois's theory of festival, developed under the aegis of the Collège de Sociologie in collaboration with Bataille, Klossowski, and Leiris, Horkheimer and Adorno also present Sade's masters and their apprentice Juliette as figures of the rationalization of pleasure, which has a long historical trajectory from the primitive festival to the modern vacation. The eighteenth-century Enlightenment represents a key moment in the demythification and secularization of pleasure, thus constituting a landmark in the long formation of the human animal through the domination of nature. Yet in Horkheimer and Adorno's reading, in the perverse activities of his libertines, Sade discloses the continuing proximity of modern leisure to primitive sacrificial ritual, which in no way contradicts the formal rationality he imposes through his cataloguing of the orgies:

> The rulers introduce pleasure as a rational measure, a tribute paid to imperfectly subdued nature; they seek at once to detoxify it and to preserve it in higher culture; to administer it to their subjects in controlled doses where it cannot be entirely withdrawn. Pleasure becomes an object of manipulation, until it finally perishes in the administrative arrangements. (*Dialectic of Enlightenment*, 83)

Like Marcuse, they too deploy an ironic analogy to Nazi "Strength through Joy," but they see Sade rather than Fourier as the precursor of totally administered leisure: "In fascism they are supplemented by the collective fake intoxication, concocted from radio, headlines, and Benzedrine" (83). The sphere of free time, which might liberate libidinal pleasures that are useless from the perspective of work, has over the course of time since Sade become the managed complement of work, as rationalized consumption. The truly perverse instincts continue to return and seek expression … in destructive frenzies of fury, crime, violence, and war—a secret truth about modern rationality that Sade, as one of the "black writers of the bourgeoisie," unflinchingly betrays. Yet implicitly, Horkheimer and Adorno also suggest that administered leisure provides an ironic hermeneutic on Sade's own text, produced in the enforced "idleness" of his prison cell, as his way of "killing time" that is anything but "free." Sade's text, they imply, uncannily anticipates the rigid schematism of manipulated leisure. Reading Sade's extended litany of outrages induces in the reader a disintegration of thought analogous to that which the "hit parade" of pseudo-novelties produces in today's consumer of Culture Industry goods.

Sade with Fourier: Benjamin

In contrast to Horkheimer and Adorno, Benjamin approached Sade from the utopian side. The utopian socialist Fourier was a central figure in his research on the Paris arcades, which, he suggests, Fourier's architecturally and passionally organized "phalansteries" anticipated. In turn, the arcades retain traces of Fourier's visions of a libidinally organized utopian society of abundance. Benjamin dedicated a whole notebook of his *Arcades Project* to notes on Fourier, for whom he reveals a persistent fascination. As Klossowski recalls, Benjamin saw Fourier's social distribution of the passions as a complement to the Marxian critique of capitalism (a view reinforced by Benjamin's parallel interest in Johann Jakob Bachofen's theory of universal promiscuity during primitive matriarchy, which returns in distorted form in modernity in the marginalized figures of the prostitute, the androgyne, and the fetishist). In a retrospective memoir in 1969, Klossowski reported that the Collège de Sociologie intellectual leadership (Bataille, Caillois, Leiris, and Klossowski himself):

> questioned [Benjamin] even more insistently about what we sensed was his most authentic basis, namely, his personal version of a "phalansterian" revival. Sometimes he talked about it to us as if it were something "esoteric," simultaneously "erotic and artisanal," underlying his explicit Marxist conceptions. Having the means of production in common would permit substituting for the abolished social classes a redistribution of society into *affective classes*. A freed industrial production, instead of mastering affectivity, would expand its forms and organize its exchanges.... [W]ork would be in collusion with lust, and cease to be the other, punitive side of the coin.[16]

Not only, however, does Benjamin take a more positive stance towards Fourier than Marcuse, recovering him as libidinal revolutionary from the nineteenth-century polemics of "scientific socialism" against "utopian socialism," most famously by Friedrich Engels in 1880. He also extends this approbation to Fourier's dark counterpart, Sade, making explicit his own redemptive view of perversion as a singularly expressed desire in which the utopian wish for a passionally configured society was latent:

> The kinship between Fourier and Sade resides in the constructive moment that is proper to all sadism.... Fourier's harmonies ... are altogether his conception, and they give to the harmony something inaccessible and protected; they surround the *harmoniens* as though with barbed wire. The happiness of the phalanstery is a *bonheur barbelé*. On the other hand, Fourierist traits can be recognized in Sade. The experiences of the sadists, as presented in his *120 Jours de Sodome*, are, in their cruelty, exactly that extreme that is touched by

the extreme idyllic of Fourier.... The sadist, in his experiments, could chance on a partner who longs for just those punishments and humiliations which his tormentor inflicts. All at once, he could be standing in the midst of one of those harmonies sought after by the Fourierist utopia.[17]

Benjamin's note recognizes the "ou-topian" aspect that Fourier's phalansterian enclosures share with Sade's isolated castles: both are imaginative "nowheres" fenced off from the world where a new logic of social and passional combination—a "*bonheur barbelé*"—can be explored. Fourier's happiness, accordingly, is pervaded by forces of repulsion as well as attraction, and spiked with the promise of organized pain as well as orchestrated pleasure. In sum, it partakes of the destructive negativity of Sade's "other place," as well as of the harmonized passions of the phalansterian "good place." Although this entry remained an isolated note that Benjamin did not develop at greater length, his confrontation of Sade's *ou-topia* with Fourier's *eu-topia* was prescient: this conjunction would again surface in the French context in the wake of the 1968 revolts, with Klossowski's late essays "Sade and Fourier" and "Living Currency" in 1970 and in Barthes's 1971 book *Sade Fourier Loyola*. Like Barthes, Benjamin not only speaks to the complementary sexual and utopian-social content of Sade's and Fourier's texts; he also implies that in their convergence, in their spark across extremes of the idyllic and the cruel, an emergent genre of modern utopian communication was being defined.

Benjamin's own exploration of forms of "mimetic" communication emerging under the impetus of new technological media—a communication that is embodied, affective, gestural and intuitive, mediated by "images"—suggests how he might have conceived the experience of reading this utopian text. Less a discursive representation of a program or an ideology, it was intended to catalyze and shape the "reader's" affective forces, in the way that Artaud imagined the spectator of his theatre of cruelty being affected, a spectator to whom, he wrote, "violent scenes have transferred their blood ... violence and bloodshed having been placed at the service of the violence of thought."[18] Through the reader's aroused body, the book might flow over into social space and engage with other bodies there in shared action. Dipping into the image-store of eighteenth-century France for an example, Benjamin in his "Theses on the Philosophy of History" cites an incident in which revolutionaries shot out the clocks in towers at multiple places in Paris at the same moment; it was for him the coming together of an impossible "mimetic" community in a charged moment of "now-time" (*Jetztzeit*). He might, however, instead have looked to Fourier and Sade for an alternative picture of such affective reading: the convergence of singular passions into the embodied community of the phalanstery, or in the mingled bodies of the libertine orgy.

From Sade to God: Bataille

From the beginnings of his oeuvre in texts of the late 1920s and early 1930s such as "The Use Value of D.A.F. Sade," through his mature theoretical works such as *The History of Eroticism* (c. 1951) intended as the second volume of *The Accursed Share* trilogy, through such late writings as *Erotism* (1957), *Literature and Evil* (1957), and *The Tears of Eros* (1961), the writings of Bataille dwelled with obsessive consistency on eroticism, especially its most extreme and perverse forms. In particular, Bataille stresses two basic connections: the association of eroticism with the experience of death and decay, and the affinity of eroticism with the sacred and the mystical. Both death and the sacred for Bataille represent the experiential limits of rationality and thought, and hence play a critical function in his deconstruction of philosophical, economic, and theological systems, as well as in his own political and literary writings.

Thus, for example, in his early "open letter to his comrades" entitled "The Use Value of D.A.F. Sade," Bataille formulates his own historico-political present as one of social decay leading a new morality first starkly formulated in Sade's writings:

> [N]othing can stop the movement that leads human beings toward an ever more shameless awareness of the erotic bond that links them to death, to cadavers, and to horrible physical pain. . . . Since it is true that one of man's attributes is the derivation of pleasure from the suffering of others . . . it is time to choose between the conduct of cowards afraid of their own joyful excesses, and the conduct of those who judge that any given man need not cower like a hunted animal, but instead can see all the moralistic buffoons as so many dogs.[19]

At this stage of Bataille's thinking, when as a renegade surrealist he still sought to reconcile his anarchic anti-morality with the necessity of a communist revolution against capitalism, he projects "two distinct phases in human emancipation," the first inspired by Lenin, the latter by Sade:

> During the revolutionary phase, the current phase that will only end with the world triumph of socialism, only the social revolution can serve as an outlet for collective impulses, and no other activity can be envisaged in practice.
> But the post-revolutionary phase implies the necessity of a division between the economic and political organization of society . . . and . . . an antireligious

and asocial organization having as its goal orgiastic participation in different forms of destruction . . .

Such an organization can have no other conception of morality than the one scandalously affirmed for the first time by . . . Sade. ("The Use Value of D.A.F. Sade," 101)

Bataille thus anticipates the actualization of Sade's system as a model of a utopian, post-revolutionary society. However, given that he has no way of conceiving the two "phases of human emancipation" as anything but radically exclusive ("During the revolutionary phase . . . no other activity can be envisaged in practice"), nor any way of showing how or why the total industrial and state organization of Soviet communism should give rise to an anarchic society of generalized perversion, his project of a Sadean society remains rigorously "utopian," also in the pejorative sense of lacking any chance of translating his visions into reality. In his writings following World War II, Bataille relinquishes his utopian hopes for collective actualization—the projection of perverse pleasure into shared happiness, however convulsive—and now accepts extreme, perverse eroticism solely as a form in which human consciousness may tragically confront "the impossible," a feature it shares with mysticism and death.

In *Erotism*, this utopian moment of Bataille's engagement with perversion has been weakened to the recognition that Sade has made it possible for the "normal man" of the present to become aware of human beings' extreme possibilities—those that may eventuate in violence, destructiveness, and perversion. In "De Sade and the Normal Man," Bataille presents the confrontation with Sade's consciousness as an existential test the normal man must today stand, even if only to preserve his normality by suppressing some of the possibilities that he has nevertheless been made aware of:

[I]t is connected with the need of the normal man of today to become aware of himself and to know clearly what his sovereign aspirations are in order to limit their possibly disastrous consequences; to accept these if it suits him but not to push them any further than he needs, and resolutely to oppose them if his self-awareness cannot tolerate them.[20]

Sade's awareness, Bataille makes clear, centers on the conjunction of horror and pleasure, which he bears forth in an ever-widening dialectic of revulsion before the intolerable and with a will to expose and experience the impossible:

The fact is that what de Sade was trying to bring to the surface of the conscious mind was precisely the thing that revolted the mind. For him the most revolting thing was the most powerful means of exciting pleasure. Not only did he reach the most singular revelations by this means, but from the very first he set before the consciousness, things which it could not tolerate. (*Erotism*, 195)

Bataille concludes that Sade's desire to mingle horror and heightened consciousness ("enlightenment") pursued antinomic aims, which could not be realized simultaneously. Sade, Bataille writes, "wanted to revolt our conscious minds, he would have also liked to enlighten them but he could not do both at the same time" (Bataille, *Erotism*, 196). Today, however:

> we realize that without de Sade's cruelty we should never have penetrated with such ease the once inaccessible domain where the most painful truths lay hidden. . . . [I]f today the average man has a profound insight into what transgression means for him, de Sade was the one who made ready the path. Now the average man knows that he must become aware of the things which repel him most violently—those things which repel us most violently are part of our nature. (196)

In the popularization of Sade's insight to "the normal man," we glimpse the last trace of Bataille's earlier projection of a Sadean utopia, in which each would live in a post-revolutionary society of generalized perversion, a society generically (dis-)organized to actualize for all the liberty of Sade's sovereign masters. Through reading, the "normal man" can now partake of Sade's consciousness "with ease," but at the cost of inhibition, before the intolerability of this awareness's contents, and relinquishment of any translation of consciousness into action. Bataille thus cuts the affective link between reading and perversion upon which Sade based his utopian community of perverts, aroused to participation by each finding his own singular passion amid Sade's exhaustive and otherwise revolting catalogue of outrages.

In *Literature and Evil*, in fact, Bataille extends this relation of consciousness and inhibited action to Sade himself. Bataille now sees Sade's confinement in the Bastille as the *positive* condition of his attainments in consciousness. Any possibility of active gratification of desire comes at the cost of the consciousness it intensifies so long as it is unfulfilled:

> We see that the consciousness of desire is hardly accessible: desire alone alters the clarity of consciousness, but it is above all the possibility of satisfaction which suppresses it . . . [H]ad he not been imprisoned, the disorderly life he led would never have given him the possibility of nurturing an interminable desire which he was unable to satisfy.[21]

The Bastille, he concludes, "was the crucible in which the conscious limitations of being were slowly destroyed by the fire of a passion prolonged by powerlessness" (103). Unwittingly, Bataille here almost reiterates the conclusions of Adorno and Horkheimer, who consider Sade's achievement as the dark chronicler of the age of self-destructive Enlightenment to be predicated on his unbroken swathes of (un)free time, within the strictures of his prison cell. Both Bataille and Horkheimer/Adorno expound the same aporia of Sade's thought: one can write (and by extension, read this writing) to become conscious of a dark truth about modernity; or one can act, but at the cost of dissipating consciousness. The truth that may be communicated via texts evaporates as soon as it begins to pass into efficacious action. Sade's utopia, therefore, is once again consigned to a nowhere, to a castle of solitude that is indiscernible from a dungeon.

In his posthumously published *History of Eroticism*, Bataille specifies this antinomy of consciousness and action for the relation of pleasure and happiness in eroticism. In essence, Bataille dissevers pleasure, which is individually experienced, from happiness, which implies at least the potential for communication and sharing. In Bataille's view, happiness can only be *ou-topic*, "out of this world" of seriousness and work:

> The truth is that we have no real happiness except by spending to no purpose. And we always want to be sure of the uselessness of our expenditure, to feel as far away as possible from a serious world, where the increase of resources is the rule. But . . . eroticism . . . is ordinarily an impulse of aggressive hatred, an urge to betray. That is why a feeling of anguish is connected with it, and also why, on the other hand, when the hatred is a powerlessness and the betrayal an abortive act, the erotic element is ludicrous.[22]

We may read in Bataille's "far away" the utopianizing vector, in which happiness can be achieved, but at the cost of any real place in which it can be experienced. Indeed, extreme eroticism—and behind Bataille's conception of it, Sade's whole monstrous catalogue of horrors—passes beyond even an intangible utopia into tragic consciousness experienced in anguish.[23]

Bataille's obscene novel *Madame Edwarda*, published pseudonymously in 1941 and 1945, then once again under his own name in 1956, illustrates the implications of this shift. *Madame Edwarda* narrates the frenzied encounter of a drunken, anguished narrator and a mentally disordered prostitute, through which Bataille explores the intolerable premise of God's incarnation in the whore and the narrator-john's devastating encounter with the numinous through her. In the final scene, Edwarda brings a cab driver into the back seat and mounts his penis while the narrator sits alongside them. As Bataille presents the scene, Edwarda becomes a base version of Bernini's Saint Theresa, ecstatic as the angel's arrow pieces her womb. The erotic act for Edwarda is the inducement of a mystic state in which orgasm, tears, and death mingle together in an eclipse of self:

> The milky outpouring travelling through her, the jet spitting from the root, flooding her with joy, came spurting out again in her very tears: burning tears streamed from her wide-open eyes. Love was dead in those eyes, they contained a daybreak aureate chill, a transparence wherein I read death's letters. And everything swam drowned in that dreaming stare: a long member, stubby fingers prying open fragile flesh, my anguish, and the recollection of scum-flecked lips—there was nothing which didn't contribute to that blind dying into extinction.[24]

The narrator witnesses Edwarda's extreme pleasure, which "went on and on, weirdly, unendingly." He himself, however, tarries in anguished emptiness, in consciousness intensified by desire rather than action to gratify it, thus suspending his participation in Edwarda's pleasure:

> [S]he saw me to the bottom of my dryness, from the bottom of my desolation I sensed her joy's torrent run free. My anguish resisted the pleasure I ought to have sought. Edwarda's pain-wrung pleasure filled me with an exhausting impression of bearing witness to a miracle. My own distress and fever seemed small things to me. But that was what I felt, those are the only great things in me that gave answer to the rapture of her whom in the deeps of an icy silence I called "my heart." (*Madame Edwarda*, 158)

As Bataille emphasizes in his preface to *Madame Edwarda*, his main interest in eroticism in this novel and more generally at this point in his thinking is not with sexuality as such, and even less so with the specific content of perversion, but rather with eroticism as an approach to the limit-experiences of death and the extinction of subjectivity—to destructive transgression of the limits set by and on human rationality. To dwell on the perversions themselves, however, even with the extremity of Sade, is to stop short of a vertiginous, direct encounter with death and extinction. They do not go to the final limit and beyond:

> Even in Sade's universe, death's terrible edge is deflected away from the self and aimed at the partner, the victim, the *other*—and, contradictorily, Sade shows the other as the most eminently delightful expression of life. The sphere of eroticism is inescapably plighted to duplicity and ruse. (*Madame Edwarda*, 142–43)

In dwelling on the perverse *pleasures* of his libertines, Sade must also maintain the world of other people and objects, even if only to systematically destroy it. For Bataille, Sade's negativity does not go far enough to abolish the world as a whole, nor could reading Sade ever catapult the reader into the fully a-rational, impossible space that Bataille seeks to experience.

Sade halts, in Bataille's view, before the threshold of a more radical ascesis of subjectivity, an emptiness beyond pleasure, that opens up the dark immensity in which religious mystics encountered God. Moreover, with his turn away from sexual pleasure, heightened and singularized in perversion, towards anguish in eroticism, Bataille likewise brackets any question of specifically *aesthetic pleasure*, pleasure in narrating and reading, which Sade perversely had intertwined with sexual pleasure and pleasure in destruction. Sade, we recall, recognized that many of the perversions he recounted in his books would horrify or disgust a reader; but given his premise of a universal *capacity* for perversion, he also postulated that an exhaustive and differentiated enough catalogue of perversions would offer each reader the chance to gratify her own singular passion. In abolishing this motif of gratified pleasure, Bataille also undermines any possibility of a utopian aesthetic community of singular readers, a perverse "aesthetic state." Reading for pleasure—normal or perverse—can only now appear to Bataille a diversion from the task of confronting the anguish of death. This anti-aesthetic conclusion returns all the way back to Bataille's intransigent denunciations of surrealist lyricism and the allure of poetry in "The Use Value of D.A.F. Sade" and other early writings.[25]

Perversion and its pleasures, pursued within the necessary lack of liberty that "the serious world" allows, offer only a laughable parody of sovereignty. The heightened consciousness that provokes this laughter looks in anguish beyond human being towards an impossible freedom: towards the unlimited negation of a "limitless revolt" (*The Accursed Share* II and III, 184), in a revulsion from the world that "retains only eroticism's transgression in a pure state, or the complete destruction of the world of common reality, the passage from the perfect Being of positive theology to that formless and modeless God of a 'theopathy' akin to the 'apathy' of Sade" (*The Accursed Share* II and III, 171). But in this limitless space of mystical or apathetic dissolution of self, the problematic of organized hedonism, even in its Sadean exasperation, simply becomes irrelevant. Pleasure and happiness now are mere specks in the limitless darkness of an a-subjective mystical imaginary. If Marcuse ultimately relinquished the specificity of the perversions by "sublimating" (in the psychoanalytic sense) them into the generality of human sensual activity, Bataille *absolutely* abolishes their singular contents, and the potential utopia of polymorphous erotics they project, in the unspeakable sublimity of God.

Will Sade Be My Neighbor?: Klossowski

In *Sade, My Neighbor*, Klossowski took up the problem of perversion as a point of entry to the paradoxical nature of Sade's communication and, by extension, the impossible "utopia" he gestures towards: a community of perverts, affected by narratives of perverse acts and connected analogically by their unconstrained pursuit of singular passions. Klossowski focuses rigorously on the nature of the pervert in Sade and formulates it with precision. What is crucial, for Klossowski, is that the pervert's relation to pleasure is constricted, compulsive, and essentially incommunicable (and thus anything but the liberty sought by the "libertine"). Indeed, the pervert's instantaneous and iterative relation to the object of craving even undercuts any narrative unfolding of time: "The pervert pursues the performance of one sole gesture; it is done in a moment. The pervert's existence becomes the constant waiting for the moment in which this gesture can be performed."[26] As such, the pervert is subindividual, "an arbitrary subordination of the habitual life functions to one sole insubordinate function, a craving for an improper object" (*My Neighbor*, 23). He is thus, at first glance, an unlikely model for Sade's cultivation of a polymorphous banquet of pleasures, for Sade's claim on liberty against subordination to law, or for his drive to exhaustively communicate, both linguistically and affectively, the outrages of his libertine protagonists.

The pervert's function is, however, exemplary in a different way for Sade: as a first term in a syllogism by which, through the generalizing mechanism of narrative and narrated argumentation, Sade establishes the principle of "universal prostitution," the surrender of private property in one's own body and its availability for use by any and all:

> [I]nasmuch as this insubordination of one sole function could only be concretized and thus become individuated in his case, [the pervert] suggests to Sade's reflections a multifold possibility of the redistribution of the functions. Beyond individuals "normally" constituted, he opens a broader perspective, that of sensuous polymorphy. . . . His existence consecrates the death of the species in him as an individual; his being is verified as a suspension of life itself. Perversion would thus correspond to a property of being, a property founded on the expropriation of life functions. An expropriation of one's own body and of others would be the meaning of this property of being. (*My Neighbor*, 22)

Taken outside of the context of other key components of Sade's outlook, such "expropriation" might even bear utopian traits, as Klossowski himself remarks with explicit reference to the Fourierist utopia of harmonized passions:

> For the expropriation of the corporal and moral self, the condition for universal prostitution, is still something that could be instituted, in the utopian sense of Fourier's phalanstery, which was based on the "interplay of the passions." As soon as this pooling together of the passions is established, there would no longer be the tension necessary for outrage, and sadism would dissipate. (19)

Klossowski thus imagines a social order that selectively interprets Sade's expropriation of property in one's own individual person and that mitigates his violence in a happy, hedonistically gratified collective. Klossowski also obliquely conjures the utopian perspectives that Benjamin and Marcuse develop, in a eudaemonistic interpretation of Sade that discerns a collective therapeutic value in perversion and the foundation of a new "norm" of a-normativity: "If the human race as a whole 'degenerated,' if there were no one left but avowed perverts—if integral monstrosity would thus prevail—one might think that Sade's 'goal' would have been reached, that there would no longer be any 'monsters' and 'sadism' would disappear" (20). But Klossowski makes clear that this is not the case and that no Sadean utopia is in fact possible, despite the apparent proximity of Sade and Fourier. Sade, he claims, made no "positive conceptual formulation" of the perversions (18), and because—here Klossowski is indebted to Bataille—outrage and transgression are ineradicable elements of Sade's system.

The use of perversion to compel transgression makes Sade not just conservative, Klossowski suggests, but *fatalistic* with respect to existing institutions and the norms that they support. Analogously, Sade treats the existence of perversions as simply given, with no explanation and no need to be explained. He has none of the curiosity of the psychoanalyst about their genesis or about their possible therapeutic remaking. Sade is interested only in what happens when perversions suddenly erupt—as they inevitably will—from the nourishing medium provided for them by norms. And because without norms to generate outrage through perversion, there is no transgression, Sade paradoxically affirms institutions and their norms in order to keep transgression coming. "In outrage," Klossowski writes, "what is outraged is maintained to serve as a support for transgression" (*My Neighbor*, 18). It is this self-regenerating dialectic of outrage in Sade that allows the intellectual movement from the sheer facticity of perversion to the logical scandal of the singular case, passing though the mediation of a generic reason that Sade's thinking sustains and transgresses.

Klossowski suggests that this mutually reinforcing tension in Sade between the acceptance of norms and the need to transgress decisively forecloses any extraction of a utopian content from Sade, whether as explicit doctrine or in more sidelong form. For as already noted, in

Sade's text "universal prostitution" and "integral monstrosity" already exist in "normal" society and depend on society continuing to exist as it is:

> Sade plants his character in the everyday world; he finds him in the midst of institutions, in the fortuitous circumstances of social life. Thus the world itself appears as the locus in which the secret law of the universal prostitution of beings is verified. Sade conceives the countergenerality to be thus already implicit in the existent generality, not in order to criticize institutions, but in order to demonstrate that of themselves institutions ensure the triumph of perversions. (*My Neighbor*, 26)

Klossowski thus denies any utopian possibililites to Sade's projected community of readers, each stimulated to discover his paradoxical commonality with other perverts by identifying that singular passion that moves him or her. Klossowski notes that this proposal is itself a sophism, a transgression of normative reason, seeking to persuade readers into complicity with transgression as such.

There are further snares, according to Klossowski, even in strong rejection of the perverse text's appeal to the reader to identify with it. Not only Sade's prescribed reader's response, arousal and orgasm ("warm you to the point of costing you some fuck"), but other strong, spontaneous movements of passions such as repulsion, fear, or disgust, viscerally affecting the body, cunningly invite the reader to identify "his own singularity—latent in him as in everyone" (*My Neighbor*, 26). From the recognition of a capacity for violent singular affect, even negative, it is only a short sophistic step to the possibility that there lurks within the reader also a capacity for singular *pleasure*, should the proper act or object be found. "It is not by arguments," Klossowski concludes, "that Sade's character can obtain the assent of his interlocutor but by complicity" (27), and this is equally true of the author's self-imputed relation to his readers.

This analysis ultimately leads Klossowski to conclude that Sade and Fourier can never form—as Benjamin argued, and in a different way Marcuse as well—convergent extremes of one utopian text, prefiguring a redeemed polymorphous-perverse society, a Sadean society without sadism. He instead arrives, in the end, at an either-or decision between Sade and Fourier. By 1970, Klossowski arrays himself on the side of Fourier and his utopia, against Sade's perversion of utopia, which ironically resembles the actual shape of late industrial modernity (as Horkheimer and Adorno also believed):

> From Fourier's perspective, Sade seemed little more than a prophet of doom, because what he created on a purely imaginative level only confirms the

persistent inequalities of the industrial world. Yet even if the evidence now tends to favor Sade, the belief that Fourier's vision of future happiness is a false or utopian prophecy is only a supposition on our part, and a fairly biased one as well. In Fourier's eyes, choosing Sade over Fourier amounts to *wanting* the inalterable.[27]

The choice of Fourier against Sade is, among other things, a choice to *unsettle* the fatality of the perversions, their mere facticity as implements of outrage and transgression in Sade, in order to recognize their creative mutability. This implies a different sort of utopian text and a different efficacy of reading than that anticipated by Sade. Reading would not be a *selective* process, identifying from an exhaustive store a latent though already virtually complete and exclusive passion that each brings to the community of perverts. Rather, it would reveal the *contingency* of readers' dispositions and their capacity to create and recreate themselves in the mold of new and collectively expressed passions. "On the whole," Klossowski concludes,

> if Fourier was or behaved like a prophet of happiness, it was because for him *nothing is set in stone*, by reason of the erotic spark itself, which is "divine" and thus essentially creative. To champion the *irreducible*, as Sade did . . . is to betray and strike at this erotic spark, which he clearly wanted to make the basis of his thought, yet nonetheless linked to institutions, thus condemning them to mutual destruction. . . . If perversity is ever to resume its place as a natural function of life, then aggressiveness must be free to create its own object: the serious business of perversion must be replaced by fun and games. (*Living Currency*, 82)

Klossowski, in the end, placed himself on the side of a socialized eroticism that has gone beyond perversion as defined by Sade, and in the cause of a collective happiness that emerges by dissolving and remaking existing institutions anew. In short, he affirms the utopian imagination of Fourier against the pseudo-utopian fatalism of Sade. And to Simone de Beauvoir's famous question, "Must we burn Sade?" this greatest expositor of Sade's writings seems to nod in response—after some hesitation—an ironic "perhaps."

Notes

1. Donatien Alphonse François, Marquis de Sade, *120 Days of Sodom, and Other Writings*, trans. Austryn Wainhouse and Richard Seaver (New York: Grove Press, 1966), 253.
2. Axel Honneth, "Rejoinder," in Honneth, *Reification: A New Look at an*

Old Idea, with Judith Butler, Raymond Geuss, and Jonathan Lear, ed. Martin Jay (Oxford: Oxford University Press, 2008), 157.
3. These issues are explored in historical and theoretical depth in James W. Steintrager, *The Autonomy of Pleasure: Libertines, License, and Sexual Revolution* (New York: Columbia University Press, 2016). In his final chapter, "Canonizing Sade: Eros, Democracy, and Differentiation," Steintrager traces the contemporary reception of Sade's thought within literary and cultural theory and in popular culture; see 263–98.
4. Dalia Judovitz, *The Culture of the Body: Genealogies of Modernity* (University of Michigan Press, 2000), 156.
5. Sade, *The Complete Justine, Philosophy in the Bedroom, and Other Writings*, trans. Richard Seaver and Austryn Wainhouse (New York: Grove Press, 1965), 202–3.
6. Roland Barthes, *Sade Fourier Loyola*, trans. Richard Miller (Berkeley and Los Angeles: University of California Press, 1976), 3.
7. In Sade's most extended and explicitly political discussion in his novels, his parodic republican treatise "Yet Another Effort, Frenchmen, If You Would Become Republicans" in *Philosophy in the Bedroom*, Sade pays tribute to his utopian lineage through the Chevalier's exposition of his idea of a republic founded on the abolition of private property in one's own body and the categorical imperative to universal prostitution: "Thomas More proves in his *Utopia* that it becomes women to surrender themselves to debauchery, and that great man's ideas were not always pure dreams" (Sade, *The Complete Justine, Philosophy in the Bedroom, and Other Writings*, 323–24). Sade appends a further footnote to his reference to More: "The same thinker wished affianced couples to see each other naked before marriage. How many alliances would fail, were this law enforced! It might be declared that the contrary is indeed what is termed purchase of merchandise sight unseen" (324).
8. Élisabeth Roudinesco, *Our Dark Side: A History of Perversion*, trans. David Macey (Cambridge: Polity Press, 2009), 35.
9. Simone de Beauvoir, "Must We Burn Sade?" in Sade, *120 Days of Sodom, and Other Writings*, 30.
10. Herbert Marcuse, *Eros and Civilization: A Philosophical Inquiry into Freud* (Boston: Beacon Press, 1966).
11. I am indebted for my discussion of Marcuse's *Eros and Civilization* to Joel Whitebook, *Perversion and Utopia: A Study in Psychoanalysis and Critical Theory* (Cambridge, MA: The MIT Press, 1995), 24ff. I note, however, that perversion is only treated in detail in Whitebook's essay on Freud's critique of civilization, while the other essays treat various aspects of utopia in psychoanalysis and Frankfurt School Critical Theory. Whitebook's explicit connection of perversion with utopia is limited to his critical discussion of Marcuse.
12. Jean Laplanche and Jean-Bertrand Pontalis, *The Language of Psychoanalysis*, trans. Donald Nicolson-Smith (New York: W.W. Norton and Company, 1976), 306.
13. Note that the polysemic German term "Freude" encompasses a range of interrelated meanings, including joy, enjoyment, pleasure, happiness, and lust.

14. Max Horkheimer and Theodor W. Adorno, *Dialectic of Enlightenment*, ed. Gunzelin Schmidt Noerr, trans. Edmund Jephcott (Stanford: Stanford University Press), 74.
15. Maurice Blanchot, *Lautréamont and Sade*, trans. Stuart Kendall and Michelle Kendall (Stanford: Stanford University Press, 2004), 9.
16. Pierre Klossowski, "Entre Sade et Fourier," in *The College of Sociology (1937–39)*, ed. Denis Hollier (Minneapolis: University of Minnesota Press, 1988), 388–89. For discussion of Benjamin's relations with the College of Sociology, see Tyrus Miller, "Mimesis, Mimicry, and Critical Theory in Exile: Walter Benjamin's Approach to the Collège de Sociologie," in *Exile, Borders, Diasporas*, eds. Elazar Barkan and Marie-Denise Shelton (Stanford: Stanford University Press, 1998), 123–33.
17. Walter Benjamin, *The Arcades Project*, trans. Howard Eiland and Kevin McLaughlin (Cambridge, MA: The Belknap Press of Harvard University Press, 1999), 639.
18. Antonin Artaud, *Selected Writings*, ed. Susan Sontag, trans. Helen Weaver (Los Angeles and Berkeley: University of California Press, 1976), 258–59.
19. Georges Bataille, "The Use Value of D.A.F. Sade (An Open Letter to My Comrades)," in *Visions of Excess: Selected Writings, 1927–1939*, ed. and trans. Allan Stoekl (Minneapolis: University of Minnesota Press, 1985), 101.
20. Georges Bataille, *Erotism: Death and Sensuality*, trans. Mary Dalwood (San Francisco: City Lights Books, 1986), 185.
21. Georges Bataille, *Literature and Evil*, trans. Alastair Hamilton (New York: Urizen Books, 1973), 102.
22. Georges Bataille, *The Accursed Share, Volumes II and III: The History of Eroticism and Sovereignty*, revised edition, trans. Robert Hurley (New York: Zone Books, 1991), 178.
23. See also Jean-Paul Sartre's critique in his review of Bataille's 1943 book *Inner Experience*: Sartre, "A New Mystic," in *Critical Essays*, trans. Chris Turner (London: Seagull Books, 2010), 219–93.
24. Georges Bataille, *Madame Edwarda*, in Bataille, *My Mother. Madame Edwarda. The Dead Man*, trans. Austryn Wainhouse (London: Marion Boyars, 1995), 158.
25. See, for example: "Poetry at first glance seems to remain valuable as a method of mental projection (in that it permits one to accede to an entirely heterogeneous world). But it is only too easy to see that it is hardly less debased than religion. It has almost always been at the mercy of the great historical systems of appropriation. And insofar as it can be developed autonomously, this autonomy leads it onto the path of a total poetic conception of the world, which ends at any one of a number of aesthetic homogeneities" (Bataille, "The Use-Value of D.A.F. Sade," 97).
26. Pierre Klossowski, *Sade, My Neighbor*, trans. Alphonso Lingis (Chicago: Northwestern University Press, 1991), 22–23.
27. Pierre Klossowski, *Living Currency, Followed by Sade and Fourier*, eds. Vernon W. Cisney, Nicolae Morar, and Daniel W. Smith (London: Bloomsbury, 2017), 82.

Chapter 9

Interdisciplinary Legacies: Critical Theory and Authoritarian Culture

This chapter considers one of the most salient aspects of contemporary critical humanistic scholarship and cultural practice: its imperative to push beyond the limits of single disciplines towards the "interdisciplinarity" necessary to apprehend complex sociocultural phenonema. If the current demand for interdisciplinarity has reached a new peak of intensity, it also has a deeper history in the legacy of critical theory. In a tribute article for Georg Simmel in 1918, Lukács had already identified as a crucial distinction of Simmel's work his methodological pressure on separate disciplines, his opening up of "new subject areas" through close attention to the "qualitative and unique" aspects of concrete objects and phenomena and the "manifold and intricate connections" between them.[1] Lukács goes on to note the impact of Simmel's interdisciplinary thrust on other key figures of German sociology: "A sociology such as is undertaken by Max Weber, Troeltsch, Sombart and others has become possible only on the ground laid by him, however much [they] may differ from him methodologically" (149). Such interdisciplinary impulses are true as well of the early twentieth-century radical intellectual circles of Budapest, including the Galilei Circle[2] and Lukács's own Sunday Circle,[3] which impacted fields such as sociology, philosophy, history, economics, film theory, and art history through figures of the later Hungarian diaspora including Karl Mannheim, Arnold Hauser, Oszkár Jászi, Karl Polanyi, Michael Polanyi, Béla Balázs, Charles de Tolnay, and Johannes Wilde. Even more enduring and influential as an interdisciplinary formation, however, was the Institut für Sozialforschung, the "Frankfurt School."

In what follows, I first offer framing observations about the Frankfurt School's conception of interdisciplinary research and its relation to interdisciplinary research in the humanities and interpretative social sciences today. I suggest that while the American reception of the Frankfurt School, particularly in the humanities and in cultural studies, has been extensive, this reception has also been one-sided and based on the prestige of a relatively small number of English-language translated texts by three major individuals within the larger group: Benjamin, Adorno, and Marcuse. In addition, I argue, the Institut für Sozialforschung itself incubated at least two distinct types of interdisciplinary research—an individual and a group research model—which were held in tension rather than synthesized into a unitary framework. Yet only one of these models has had a significant impact on present-day humanities research, at least in Anglophone universities. Though I do not question the productivity of that reigning interdisciplinary paradigm, I also wish to recall the group dimensions of interdisciplinarity that characterized the Frankfurt School's research activity and consider whether they might have value as alternatives within discussions and debates about disciplinarity and interdisciplinarity in the contemporary university.

In the second section, I take up the case of an explicitly interdisciplinary special project of the Institut für Sozialforschung, published in 1936 as *Studien über Authorität und Familie*, which engaged a wide range of expertise across disciplines and demonstrated the methodological implications of the pre–World War II Frankfurt School's vision of interdisciplinary research.

In the third and final part of the chapter, I depart from the Frankfurt School framework to consider a more contemporary analogue to their interdisciplinary focus on authoritarianism: the post-socialist musealization of "totalitarianism" by digital artist George Legrady (*An Anecdoted Archive of the Cold War*, 1993) and film designer and architect Attila F. Kovács (Budapest's *Terror Háza*/House of Terror and his related *Emlékpont*/Memory Point in Hódmezővásárhely). I consider Legrady's and Kovács's problematic interdisciplinary approaches as complementary if antithetical perspectives on Hungary's dictatorships, which continue to resonate in post-socialist artistic attempts to come to terms with the historical traumas of the twentieth century.

The Frankfurt School and Models of Interdisciplinarity

The Institut für Sozialforschung was centered on its director and his inner circle of about six to eight close collaborators, an advisory and editorial circle including representatives of several specialized disciplines. This inner circle made assignments and assessed the written studies of an outer layer of affiliated contributors. There was also a much wider circle of scholars friendly to their project with whom they remained in looser contact, mostly through the extensive review section of the journal and occasional collaboration and consultation on particular studies and projects; as noted, even Lukács figured among this outer circle of contributors. Among the Frankfurt School's principal scholars, however, there developed two major analyses of the *limits* of specialized disciplinary knowledge in the modern age and two models of how to go beyond these limits and practice interdisciplinary research. These two models were held in tension in the operation of the Institut: on the one hand, there were *topical, problem-based* ventures into interdisciplinary criticism by individual scholars, and on the other hand, the larger *group-oriented* inter- and multi-disciplinary research activity represented by the Institut as a collective, embodied most importantly in the editorial practice of its journal, the *Zeitschrift für Sozialforschung*.

In the first model of interdisciplinary criticism, the individual scholar deploys a variety of disciplinary materials and frameworks in a unique, singular constellation to analyze and criticize a particular object of study—for example, in Adorno's case, his critique of popular music that constellates Lukácsian-Marxist concepts of reification and commodity fetishism with Freudian psychoanalysis, formal analysis of music, and sociological study of listening. This model has proven very influential in the contemporary humanities. Recent scholarship has carried the thought of Benjamin and Adorno into a wide range of otherwise diverse approaches, including cultural studies, film theory and criticism, visual culture studies, and historicist literary criticism. Martin Jay aptly describes the Benjamin-Adorno model as deriving from a preliminary *acceptance* of the irreducible multiplicity of disciplines and disciplinary knowledge, a condition that Lukács had also confronted in his early work in Heidelberg with Weber and the neo-Kantian philosophers there. As Jay writes, there is "no methodological remedy to the fragmentations of knowledge expressed in the chaos of competing disciplines. The goal of a fully integrated interdisciplinary project [is] thus unattainable at present."[4] Rather than striving towards a reconstructed totality by developing a new, holistic interdisciplinary paradigm, Benjamin and Adorno proceeded, like the early Lukács, provisionally and essayistically. In their view, Jay concludes, "the dissonant juxtaposition of disciplines rather than their smoothly integrated harmonization was more genuinely critical in this time of social and cultural detotalization" (115). Benjamin's articulation of this model for his massive, uncompleted cultural history of nineteenth-century Paris was closely related to his outsider position as an independent researcher and journalistic writer who made idiosyncratic use of academic writing and who felt no necessity to conform to the disciplinary protocols of the German university that had excluded him, first as an individual who failed in a key phase of his university credentialing and after 1933 as a left-wing intellectual and exiled Jew. Adorno, in a sense, brought Benjamin's outlaw methodology partially back into the fold of the academic institution. If Benjamin's version of this paradigm was fully extra-academic and linked to avant-garde artistic procedures of collage and montage in his handling of historical material, Adorno evolved a micrological, almost cubistic style of philosophical interpretation.

Already back in the 1930s, Benjamin's and Adorno's approaches presupposed the contemporary crisis of social science and humanistic disciplines and loss of a master discourse of totalization once fulfilled by philosophy, a crisis analyzed in various ways by Weber, Heidegger, and Edmund Husserl in the first few decades of the twentieth century. This sense of fragmentation, loss of authoritative frameworks, and discrediting of metanarratives has returned in intensive ways in postmodernist and poststructuralist-influenced interdisciplinarity in the humanities since the 1980s. For scholars who have wanted to hold onto a way of lending their research relevance with respect to social and political contexts, Benjamin's and Adorno's example offered powerful theoretical tools and helped open new themes and social problematics for humanistic research. It has vastly increased communication between disciplines such as literature, history, art history, film, and media studies, and it has given scholars new interpretative means for relating individual works of art and culture to emancipatory interests, ideologies, and agents.

This model of interdisciplinarity as practiced by an individual scholar, we should note, has also been encouraged and rewarded by Anglo-American university institutions since the "theory boom" started in the late 1970s. The work of Benjamin and Adorno has been absorbed by the most prominent figures of literary and cultural theory—for example, in the enormously influential work of Jameson, whose critical essays on everything from nineteenth- and twentieth-century novels to architecture, video, and film helped teach the work of the Frankfurt School to more than one generation of literary scholars. We might also single out the work of Jay, who moved organically from being a disciplinary intellectual historian writing about the interdisciplinary research of the Frankfurt School to himself practicing erudite interdisciplinary scholarship in later books such as his 1993 study *Downcast Eyes*, which lent important impetus to the establishment of "visual studies" as a new field with its own journals, conferences, programs, and even departments. Such qualities as breadth, scope, and range—understood in terms of this individual interdisciplinary paradigm—are essential for many academic humanities departments in defining new positions and evaluating new hires; they are also crucial to demonstrate if one is to succeed in publishing in the most prestigious journals and university presses. There is, however, another model of interdisciplinarity to which I have alluded, a sort of "road not taken," at least within the humanities in the United States, where group projects, research teams, and independent research institutes with defined, collectively executed and authored projects remain marginal to the production of humanistic knowledge (though work in the digital humanities may represent a new inroad in this direction).

In his inaugural address entitled "The Present Situation of Social Philosophy and the Tasks of an Institute for Social Research," delivered upon his assumption of the directorship of the Institut in 1930, Horkheimer evoked a situation in which the accumulation and differentiation of disciplinary research had outstripped the capacity of any individual researcher. Yet he retained an orientation towards the social totality as the context within which the data and results of disciplinary research reveal their social meaning and value and could be assessed for their contribution to social emancipation. As Horkheimer said:

> the question today is to organize investigations stimulated by contemporary philosophical problems in which philosophers, sociologists, economists, historians, and psychologists are brought together in permanent collaboration to undertake in common that which can be carried out individually in the laboratory in other fields. . . . [Q]uestions become integrated into the empirical research process; their answers lie in the advance of objective knowledge, which itself affects the form of the questions. In the study of society, no one individual is capable of adopting such an approach, both because of the volume of material and because of the variety of indispensable auxiliary sciences.[5]

Horkheimer believed that this function could be carried out by social research only if it moved beyond disciplinary limits, but also only if it moved beyond the capacities of the traditional individual scholar in a new organization of knowledge that would be not only interdisciplinary, but also trans-individual. The new "subject" of social knowledge would be a research team, bringing together individual disciplinary expertise within planned projects, in which group discussion would clarify the problems to be pursued, the methodologies, the disciplinary contributions and their limits, and the synthetic outcomes of the collaboration.

This interdisciplinary group work was dramatically embodied by the Institut's journal, the *Zeitschrift für Sozialforschung* (Figure 9.1).[6] The commissioning of articles followed from the theoretical presuppositions of the group and the editorial collective's decisions; all articles were read and discussed by the core group as well. Taking as an illustration the major essays from the first year, 1932, we can see the impressive range

Figure 9.1 *Zeitschrift für Sozialforschung 1* (1932), table of contents.

of specialized topics contributing to the synthetic picture of the social situation of the age. Even more important for the practical implementation of interdisciplinarity, however, was the book review section, which encompassed half the journal's page-space and averaged more than 350 reviews a year. As Habermas remarks in an essay about the *Zeitschrift*:

> The literature deployed and discussed in the book review section provided the difficult material that fits almost naturally into the theoretical framework; it provided a test for the organizing power of the central research interests. The book review section was divided into Philosophy, General Sociology, Psychology, History, Social Movement, Social Policy, Specialized Sociology, and Economics. Subdivisions of Specialized Sociology included political science, cultural anthropology, and theory of law. Never again ... has the unity of the social sciences been so convincingly portrayed as here, from the perspective of an unorthodox modified "Western Marxism."[7]

We can draw a few tentative conclusions about these two models of interdisciplinarity represented by the Frankfurt School and held in unresolved tension in its activities. First, the *Zeitschrift für Sozialforschung* demonstrates how much is required to achieve such a comprehensive and multi-perspectival interdisciplinary view. The *Zeitschrift* was the focal point of group activity, with an editorial collective totally involved with all that appeared in the journal, and at least two concentric circles of contributors sustaining its very extensive range of studies and reviews. At the same time, as a focal point of a vast amount of social science theory and research in several specialized fields, the journal was also to serve as the *pedagogical* instrument for developing the interdisciplinary competence of editors, contributors, and ulterior readers. Second, it is not accidental that the Institut für Sozialforschung, though loosely associated with universities, was autonomous in its funding and animated by concerns to resist fascism and antisemitism and to advance social and political emancipation. A journal of this sort demanded a tremendous amount of work and personal sacrifice, and for a time, the scholars involved set aside their individual professional ambitions to a substantial degree in pursuit of these collective aims. Finally, in the legacy of the Frankfurt School in the present-day American academy, this collective model of interdisciplinary research has been largely eclipsed by the individual model I described earlier, which, as I have suggested, is more in tune with the evaluation and reward system of university institutions, at least in the humanities and some social science disciplines. Even with current gestures towards strengthening interdisciplinary collaboration, coauthored publication, and group work in these disciplines, it remains to be seen whether the institutional conditions to support such work sustainably are anywhere on the horizon.

Authoritarianism as Interdisciplinary Object: *Studien über Authorität und Familie*

In the mid-1930s, as fascism spread across Europe, the Institut für Sozialforschung published a compendious "research report" on the topic of "authority and the family," an important precursor to Adorno's post–World War II social psychological group study *The Authoritarian Personality*.[8] Completed in New York in 1935 and published the next year in 1936, the report attempted to bring to light the wide-ranging investigations of the Institute and its collaborators concerning authority and its social and psychological genesis within the European family. Horkheimer notes that, despite its fragmentary character—a product of the displacement of the research organization and its members— the study carried an "essential programmatic character." The rise of authoritarianism in Europe, the direct cause of the upheavals in the Institute's scientific activities, made the question of authority not only of holistic, interdisciplinary, and international interest, but also of political and personal survival. In the textual architecture of an extensive (900 pages) publication on a single critical social-cultural topic, the project instantiated the methodological premises of the critical, interdisciplinary group research that Horkheimer had announced in his inaugural address on assuming the directorship of the Institute, "The Present Situation of Social Philosophy and the Tasks of an Institute for Social Research" (1931), which I quoted above.

Horkheimer underscores the project's collaborative nature, noting that the identification and articulation of the theme authority/family had taken place through "seminar-like meetings in the Institute" and that it consequently "belongs to no sole member of our group"; he does single out Erich Fromm, Leo Lowenthal, the economic historian Karl August Wittfogel, and the leader of the Geneva Office of the Institute, Andries Sternheim, as particular important voices in those discussions. The book is complexly designed, composed of three major sections: the first a three-part "Theoretical Outline" of the problem of authority and the family, primarily edited by Horkheimer; the second, a presentation of surveys on family structure, character structure, and attitudes towards authority, edited primarily by Fromm; and a set of individual contributions and literature reviews, edited primarily by Lowenthal. Further spinning the web of collaboration, as Horkheimer notes, was also an extensive correspondence on key issues with contributors, whose work often existed in multiple redactions.

Horkheimer mentions that the whole second ("empirical") section was informed by new experiences gained through very recent contact with American social scientists, using methods that were largely unfamiliar to the European investigators. It has, he says, the "character of an experiment," and rather than offering solid statistical proof, should be seen as means to a "productive construction of a typology" (*Studien*, x). The surveys were in fact, for the most part, never applied beyond a small pilot population. The third section, comprising more than half the book's pages, is composed of commissioned studies and literature reviews rich in scope and relevant perspectives on the authority/family nexus. It includes Wittfogel's study of the economic historical bases of the development of family authority; several essays touching on various historical, legal, and political aspects of the family in France, Belgium, Germany, and Austria; an essay by the neuropsychologist Kurt Goldstein on the significance of biology in the sociology of authority; a literature review by Marcuse about authority and the family in German sociology up to 1933; an essay by Hans Meyer on authority and family in anarchist theory; and much more. Yet as Horkheimer suggested in correspondence, these were intended above all to expand the perspectives of the Institute's members, and accordingly there is little organic integration of this extraordinarily diverse assemblage of expert knowledge into the theoretical contributions by Horkheimer, Fromm, and Marcuse—as would have been the case had Horkheimer genuinely realized his programmatic aim of a mutual productive dialectic of theory and empirical research across disciplines. Several commentators have noted this relative lack of constructive integration of the parts of the book, which renders it more an anthology of loosely related, yet substantially heterogeneous materials rather than an achieved architecture of interdisciplinary research.

The project represented by "Studies on Authority and the Family" is rightly seen as a landmark in Horkheimer's early interdisciplinary research program, second only to the editorial structure and process of the Institute's journal, the *Zeitschrift für Sozialforschung*, which remains the greatest achievement of this collaborative intellectual complex. Yet its character, as several commentators have pointed out, was incomplete and more valedictory than catalytic of further work of the sort. As Leo Lowenthal noted in a conversation with Helmut Dubiel:

> The work was uneven. Yet the first part, containing the theory of authority in modern society ... would presumably have remained unchanged in a more developed version of the project. I myself would probably have written more on how this program was reflected in literature. And were it not for Hitler, the empirical research would have included additional sections. ... Had we the means and personnel, we would have undertaken comparative studies in other European countries. ... Perhaps all of this might have developed in such a way that the *Zeitschrift für Sozialforschung* would have published research reports on other inquiries. The book was not very successful. But how could it have been otherwise?[9]

No other collective publication of the sort would appear from the Frankfurt School for many years, and it marks a turning point from the early program of an emancipatory, interdisciplinary social science towards the theoretical directions represented by Horkheimer and Adorno's *Dialectic of Enlightenment*, focused upon human reason's self-destructive dynamics and the abolition of freedom in the manipulated thought-schemas of fascism and industrially produced culture. Whether, like Dubiel, one believes that this programmatic ideal can be reconstructed and the shortcomings of *Studies on Authority and the Family* measured against this ideal,[10] or whether, like Wiggershaus, one finds in it evidence for skepticism about whether the program ever coherently existed,[11] we can in any case conclude that the *Studies* are an incomplete and inconclusive monument, despite their impressive scope and bulk. Wiggershaus even implies that the gesture towards empirical work was something of a mask for Horkheimer's consolidation of a philosophically oriented theoretical project, articulated in concert with a limited circle of collaborators including Marcuse, Lowenthal, and ever more prominently, Adorno.

The theoretical section, indeed, can be situated in the core of the Institute's theoretical concerns, both before and after the appearance of the *Studien*. The most obvious context and, in many cases, explicit thematic focus of this theoretical work as well was the accession to power of authoritarian states in Europe, both in the form of state-corporatist fascism and Nazism and in Stalin's consolidation of Soviet communism, which had seen intensive industrialization, collectivization of agriculture, bureaucratization, and state terror in the late 1920s and 1930s. The theoretical section contains a "general part" written by Horkheimer, a "social psychological part" written by Fromm, and a "history of ideas part" written by Marcuse.[12] There was to have been a fourth theoretical essay on economics by Friedrich Pollock, another member of the institute's inner circle, but it was considered incomplete at the time of publication. All three essays published in this section synthesize insights developed earlier by Horkheimer, Marcuse, and Fromm, and would receive subsequent elaboration, notably in essays in the *Zeitschrift für Sozialforschung*.

Horkheimer's introduction, as already noted, explicitly referred to his program for interdisciplinary social research, which also tacitly counterpointed authoritarianism's concentration and forcible integration of separated liberal political, economic, and cultural spheres. Moreover, it drew upon his own historical accounts of the contradictory evolution of bourgeois political and moral thought, such as his study, "Egoism and the Freedom Movement," published in 1936 in the *Zeitschrift für Sozialforschung*. Horkheimer would continue this focus as his American exile extended into the war years in essays such as "The Authoritarian State" (written in 1940) and "The End of Reason" (1941).

Similarly, Marcuse developed a consistent thread of reflection on authoritarianism throughout the 1930s. In his essay "The Struggle against Liberalism in the Totalitarian View of the State," which appeared in 1934 in the *Zeitschrift für Sozialforschung*, Marcuse analyzed the displacement of liberal capitalist ideology by a new *Weltanschauung* supporting the authoritarian abolition of liberal divisions between public and private, culture and politics, the individual and the community, the party and the state. In his well-known essay "The Affirmative Character of Culture," published a year after *Studien über Authorität und Familie*, Marcuse likewise explored the shift in function undergone by culture in the transition to the authoritarian state. Under liberal capitalism, in

Marcuse's view, culture had offered an illusory, idealistic, and socially harmless haven from the conflicts of the economic and political realms; under authoritarianism it was losing even this feeble capacity, as a no longer even relatively autonomous culture was integrated into state and communal functions as a direct instrument of domination.

Fromm, building upon his Marxist-Freudian social psychology in essays such as "The Method and Function of Analytic Social Psychology: Notes on Psychoanalysis and Historical Materialism" and "Psychoanalytic Characterology," both published in 1932 in the *Zeitschrift*, and further influenced by Wilhelm Reich's *Character Analysis* and *The Mass Psychology of Fascism*, introduced in *Studies on Authority and the Family* the concept of the "sado-masochistic character type" as the characterological correlate of authoritarian social structures and their supporting ideologies. Fromm suggested a dialectical interplay between authoritarian social and political developments and this authoritarian character type: the sado-masochistic type at once internalized social authoritarianism within the structure of the individual psyche and actively contributed to the preservation of authority by making it an object of desire and motivation.

I will focus my remaining discussion on Horkheimer's contribution, which I consider the most theoretically innovative of the three (despite Fromm's influential framing of the authoritarian character type, which would be further, and differently, elaborated by Adorno in *The Authoritarian Personality*). Horkheimer's theoretical essay, a general introduction, is set out in three sections: "Culture," "Authority," and "Family." He thus somewhat misleadingly suggests a correlation with the tripartite organization of the book as a whole, though closer consideration reveals that this is not the case, since the macro-structure is, as I have already indicated, a theoretical section, a section encompassing survey questions and preliminary data, and a capacious sample of specialized research and surveys of disciplinary literature. Since his inclusion of headings on "Authority" and "Family" are rather self-explanatory in a general introduction to a book on authority and the family, it is the first heading, on "Culture," that stands in need of explanation. Indeed, Horkheimer begins his essay in a surprising way: with a reflection on historical periodization and the categories by which we divide and order historical processes:

> The history of mankind has been divided into periods in very varying ways. The manner in which periodization has been carried out has not depended exclusively on the object . . .; the current state of knowledge and the concerns of the knower have also played a part. Today the division into antiquity, Middle Ages, and modern times is still widely used. It originated in literary

studies and was applied in the seventeenth century to history generally. It expresses the conviction, formed in the Renaissance and consolidated in the Enlightenment, that the time between the fall of the Roman Empire and the fifteenth century was a dark era for mankind, a sort of hibernation of culture. ... In contemporary scholarship this particular periodization is considered highly unsatisfactory. One reason is that the "Middle Ages" were in fact a time of important progress even from a purely pragmatic viewpoint, since they saw decisive advances in civilization and produced revolutionary technical inventions. A further reason is that the usual criteria for making the fifteenth century a dividing point are partly indefensible, partly applicable in a meaningful way only to limited areas of world history.[13]

What, we may justifiably ask, does this have to do with authority and the family? Horkheimer goes on for several pages in this highly abstract vein before we begin to get an inkling of what might be his intention here.

Horkheimer, it transpires, seeks to negotiate a role for culture in our concepts of history that would avoid, on the one hand, classical Marxism's underestimation of culture's efficacy in relation to the transformations impelled by the economic forces and relations of production; and on the other, idealist conceptions of history that hypostatize culture into period "essences," as in German *Geistesgeschichte* and *Kulturmorphologie*. Horkheimer wants to account for the role that culture and its institutions play in the processes of historical change that should be reflexively incorporated into periodizing concepts. He raises the possibility of a differential historicity that traverses the social whole, impacting back on the concepts by which we understand history: "The process of production influences men not only in the immediate contemporary form in which they themselves experience it in their work, but also in the form in which it has been incorporated into relatively stable institutions which are slow to change, such as family, school, church, institutions of worship, etc." (54). We can note that these institutions, though Horkheimer does not yet explicitly say so, are those we typically see as framing relations of authority: parent to child, teacher to pupil, priest to follower, and so on. Horkheimer does, however, suggest that such cultural institutions "in so far as they influence the character and behavior of men at all, are conservative or disruptive factors in the dynamism of society. Either they provide the mortar of the building under construction, the cement which artificially holds together the parts that tend toward independence, or they are part of the forces which will destroy the society" (54).

It is only in the second section of the essay that Horkheimer explicitly connects these reflections to the matter of authority, which he sees as one of the primary mechanisms by which the conservative, or disruptive, effects of culture express themselves through human actions and choices:

> [T]he strengthening or weakening of authorities is one of those characteristics which make culture a dynamic factor in the historical process. The weakening of relationships of dependence which are deeply rooted in the conscious and unconscious life of the masses is among the greatest dangers that can threaten a societal structure and indicates that the structure has become brittle. Conscious exaltation of the status quo is evidence that a society is in a critical period and even becomes a "main source of danger." (72)

The rest of the essay is dedicated to two further themes, which are fairly familiar elements of Frankfurt School thought: the gradual shift from bourgeois emancipation from traditional authority to the reinvention of the authority of the "free market," up to the current crisis in which bourgeois liberalism is being abolished by authoritarian state capitalism; and the historical role of the family in the psychic economy of authority for the bourgeois individual.

More novel, however, is Horkheimer's motif of culture itself, which as articulated through authority, becomes a conservative or disruptive force in the historical process. Although he does not quite use these terms, implicit in his essay is the idea that authority, invested in culture and effectuated through institutions, may slow or accelerate the pace of historical change due to its fundamental impulse, as Horkheimer's underlying Marxist orientation suggests, from the forces and relations of production at a given moment and place. It is fairly evident that Horkheimer views authoritarian tendencies in modern societies—as well as the open authoritarian developments on the European continent—as "frustrations" laid upon a history that should, by its underlying economic, technological, and organizational features, be tending towards socialism, and this is no doubt the dominant and rather pessimistic *Grundton* of his essay. Yet Horkheimer leaves open the question of a potential conjunction of culture and authority in the direction of an acceleration of history as well, as a disruptive force that breaks the lock on historical development and allows its rapid surge forward.

Did Horkheimer in 1936 imagine an alternative convergence of culture and authority that could restart and accelerate a stalled history, an authoritative political will-formation that could oppose itself to the reactionary authoritarianism that was everywhere in evidence? It is difficult to say. By 1940, in any case, very little room remained in Horkheimer's perspective to mediate critical theory and historical action, which, as he himself had suggested, might depend on the exercise of political authority. Horkheimer is thus constrained to give witness to the debilitation of political will and the absence of any practical emancipatory direction. An exemplary expression of this predicament is his essay on "The Authoritarian State," which he intended to publish in a memorial volume for Benjamin, who was one of the tragic victims of the current historical circumstances:

> The readiness to obey, even when it sets out to think, is of no use to theory. ... Thought is not absolutely opposed to command and obedience, but sets them for the time being in relationship to the task of making freedom a reality. This relationship is in danger. Sociological and psychological concepts are too superficial to express what has happened to revolutionaries in the last few decades: their will toward freedom has been damaged, without which neither understanding nor solidarity nor a correct relation between leader and group is conceivable.[14]

Totalitarian Interdisciplinarity: Critical Art and Post-Socialist Cultural Politics

Many practitioners of contemporary art in the United States and Western Europe have embraced interdisciplinarity as a programmatic basis of their artistic practice, and in parallel, research into the arts has developed a number of interdisciplinary tributaries, including new museological studies and visual cultural studies. Such developments, similarly, have not been lacking in the artistic and art-scholarly spaces of former socialist "East Bloc" countries or in "unaligned" nations such as the ex-Yugoslavia. However, given the particular histories—nationalist, fascist, socialist, and post-socialist—that transpired in these countries, the nature and content of contemporary interdisciplinarity may be significantly different there than in apparently similar cases elsewhere.

In recent art-critical discussions, interdisciplinarity in the arts is often seen as a response to the boundaries drawn by traditional and modernist presuppositions about medium specificity, decontextualized form- and style-concepts, and context-insensitive narratives of "art history." While it is indeed true that traditional and modernist criteria prevailed for many years under state socialism and have substantially persisted in post-socialism, interdisciplinary investigation has received impetus from an unlikely quarter: from artistic engagement with the historical legacy of "totalitarian" culture and the totalizing conceptions of cultural politics that legitimated it. Both Nazi-fascist culture and Stalinist culture have provided material for contemporary post-socialist projects that mix artistic practice with historical and museological reflection, the most striking of which is the Slovenian neo-avant-garde movement *Neue Slowenische Kunst* and its affiliated entities such as the Irwin artist group and the Laibach rock band.[15] Such projects are, in a sense, intrinsically "interdisciplinary" because of the unifying, concentrating nature of totalitarian conceptions of culture that they take as their object of reflection and formal inspiration, in however ironic and subverting a way. Such artists investigate historical forms of culture which, in instantiating the programmatic desire to remake the whole domain of culture and everyday life in the image of the ideology of the total state, had *already* programmatically blurred disciplinary boundaries—the lines between image and discourse, art and publicity, education and political indoctrination, visuality and performativity, and popular and elite culture in collectively lived space. Moreover, their contemporary works reflexively employ those discipline-crossing (multi)media in which the greatest utopian aspirations were originally invested by artists of the politicized avant-gardes, especially architecture and film (or its latter-day avatars in the digital sphere).

Péter György notes that after the imposition of dictatorship in Hungary in 1949, the adjective "Soviet" took on an omnipresence in many spheres of cultural life. In his examples of Hungarian publications started during these years, we catch a glimpse of a monistic will to reunify under "Soviet" the division of labor and fragmentation of specialized, professionalized disciplines conceived to be the hallmark of modernity in the classical social theories of Marx, Weber, and Durkheim.

Soviet Culture, Soviet Architectural Review, The Soviet Village, Soviet People, Soviet Youth, Soviet Applied Arts, Soviet Art History, Soviet Ethnography, Soviet Linguistics, Bulletin of Soviet Medicine, Soviet Archaeology, Review of Soviet General Industries, and *Collected Studies on Soviet Law.*[16]

The word "Soviet" here functions as a signal that any division between spheres of knowledge and culture, any incommensurability or incommunicability among their respective discourses, is only apparent. The governing heights of the Party-State and the oversight of science, culture, economy, and everyday life by centrally coordinated organs guarantee that everything will be connected to everything else in a maximally productive way. As Claude Lefort writes in his essay "The Logic of Totalitarianism," "What is being created is the model of a society which seems to institute itself without divisions, which seems to have mastery of its own organization, a society in which each part seems to be related to every other and imbued by one and the same project of building socialism."[17]

I will discuss in greater detail two significant examples from the years following the 1989 political changes in Hungary that engage the legacy of Hungarian socialism and its relatively brief "totalitarian"-dictatorial aspirations from 1949 up to 1953, along with the Soviet invasion in response to the 1956 uprising. These are: George Legrady's digital *Anecdoted Archive from the Cold War*, which superimposes a personal collection of Eastern European and communist materials with the virtual floor plan of the now-closed Museum of the Worker's Movement, a socialist educational and propagandistic display; and Attila F. Kovács's self-reflexively totalizing, architectural-museological and propagandistic *Gesamtkunstwerk*, the Budapest "House of Terror" on historic Andrassy Avenue, which was opened by the right-wing government of Viktor Orbán amid the contentious 2002 elections that ushered in a short-lived coalition government of socialists and free democrats. To anticipate my conclusions: despite being made by skilled and highly conscious artists and being, as such, accomplished works of art, both works remain highly problematic. Not for formal-artistic reasons, but rather because in light of their relation to their historical and political contexts they struggle to find a perspective—to use a Lukácsian concept—from which to form and illuminate the historical material they encompass. In making this judgment, however, I also want to suggest that their respective artistic difficulties lend greater critical insight into the problem of "totalitarianism" than a more evident museological or historiographic "success" might have. The artists' struggles to master this historical material points to the conceptual instability in the very notion of totalitarianism—which also raised problems even for its most brilliant theoreticians, such as Arendt and Lefort—for its disquieting combination of novelty and extirpation of creativity, its totalizing and atomizing impulses, its claims to omnipotence and its internal inefficiency. One is inclined to agree with Žižek when he claims that "the notion of 'totalitarianism,' rather than a theoretical concept, is a kind of discursive *stopgap*: rather than enabling insight into the historical reality it points to, it puts obstacles in the way of understanding, or even actively produces blindspots."[18]

Moreover, such difficulties in wrestling meaningful narratives or artistic forms from totalitarian culture points us back to a basic issue of interdisciplinarity, the degree to which success in moving across disciplinary lines and fusing the hermeneutic horizons of specialized discourses and practices depends on particular constellations of institutional and political forces. Without an authorizing framework, interdisciplinarity can fall into mere dilettantism or arbitrary montage. Yet if that authorization is overly strong, it becomes a compulsory fusion that overwhelms the internal criteria of scientific knowledge, short-circuiting it in the name of an ideological project, as with proletarian science or more recently, the merger of theology and biology in the notion of "intelligent design." To a crucial extent, interdisciplinarity hinges on the relation between the relatively impersonal, falsifiable, and iterable domain of knowledge and the collective, institutionally articulated "subjectivity" that authorizes it and renders it socially communicable. I want to suggest, then, that it is not accidental that Legrady's and Kovács's works shuttle between two key metaphors for how culture under dictatorship was individually experienced, *chance* and *terror*. For "totalitarianism" is a kind of placeholder for a range of "pathologies of reason" (Honneth) in the relationship between knowledge and collective authorization. Chance is the avatar of total historical contingency, here marked by the witty allusion of Legrady's title to Daniel Spoerri's Fluxus-oriented work (originally from 1962 though changing and growing in subsequent editions, hence paralleling the development of the Kádár regime): the *Anecdoted Topography of Chance*,[19] which suggests disorder and arbitrariness underlying the rigid ideological architectonics of an official socialist history museum. Terror, in contrast, marks the logic of inexorable historical necessity driven by a coercive ideology. Notably, the notion of totalitarianism fuses these two polar extremes. In totalitarianism, chance and terror become indiscernible as authorizing instances of knowledge and culture, which in turn reflexively creates problems for giving a coherent theoretical or artistic account of that which has been designated by the term "totalitarian." It is thus above all in the "objective" historical material itself and not in any practical shortcoming of the artists that the problematic character of Legrady's and Kovács's works resides.

Legrady: *An Anecdoted Archive from the Cold War*, 1993

George Legrady was born in Budapest in 1950 and left Hungary with his family in the wake of the 1956 uprising; he grew up in Canada and now teaches digital arts at the University of California in Santa Barbara. Legrady speaks of *An Anecdoted Archive from the Cold War* as a "non-linear index" that allows access to Cold War history through his own "particular hybridized history in relation to the Cold War." The "anecdoted archive" is closely tied to his personal family history and incorporates several intimate items: home movies, artifacts, ID cards, drawings of family memories, photographs of their residence. Also included are items of more distant connection, including propaganda materials, official photographs, street signs, books, and money. It is the conjunction between the materials and the contingent (but not arbitrary) meanings they generate in their shifting associations that is of interest to Legrady.[20]

In his discussion of the work, Legrady has made explicit his interest in its disciplinary or classificatory aspect, which is also signaled by his use of the metaphor of the museum, through the incorporation of the layout of the floor plan of the defunct Museum of the Workers' Movement as the virtual "architecture" of his digital design. Notably, also, for a decade following the closure of the Museum of the Workers' Movement, its space in the Buda Castle housed the Ludwig Museum of Contemporary Art, which makes Legrady's mapping of his own contemporary digital art onto pre-digital propaganda all the more resonant.

Legrady self-consciously addressed his work to the problem of meaning-making out of the recalcitrant material of a fragmented, traumatically charged, and often falsified or repressed historical past. In a 2001 interview with Sven Spieker, Legrady said of the *Anecdoted Archive*:

> The initial idea with the *Anecdoted Archive from the Cold War* was to create an archive that would integrate all the odd bits of information I had at hand (and in storage) about my leaving Hungary and growing up in Canada during the Cold War. The challenging question for the work was "how can I develop a coherent narrative out of odds and ends and multiple ideological and cultural perspectives?" or "How can I make sense of my own history through these things I have kept and is it possible to convey the personal value they have for me to others." The first solution was to come up with an organizing device that also had a multiple play of expectations. I used the floorplan of the Budapest official propaganda museum as a way to organize all my things to be included in the archive. In this official symbolic structure, I inserted official and personal material, a lot of which you would normally not find grouped together.
>
> I realize of course that any story I construct with these scattered objects cannot be comprehensive or complete. All that can be done is a kind of sampling, organizing a particular set of data into some kind of system or logic.... The thing about digitalization is that through databases and through various forms of information processing and data mining you can very effectively organize data and reduce the differentiating markings that separate official and personal sources. So my idea was to construct a digital archive where if you select one thing the program goes and dynamically tries to find other related things, similar to search engines today. That was the original plan but I didn't have the means to realize it at the time.[21]

About the classificatory aspect of the work, he points to his interest in Foucault's account of classificatory change in *The Order of Things*. He also notes how, after 1989, with the simultaneous fall of the Berlin Wall and the death of his father—the loss of both a personal and a collective symbolic order, as it were—digital technology offered remediation of the broken connection of the personal and historical:

The project's primary intent was to give coherent form to the diverse set of references and 'invested objects' at hand that defined my sense of history following the collapse of the Berlin wall which coincided with the death of my father. I am not a historian, sociologist, archivist, or museologist but made use of methodologies borrowed from these disciplines to produce this interactive archive. It is not intended as an official history. It is rather about a way to situate stories through technological media. For instance, to create a platform where one's stories can engage in discourse with official history since one of the capabilities of the digitization process is that it reshapes information, erasing differences traditionally easily identifiable as belonging to official or personal documents.[22]

Legrady goes on to discuss the non-linear, interactive quality of the archive, which renders the meanings of history not necessary but contingently possible, a product of chance and choice. In this sense, the anecdoted archive—as opposed to the official propaganda museum that it supplanted—dramatizes in microcosm the liberal pluralization of state socialism's ideologically structured past, as individuals make of the historical archive what they can and will, in interaction with the capacities of digital media for unexpected remixes of materials. "Based on chance, and the choices that viewers follow," he writes, "each viewer walks away with a slightly different story from this Archive based according to their own ideological beliefs. . . . In other words, the sequence and choices that each viewer selects becomes a visible reflection of their own cultural/political perspective."[23] Yet despite this interpretation of his chosen medium, conceiving the *Anecdoted Archive*'s digital interactivity as sort of miniature "open society," a tension persists between the two statements just quoted. For in a certain sense, Legrady ascribes to the new artistic technologies a utopian ability to overcome—or at least mitigate—the splits that constituted his own family history (and perhaps in a more personal sense, to pay memorial homage to his deceased father). Notably, however, he discusses such an overcoming of this division in terms that might describe the very cultural and political dynamics of totalitarianism, its erasure of the differences between the official and the personal, the collapse of the distance between the ideological-political and the "social" sphere of production and everyday life.

It would be unfair to exaggerate the degree to which this "totalitarian" trace is technologically actualized rather than latently reflected in Legrady's archive, as if his "anecdoted archive" were to bear out Žižek's sinister assertion that "The digitalization of our daily lives, in effect, makes possible a Big Brother control in comparison with which the old Communist secret police supervision cannot but look like primitive child's play" (*Did Someone Say Totalitarianism?*, 256). Yet it must also be admitted that the "freedom" offered by its interactivity—especially viewed from the distance of almost thirty years of rapid development of digital arts technology—remains unrealized. As Legrady himself notes in his interview with Spieker, mobilizing the estranging powers of digital technologies and their capacity to associate data in unexpected ways was a technical challenge he could take up only in subsequent work. What is of greater consequence, and perhaps the most authentic achievement of the work in retrospect, is its highlighting of just this unresolved presence of opposed impulses in a work dealing with the historical legacy of East–Central European state socialism. Legrady's work illustrates poignantly, to adopt Adorno's famous metaphor, how difficult it may be, despite subjective intentions, to reassemble its torn bits into a coherent whole.

Attila F. Kovács: House of Terror Museum, Budapest, 2002, and Memory Point Museum, Hódmezővásárhely, 2006

Attila Kovács, born in 1951, is almost an exact contemporary of Legrady, although unlike Legrady, he remained in Hungary and was associated with the skeptical, semi-dissident art scene of late socialism. He designed film sets for such directors as István Szabó, Sándor Pál, and András Jeles, including his renowned "Stone Room" for Jeles's banned film *Dream Brigade* (Figure 9.2), which as György has pointed out, offered one of the most effective images of the stagnation of society in the late Kádár period, while resonating with other Central European

Figure 9.2   Attila F. Kovács set from András Jeles, *Dream Brigade*, 1983. Film still.

socialist bloc works of this period such as the "Dead Class" of Tadeusz Kantor.[24] Kovács also helped Jeles create a brilliant visual allegory of an orthodox bureaucratic society in the Byzantium section of the film *The Annunciation*, which adapts Imre Madách's nineteenth-century drama *The Tragedy of Man*. In the recent socialist past, Madách's historical dream-vision had been the object of one of Lukács's most notorious critiques, on grounds of its "anti-democratic world-view" and its "pessimistic lack of perspective." Lukács's essay, reportedly, was written on the prompting of the Stalinist leader Rákosi[25] and may have justified the official ban on its performance during socialism (although, it is worth noting, Lukács had harshly criticized Madach's play on similar grounds already in his early *Developmental History of Drama* in 1910–11).[26] Jeles's film also includes an episode representing the terror in the French Revolution, which, along with Madach's negative representation of a future phalanstry, no doubt offended the ideological sensibilities of socialist Hungary's authorities. Kovács's 1987 exhibition *Necropolis* similarly presented geometrical, industrial forms in tarred metal as sculptural depictions of the static, lifeless space of the late socialist environment. His work at this juncture heightened to oneiric uncanniness the banal, impoverished environments of everyday life and work under state socialism. His artistic presentation of socialism finds parallels in recent scholarship about late and post-socialism that highlighted the strange, even delirous aspects of Soviet and East Bloc socialist culture—for example, Susan Buck-Morss's *Dreamworld and Catastrophe: The Passing of Mass Utopia in East and West* and the work of anthropologist Katherine Verdery on post-socialist reburials.[27] Kovács has made several important theatre and opera set designs, including the paradigmatic Wagnerian *Gesamtkunstwerk*, the *Ring* cycle. He is also a notable architect and interior designer for private and commercial spaces. Following the opening of Budapest's House of Terror, four years later Kovács designed a satellite museum of socialism in Hódmezővásárhely, in southern Hungary, called Memory Point (Figures 9.3 and 9.4).

The Budapest House of Terror, however, remains his most ambitious and accomplished work, and it is by this work that his reputation will undoubtedly be measured. The House of Terror opened in the midst of the election campaign in February 2002, with a rally of Orbán supporters outside, a videotape of which now concludes one's museum visit. It is important to emphasize this post-socialist political context, because there are many respects in which the presentation of the history of "terror" in Hungary is propagandistically arrayed against the (now oppositional) Hungarian Socialist Party in the present, depicting today's socialists as the immediate heirs of a grim tradition of terror, and Orbán, a perfected

Figure 9.3   Central foyer of Terror Háza Muzeum, Budapest. Fred Romero, 2017. Permission for use by Creative Commons Attribution Generic 2.0 License.

Figure 9.4   Statues in courtyard of Memory Point, Andrassy Street 34, Hódmezővasárhely. Unnamed photographer ("Globetrotter19"), 2021. Permission for use by Creative Commons Attribution Share-Alike 3.0 License.

instance of what Solzhenitsyn termed the Egocrat, as Hungary's elected savior from it. Kovács's architectural and display designs are not only spatially complicit with this tendentiously ideologized historical presentation, they are powerful, compulsory, dynamic embodiments of it.[28] Although clearly a walk through a museum in present-day Budapest is a far cry from the real fear and violence people suffered during the years of the dictatorship or the clampdown following the 1956 revolt, the point remains: while seemingly denouncing the history and means of terror, the museum itself draws its aesthetic sustenance from totalitarian means, including state propaganda and terror. This paradox of an artistic critique of totalitarianism being instrumentalized in the service of an increasingly authoritarian "foe" of totalitarianism had, indeed, already been anticipated in the suppression of the Soviet political avant-gardes by the official aesthetics of the Stalin era, as Boris Groys has suggested. Socialist realism's apparent reversal of the early Soviet avant-garde in fact covertly completed that which the avant-gardes themselves could only imperfectly realize: total homologization of the artistic field with the field of politics.[29] Kovács's neo-avant-garde treatment of totalitarianism is a microcosmic image of a Hungary in which the Orbán government's instrumentalization of media and culture has been fully consummated.

I believe this to be key to Kovács's museum-*Gesamtkunstwerk* in two important senses. The first is epistemic and relates to the question of interdisciplinarity raised at the outset. The artist has put all the means at his command, from architecture to scenography, and from sculptural installation to digital technology, in the service of a monolithic, pseudo-historical narrative. Interdisciplinarity is thus subsumed by a tautological intent, to demonstrate viscerally that terror feels terrible, and that "socialism" is the proper reference of this terrible gut feeling. In case it be thought that I am exaggerating the crudely tautological nature of the message that underlies the museum's sophisticated aesthetic means, consider this quotation from the *International Herald Tribune* attributed to Maria Schmidt, a historian who is the museum's director and adviser to Orbán: "Is there anything in history that is not related to politics? ... The political motivation of those who work here is to show that the system of terror was terrible—the Communist terror was terrible."[30] There is, in fact, no historical narrative to expound; the House of Terror is an environment for instantiating the timeless, because tautological, proposition that "terror is terrible."[31]

The other sense in which the museum mimics the logic of totalitarianism is its purgation of contingency by imposing a spatialized necessity onto the historical past and present. As Lefort suggests in his analysis of the logic of the Terror in the French Revolution, terror-space is strictly binarized and moralized, with the position of the revolutionary closely locked to that of the enemy.³² Dramatically redoubling the structure of terror putatively to criticize it, the Budapest House of Terror replicates the oppressive bunker-like closure of its overall architecture and its mandatory "no exit" trajectory within the rigidly organized "cells" of its displays. Artistically, the tautological yet compulsory nature of the content is realized in an exhaustively spatialized image of Hungary's recent past and contemporary history, petrified into an unchanging, unambiguous geometry of political fear.

This already begins with the choice of the museum's location, 60 Andrassy Avenue, which possesses a special *genius loci*, having been the offices first of the Nazi collaborationist Arrow Cross movement, then the Gestapo headquarters, then the communist secret police headquarters and interrogation center; in the later, less repressive Kádár years, it was a communist youth center. Although it might be argued that this history makes it appropriate as a site of memory, Kovács's Terror Museum also mobilizes this history as part of its aesthetic frisson of "Terror"; even its signature architecture, which includes the symbolically connotative "blades-walls," literally projects the rigid signifier of Hungary's recent past into the public space of Budapest's post-socialist present (Figure 9.5). As István Rév describes:

Figure 9.5 Exterior view of Terror Háza Muzeum, Budapest. Fred Romero, 2017. Permission for use by Creative Commons Attribution Generic 2.0 License.

Around the completely grey façade of the House of Terror (even the glass of the windows is painted grey) the architect designed a black metal frame. . . . Around the roof, as part of the black frame there is a wide perforated metal shield with the word "TERROR," inscribed backward, the five-pointed star [symbol of communism] and the arrow-cross [symbol of Hungarian Nazi-fascism]. When exactly at noon, the sun is supposed to shine through the perforation, the word "TERROR" and the signs of autocracy hypothetically cast a shadow on the pavement. The presumed "Darkness at Noon" harks back to the Hungarian-born Arthur Koestler's Nicolas Salmanovich Rubashov, the most famous fictional Communist show trial character.[33]

One is meant to enter the House of Terror as a haunted space, full of dark nooks and luminous apparitions, and though a few rooms are perfunctorily dedicated to the Nazi Arrow Cross movement, the specter haunting the House of Terror Musuem is emphatically that of communism. Moreover, the choice of *genius loci* is not an innocent one with respect to the history of terror in Hungary. By focusing on the Arrow Cross movement, which took over the building in 1937, it could be conveniently forgotten that there was *already* a substantial history of terror in Hungary that preceded the Arrow Cross regime, including Red terror during the short-lived socialist commune of 1919 and the White terror that followed under the Horthy regime, which saw, for example, antisemitic pogroms as well as the institution of forced labor for Jews well before the Nazi collaborationist regime was established. Horthy has been recanonized by the Hungarian nationalist right as a patriot and national savior, rather than a clerico-military fascist strongman and, in his own way, an important ally of Hitler.

The museum depends on a highly codified pathway through its displays, including an obligatory final descent from the first floor in a slow elevator into the basement, where dungeon-like interrogation and torture cells are on display. In a literally architectural sense, the House of Terror instances that defining feature of totalitarianism that Lefort aptly called "the phantasmagoria of the Plan" (288). Indeed, the floor plans are included on the House of Terror's website, and incorporated into them are arrows indicating the obligatory pathway museum visitors must follow to animate the intense but iterative messaging of its displays and spaces. The plan incorporates the museum spectator into its artificial, sublimely overpowering body, which is traversed by strange bursts of light and sound, material textures, colors, and darknesses (Figure 9.6). In one of the most remarkable parts of the museum—with a nod to Joseph Beuys's sculptures in fat such as "Fat Chair" (1964) and "Fat Corner" (1968), which themselves index the confrontation of Nazi and Stalinist dictatorships in World War II—Kovács even concretizes this

Figure 9.6 Permanent installation at Terror Háza Muzeum, Budapest. Unnamed photographer ("n1207"), 2017. Permission for use by Creative Commons Attribution Share-Alike 3.0 License.

bodily metaphor with a rubberized wall representing bricks of pork fat, referring to a campaign of agricultural expropriation in which János Kádár had a hand. The message is that Kádár was part of the pre-1956 dictatorial terror as well as the presiding figure of post-1956 "Goulash communism." Therefore, his socialist party successors—such as Orbán's 2002 election rival Péter Medgyessy—are also heirs of terror. From vantage after vantage, the same statement is repeated: socialism is terror, and terror is terrible.

A Provisional Conclusion

In the museological artworks of both Legrady and Kovács, we detect that the primary problem of the artists in confronting the material of totalitarianism is not, first and foremost, a technical one. It is, instead, what Lukács called "perspective": namely, what stance does the artist take towards his material in order to achieve a "truthful" presentation of it? One is tempted to translate the respective approaches of Legrady and Kovács, chance and terror, into Lukács's Hegelian vocabulary, and argue that they fall into the twin but complementary traps of *subjective immediacy*, in which the link between the individual artifact or memory and the historical context remains arbitrary, and *abstract subjective idealism*, in which the necessary linkage of individual and history appears imposed and willful. Certainly other approaches are possible that would offer solutions to the problem of perspective, and one might imagine different treatments of this same historical material. However, we should also be led to ask whether it is merely accidental that these two Hungarian artists of the same generation, both making museological works about that country's socialist legacy, should have foundered on just this problem of perspective. The thinking and feeling subject, as Adorno reminds us, is also a historical product and, like the work of art, a complex resultant of relations of domination. Beyond any subjective shortcoming or artistic error, in the limits of these works, we glimpse the subjective costs that state socialism continues to exact from artists, even as the system itself fades into collective memory and selective musealization.

Notes

1. Georg Lukács, "Georg Simmel" (1918), trans. Margaret Cerullo, *Theory, Culture & Society* 8 (1991): 148.
2. On the Galileo Circle, see Péter Csunderlik, *Radikálisok, szabadgondolkodók, ateisták. A Galilei Kör története*, 1908–1919 (Napvilág Kiadó, Budapest, 2017).
3. On the Sunday Circle, see: *A Vasárnapi Kör. Dokumentumok. Összeállította*, eds. Éva Karádi and Erzsébet Vezér (Budapest: Gondolat Kiadó, 1980); Zoltán Novák, *A Vasárnapi Társaság* (Budapest: Kossuth Könyvkiadó, 1979); Júlia Bendl, *Lukács György élete a századfordulótól 1918-ig* (Budapest, 1994, Scientia Humana Társulás); Lee Congdon, *The Young Lukács* (Chapel Hill: University of North Carolina Press, 1983); Mary Gluck, *George Lukács and His Generation, 1900–1918* (Cambridge, MA: Harvard University Press, 1991).
4. Martin Jay, "Positive and Negative Totalities: Implicit Tensions in Critical Theory's Vision of Interdisciplinary Research," in Jay, *Permanent Exiles: Essays on the Intellectual Migration from German to the America* (New York: Columbia University Press, 1986), 114.
5. Max Horkheimer, "The Present Situation of Social Philosophy and the Tasks of an Institute for Social Research," in Horkheimer, *Between Philosophy and Social Science: Selected Early Writings*, trans. G. Frederick Hunter, Matthew S. Kramer, and John Torpey (Cambridge, MA: The MIT Press, 1993), 9–10.
6. For discussion of Frankfurt School-style "interdisciplinarity" see also, along with Martin Jay's essay cited in note 4, Richard Wolin, "The Frankfurt School: From Interdisciplinary Materialism to Philosophy of

History," in Wolin, *The Terms of Cultural Criticism: The Frankfurt School, Existentialism, Poststructuralism* (New York: Columbia University Press, 1992), 45–61.
7. Jürgen Habermas, "The Inimitable *Zeitschrift für Sozialforschung*: How Max Horkheimer Took Advantage of a Historically Oppressive Hour," *Telos* 45 (1980): 117.
8. Max Horkheimer et al., *Studien über Authorität und Familie*, reprint of 1936 Paris edition (Lüneberg: Dietrich zu Klampen Verlag, 1987). Cf. Theodor W. Adorno et al., *The Authoritarian Personality* (New York: Harper & Brothers, 1950).
9. Leo Lowenthal in *An Unmastered Past: The Autobiographical Reflections of Leo Lowenthal*, ed. Martin Jay (Berkeley and Los Angeles: University of California Press, 1987), 73–74.
10. Helmut Dubiel, *Theory and Politics: Studies in the Development of Critical Theory*, trans. Benjamin Gregg (Cambridge, MA: The MIT Press, 1985).
11. Rolf Wiggershaus, *The Frankfurt School: Its History, Theories, and Political Significance*, trans. Michael Robertson (Cambridge, MA: The MIT Press, 1994), 149–56. For further discussion of the *Studien*, see Chapter IV of Martin Jay, *The Dialectical Imagination: A History of the Frankfurt School and the Institute of Social Research, 1923–1950* (Boston: Little, Brown and Company, 1973), 113–42; and Emil Walter-Busch, *Geschichte der Frankfurter Schule: Kritische Theorie und Politik* (Munich: Wilhelm Fink, 2010), 116–37.
12. Marcuse's essay was reprinted in English translation as "A Study on Authority," in Herbert Marcuse, *Studies in Critical Philosophy*, trans. Joris de Bres (Boston: Beacon Press, 1973), 49–155.
13. Max Horkheimer, "Authority and the Family," in *Critical Theory: Selected Essays* (New York: Continuum, 2002), 47.
14. Max Horkheimer, "The Authoritarian State," *Telos* 15 (1973): 19–20.
15. See Alexei Monroe's 2005 study, *Interrogation Machine: Laibach and NSK* (Cambridge, MA: The MIT Press, 2005).
16. Péter György, "The Mirror of Everyday Life, or the Will to a Period Style," trans. Chris Sullivan, in *Art and Society in the Age of Stalin*, eds. Péter György and Hedvig Turai (Budapest: Corvina, 1992), 16.
17. Claude Lefort, "The Logic of Totalitarianism," in *The Political Forms of Modern Society: Bureaucracy, Democracy, Totalitarianism*, ed. John B. Thompson (Cambridge, MA: MIT Press, 1986), 284.
18. Slavoj Žižek, *Did Someone Say Totalitarianism?* (London: Verso, 2011), 3.
19. See Daniel Spoerri, *An Anecdoted Topography of Chance*, trans. Malcolm Green (London: Atlas Press, 1995).
20. Though he is not directly discussed, Sven Spieker's study *The Big Archive: Art from Bureaucracy* (Cambridge, MA: The MIT Press, 2008) provides critical and historical context for Legrady's project in a broad spectrum of modern and contemporary art's dialogue with archives. See also Spieker's 2001 interview with Legrady, quoted below.
21. Sven Spieker, "Pockets Full of Memory: A Conversation with George Legrady," *ArtMargins*, December 15, 2001, https://artmargins.com/pockets-full-of-memory-a-conversation-with-george-legrady/ (accessed December 31, 2021).

22. From George Legrady, "Concept: An Anecdoted Archive from the Cold War, 1993," https://www.mat.ucsb.edu/~g.legrady/glWeb/Projects/anecdote/Anecdote.html (accessed December 31, 2021).
23. Ibid.
24. Péter György, "Hungarian Marginal Art in the Late Period of State Socialism," in *Postmodernism and the Postsocialist Condition: Politicized Art under Late Socialism*, ed. Aleš Erjavec (Berkeley and Los Angeles: University of California Press, 2003), 197.
25. According to István Eörsi, "The Unpleasant Lukács," *New German Critique* 42 (1987): 3–4.
26. György Lukács, "Madách tragédiája," in Lukács, *Magyar Irodalom, Magyar Kultúra* (Budapest: Gondolat Kiadó, 1970), 560–73. For Lukács's early critique of Madách, see *Entwicklungsgeschichte des modernen Dramas*, 542–43, where he argues that *The Tragedy of Man* is no drama, but rather an unsuccessful mélange of epic and didactic poetry—a criticism that echoes Lukács's later view of Brecht. For discussion of Lukács's criticisms of Madách, see also János Kelemen, "Art's Struggle for Freedom: Lukács, the Literary Historian," in *Georg Lukács Reconsidered: Critical Essays in Politics, Philosophy and Aesthetics*, ed. Michael J. Thompson (London: Continuum, 2011), 123–25.
27. Susan Buck-Morss, *Dreamworld and Catastrophe: The Passing of Mass Utopia in East and West* (Cambridge, MA: The MIT Press, 2000); Katherine Verdery, *The Political Lives of Dead Bodies: Reburial and Postsocialist Change* (New York: Columbia University Press, 1999). See also the catalogue and essays from the Schirn Kunsthalle Frankfurt's exhibition *Traumfabrik Kommunismus/Dream Factory Communism: The Visual Culture of the Stalin Era*, eds. Boris Groys and Max Hollein (Ostfildern-Ruit: Hatje Cantz Verlag, 2003).
28. For discussion of the House of Terror's ideological presentation of history, see Magdelena Marsovszky, "'Die Märtyrer sind die Magyaren': Der Holocaust in Ungarn aus der Sicht des Hauses des Terrors in Budapest und die Ethnisierung der Erinnerung in Ungarn," in *Die Dynamik der europäischen Rechten: Geschichte, Kontinuitäten und Wandel*, eds. Claudia Globisch, Agnieszka Pufelska, and Volker Weiß (Wiesbaden: VS Verlag für Sozialwissenschaften, 2011), 55–74; Anna Manchin, "Staging Traumatic Memory: Competing Narratives of State Violence in Post-Communist Hungarian Museums," *East European Jewish Affairs* 45/2–3 (2015): 236–51; and Zsófia Frazon and Zsolt K. Horváth, "The Offended Hungary: The House of Terror as a Demonstration of Objects, Memorial, and Political Rite" (2019 republication of 2002 original), http://mezosfera.org/the-offended-hungary-the-house-of-terror-as-a-demonstration-of-objects-memorial-and-political-rite-2002/ (accessed December 31, 2021).
29. Boris Groys, *The Total Art of Stalinism: Avant-Garde, Aesthetic Dictatorship, and Beyond*, trans. Charles Rougle (Princeton: Princeton University Press, 1992).
30. Maria Schmidt, quoted in Thomas Fuller, "Stark History/Some See a Stunt: Memory Becomes Battleground in Budapest's House of Terror," *The New York Times*, August 2, 2002, https://www.nytimes.com/2002/08/02/news

/stark-history-some-see-a-stunt-memory-becomes-battleground-in-budapests.html (accessed December 31, 2021).
31. The literature on museums and memory politics is vast. I will mention here only two works that deal with historical debates in the analogous context of memorialization of the Nazi past in post-war, divided, and post-reunification Germany: Charles S. Maier, *The Unmasterable Past: History, Holocaust, and German National Identity* (Cambridge, MA: Harvard University Press, 1988); and Jeffrey Herf, *Divided Memory: The Nazi Past in the Two Germanys* (Cambridge, MA: Harvard University Press, 1997).
32. Claude Lefort, "The Revolutionary Terror," in *Democracy and Political Theory*, trans. David Macey (Minneapolis: University of Minnesota Press, 1988), 81.
33. István Rév, *Retroactive Justice: Prehistory of Post-Communism* (Stanford: Stanford University Press, 2005), 282.

Chapter 10

Prophecies of Mass Deception: Dewey, Trotsky, and the Moscow Show Trials

In this last of my major chapters, I explore the event and context of the Moscow show trials of the 1930s from a wide angle: as an instance of what Horkheimer, in his introduction to Leo Lowenthal and Norbert Guterman's 1947 study of right-wing agitators, *Prophets of Deceit*, characterized as the "manufacture" of "attitudes and reactive behavior" through "calculated techniques of communication" and of the "mass deception" Horkheimer and Adorno diagnosed more generally in the Culture Industry.[1] Lukács witnessed the trials up close from Moscow, viewing them, as he later claimed, through the lens of the French revolutionary tribunals, but also through the literary mediation of Georg Büchner's nineteenth-century drama *Danton's Death* and other historical dramas about which he was writing at the time. The Moscow trials are more submerged in the Frankfurt School's history, not least because its principals, as Jay (and Žižek after him) has pointed out, "never focused the attention of Critical Theory on the left-wing authoritarianism of Stalin's Russia."[2] Yet as Lowenthal testified, among the members of the Institute a "basic conflict involved the Soviet Union and the trials. There was quite a split about that, and it frequently resulted in heated conversations and unpleasant scenes."[3]

Even Adorno, however, advised keeping this conflict under tight wraps. To Horkheimer in late 1936, after the first Moscow trial, Adorno wrote: "the most loyal attitude to Russia at the moment is probably shown by keeping quiet," and "in the current situation ... one should really maintain discipline (and no one knows the cost better than I!) and not publish anything that might damage Russia."[4] In his tape-recorded interviews late in his life, Lukács too justified his acceptance of the trials and opposition to Trotskyism on the basis of their impact on public opinion about the Soviet Union in the West:

> *Int.*: Comrade Lukács, you seem to be saying that Trotsky did more damage to the Soviet Union in the eyes of American public opinion than did the trials? I have the feeling that the trials caused the greater damage.
>
> *G.L.*: These things cannot simply be weighed against each other. There is no doubt that the trials caused damage. It is also beyond doubt that they did damage simply because they took place. I think we are talking about a complex issue here. What was at stake at the time was the whole question of the Stalinist leadership, of whether Stalinism had given rise to a worse dictatorship than was to be expected of Trotsky and his supporters. Of course, we answered this in the negative.
>
> *Int.*: But in the last analysis the question was not whether we should strive for a Stalinist or Trotskyist dictatorship.[5]

Lukács and, more improbably, Adorno were concerned less with confronting the trials as a manifestation of Stalinism's consolidation in the USSR and the organs of international communism, than they were about the negative impact on the Soviet Union's reputation in the international public sphere. As we shall see, this position was echoed by a substantial number of American liberals as well. Occluded by this lesser-of-two-evils, Stalin-versus-Trotsky framework, however, was precisely the role of an informed democratic public to weigh the evidence and exercise independent judgment. Instead, intellectuals—communist, independent leftist, and liberal alike—propagated or at least let stand that particular Platonic lie that they considered it best for the masses to believe. Across the manifest ideological divides, I would argue, each contrived to stifle the most crucial question the trials had in fact posed in a moment of extreme international danger: that of democracy's radical vocation, both in capitalist and in socialist society.

The ideological falsifications perpetrated in the Moscow trials of the 1930s, and the justifications by American liberals for accepting or remaining agnostic about the "evidence" for Trotskyite conspiracies, anticipated later developments in the manufacture of mass deception, including those we grapple with today in our media-saturated "post-truth" public sphere. In connection with this theme, I suggest, we may still find instructive the response of the philosopher and progressive stalwart John Dewey, who in 1937 headed up a commission of investigation to establish the facts and offer a reasoned judgment about Trotsky's guilt or innocence of the charges made against him in the Moscow trials, motivated by his consistent commitment to progressive democracy.

Otto Kirchheimer and Political Trials

Before embarking on the specific circumstances of Dewey's involvement in the Trotsky commission, I turn to the Frankfurt School legal scholar and political scientist Otto Kirchheimer, who in 1961 published his study *Political Justice: The Use of Legal Procedure for Political Ends*. Kirchheimer discusses show trials in both Nazi Germany and the Soviet Union in the 1930s and, at greater length, the related structures of "socialist legality" in the post-war German Democratic Republic.[6] Comparing the Moscow show trials with the Nazi trial of Herschel Grynszpan, who had assassinated a German diplomat in Paris and around whom the Nazis unsuccessfully sought to conjure up a broader conspiracy, Kirchheimer notes that the Stalin-era trials managed to fuse the machinery of orchestrated trials tightly with their predetermined certainty of outcome, towards "the creation of a political imagery appropriate for present needs" (*Political Justice*, 105). This led to a widely accepted narrative of "an alternative reality, consisting of dangers which would have come to pass but for the vigilance of the official hierarchy" (106).

Kirchheimer tended to see the Moscow show trials—and their counterparts throughout the socialist bloc following World War II—as inauthentic *political* trials because their outcomes were predetermined and procedures manipulated to lead inexorably to those outcomes. Notably, however, their character as "spectacle" did not disqualify them for Kirchheimer, since he in fact emphasizes the dramaturgical aspects of political trials, using the theatrical language of "roles" and referring to certain "age-old," almost archetypal dramatic figures such as "the informer and the turncoat"[7] in these courtroom dramas in which individuals enacted their political beliefs and the state demonstrated their baleful implications. Kirchheimer emphasized the trials' function of condensing messy, complex historico-political realities into images, conveyed by dramatic personifications and representative acts.[8]

In connection with the Alger Hiss trial of 1949–50, which took place almost concurrently with the paradigmatic Hungarian show trial of Lukács's friend László Rajk,[9] Kirchheimer compared the political trial to a popular movie:

> The process of translating and transforming fragmentary acts into a simplified picture of political reality ... is a collective process that takes place simultaneously in millions of minds, and it is more intensive than the more passive reception of the artificial reality prefabricated for the purposes of the totalitarian trial. In the minds of millions, the fixed, cinematic episode

is totally identified with the political beliefs with which the defendant is presumably identified though not charged. (*Political Justice*, 113–14)

The Moscow trials, accordingly, drew contemporary commentators ineluctably to theatrical references and metaphors, given the shadow of theatricality over the trials.

In a 1967 interview with Ilse Siebert, Lukács noted that "having been in part brought up in the traditions of the French Revolution, during the great trials we very often thought of the trials against the Girondists and Dantonists, in which likewise not all the formalities had been observed, and nevertheless we were on the side of Robespierre against the Dantonists. This analogy . . . played a large role."[10] Yet in February 1937—just after the Pyatakov-Radek trial in January 1937—Lukács had published from Moscow his essay "On the Fascistically Falsified and the Real Büchner," which trained attention particularly on Büchner's historical drama of the French Revolution, *Danton's Death* (1835). In dramatizing the great historical clash of Danton with Robespierre and Saint Just, Lukács's Büchner is no partisan of one or the other, but rather the tragic dialectician who mediates between two flawed revolutionary leaders and their incomplete political positions. "Neither Danton nor Saint Just alone is the mouthpiece of the poet," Lukács writes. "Of course, Saint Just's position comes closest to Büchner's own solution to the question of hunger. . . . But [he] stands nearer in his feelings to Danton than to the more politically-akin Saint Just."[11] Given the coincidence of the hundredth anniversary of Büchner's death in February 1937, it is irresistible to think not only that the Moscow trials inflected Lukács's interpretation of Büchner's play, but also that Büchner's drama mediated Lukács's perception of the trials themselves as tragically "necessary."

In fact, Lukács would employ other theatrical metaphors in his reference to the trials as well. Thus, in the closed meetings of the German writers convened in 1936 in Moscow, which echoed the trials themselves in the denunciations and self-recriminations they elicited, Lukács ominously characterized the Soviet Union's new phase of conspiracies and trials in terms of "masked figures," echoing a common figure of speech in Stalin's own discourse. Lukács is recorded as having said that

> in the question of vigilance a wholly new problem emerged, something already there in the Kirov Trial [1934] but now comes forward with complete clarity. [Earlier] we could analyze: this man is a Bukharinite, this a Trotskyite, etc. The present enemies of the party have no platform, *rather they appear in the mask* of loyal men of the party.[12]

Similarly, in the American context, in his apologetic review of the record of the January 1937 trials, Malcolm Cowley both affirms and disavows the theatrical nature of the trials: "Judged as literature," he writes, "'The Case of the Anti-Soviet Trotskyite Center' is an extraordinary combination of true detective story and high Elizabethan tragedy with comic touches. I could accept it as a fabricated performance only on the assumption that Marlowe and Webster had a hand in staging it."[13] And in a review of the same trial report, the pro-Stalin British lawyer Dudley Collard disavowed the evident theatrical nature of the reports in order to assert their veracity as juridical documents: "No one who takes the trouble to read through this report, whatever his other doubts, could still believe that the whole proceedings were staged and that some playwright wrote these 580 pages in advance for the defendants to act."[14]

Kirchheimer himself implies that dramatic mediation of the political trial is intrinsic to its political functioning, and that therefore to the extent that the juridical decision in the Stalinist show trials had been predetermined and the unexpected foreclosed, their dramatic efficacy was in fact diminished. In an interview conducted late in his life, Lukács, however, gives this argument a twist, claiming that in fact the effective message of the Rajk trial lay with its manifest *inauthenticity*, its "show" quality, which was paralleled in the confectedness of the party's concurrent attacks on his writings. "The fact is," Lukács asserts,

> they simply got rid of anyone who was suspected of not endorsing Stalin's line with sufficient enthusiasm. . . . The whole [Lukács] debate simply proves that the dictatorship which prevailed in the fifties was a dictatorship from the very start, and that it is a myth that it was preceded by a democratic phase. . . . I also learned the lesson that if such absolutely orthodox people as Rajk could be executed, it was not possible to imagine any alternative. Such a fate seemed to lie in store for anyone whose opinions deviated from the orthodox line.[15]

In an unpublished essay for a memorial volume that Rajk's widow Júlia was assembling, Lukács similarly stressed the "preventive" character of the Rajk trial. Lukács explicitly contradicted Júlia Rajk's assertion that her husband had in any way been oppositional.[16] Yet precisely because of his close ideological alignment with Rákosi and his Stalinist inner circle, Rajk represented a *potential* alternative to them as a leader and was thus preemptively eliminated.

Show trials, Kirchheimer explains, focus on political leadership and ultimately hinge on real or imagined implications of dissension within a leadership group:

> The defendants were individuals who presumably wanted or at least were able—should objective conditions show a change of policy—to substitute for

the present leadership. The presumption was based on their former record of opposition within the party, in some instances on a more recent dissension, but often exclusively on their official position. (*Political Justice*, 105)

He goes on to describe how the judicial proceedings of show trials use "rules of translation" to generate from "a collection of motley facts in which real occurrences were inextricably bound up with purely fictitious happenings" a "prefabricated and alternative reality," to which the defendants were in the process compelled to concede. The dramaturgical mechanisms of the political trial sharpen such dissensions into essential, if often merely possible conflicts between leaders, routing them into narrative chains of historical necessity that invest even trivial acts and utterances with fatal significance:

> Under the defendants' sometimes willing, sometimes grudging cooperation, certain of their thought and discussion patterns were translated into the realm of action and debited to the hypothetical consequences. Thus [Moscow trial prosecutor] Vishinsky ... led [his] victims close to admitting that foreseeing certain contingencies is tantamount to supporting them. They took the defendants through the remotest possible situations that could arise from what they made them admit were consequences of their political action. They always forced on them interpretations that were in line with the prosecution's theory of how the defendants would have acted had these situations arisen. (*Political Justice*, 107)

Lastly, citing the 1937 report of the Dewey Commission that investigated the putative "crimes" of Trotsky, Kirchheimer notes: "Whenever independent checks could be made on those in foreign countries who were implicated in the tales of the prosecution and the defendants, these persons not only vigorously denied all the factual allegations but in many instances proved the physical or logical impossibility of the events admitted at the trial" (107).

The Moscow Trials and the Dewey Commission

The "Moscow trials" refer to three political trials held between 1936 and 1938, in which nearly the entirety of the remaining Bolshevik leadership of the Russian Revolution was put on the docket, convicted of conspiracy against the Soviet Union, and executed; there was, in addition, a further secret trial of generals of the Red Army in 1937. All these trials centered on the premise that the exiled revolutionary leader Trotsky—who opposed Stalin's consolidation of power and propagation of "socialism in one country" against Trotsky's own calls for world revolution—had conspired within the Soviet Union and with agents of foreign fascist governments to assassinate Soviet leaders, carry out acts of sabotage against industry and infrastructure, and encourage invasion of the Soviet Union and the restoration of capitalism.

In a speech of March 3, 1937 to the Plenum of the Central Committee of the Communist Party of the Soviet Union, Stalin laid out three "indisputable facts" he claimed had been established:

> First, the wrecking and diversionist-espionage activity of the agents of foreign states, among whom a pretty active role was played by the Trotskyites, has affected in one degree or another all or nearly all our organizations—economic, administrative and Party. Second, agents of foreign States, including Trotskyites, penetrated not only into subordinate organizations, but also to certain responsible posts. Third, some of our leading comrades . . . not only failed to discern the real countenance of these wreckers, diversionists, spies, and murderers, but proved so unconcerned, complacent and naive, that at times they themselves assisted in promoting the agents of the foreign States to one or other responsible post.[17]

The transcripts of the trials were published and translated worldwide, and communist presses promulgated the official version of events, accusing anyone who doubted it of being themselves Trotskyites and fascist sympathizers (Figure 10.1).[18]

Figure 10.1 Trotsky "Whitewash" Cartoon, *The Daily Worker*, April 26, 1937.

The trials roiled the ranks of the New York liberal intelligentsia, which widely admired Stalin's rapid industrialization of the Soviet Union against the background of Depression-era capitalism and, even more importantly, saw the USSR as a bulwark against fascism and a new world war. Following the disaster of the Comintern's "Third Period" policy, which had cast other socialist tendencies as the communists' main enemy and helped smooth the way to the Nazi seizure of power, the Comintern pivoted towards the policy of the Popular Front, which encouraged the forging of alliances of all progressive forces, downplaying class struggle ideology in favor of broad opposition to fascism, and defending the workers' state against its hostile neighbors. Openly courted to this new alignment of Popular Front forces were intellectuals—writers, journalists, and academics among them—such as those who constituted the editorial mastheads and regular contributors of magazines of liberal opinion such as *The Nation* and *The New Republic*. The dubious character of the Moscow trials and executions that followed, however, represented uncomfortable intrusions into the Popular Front's dream of liberal common cause with Stalinist communism in the progressive struggle against fascism. The trials were met in liberal intellectual circles with a shifting combination of denial, evasion, agnosticism, disavowal, special pleading, name-calling, and divisive squabbling—but still, as might now seem remarkable, with a majority view that the trials were, if not wholly proper, at least in broad outlines authentic, necessary, and justified.[19]

It was in this context that Dewey made his charged and, given his age (almost eighty) and the opposition of family and friends, somewhat surprising decision to head up the Trotsky investigation. True, Dewey had previously grappled with abuses of political justice following the execution of the anarchists Sacco and Vanzetti in his article in *The New Republic* entitled "Psychology and Justice," in which he characterized the whole affair as "extrajudicial."[20] After the first Moscow trial, a committee of prominent academics and intellectuals—including the theologian Reinhold Niebuhr, philosopher Sidney Hook, anthropologist Franz Boas, novelist John Dos Passos, and others—had formed a committee for the defense of Trotsky ("defense" meaning that they supported asylum for Trotsky and advocated investigation of the charges arrayed against him). Trotsky delivered a barrage of speeches and articles defending himself, as well, including a February 9, 1937 radio address to a New York audience that was subsequently published, at Hook's urging, as a pamphlet entitled *I Stake My Life* (Figure 10.2).[21] Having undertaken on Trotsky's request to constitute a commission of inquiry and conduct an investigatory judicial process, the committee solicited Dewey to chair it.

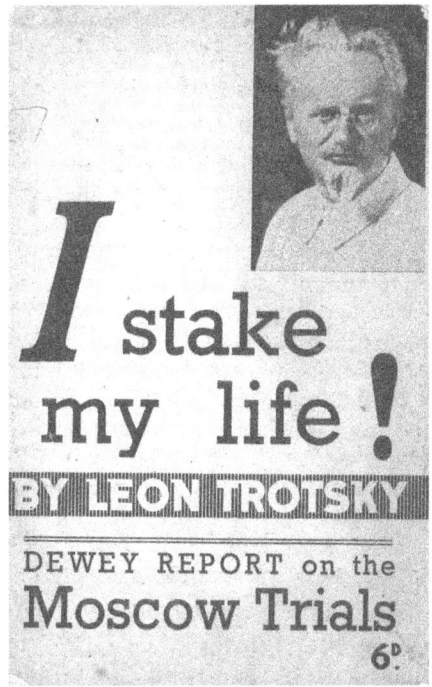

Figure 10.2 Cover of Leon Trotsky, *I Stake My Life!*, 1937.

Like the Moscow trials themselves, Dewey's Trotsky commission exemplified a novelty in international law. Dewey's was only the second major international citizens' tribunal, the first having been the Commission of Inquiry into the Origins of the Reichstag Fire, just prior to the Nazi trial of the Bulgarian communist Georgi Dimitrov and his co-defendants.[22] The Dewey Commission's eleven members, plus the lawyer for the commission and Trotsky's counsel, traveled to Mexico to conduct its "trial" from April 10 to April 17, 1937, publishing its findings six months later as *The Case of Leon Trotsky*, which provided day-by-day transcripts of the process, and as *Not Guilty*, which presented the commission findings and eponymous verdict.[23] That closing verdict read:

> [W]e find that the trials have served not juridical but political ends. On the basis of all the evidence herein examined and all the conclusions stated, we find that the trials of August, 1936 and January, 1937, were frame-ups. On the basis of all the evidence herein examined and all the conclusions stated, we find Leon Trotsky and Leon Sedov not guilty. (*Not Guilty*, 499)

Throughout the process, from the formation of the commission to the publication of its findings, Dewey and others were pressured not to participate or to resign, as well as subjected to vituperation as Trotskyite dupes, stooges, or secret supporters in the communist press. In a letter to the February 19, 1937 *News Bulletin of the American Committee for the Defense of Leon Trotsky*, for example, the Marxist art historian Meyer Schapiro (also, notably, a friendly New York contact for the recently arrived Frankfurt School leadership) gives a glimpse into this orchestrated pressure campaign against intellectuals involved in the defense of Trotsky:

> Mr. Kenneth Durant, the director of the American branch of TASS, the Official Soviet news agency, called me ... on Friday, February 5, in order to find out—as a matter of journalistic fact—whether I was still a member of the Committee for the Defense of Leon Trotsky. He informed me that several members had resigned and urged me, as a known friend of the Soviet Union to do the same before it was too late. He characterized the committee as a tool of Trotskyites and a dangerous fascist counter-revolutionary force. The effort of Durant to detach me from the committee is part of an organized mission of members of the Communist Party to destroy the committee.[24]

Besides cruder attacks in the communist press, the campaign to discredit the Dewey Commission also included "An Open Letter to American Liberals," published in the March 1937 issue of the fellow-traveler journal *Soviet Russia Today* and signed by eighty-eight leftist intellectuals, journalists, artists, and writers including Malcolm Cowley, Theodore Dreiser, Louis Fischer, Lillian Hellman, Dorothy Parker, Henry Roth, Paul Sweezy, Max Weber (the painter), and Nathanael West. The letter posed four highly leading questions: whether Dewey committee members were motivated by adherence to Trotskyism or liberal principles; whether they wished to align themselves with political movements opposed to progress in the Soviet Union; whether they wanted to further the interests of fascism; and whether they opposed the Soviet Union's protecting itself against treason.[25] The goal was to insinuate the worst and sow doubt about the commission's aims and integrity.

Whitewashing the Trials: Journalists and Scholars

It is worth recalling how mainstream pro-Stalinist views of the trials were at the time. The now-notorious special correspondent for the *New York Times* Walter Duranty, who won the Pulitzer Prize for his reporting from the Soviet Union in 1932, opined in an article of January 31, 1937, "There is little doubt that this trial has accomplished what the Kameneff-Zinoviev affair may have failed to accomplish, the convincing of the whole Soviet Nation that Trotskyism not only is counter revolutionary but also an ally of fascism and a stimulus to war."[26] In a subsequent article on February 7, 1937, Duranty explained:

> Trotsky's mainspring was personal ambition, whereas Stalin was "Lenin's disciple and a prolonger of Lenin's work," as he told me himself on Christmas Day of 1933.... Stalin from the outset was true to the Bolsheviks' ideology, whereas Trotsky from the outset to his present lamentable position was a Trotskyist first, last, and always. (Duranty quoted in Heilbrunn, 91)

In an article published in *The New Republic* on July 14, 1937, entitled "The Riddle of Russia: What Lies behind Recent Events in the USSR?" Duranty offered his account of the trial evidence and provided readers with the following "final synthesis," seeking to dispel any doubts they might have about the trials' bases and proceedings:

> Trotsky was fanatically determined to overthrow the Stalinist regime.
> Hitler was fanatically determined to "expand eastwards" at the expense of the USSR.
> Both Hitler and Trotsky had at their disposal efficient organizations to develop conspirative action, sabotage and espionage within the USSR and to conduct propaganda abroad.
> Opportunities for contact between Germany (and Japan) and anti-Stalinist conspirators both inside and outside the USSR were not lacking.
> The conclusion is inevitable.
> It cannot be negatived [sic] by foreign bewilderment over the "mystery" of the trials and of the confessions made by the accused, or by foreign belief that the morale of the Red Army has been gravely impaired and that the whole of the USSR has been engulfed in a flood of hysterical witch-hunting. The Kremlin's enemies have used this belief and bewilderment to weaken ... the international prestige of the USSR, but that does not alter the fact that their Trojan Horse is broken and its occupants destroyed.[27]

Such opinions, in fact, had already been anticipated by the articles on Soviet Russia for which Duranty had previously received the Pulitzer Prize. Along with reports covering up the deadly famine in the Ukraine, one of Duranty's articles considered by the Pulitzer committee was entitled "Stalinism Smashes Foes in Marx's Name," which, though dating from 24 June, 1931, might have been a headline from the trials six years later.[28] Summing up the quality of Duranty's bestselling books, such as his 1941 *The Kremlin and the People*, Jacob Heilbrunn remarks that "An inspection of Duranty's books further reveals the character of his extraordinary dispatches, almost unequaled in the history of modern journalism for their mendacity" (Heilbrunn, 96).

Early in 1937, a member of the American Committee for the Defense of Leon Trotsky, the journalist and editor Mauritz Hallgren, who wrote for *The Nation* and later *The Baltimore Sun*, turned against the committee and released a communist-published pamphlet entitled "Why I Resigned from the Trotsky Defense Committee."[29] Hallgren argued that when Trotsky was granted asylum in Mexico the committee's work was done, and the argument for an investigation of the Moscow trials was a sign of Trotskyite machinations. Hallgren summed up his own view of the trials as follows:

> On the one hand we have the confessions of the Moscow defendants, the court record, the statements of disinterested observers at the first trial, and the reports on the second trial of such reputable journalists as Walter Duranty. These provide... an abundance of evidence tending to prove that the defendants were fairly tried and that their guilt in conspiring to overthrow the Soviet government has been established. They also tend to prove that Trotsky participated in the conspiracy, or that he at least had guilty knowledge of it, though the direct proof of his part in the crime is not so substantial as that involving the men on trial. However, we also have his writings and they tend greatly to strengthen the presumption, if not of actual guilt, at least of moral responsibility. On the other hand, we have nothing concrete with which to offset the charge of conspiracy. ("Why I Resigned," 11–12)

Cowley, as literary editor of *The New Republic*, was one of the most vociferous apologists for the Moscow trials in the liberal camp. In a long article for *The New Republic* in April 7, 1937 reviewing *The Case of the Anti-Soviet Trotskyite Center*, Cowley expressed distaste for "big-city intellectuals of [Trotsky's] type"[30] and argued that while some details of the Moscow trials required suspension of judgment, the basic facts in the case were nevertheless beyond reasonable doubt. Such established "facts," in Cowley's view, included:

> The defendants had been fighting their own government by sabotage and terrorism. They had plotted against the lives of Stalin and his chief collaborators. They had caused a series of railroad accidents in West Siberia and the Urals, including one wreck in which twenty-nine Red Army men were killed. They had been responsible for fatal explosions in power and chemical plants. They had deliberately drawn bad plans for factories and mines, so that production was delayed and accidents increased. They had delivered three important chemical secrets to agents of the German government, and they had given the mobilization plans for the Siberian railroads to Japanese spies. All this they had done under the impression that they were faithfully carrying out "directives from the center," in other words, from Trotsky himself. ("Record of a Trial," 268)

Throughout 1937 and 1938, the general editorial position of *The New Republic* did not question that the Moscow trials were grounded in established evidence of a Trotskyite conspiracy and collusion with foreign powers, though it did express growing worry about their impact on the USSR's international standing and its ability to resist the threat from Germany and Japan. This worry led even to a cringeworthy open letter from Cowley's fellow editor Bruce Bliven to Stalin, in which he advises the Russian leader to follow Anglo-Saxon or Roman law convention in any future trials; to make more of the underlying evidence available to the world public; to abolish the death penalty; to provide an amnesty to those not currently charged under the normal civil code; and to organize those amnestied into a *legal* opposition![31]

For his part, Cowley stuck to a more active defense of the trials, for instance, in his May 18, 1938 review of the Radek and Bukharin trial reports, "Moscow Trial: 1938," in which he summarized several conclusions from his reading of the transcripts. Cowley offers his readers six summary points: 1) that there was a loose alliance of all anti-Stalin oppositional elements; 2) that the weakness of the conspirators made them seek out the USSR's enemies; 3) that the different factions prosecuted their conspiratorial activities along different lines, in industry, the army, etc.; 4) that the aim of the defendants was to seize power; 5) that the conspirators were timing their action to coincide with the outbreak of war, which they sought to hasten; and 6) that we may expect further conspiracies against Stalin, and thus the trials will continue.[32] Continuing the following week with reflections on the 1938 trial reports in "Moscow Trial: II," Cowley expressed ethical qualms about the trial and "new respect and affection for the political virtues of the old-fashioned liberals," but continued to assert the factual existence of a Rights-Trotskyite political alliance that had sought to carry out a "series of schemes for political assassinations and palace insurrections that ended with their trial."[33]

In response to Cowley's April 1937 review of the trial reports, his friend Edmund Wilson admonished him and expressed skepticism about the trials:

> I believe you are mistaken about the trials. . . . [Y]ou sound as if you had read nothing but the official report. . . . I guess that all the trials have been fakes since the time of the Ramzin sabotage trial [the "Industry Party Trial" of 1930]. They have always been intended to provide scapegoats and divert attention from more fundamental troubles. In the case of these recent trials, I imagine that not a word of these confessions was true. The victims had, I suppose, been guilty of some sort of opposition to the regime; and the technique is evidently to tell them that they can only vindicate themselves by putting on acts which will be helpful to the USSR.[34]

But Wilson was in a minority.

Even respectable academic opinion genteelly resonated with the more brutal views of Duranty, Hallgren, and Cowley. In a May 19, 1937 editorial note in *The New Republic*, the editors report that they have sent the trial reports and the published materials from "the Trotsky side" to a Yale Law School professor, Fred Rodell, to read as a legal expert. Rodell pleaded complete agnosticism in the case, since the main effect of examining the evidence, he stated, was to heighten his uncertainty about the truth of the matter:

> After reading all the material, I feel that I know just as little about what really happened as before I started. . . . So far as I'm concerned the whole thing might still have been a frame-up or every word might have been gospel truth. . . . The two cancel each other out and leave, to my skeptical mind, exactly nothing.[35]

In a scholarly article in the October 1937 issue of *Foreign Affairs* entitled "The Moscow Trials: A Legal View," UC Berkeley law professor Max Radin went beyond Rodell's skepticism, offering several conclusions following a meticulous rehearsal of the case. Radin argued that "it is clear that no judgment that will command assent can be reached on the basis of the available evidence," because neither the published evidence of the trials nor the evidence subsequently evinced by the Dewey Commission's investigation was complete.[36] Noting that the Moscow trials' complete lack of any documentary evidence and inconsistency in some key details constituted "weakness" in the prosecution's case, Radin nevertheless argues for the likely authenticity of the confessions of the defendants. "[T]he public confessions of all the defendants are," he writes,

> extremely difficult to explain on any plausible ground unless they were actually guilty. It is unprecedented that men of this type . . . should have acted as they did without any reasonable ground to believe that they would escape the death penalty and without any specific evidence of torture. We should further have to assume that the prosecution forced them to enter into a conspiracy to incriminate Trotsky and his son without advantage to themselves and without thereby making the seizure and punishment easier for the government. This is possible, just as it is possible that there are adequate if undisclosed reasons for the absence of documentary evidence. ("The Moscow Trials: A Legal View," 79)

However, Radin concludes, "If we must make some estimate of the weight of probability, I think it is still in favor of the prosecution as far as the Moscow defendants were concerned. In the case of Trotsky and Sedov [Trotsky's son] themselves nothing except a suspension of judgment is possible" (79). Lastly, with respect to the executions of the accused: "The extent of punishment is a matter of policy. As long as capital punishment is part of a criminal system, the justification for its application must depend on considerations that cannot be easily estimated at a distance and by foreigners. But English and American observers will not readily overcome their repugnance to capital punishment inflicted wholesale on groups of thirteen and sixteen people" (79). To sum up Radin's position in other words: On the basis of the evidence we cannot make any reliable judgment about the case, but we may nevertheless infer that the Moscow defendants were probably guilty of much of what they were accused of. While we may personally find mass executions repugnant, capital punishment is really a matter of local policy.[37]

Radin's views appear to have been consonant with those of other legal experts as well. In his 1941 bestselling book *Mission to Moscow*, Joseph Davies, Roosevelt's ambassador to the Soviet Union from 1936 to 1938, reports having bought "fifty or sixty copies" of the proceedings of the two purge trials to date, which he sent to friends in the United States. He reports that—

> two very eminent lawyers, one an Assistant Attorney General under President Wilson's Administration, the Honorable Charles Warren, author of the recent standard book on the Supreme Court of the United States, and the other the Honorable Seth W. Richardson, Assistant Attorney General under the Hoover Administration, told me that they had found interest in reading the proceedings with care and that each had arrived at the conclusion that no other judgment but guilty, in their opinion, could have been sustained by the evidence.[38]

Davies does not, we may note, report the reactions of the other forty-eight to fifty-eight of his friends in the US. When *Mission to Moscow* was adapted into a Hollywood film in 1943—by then, explicitly functioning as wartime propaganda to dispel concerns about the Soviet Union as a military ally—Davies's presentation of the trials in his book, which hedges to some degree about their veracity and quotes dissenting views among diplomats, now becomes sheer one-sided falsification. The trials are dramatized as if the guilt of the defendants was definitively established; the Stalin–Hitler pact is rationalized as an unfortunate necessity imposed upon the sincere, westward-yearning Stalin; and the damaging purges of the Red Army general staff are covered over with reassuring scenes of Soviet military parades using spliced-in documentary footage. Notably, this closure of the film around a cosmos of alternative facts was not simply a function of Hollywood vulgarization or even the exigencies of wartime propaganda. Ambassador Davies himself had retained absolute control of the script, even rejecting one version and demanding a new screenwriter be brought in by Warner Brothers.[39]

The film dramatizes the third Moscow trial, with the closing speech of the Bolshevik leader Nikolai Bukharin,[40] upon whom Arthur Koestler loosely based his prisoner Rubashov in his novel *Darkness at Noon*.

Bukharin's bizarrely inconsistent speech is notorious for the disturbing probability, still clearer from evidence of Stalin's own hand-editing of the transcripts, that Bukharin was ironizing his own confession, when the defendants' confessions and their denunciations of one another constituted the sole publicly available documentary evidence in the trials. For example, in a passage which, remarkably, made it into the transcript, Bukharin says, "The confession of the accused is not essential. The confession of the accused is a medieval principle of jurisprudence."[41] He goes on to make the absurd and possibly ironic assertation that he could "infer *a priori* that Trotsky and my other allies in crime as well as the Second International . . . will endeavor to defend us, especially and particularly myself" (Bukharin in *Report of Court Proceeding*, 778–79). In another passage that Stalin hand-penciled out of the transcript, Bukharin offers the following self-incrimination: "I accept responsibility even for those crimes about which I did not know or about which I did not have the slightest idea."[42] None of the exasperated twists of logic that entered the trial record are to be found in *Mission to Moscow*'s Bukharin, who in his final speech to the court earnestly confesses his crimes against the proletarian state and contritely invites the ultimate punishment (Figure 10.3).

Figure 10.3 Bukharin scene at Moscow trial, *Mission to Moscow*, 1943. Film still.

James Rorty and the Liberal Apologists

A letter to *The Nation* dated February 16, 1937, entitled "Harsh Words from a Friend," offered an angry response to the editorial "Behind the Soviet Trials" which *The Nation* had published in its February 6 issue. The editorial had taken studied distance from any judgment on the facts of the trials, claiming "It is possible that it will be another hundred years before all the actual facts about the recent Soviet trials are known."[43] But the editorial writer still had argued that in all probability the confessions of the conspirators were authentic; that the most disturbing aspects of the trial to the Western observer were due to the differences in the Soviet legal system; that the accusations of terrorism, conspiracy, and even collusion with foreign powers were plausible given Trotsky's opposition to Stalin and his belief that world revolution would engulf the imperialist countries in case of war; that the trials were instrumental to achieving the unity required to defend the USSR against its enemies; and that terrorism and conspiracies are understandable as an outgrowth of the Soviet Union's dictatorial suppression of the legitimate means of political opposition typical in a democracy. On the last point, in a tour de force of convoluted reasoning, the editors conceded that liberals could take up certain warranted criticisms of the current Soviet Union on behalf of the opposition, while, at the same time, they should not question the overall legitimacy of the Moscow trials. "Meanwhile," they concluded, "the sympathetic outside observer must offer the Russian government a measure of that criticism which a legal opposition provides the government of a democracy. He must point out the dangers inherent in a prolonged dictatorship, while refusing to use the trial as the enemies of the Soviet Union." ("Behind the Moscow Trials," 145). In the interest of the progressive unity of the Popular Front, the editorial suggested, liberals should dispel their misgivings about the trials and the resulting liquidations, to use the phrase of the moment.

The author of the February 16th letter was having none of this. He writes:

> Dear Sirs:
> For nearly twenty years I have read *The Nation* and written for it. During that period I have always felt that no matter how sharply I differed with the opinions and attitudes of particular editors ... I could always count on one thing: that *The Nation*, when confronted with a situation involving fundamental issues of truth, justice, and moral and intellectual integrity, would deal with it honestly and courageously.
> *The Nation* faced a test of this kind during the last war and met it more

creditably than most . . . of its contemporaries. *The Nation* faced such a test in connection with the Moscow trials, and in my opinion failed—patently, grossly, disgracefully . . . [W]hen you printed Behind the Moscow Trials you made your debut in a way of thinking and writing that violates every standard that three generations of editors and writers have labored to establish for *The Nation*. You admit, by implication at least, that the frame-up of Trotsky *was* a frame-up. Yet you condone this frame-up on the ground of political expediency . . .[44]

The letter's author refers to Trotsky's written refutations of the Moscow trials' accusations against him. He alludes to inconsistencies in the prosecutor's case, pointing towards its falsification: for instance, that Copenhagen's Hotel Bristol, where Trotsky's son allegedly had met with the conspirator Holtzman in 1932, had actually been torn down already in 1917; that the confession of Pyatakov, who allegedly flew from Berlin to Oslo in December 1935 to meet with Trotsky, was contradicted by the head of the airport's assertion that no flights from Germany had landed during the entire month of December; that Trotsky and his son, under close police watch at their residence in the French countryside, had not been in Paris at the time they were supposed to have met with Romm there. About six weeks after the appearance of this letter, the Dewey Commission, convening for an investigatory trial of Trotsky in the house of painter Diego Rivera in Mexico in April 1937, would review just such inconsistencies in copious detail. The letter's author was a poet, journalist, and founding editor of the leftist magazine *The New Masses* named James Rorty, the father of the contemporary philosopher Richard Rorty.[45]

In the late 1920s and early 1930s James Rorty had been associated with the Communist Party. However, by the mid-1930s, he had fallen afoul of Stalinist orthodoxy and embraced an independent socialist but Trotsky-friendly orientation, which made him a regular object of scorn and criticism by the communist press. As Judy Kutulas notes of dissident Marxists such as Rorty and Herbert Solow, they "reinforced the CPUSA's suspicion of nonaffiliated intellectuals by being belligerent, disruptive, and deliberately provocative. . . . They were not intimidated by Communist functionaries and joined fronts without any intention of playing by their unspoken rules."[46] As was evidenced by his 1934 study of advertising, *Our Master's Voice*, Rorty was also a sophisticated critic of the mass media and its potential for persuasion, spin, manipulation, and propaganda.[47] As Jefferson Pooley notes in his introduction to a reissue of *Our Master's Voice*, Rorty joined for a short time Paul Lazarsfeld's Princeton Radio Project in 1937, where Adorno also began working in 1938. Though both were troublesome personalities, Lazarsfeld tended to defend Adorno and contrasted him to Rorty: "It is true that I still have some difficulty in getting W [Wiesengrund-Adorno] down to earth but there can be no doubt of his originality and the fruitfulness of his approach. With R [Rorty], I do not even know whether he has produced a new aspect."[48] Following critical remarks Rorty made in the *Socialist Call* newspaper about the 1937 League of American Writers Second Writers' Congress in New York, Rorty was taken to task by his previous magazine *The New Masses* in an article entitled "From Rorty to Hearst," which accused him of furnishing the Hearst Press with ammunition to attack the Popular Front.[49] The Communist Party's *Daily Worker* dutifully toed this line as well, lampooning Rorty in a cartoon as a trained seal fed by William Randolph Hearst (Figure 10.4).[50] The *Socialist Call*

Figure 10.4   James Rorty as William Randolph Hearst's Trained Seal, *The Daily Worker*, June 11, 1937.

itself carried a reply to Rorty by the writer Claude McKay, who was by this time highly critical of communism. McKay argued that Rorty's and fellow intellectuals' criticisms of the League were insufficient; they needed to declare their independence from any regime and organize a truly autonomous writers' union.[51]

Philosophy on Trial?

It is not prima facie improbable that we could take the Moscow trials to be a *philosophically* significant event, as a novel historical occurrence that provoked philosophical reflection, especially given the engagement of a philosopher of the stature of Dewey in examining their factual basis and their distortions of juridical procedure. That was certainly later the case for Maurice Merleau-Ponty, who in his 1947 book *Humanism and Terror* focuses on the Moscow trials to reflect on questions such as the role of violence in human relations, the tension between human agency and responsibility within a deterministic philosophy of history, the subjective and objective conditions of legal guilt and innocence, and the epistemological and existential status of self-accusation and confession.[52] Even closer at hand, Dewey's friend and follower Sidney Hook—who introduced ideas from Lukács's *History and Class Consciousness* to the United States and Karl Korsch to American readers in his 1933 book *Towards an Understanding of Karl Marx*—explicitly avowed that the trials and the commission's work had affected his own philosophical views, particularly about the nature of historical truth.

In his 1987 autobiography *Out of Step*, Hook amplifies the specifically philosophical impact of the trials on his Dewey-influenced left pragmatism, which he characterized as "objective relativism":

> The upshot of the Moscow trials affected my epistemology, too. I had been prepared to recognize that understanding the past was in part a function of our need to cope with the present and future, that rewriting history was in a sense a method of making it. But the realization that such a view easily led to the denial of objective historical truth, to the cynical view that not only is history written by the survivors but that historical truth is created by the survivors—which made untenable any distinction between historical fiction and truth. . . . Because nothing was absolutely true and no one could know the whole truth about anything, it did *not* follow that it was impossible to establish any historical truth beyond a reasonable doubt.[53]

Hook's use of the phrase "beyond a reasonable doubt" suggests aligning the criteria of historical truth with a pragmatic legal standard of proof, rather than a stronger epistemological claim based on representational correspondence to an uncontestable, non-discursive reality.

Dewey was less ready to admit any philosophical significance of his activities around Trotsky. Selden Rodman, one of the editors of the independent leftist journal *Common Sense*, had published an article entitled "Trotsky in the Kremlin: An Interview. What the Exiled Bolshevik Leader Might Have Done In Stalin's Place,"[54] which earned the ire of Trotsky and dismissal of the magazine's circle as "reactionary snobs."[55] The article had opined about Trotsky's own dogmatic mindset, his adherence to Bolshevik principles, and his history of using violence in the suppression of his enemies. Referring to the Dewey Commission's findings and the transcripts of the Moscow trials, Rodman expounded the following views:

> That Trotsky certainly, and the Moscow defendants probably, were guilty neither of terrorism nor of plotting with foreign powers;
> That the Moscow Trials ... are not primarily manifestations of some sinister latter-day sorcery known as Stalinism, but are a direct result of the Marxist-Leninist philosophy in which the end is made to justify the means ...;
> That similarly it can be argued fairly that Trotsky and the Oppositionists would have acted in the same way, given the opportunity;
> That the Commission itself being composed of two ardent admirers of Trotsky, two Liberals and one inaudible Herr Doktor, could prove nothing finally;
> That one of the liberals became so irritated with the partisans and with Trotsky's innate inability to answer a simple question without making a speech, that he asked unfair questions and precipitated his own resignation ...;[56]
> *That the other liberal was right and courageous in demanding a hearing for Trotsky but hesitant to identify the common philosophy that led to only apparently different actions*;
> That the case will never be proved because if One True Church cannot be wrong, neither can Two. (Rodman in Dewey, *The Later Years* 13, 395–96; emphasis mine)

From all this, Rodman concluded: "the time has come for American radicals to stop juggling with the comparative merits of the philosophy and tactics that underlie both" (400), a view echoed by the Stalinophile *New Republic*, which published conflicting letters on the Moscow trials' validity under the title "Both Their Houses," echoing Mercutio's famous curse in *Romeo and Juliet*.[57]

Dewey's response, entitled "In Defense of the Mexican Hearings," was published in the January 1938 issue of *Common Sense*.[58] He offers a couple of factual corrections, but more substantively notes that the commission made no assessment of the underlying political philosophy that Stalin and Trotsky share, that of Bolshevism or of Marxism more broadly. The commission, Dewey asserts, was not charged with considering matters of philosophy but solely "to hear whatever evidence Trotsky had to present bearing on the charges brought against him in the Moscow trials, and to examine and weigh that evidence, oral and especially documentary. . . . To arrive at a conclusion on the point of guilt was the entire and sole purpose of the investigation which the full Commission of Inquiry has conducted" ("In Defense," 348). He goes on to write, "It is an interesting question whether, as Mr. Rodman says, 'Trotsky and the Oppositionists would have acted in the same way, given the opportunity.' But, in the first place, it is a question of argument not of fact, and in the second a question outside the scope of the Commission" (348). The commission at most raised matters for later philosophical reflection—for instance, as Dewey writes, leading "radicals to consider more fully than they have done in the past the alternative philosophies of social change which underlie different strategies and tactics" (348)— but it should not be criticized for not pursuing such philosophical questions itself.

Philosophy, Democracy, and the Dewey Commission

Accepting then that we should not take Dewey to have had any direct philosophical intent in his investigations of the Moscow trials, nor to have offered any direct philosophical reflection on his experience with Trotsky, we may nevertheless, in conclusion, find resonances of Dewey's Trotsky-related activities with the theoretical concerns of the Frankfurt School, with mass deception and even, perhaps, with Lukács's late concerns with democratization and what we might call the "socialist public sphere." If so, I suggest, these resonances may be found in Dewey's pragmatist's nexus of practical engagement and theoretical reflection, the interplay of means and ends, processes of inquiry and warranted claims to truth, and his commitment to democracy as the basis of social problem-solving and progressive change. I will indicate three areas of interest.

First, Dewey's encounter with Trotsky and the full enormity of the Moscow trials stiffened Dewey's criticisms of Marxism's philosophy of history, which he thought reduced the plurality of human motivations and action-forms to a single type, the class struggle. In the 1920s in the Soviet Union there had been attention to and even some application of Dewey's educational ideas, and Dewey had in turn followed the Soviet social experiment with interest, publishing in 1929 a positive account of his visit, *Impressions of Soviet Russia and the Revolutionary World*.[59]

But, as he stated in a February 1938 interview with Agnes Meyer on "The Significance of the Trotsky Trial,"

> The great lesson to be derived from these amazing revelations is the complete breakdown of revolutionary Marxism. . . . The great lesson for all American radicals and for all sympathizers with the USSR is that they must go back and reconsider the whole question of means of bringing about social changes and of truly democratic methods of approach to social progress.[60]

As with Lukács in his debate with Adorno, Dewey's implied point of criticism is primarily practical and pedagogical rather than theoretical: How can we prepare most effectively to confront social challenges and fully develop the potentials of our society? In pursuit of this evolving goal, Dewey looked to an experimental, adaptive collective practice, supported by democratic education and public discussion of matters of common concern.

Dewey also responded to the June 1938 essay of Leon Trotsky entitled "Our Morality and Theirs," in which Trotsky argues that all morality is class morality and that the rules of moral conduct derive from the class struggle. In his response "Means and Ends," published in August 1938, Dewey criticizes Trotsky for deducing means to a moral end—the liberation of humanity—from a putative law of history. Thus lost, Dewey argues, is the interdependence of means and ends that entails consideration of the variety of means according to their possible consequences.[61] Dewey here forms the antipode to Lukács's tormented early ethical reflections on ends and means in revolutionary action, which Lukács describes in quasi-theological (and dramaturgical) terms of destiny, tragedy, guilt, and sacrifice.[62] Closer to Dewey, however, is Lukács's later, "realist" conception of action within constrained but mutable contexts, which commits him to account for the contingency in all historical situations and to recognize that even false starts, defeats, and delays may, in the long view, represent critical collective learning processes.

Second, as Hook underscores, Dewey interrupted years of work on his late magnum opus *Logic: The Theory of Inquiry*, which was only published in 1938. While doubtlessly there is little direct trace of the Trotsky experience in the arguments of the book, it is useful to consider, as Alan Spitzer did in his 2000 book *Historical Truth and Lies about the Past*, Dewey's Trotsky investigation in light of the *Logic*'s exposition of "judgments recognized to be historical" in the longer section dedicated to "Narration-Description."[63] Here, Dewey offered a strongly hermeneutical and historicist conception of historical writing, emphasizing the activity of selecting and composing a historical account of the past from the perspective of the present—analogous in this respect to Lukács's arguments about the fusion of past and present horizons in the historical novel and drama. "All historical construction is necessarily selective," Dewey writes:

> Everything in the writing of history depends upon the principle used to control selection. This principle decides the weight which shall be assigned to past events, what shall be admitted and what omitted; it also decides how the facts selected shall be arranged and ordered. Furthermore, if the fact of selection is acknowledged to be primary and basic, we are committed to the conclusion that all history is necessarily written from the standpoint of the present, and is, in an inescapable sense, the history not only of the present but of that which is contemporaneously judged to be important in the present.[64]

It might seem that Dewey is granting wide latitude to "anything-goes" historical relativism in which one might, if not justify, at least not be able to disqualify a slanted selection of facts such as the Moscow trials frame-ups. But Dewey rejects in strong terms any premise that the intrinsic fluidity and changeability in historical interpretation implies an equivalent lability of its underlying evidentiary basis. He writes:

> The first task in historical inquiry [is] the collection of data and their confirmation as authentic. Modern historiography is notable for the pains taken in these matters and in development of special techniques for securing and checking data as to their authenticity and relative weight. Such disciplines as epigraphy, paleography, numismatics, linguistics, bibliography, have reached an extraordinary development as auxiliary techniques for accomplishing the historiographic function. (*Logic*, 231–32)

While there may indeed be no deeper, foundational anchor that allows us to say of a historical account that it represents the past absolutely "as it really was," the institutionalized protocols of historical inquiry and the auxiliary techniques that support them are enough to produce historically valid (if fallible and correctable) statements about the past. That is, "true" in the only way that historical statements could ever be true, in Dewey's view: as warrantable assertions based on legitimate processes of inquiry.

We can see a practical instance of Dewey's conception of historical truth in an anecdote from his engagement with the Trotsky case. After the Dewey Commission did its investigation and published its verdict, a third Moscow trial took place, the Rykov-Bukharin trial. The pro-Stalin socialist philosopher Corliss Lamont sent Dewey an angry telegram accusing him of betraying his experimental method by continuing to assert that the trials were a frame-up without having considered the further evidence that the new trial presented about Trotsky's putative conspiratorial activities. Dewey retorted:

> Experimental method does not prevent use of intelligence and authentic knowledge previously obtained. On the contrary scientific method demands application of knowledge previously had by its use to judging related present and future conditions. Material given out by the commission of inquiry has had my prior authorization. I accept full responsibility. No cause for worry.[65]

Dewey's hermeneutical and historicist understanding of historical writing did not, then, in his view foreclose, but rather entailed the necessity to draw valid historical inferences from authenticated data.

The final point concerns what Hilary Putnam has called Dewey's "epistemological justification of democracy," which Putnam formulates as: "Democracy is not just a form of social life among the other workable forms of social life; it is the precondition for the full application of intelligence to the solution of social problems."[66] Putnam suggestively compares Dewey's epistemological justification of democracy with the communicative action theories of the second-generation Frankfurt School, with Habermas's and Karl-Otto Apel's attempts to ground social critique in the normative bases of undistorted intersubjective communication. Honneth brings Dewey still closer to Habermas's communicative action model, wherein public discussion of issues and problems is seen as a means by which institutions are democratically steered and decisions are shaped by collective intelligence and will. But in conceiving of the public sphere as performing such a function, Dewey emphasizes shared processes of inquiry, social problem-solving, and social learning, going so far as "to conceive of the process of public will formation as a large-scale experimental process in which, according to the criteria of the rationality of past decisions, we continually decide anew how state institutions are to be specifically organized and how they are to relate to one another in terms of their jurisdiction."[67]

For his part, far distant from Dewey in his political outlook and historical moment, Lukács took up after the suppression of the Prague Spring in 1968 this very question of "public opinion" in the socialist bloc and the need for extensive factual and theoretical correction of the Stalinist legacy, in the interest of the democratization of actually existing socialist society. Lukács reflected on state socialism's failure to allow a genuine public sphere to flourish and the consequent forcing of public discussion into subterranean channels of gossip, euphemism, and conversation in secret. On the one hand, he noted, "The participants are deeply convinced that taking part in [public] discussions has practically no significance for the issues themselves, or can frequently cause the participants personal harm."⁶⁸ On the other hand, he continues, in the cultural sphere:

> vibrant and free public opinion exists, but in an underground and subterranean form. . . . Within Eastern European society, and dealing with all aspects of social life, this public opinion is primarily a matter of private conversation, of immediate and spontaneous discussions between two people. The real influence of such a secretive world is extraordinarily various. However, it would be wrong to underestimate it, or to judge it as completely ineffectual. I mention only in passing that it has been my personal experience for decades that success in the cultural areas is determined by this subterranean public opinion. Whether a work has artistic merit or is superficial, whether a novel has been successfully adapted into film, are questions decided on more by this secretive world than by the published critics (above all, by the official writers). (*Democratization*, 150)

Similar to Dewey, Lukács lay emphasis on historical *authentication*, including the need to correct falsifications and distortions of the evidentiary basis of historical writing. This necessary "cleansing of the historical record," inherited from Stalinism, he writes,

> will neither be immediate nor final, for it is impossible at this point to have a concrete grasp of all the problems and cases to be faced because so much of the present is still hidden in the unexamined Stalinist past. . . . Decades of omissions, confusions, distortions can only be put aside through many years of investigative work, through factual discussions concerning fundamental issues of theory and history. (*Democratization*, 161)

By 1968, in his emphasis on public discussion and historical truth-telling in this late text, the octogenerian Lukács had thus begun to sound rather like the near-octogenerian Dewey in 1938. This is not completely by accident: as a letter in September 1968 to Frank Benseler notes, Lukács was pondering the general significance of democracy in *both* capitalism and socialism. He projected "a larger essay on the social-ontological problems of today's democratization (in both systems)."⁶⁹ With respect to his own context of actually existing socialism, as Norman Levine has argued, Lukács envisioned both a reconstruction of and a new direction for the idea of the "transition of socialism to communism." Lukács, Levine writes, "substitutes the idea of a deeper democratization of socialist society for the idea of communism" as the goal of systemic change.⁷⁰ Lukács had intended to publish his democracy book in a German and an Italian edition, for which a contract had even been drafted. Yet unfortunately the book would not appear in print until the mid-1980s, when the Soviet Union and the East–Central European socialist societies were already headed towards a very different fate than the democratized socialism which Lukács hoped was still possible.⁷¹

And as for Dewey? His epistemological as well as practical-political concept of democracy sheds new light on the significance of the Trotsky Commission as well as, implicitly, on that retrospective authentication of socialist history that Lukács envisioned as the necessary preparation for genuine democratization. Neither a general sense of obligation to find out the truth, nor the personal moral sympathy Dewey might have felt for Trotsky in his peril can alone account for the philosopher's accepting the onerous task of heading the commission. It was rather his deep-seated commitment to democracy, both practical and philosophical, which demanded a properly conducted process of inquiry in this matter of urgent public concern. Where democracy itself, as a condition for truth and positive social change, was at stake, Dewey—like Lukács in his greatest moments of civic courage—could not take his place on the sidelines.

Notes

1. Max Horkheimer, "Introduction" to Leo Lowenthal and Norbert Guterman, *Prophets of Deceit: A Study of the Techniques of the American Agitator* (New York: Harper and Brothers, 1947), xi–xii.
2. Martin Jay, *The Dialectical Imagination: A History of the Frankfurt School and the Institute for Social Research, 1923–1950* (Boston: Little, Brown and Company, 1973), 20.
3. Leo Lowenthal, *An Unmastered Past: The Autobiographical Reflections of Leo Lowenthal*, ed. Martin Jay (Berkeley and Los Angeles: University of California Press, 1987), 66.
4. Adorno to Horkheimer, October 26, 1936 and November 28, 1938, quoted in Rolf Wiggershaus, *The Frankfurt School: Its History, Theories, and Political Significance*, trans. Michael Robertson (Cambridge, MA: The MIT Press, 1994), 162.
5. Georg Lukács, *Record of a Life: An Autobiographical Sketch*, ed. István Eörsi, trans. Rodney Livingstone (London: Verso, 1983), 108.
6. Otto Kirchheimer, *Political Justice; The Use of Legal Procedure for Political Ends* (Westport, CT: Greenwood Press, 1961). See also Kirchheimer's earlier essay "Politics and Justice" (1955), in Otto Kirchheimer, *Politics, Law, and Social Change*, eds. Frederic S. Burin and Kurt L. Shell (New York: Columbia University Press, 1969), 408–27. For discussion of Kirchheimer's conception of political justice, see: Ruben Hackler and Lucia Herrmann, "'Political Justice' in the Making: Otto Kirchheimer and His Late Work in Historical Perspective," *Redescriptions* 19/2 (2016): 146–72; Frank Schale, Lisa Klingsporn, and Hubertus Buchstein, "Otto Kirchheimer: Capitalist State, Political Parties and Political Justice," in *The SAGE Handbook of Frankfurt School Critical Theory* (London: SAGE Publications, 2018), 105–22; Annette Weinke, "A Case of Schmittian-Marxian Syndrome? Criminals, Enemies, and Other Foes in Otto Kirchheimer's Reflections on

Nazi Law and Nazi Criminality," in *Criminal Enemies*, eds. Austin Sarat, Lawrence Douglas, and Martha Merrill Umphrey (Amherst, MA: University of MA Press, 2019), 44–72. It is also worth recalling that Kirchheimer's work came out in 1961 as one of a number of other important post-World War II considerations of political trials by philosophers, including Maurice Merleau-Ponty's *Humanism and Terror* (1947), Hannah Arendt's *Eichmann in Jerusalem: A Report on the Banality of Evil* (1963), and Judith Shklar's *Legalism: Law, Morals, and Political Trials* (1964).

7. Kirchheimer, *Political Justice*, 112. For explications of the connections between theatre and the courtroom in the Soviet Union, see Julie A. Cassiday, *The Enemy on Trial: Early Soviet Courts on Stage and Screen* (DeKalb: Northern Illinois University Press, 2000); Elizabeth A. Wood, *Performing Justice: Agitation Trials in Early Soviet Russia* (Ithaca, NY: Cornell University Press, 2005); Stephan Kossmann, "Die Moskauer Prozesse der Jahre 1936 bis 1938—Monströse Lehrstücke theatraler Entgrenzung," *Slavica TerGestina* 13 (2011): 117–41; Vanessa Voisin, "Du 'procès spectacle' au fait social: historiographie de la médiatisation des procès en Union sovietique," *Critique Internationale* 75 (2017): 159–73.

8. Yasco Horsman has analogously explored the idea of political trials in Hannah Arendt, Bertolt Brecht, and Charlotte Delbo as a form of didactic theatre. See Horsman, *Theaters of Justice: Judging, Staging and Working Through in Arendt, Brecht, and Delbo* (Stanford: Stanford University Press, 2011).

9. For documentation of the Rajk trial, see *Rajk László és társai a népbíróság elott* (Budapest: Szikra, 1949); *László Rajk und Komplicen vor dem Volksgericht* (Berlin: Dietz Verlag, 1950); *Rajk Per*, ed. Gábor Paizs (Budapest: Ötlet, 1989).

10. Georg Lukács with Ilse Sieburt, "'Eine Art Freundschaft': Gespräch mit Georg Lukács" [1967], in Georg Lukács, *Werke* 18, eds. Frank Benseler and Werner Jung (Bielefeld: Aisthesis Verlag, 2005), 359.

11. Georg Lukács, "Der faschistisch verfälschte und die wirkliche Georg Büchner: Zu seinem hundertsten Todestag am 19. Februar 1937," in Lukács, *Deutsche Realisten des 19. Jahrhunderts* (Berlin: Aufbau-Verlag, 1953), 80.

12. György Lukács, "Sitzung der deutschen Schriftsteller am 4.9.1936," in *Die Säuberung: Moskau 1936: Stenogramm einer geschlossenen Parteiversammlung*, ed. Reinhard Müller (Reinbek bei Hamburg: Rowohlt, 1991), 184–85, emphasis mine. In her discussion of culture during the Moscow trial period, Katerina Clark employs the concept of theatricality broadly, but also directly in connection with theatre, such as the canonization of Stanislavsky at this time. See "Face and Mask: Theatricality and Identity in the Era of the Show Trials (1936–1938)," in Clark, *Moscow, the Fourth Rome: Stalinism, Cosmopolitanism, and the Evolution of Soviet Culture, 1931–1941* (Cambridge, MA: Harvard University Press, 2011), 210–41.

13. Malcolm Cowley, "The Record of a Trial," *The New Republic* (April 7, 1937): 267.

14. Dudley Collard, "Review of *The Case of the Anti-Soviet Trotskite Center* and *The Moscow Trials*," *International Affairs* 16/4 (1937): 640. Collard

also published a book-length defense of the trials in the Left Book Club series: Dudley Collard, *Soviet Justice and the Trial of Radek and Others* (London: Victor Gollancz, 1937).
15. Lukács, *Record of a Life*, 114–15.
16. György Lukács, "Emlékeim Rajk Lászlóról," in Lukács, *Curriculum Vitae*, ed. János Ambrus (Budapest: Magvető Kiadó, 1982), 350. For correspondence between Lukács and Júlia Rajk concerning the memorial book essay, see the four letters from 1969–1970 in the Lukács Archive, Magyar Tudományos Akadémia, at http://real-ms.mtak.hu/20350/1/Lukacs_lev_34_1451_Rajk_Laszlone_1.pdf (accessed October 31, 2021).
17. Joseph Stalin, "Speech at the Plenum of the Central Committee of the Communist Party of the Soviet Union, 3 March 1937," in *The Moscow Trial (January 1937) and Two Speeches by J. Stalin*, ed. W.P. Coates and Zelda K. Coates (London: The Anglo-Russian Parliamentary Commission, 1937), 249.
18. *Report of Court Proceedings: The Case of the Trotskyite-Zinovievite Terrorist Centre Heard before the Military Collegium of the Supreme Court of the USSR, Moscow, August 19–24, 1936* (Moscow: People's Commissariat of Justice of the USSR, 1936); *Report of Court Proceedings in the Case of the Anti-Soviet Trotskyite Centre Heard before the Military Collegium of the Supreme Court of the USSR, Moscow, January 23–30, 1937*; *Report of Court Proceedings in the Case of the Anti-Soviet "Bloc of Rights and Trotskyites" Heard before the Military Collegium of the Supreme Court of the USSR, Moscow, March 2–13, 1938* (Moscow: People's Commissariat of Justice of the USSR, 1938).
19. For a survey of the journalistic reception of the trials, see James K. Libbey, "Liberal Journals and the Moscow Trials of 1936–38," *Journalism and Mass Communication Quarterly* 52/1 (1975): 85–92, 137.
20. John Dewey, "Psychology and Justice," *The New Republic* (November 23, 1927): 9–12.
21. Leon Trotsky, *I Stake My Life! Trotsky's Address to the New York Hippodrome Meeting* (New York: Pioneer Publishers, 1937).
22. Arthur Jay Klinghoffer and Judith Apter Klinghoffer, *International Citizens' Tribunals: Mobilizing Public Opinion to Advance Human Rights* (New York: Palgrave, 2002).
23. John Dewey, *The Case of Leon Trotsky: Report of the Hearings on the Charges Made against Him in the Moscow Trials by the Preliminary Commission of Inquiry* (New York: Harper and Brothers, 1937); *Not Guilty: Report of the Commission of Inquiry into the Charges against Leon Trotsky in the Moscow Trials* (New York: Harper and Brothers, 1938). For further details about the Dewey Commission's work, see also the writings on the Trotsky Inquiry collected in John Dewey, *The Later Works, 1925–1953, Volume 11: 1935–1937*, ed. Jo Ann Boydston (Carbondale: Southern Illinois University Press, 2008), 303–36; Alan Ward, "Memories of the John Dewey Commission: Forty Years Later," *The Antioch Review* 35/4 (1977): 438–51; Xenia Zeldin, "John Dewey's Role on the 1937 Trotsky Commission," *Public Affairs Quarterly* 5/4 (1991): 387–94; Jay Martin, "John Dewey and the Trial of Leon Trotsky," *Partisan Review* 68/4 (2001): 519–35; David C. Engerman, "John Dewey and the Soviet Union:

Pragmatism Meets Revolution," *Modern Intellectual History* 3/1 (2006): 33–63.
24. Meyer Schapiro, letter of February 8, 1937, *News Bulletin of the American Committee for the Defense of Leon Trotsky* (February 19, 1937): 3.
25. "An Open Letter to American Liberals," *Soviet Russia Today* (March 1937): 14–15.
26. Walter Duranty, quoted by Jacob Heilbrunn, "The New York Times and the Moscow Show-trials," *World Affairs* 153/3 (1991): 90–91.
27. Walter Duranty, "The Riddle of Russia: What Lies behind Recent Events in the USSR?" *The New Republic* (July 14, 1937): 272.
28. For a sample of Duranty's reporting on the Soviet Union up to 1934, see Walter Duranty, *Duranty Reports Russia*, ed. Gustavus Tuckerman, Jr. (New York: The Viking Press, 1934). For further on Duranty, see James William Crowl, *Angels in Stalin's Paradise: Western Reporters in Soviet Russia 1917 to 1937, A Case Study of Louis Fischer and Walter Duranty* (Washington, DC: University Press of America, 1982); S.J. Taylor, *Stalin's Apologist: Walter Duranty: The New York Times's Man in Moscow* (Oxford: Oxford University Press, 1990).
29. Mauritz A. Hallgren, *Why I Resigned from the Trotsky Defense Committee* (New York: International Publishers, 1937).
30. Malcolm Cowley, "The Record of a Trial," 267. Cowley had already expressed aversion to Trotsky in his review of Trotsky's autobiography *My Life*, "Comrade Trotsky," *The New Republic* (April 8, 1936), reprinted in Malcolm Cowley, *Think Back on Us ...: A Contemporary Chronicle of the 1930s*, ed. Henry Dan Piper (Carbondale: Southern Illinois University Press, 1967), 109–12.
31. Bruce Bliven, "A Letter to Stalin," *The New Republic* (March 30, 1938): 216–17.
32. Malcolm Cowley, "Moscow Trials: 1938," *The New Republic* (May 18, 1938): 51.
33. Malcolm Cowley, "Moscow Trial: II," *The New Republic* (May 25, 1938): 79.
34. Edmund Wilson to Malcolm Cowley, letter of April 15, 1937, in Edmund Wilson, *Letters on Literature and Politics, 1912–1972*, ed. Elena Wilson (New York: Farrar, Straus and Giroux, 1977), 286.
35. "Agonisticism in the Moscow Trials," *The New Republic* (May 19, 1937): 33.
36. Max Radin, "The Moscow Trials: A Legal View," *Foreign Affairs* 16/1 (1937): 78.
37. The historian Frederick L. Schuman, who had been part of the international tribunal for the Bulgarian communists in the trial that followed the Reichstag fire in 1933, offered his own similar analysis of the Moscow trials and Trotsky's alleged treason in "Leon Trotsky: Martyr or Renegade?", *The Southern Review* 3/1 (1937); 51–74; see also Sidney Hook's response to Schuman, "Liberalism and the Case of Leon Trotsky," *The Southern Review* 3/2 (1937): 267–82. In his June 9, 1937 letter to *The Southern Review*, Malcolm Cowley warmly affirmed Schuman's article, which he saw in advance proofs: "I thought that Professor Schuman's article was about the soundest of all written on the controversy that has spread so widely

since the last Moscow trials. I agree with almost all of his conclusions. . . . The liberals who get mixed in the controversy on moral grounds are stooges and suckers. Schuman might have added that if the latest Moscow trial was a frame-up then Stalin was its principal victim." See Malcolm Cowley, "Correspondence," *The Southern Review* 3/1 (1937): 199.
38. Joseph E. Davies, *Mission to Moscow* (New York: Simon and Schuster, 1941), 51.
39. For further historical context on Joseph Davies, his book, and the Warner Brothers film made from it, see David Culbert, "Revisiting a Stalinist Puzzle: *Mission to Moscow*," *American Communist History* 12/2 (2013): 117–35.
40. Ernst Bloch focused on Bukharin's final speech in a notorious defense of the Moscow trial, "Bucharins Schlußwort" (Bukharin's last word, 1938), in *Von Hasard zur Katastrophe: Politische Aufsätze, 1934–1939* (Frankfurt am Main: Suhrkamp Verlag, 1972), 351–59; in the same volume, see "Kritik einer Prozeßkritik," 175–84. Bloch's apology for the trials occasioned a rift with the Frankfurt School, as Jay and Wiggershaus point out; see notes 2 and 4 above.
41. Bukharin in *Report of Court Proceedings in the Case of the Anti-Soviet "Bloc of Rights and Trotskyites,"* 778.
42. Bukharin, quoted by Paul Gregory, *Hoover Digest* 3, 2010, https://www.hoover.org/research/martyred-communism (accessed October 31, 2021). See, in addition, Jochen Hellbeck, "With Hegel to Salvation: Bukharin's Other Trial," *Representations* 107/1 (2009): 56–90.
43. "Behind the Soviet Trials," *The Nation* (February 6, 1937): 143.
44. James Rorty, "Harsh Words from a Friend," *The Nation* (February 27, 1937): 252.
45. For biographical information on James Rorty and his career, see chapter 1, "James Rorty," in Neil Gross, *Richard Rorty: The Making of an American Philosopher* (Chicago: University of Chicago Press, 2008), 29–62. See also Richard Rorty, "Trotsky and the Wild Orchids," in *Philosophy and Social Hope* (New York: Penguin Books, 1999), 5–6: "When I was 12, the most salient books on my parents' shelves were two red-bound volumes, The Case of Leon Trotsky and *Not Guilty*. These made up the report of the Dewey Commission of Inquiry into the Moscow Trials. . . . I thought of them in the way in which other children thought of their family's Bible: they were books that radiated redemptive truth and moral splendor. If I were a really good boy, I would say to myself, I should have read not only the Dewey Commission reports, but also Trotsky's *History of the Russian Revolution*, a book I started many times but never managed to finish. For in the 1940s, the Russian Revolution and its betrayal by Stalin were, for me, what the Incarnation and its betrayal by the Catholics had been to precocious little Lutherans 400 years ago. My father had almost, but not quite, accompanied John Dewey to Mexico as PR man for the Commission of Inquiry which Dewey chaired. Having broken with the American Communist Party in 1932, my parents had been classified by the *Daily Worker* as 'Trotskyites,' and they more or less accepted the description."
46. Judy Kutulas, *The Long War: The Intellectual People's Front and Anti-Stalinism, 1930–1940* (Durham, NC: Duke University Press, 1995), 63.

47. James Rorty, *Our Master's Voice: Advertising* (New York: The John Day Company, 1934).
48. Paul Lazarsfeld, quoted by Jefferson Pooley, "James Rorty's Voice: Introduction," in James Rorty, *Our Master's Voice* (Bethelem, PA: mediastudies.press, 2020): xxx–xxxi.
49. "From Rorty to Hearst," *The New Masses* (June 22, 1937): 14–15.
50. Ellis, "Willy's Trained Seal," cartoon in *The Daily Worker* (June 11, 1937): 6.
51. Claude McKay, "An Open Letter to James Rorty," *Socialist Call* (July 17, 1937): 8; reprinted in *The Passion of Claude McKay: Selected Poetry and Prose, 1912–1948*, ed. Wayne F. Cooper (New York: Schocken Books, 1973), 226–27.
52. Maurice Merleau-Ponty, *Humanism and Terror: An Essay on the Communist Problem*, trans. John O'Neill (Boston: Beacon Press, 1969).
53. Sidney Hook, *Out of Step: An Unquiet Life in the 20th Century* (New York: Harper and Row, 1987), 218–19.
54. Selden Rodman, "Trotsky in the Kremlin: An Interview," *Common Sense*, No. 6 (December 1937), 17–21; reprinted in John Dewey, *The Later Works, 1925–1953, Volume 13: 1938–1939*, ed. Jo Ann Boydston (Carbondale: Southern Illinois University Press, 2008), 391–400.
55. Leon Trotsky, John Dewey, and George Novack, *Their Morals and Ours* (New York: Pathfinder Press, 1973), 15.
56. Rodman alludes here to the leftist journalist Carleton Beal, who resigned from the Trotsky Commission and published his own negative account of the inquiry in Mexico, which concluded with a curse of "a plague on both your houses," in the mainstream *Saturday Evening Post*: Carleton Beal, "The Fewer Outsiders the Better," *Saturday Evening Post* (June 12, 1937): 23, 74–78.
57. "Both Their Houses," *The New Republic* (June 2, 1937): 104. In their captioning of these letters, the *New Republic* editors reached for the same Shakespearean metaphor as Carleton Beal would a few days later.
58. John Dewey, "In Defense of the Mexican Hearings," in Dewey, *The Later Works, Volume 13*, 347–48.
59. John Dewey, *Impression of Soviet Russia and the Revolutionary World* (New York: The New Republic, 1929).
60. John Dewey, "Significance of the Trotsky Inquiry," interview with Agnes Meyer in *The Washington Post* (December 19, 1937): 3–4; reprinted in Dewey, *The Later Works* 11, 330–36.
61. See Dewey, "Means and Ends," in Trotsky, Dewey, and Novack, *Their Morals and Ours*, 67–73.
62. See, for example, Lukács's "Tactics and Ethics," in *Tactics and Ethics: Political Essays, 1919–1929*, ed. Rodney Livingstone, trans. Michael McColgan (New York: Harper and Row, 1972). Compare also Lukács's "Bolshevism as a Moral Problem," in *The Lukács Reader*, ed. Arpad Kadarkay (Oxford: Blackwell, 1995), 216–21, written shortly before his conversion to communism and arguing the case of Dostoyevsky versus Lenin. Lukács, notably, still chose Dostoyevsky at this moment.
63. Alan Spitzer, *Historical Truth and Lies about the Past* (Chapel Hill: University of North Carolina Press, 1996), 27.

64. John Dewey, *Logic: The Theory of Inquiry*, in *The Later Works, 1925–1953, Volume 12: 1938*, ed. Jo Ann Boydston (Carbondale: Southern Illinois University Press, 2008), 234.
65. John Dewey to Corliss Lamont, quoted in Hook, *Out of Step*, 240.
66. Hilary Putnam, "A Reconsideration of Deweyan Democracy," *Southern California Law Review* 63/6 (1990): 1671–1698.
67. Axel Honneth, "Democracy as Reflexive Cooperation: John Dewey and the Theory of Democracy Today," trans. John M.M. Farrell, *Political Theory* 26/6 (1998): 778. For an early attempt to develop Dewey's thought as the basis of a concept of democratic socialism, see Jim Cork, "John Dewey, Karl Marx, and Democratic Socialism," *The Antioch Review* 9/4 (1949): 435–52.
68. Georg Lukács, *The Process of Democratization*, trans. Susanne Bernhardt and Norman Levine (Albany: State University of New York Press, 1991), 150.
69. Georg Lukács to Frank Benseler, September 2, 1968, quoted in the editor's afterword to Lukács, *Democratisierung Heute und Morgen*, ed. László Sziklai (Budapest: Akadémiai Kiadó, 1985), 216.
70. Norman Levine, "On the Transcendence of *State and Revolution*," introduction to Lukács, *The Process of Democratization*, 33.
71. See the article Lukács archivist László Sziklai published in the official paper of the Hungarian Socialist Workers Party shortly before the 1989 political changes: "Megkésett prófécia? Lukács György testamentuma," *Népszabadság* (December 31, 1988): 7.

Chapter 11

Tell-Trials, or, Gyuri the Radio Play

Enough, it's time it ended . . .
And yet I hesitate, I hesitate to . . . to end.
—Samuel Beckett, *Endgame*[1]

On December 18, 2021, Klubrádió, a Hungarian left-liberal talk radio station whose broadcast license had been revoked ten months early by Orbán's right-wing government,[2] transmitted over the internet a new radio-play production of István Eörsi's drama *Az Interjú* (The Interview). Eörsi had originally composed his play in 1981, published it in samizdat version in 1985, and revised it in 1989 as an "absurd documentary play for radio" and for stage performance as well, just ahead of the end of the Hungarian People's Republic that had assumed power forty years earlier.[3] The play was based on Eörsi's personal memories of Lukács, whom he had befriended in the 1950s and whose gigantic late *Aesthetics* and *Ontology* he had translated from German into Hungarian. But it also materially derived from the tape-recorded autobiographical interviews he and Erzsébet Vezér had conducted with Lukács not long before the philosopher's death from cancer in 1971.[4] Now, more than thirty years since the collapse of state socialism in Hungary and the death of the playwright himself in 2005, Eörsi's *Interview* was rebroadcast under conditions that recall the state control and censorship of the public sphere that Hungarians had earlier experienced under Kádár.[5]

At the center of Eörsi's play is his tense, ongoing dialogue with Lukács, in many cases drawn directly from the taped interviews. Several scenes, in fact, represent Eörsi conducting the interviews with the aged and sick Lukács, whose attention wanders and who is regularly interrupted by his assiduous relative Marian, who brings his meals, answers the phone, and tends to his literary legacy ("administering his immortality," as the 1989 stage version sarcastically puts it).[6] For example, from Lukács's remarks about Trotsky in his interview (partly quoted at the beginning of my previous chapter), Eörsi condenses the following exchange:

> LUKÁCS: At that time I got the impression that had Trotsky come to power he would have constructed the same cult of personality as Stalin, if not a bigger one.
> EÖRSI: Bigger?
> LUKÁCS: Let's say the same. In his personality, something ... Lenin characterized it very aptly ... there was in him something ... something ...
> EÖRSI: Of Lassalle.
> LUKÁCS: Of Lassalle, and that already bothered me then. Don't you find the comparison precise?
> EÖRSI: I don't know Lassalle well enough.
> LUKÁCS: In everything he resembled Trotsky. (30)

Eörsi accurately conveys Lukács's substantive views in the interviews, yet in his rearrangement subtly underscores the frequent circularity and closure of Lukács's judgments as well. Over the course of the play, as his illness progresses, Lukács's ability to carry on with the interviews becomes increasingly compromised, until by the end, he is reduced to stammering out dialectical mannerisms, "On the one hand ... on the other ... subjectively ... objectively ...," while the now-dominant interviewer fills in most of the content of what he infers Lukács intended to say.

Departing from the verisimilitude of the scenes that depict the recording of Lukács's historical interviews, in other episodes Eörsi opens up a subjective space of memory and fantasy, continuing the discussion and debate even after his interlocutor's death. In some scenes, for instance, the younger writer sits atop the philosopher's grave, smokes cigars, and converses with the posthumous Lukács, who joins him up on the tomb. These cemetery encounters are pitched, in Eörsi's own words, towards the "absurd," which, he notes, was already manifest at Lukács's burial: "There I was at the burial, what a dog's farce that was ... 'Rest in peace,' on a communist grave—don't you find that absurd? Aren't life's everyday facts even more absurd as we find them today?"[7] In one humorous scene, the deceased Lukács recounts that he has recreated his workspace and library out of clouds, suggesting that in the workers' paradise the work continues even after death:

> EÖRSI: ... What kind of desk is that?
> LUKÁCS: A cloud. Here we decide the shape of the clouds for our personal use.
> EÖRSI: And how many clouds per person do you get?
> LUKÁCS: To each according to his needs. (45)

But interrupting this lighthearted idyll, Eörsi informs Lukács about the rise of Solidarność in Poland, which by the time of Eörsi's writing had grown to ten million members. "In Poland," Eörsi tells Lukács, "the workers are again demonstrating. It seems that they don't want to realize that they are already in power" (45).

In addition to the posthumous Lukács himself, his first wife Jelena Grabenko, a former Russian Social Revolutionary with whom he lived in Heidelberg until his return to Budapest in 1915, and his second wife and decades-long partner Gertrúd Bortstieber, who died eight years before Lukács, also make appearances, adding comments to the discussion and throwing shade on Lukács from their own ironizing perspectives. "Ljena," for instance, asks him why, when he was in the Soviet Union, he didn't look for her. He answers that he did, but he couldn't find her. She responds, "Did you look hard enough?" and adds, "If I'd had a tombstone, you wouldn't have found the second date on it" (27)—in fact, we only know that she died sometime after 1930 in unknown circumstances. In another scene, Eörsi takes Gertrúd aside to tell her what has happened with socialism since her death in 1963:

EÖRSI: First the Soviet Union and China turned against one another . . .
GERTRÚD: Please, don't say . . .
EÖRSI: In Cuba . . .
GERTRÚD: Don't!
EÖRSI: Should I confine myself to Europe?
GERTRÚD: You should talk about Gyuri [György]. (37)

Gertrúd's blurting out "Please, don't say . . ." with " . . . anything to Gyuri" being left unspoken suggests that even from the afterlife she is shielding Lukács and his vision of socialism from the actually existing history foreclosing his future ideal's coming to pass.

We would be mistaken, however, to see in Eörsi's play merely a settling of accounts with his late master and mentor, increasingly estranged in the distance of hindsight and later experience. It is equally a dramatization of an unresolved work of mourning for Lukács, Eörsi's "melancholy of resistance," in László Krasznahorkai's apt phrase, both towards Lukács himself and his ambiguous legacy. As the Lukács archivist and scholar László Sziklai summed up in a roundtable discussion with Eörsi on the occasion of the 1989 performance, "An Interview about *The Interview*":

Not only [are there] many Lukácses, there are also many "Lukács cases," and indeed, Eörsi has his own separate Lukács case that he wanted to close in this piece, to dispose of it. . . . The many Lukácses, his reduplication, goes together with the question of belief, which not only runs through the play, but also provides its ultimate closure—namely Lukács's belief that "on the one hand, I am correct, but on the other, I am absolutely right." Eörsi puts in question Lukács's absolute rightness, thus here, in essence it's a matter of once again retrying his case.[8]

Notably, a decade later, Sziklai himself helped to publish another set of "autobiographical" interviews with Lukács, dating to 1941, in which a "Lukács case" had earlier been tried: the transcripts of Lukács's interrogation by the NKVD, the Soviet internal police, in their Lubyanka headquarters following his arrest in June of that year, shortly before the German invasion of the USSR.[9] He managed to escape execution, in part through sheer luck and in part through the help of Georgi Dimitrov, whom Lukács had met already in his Vienna exile.

Eörsi's dramatized resistance to Lukács is not just a personal affair of the playwright alone. It touches closely on Lukács's repeatedly renegotiated place in the tradition of radical thought, and, as well, on the disappointed dreams for the future inextricably entangled with his legacy. My own book, indeed, can do nothing to dispel that "left-wing melancholy"—as Benjamin put it—or the resistance to Lukács it has nourished; I have not sought to "acquit" him, nor to "convict" him and send him away. No ultimate verdict has been pronounced either about Lukács himself or about the position he might hold in a future critical theory that for many decades has mostly sought to monumentalize him or keep him discreetly out of sight. In this ending, which hesitates to end, I do however hope to have achieved at least a more modest aim: to underscore that when the Lukács case seems at last to have been laid to rest, he may yet unexpectedly appear once more to pick up again the thread of its unfinished argument.

Notes

1. Samuel Beckett, *Endgame: A Play in One Act* (New York: Grove Press, 1958), 3.
2. See Eva S. Balogh, "Klubrádió: Ask Alexa, Not the Media Council," *Hungarian Spectrum* blog, March 11, 2021.
3. For the 2021 performance, see https://www.klubradio.hu/archivum/hangjatek-2021-december-18-szombat-1400-21929 (accessed December 31, 2021). Published versions: István Eörsi, *Az Utolsó Szó, Jogan* (Budapest: Független Kiadó, 1985); Eörsi, *Az Interjú: Rádióra Alkalmazott Abszurd Dokumentumjáték* (Budapest: Háttér, 1989); Eörsi, *Az Interjú, Színház Drámamelléklet* (January 1989), online at http://adattar.vmmi.org/dramak/159/159.pdf (accessed December 31, 2021).
4. Published in English as Georg Lukács, *Record of a Life: An Autobiographical Sketch*, ed. István Eörsi, trans. Rodney Livingstone (London: Verso, 1983).

5. Melinda Kalmár has documented how Kádárism focused control especially on the press and mass media to produce a distinctive "simulated publicness" See Kalmár, *Ennivaló és Hozomány: A Kora Kádárizmus Ideológiája* (Budapest: Magvető, 1998).
6. *Színház* (January 1989): 1.
7. Eörsi, *Az Interjú, Színház Drámamelléklet*, 7.
8. László Sziklai, "Interjú—Az interjúból," in Eörsi, *Az Interjú: Rádióra Alkalmazott Abszurd Dokumentumjáték*, 62.
9. *Vallatás a Lubjankán: Lukács György Viszgálati Ügyiratai, Életrajzi Documentumok* (Budapest: Argumentum Kiadó, 2002).

Index

abstract art, 85, 89–92, 105
abstract expressionism, 95
Adorno, Theodor W., 1–19, 21–2, 88, 92, 99, 169–70, 178–81, 186, 191, 196–8, 201, 203–5, 214, 221, 225–6, 242–3, 247
  Aesthetic Theory (book), 21, 105–12, 115–16, 127
  Alban Berg (book), 150
  The Authoritarian Personality (book), 201, 205
  "Berlin Opera Memorial" (essay), 147
  "Bourgeois Opera" (essay), 145–6
  Composing for the Films (book), 154–5, 158
  Dialectic of Enlightenment (book), 10, 108, 126, 145, 147, 153, 179–80, 203
  Erziehung zur Mündigkeit (book), 19
  "Extorted Reconciliation" (essay), 3, 11–12, 15, 17, 129
  "Fragen des gegenwärtigen Operntheaters" (essay), 139–40
  "The Idea of Natural History" (essay), 9
  In Search of Wagner (book), 147, 153
  Introduction to the Sociology of Music (book), 146, 154
  "Is Art Lighthearted?" (essay), 129–30
  Kierkegaard: Construction of the Aesthetic (book), 8
  "Kitsch" (essay), 126–8
  "Kurt Weill" (obituary), 138–9
  "Kurt Weill: Kleine Dreigroschenmusik für Blasorchester" (review), 137–8
  "Looking Back on Surrealism" (essay), 21, 112–13
  "Mahagonny" (review), 129
  Mahler: A Musical Physiognomy (book), 128, 135
  "Marginalia to Theory and Practice" (essay), 17–18
  Minima Moralia (book), 161
  "Music in the Background" (essay), 134–5
  "Musik im Fernsehen ist Brimborium" (interview), 156–57
  "Nach einem Vierteljahrhunderts" (essay), 139
  Negative Dialectics (book), 7–9, 17–18, 107
  "New Opera and Public" (essay), 145
  "On the Social Situation of Music" (essay), 112, 115
  "Opera and the Long-Playing Record" (essay), 151–2
  Philosophy of New Music (book), 112
  "Questions of the Contemporary Opera-Theatre" (essay), 139–40
  "The Radio Symphony" (essay), 149
  "Rückblick," (essay), 108, 114
  Der Schatz des Indianer-Joe (Singspiel), 131

Adorno, Theodor W. (*cont.*)
"The Schema of Mass Culture" (essay), 126
"Schubert" (essay), 133–4
"Stravinsky" (essay), 113
Towards a Theory of Musical Reproduction (book), 130
"Über die musikalische Verwendung des Radios" (essay), 152, 155
"Valéry Proust Museum" (essay), 151
"Vortrupp und Avantgarde" (essay), 140–1
"What a Music Appreciation Hour Should Be" (essay), 148
"Zum *Anbruch*: Exposé" (essay), 126
"Zur Dreigroschenoper" (essay), 137
Ady, Endre, 11, 40, 45–8
Aeschylus, 56, 61
Alighieri, Dante, 39, 60, 84
Antheil, George, 147, 161
Antonioni, Michelangelo, 82, 105
Apel, Karl-Otto, 249
Aragon, Louis, 109–10
Arendt, Hannah, 13, 210
Aristotle, 56–7, 60
Artaud, Antonin, 162, 170, 182
Asor Rosa, Alberto, 10–11
avant-gardes, 11–12, 21, 31, 82, 92–4, 105–11, 115–20, 125–9, 138–41, 147, 152, 198, 209, 217

Bachofen, Johann Jakob, 61, 181
Badiou, Alan, 14
Balázs, Béla, 6, 195
Balzac, Honoré de, 60
Barthes, Roland, 108, 173, 182
Bartsch, Rudolf Hans, 133
Bataille, Georges, 22, 107–8, 114–15, 120, 170, 178, 180–1, 183–88, 190
Baudelaire, Charles, 61–2, 105
Beauvoir, Simone de, 175, 192
Beckett, Samuel, 14, 82, 105
Beethoven, Ludwig van, 93, 147, 149–50
Benjamin, Walter, 9, 19, 21–2, 38, 92, 105, 107–9, 112–20, 131, 147, 151–2, 158, 162, 170, 178–9, 181–2, 190–1, 196–8, 208, 261
Arcades Project (book), 116, 131, 181
"Theses on the Philosophy of History" (essay), 182
Benseler, Frank, 250
Berg, Alban, 5, 124, 135–6, 147–8, 150, 155
Berté, Heinrich, 133
Beuys, Joseph, 105, 219
Bibó, István, 90
Bizet, Georges, 148
Blanchot, Maurice, 22, 179
Bliven, Bruce, 237
Bloch, Ernst, 6–8, 18, 20, 31–2, 34–40, 42, 48–52, 81, 99, 160
"Actuality and Utopia" (review), 6–7
"Gedenkbuch für Else Bloch-Von Stritzki" (essay), 48, 50–1
Spirit of Utopia (book), 31, 36–7, 42, 160
Tendency-Latency-Utopia (book), 48
Thomas Münzer als Theologe der Revolution (book), 37, 48
Bloch, Karola, 48
Bloch-von Stritzki, Else, 40, 48
Blumenbert, Hans, 37
Bolter, Jay, 145
Bortstieber, Gertrúd, 260
Brahms, Johannes, 150
Brecht, Bertolt, 105, 131–2, 140
Bremer, Thomas, 32
Breton, André, 110–11, 114, 117–18
Büchner, Georg, 225, 228
Buck-Morss, Susan, 215
Bukharin, Nikolai, 237, 239–40
Buñuel, Luis, 105, 114
Bürger, Peter, 21, 107–8, 117–20
Busoni, Ferruccio, 139, 147

Cage, John, 93, 106, 124
Caillois, Roger, 108, 114, 180–1
Calasso, Roberto, 108–9
Carter, Huntley, 71–2
Clark, Katerina, 163
Collard, Dudley, 229
comedy, 60
Corneille, Pierre, 56, 66

Cowley, Malcolm, 228–9, 234, 236–7
Cronan, Todd, 117–18
Culture Industry, 21, 107, 124–6, 133, 145, 147, 153–4, 156–7, 180, 225

Davies, Joseph, 239
Deborin, Abram, 7, 13
De Man, Paul, 32–4
Demetz, Peter, 62, 69–70
democracy, 18, 89, 226, 241, 246–7, 249–51
  people's, 3, 20, 84–5
  socialist, 98
democratization, 3, 19, 23, 246, 249–51
Derrida, Jacques, 120
Dewey, John, 3, 22–3, 226–7, 230, 232–4, 238, 242, 244–51
Dimitrov, Georgi, 233, 261
Dostoevsky, Fyodor, 33–4
Dubiel, Helmut, 203
Duchamp, Marcel, 106
Duranty, Walter, 234–7
Dutschke, Rudi, 92–3

Eisler, Hanns, 124, 129, 147, 154–5, 158
Eörsi, István, 6, 23, 35, 82, 258–61
epic, 32, 34, 62–4, 84
  -theatre, 132, 138
Ernst, Max, 111–15
Ernst, Paul, 20, 45, 47–8, 67
ethics, 35, 40, 51, 60, 85, 94

fascism, 13, 18, 89–90, 131, 140, 180, 201, 203–5, 219, 232, 234–5
Fehér, David, 97
Fehér, Ferenc, 64, 67
Fiedler, Konrad, 86
film, 21–2, 58, 64, 82, 144–5, 147, 151, 153–9, 161–3, 214–15, 239–40
Flaubert, Gustave, 33, 61–2
Fluxus, 99, 105, 211
Foucault, Michel, 120, 212
Fourier, Charles, 19, 22, 117, 170, 173, 175, 178, 180–2, 190–2
French Revolution, 74, 215, 217, 225, 228

Freud, Sigmund, 49, 175, 178
Fromm, Erich, 202–5
  "The Method and Function of Analytic Social Psychology" (essay), 205
  "Psychoanalytic Characterology" (essay), 205

Gauguin, Paul, 83–4
George, Stefan, 35, 111
Gershwin, George, 131
Giacometti, Alberto, 105, 114
Giotto [di Bondone], 84–5
Godard, Jean-Luc, 14, 105
Goehr, Lydia, 153
Goethe, Johann Wolfgang von, 49, 61–2, 70, 75, 93
Goldstein, Kurt, 202
Grabenko, Jelena, 260
Greenberg, Clement, 86, 95, 125
Grosz, Georg, 105, 127
Groys, Boris, 217
Grünberg, Carl, 4
Grusin, Richard, 145
Grynszpan, Herschel, 227
Guilbaut, Serge, 95
Guterman, Norbert, 225
György, Péter, 91, 209, 214–15

Habermas, Jürgen, 1–2, 98, 200, 249
Hallgren, Mauritz, 235–7
Hamvas, Béla, 89–90
Harrison, Charles, 90
Hauser, Arnold, 34, 195
Heartfield, John, 4, 105
Hegel, G. W. F., 8, 57, 60–1, 65, 105, 107
Heidegger, Martin, 3, 15–16, 32, 198
Heilbrunn, Jacob, 235
Heißenbüttel, Helmut, 107
Heller, Agnes, 48, 75–6, 94
Herzfeld, Wieland, 4
Hindemith, Paul, 112, 129
Hiss, Alger, 227
Hitler, Adolf, 62, 71, 203, 219, 235, 239
Hoberman, J., 82
Hofmannsthal, Hugo von, 155
Honneth, Axel, 1–3, 23, 169, 211, 249

Hook, Sidney, 22, 232, 244, 247
Horkheimer, Max, 1, 5, 9–10, 13, 22, 108, 124, 145, 147, 169–70, 178–81, 186, 191, 199, 201–8, 225
  "The Authoritarian State" (essay), 204, 208
  "Authority and the Family" (essay), 205–7
  Dialectic of Enlightenment (book), 10, 108, 126, 145, 147, 153, 179–80, 203
  "Egoism and the Freedom Movement" (essay), 204
  "The End of Reason" (essay), 204
  "The Present Situation of Social Philosophy and the Tasks of an Institute for Social Research" (essay), 199, 202
Horthy, Miklós, 219
Horváth, Márton, 91
Hughes, Langston, 132
Hulllot-Kentor, Robert, 9, 148
Humboldt, Wilhelm von, 49
Humperdinck, Engelbert, 147, 149
Hungarian Revolution of 1919, 5, 35–8, 57–9, 219
Hungarian Uprising of 1956, 12–14, 76, 94, 98, 210–11, 217, 220
Husserl, Edmund, 5, 198
Huyssen, Andreas, 153

Ibsen, Henrik, 50, 61–2
impressionism, 40, 43, 85, 87
Institut für Sozialforschung, 4–5, 13, 22, 157, 195–208
  Studien über Autorität und Familie (book), 22, 196, 201–7
  Zeitschrift für Sozialforschung (journal), 4–5, 148, 197, 199–201, 203–5

Jameson, Fredric, 3–4, 18, 31, 39, 72, 99, 198
Janáček, Leoš, 147, 159
Jancsó, Miklós, 82
Jaspers, Karl, 34
Jay, Martin, 197–8, 225
Jeles, András, 214–15

Jenny, Laurent, 114
Judovitz, Dalia, 170, 172

Kádár János, 211, 214, 218, 220, 258
Kafka, Franz, 11, 38, 82
Kállai, Ernő, 89–90
Kalotai, László, 57
Kant, Immanuel, 61, 105, 107, 175, 179
Kantor, Tadeusz, 215
Károlyi, Mihály, 57
Kemény, Katalin, 89–90
Kernstok, Károly, 43–4
Khrushchev, Nikita, 14, 94
Kierkegaard, Søren, 5, 8–9, 34, 36, 49–50
Kirchheimer, Otto, 23
  Political Justice (book), 227–30
kitsch, 19, 21, 107, 125–30, 133, 139, 141, 149, 152, 156, 161
Klossowski, Pierre, 22, 170, 178, 180–2, 189–92
Kluge, Alexander, 21–2, 145, 157–63
Koegler, Horst, 140–1
Koestler, Arthur, 219, 239
Kolisch, Rudolf, 130
Korsch, Karl, 4, 6–8, 244
Koselleck, Reinhold, 39
Kovács, Attila F., 22, 196, 210–11, 214–15, 217–21
Kozloff, Max, 95
Kracauer, Siegfried, 5–9, 13
Krasznahorkai, László, 260
Křenek, Ernst, 124, 129–30, 132, 134–7, 147, 161
Kun, Béla, 6, 36, 57
Kutulas, Judy, 242

Lacan, Jacques, 120
Lafargue, Paul, 61
Lakner, László, 96–9
Lamont, Corliss, 248–9
Lang, Fritz, 157, 161–2
Laplanche, Jean, 177
Lask, Emil, 34–5
Lassalle, Ferdinand, 20, 68–72, 259
Lazarsfeld, Paul, 242–3
Lefort, Claude, 209–10, 217, 219

Legrady, George, 22, 196, 210–14, 220–1
Leiris, Michel, 108, 180–1
Lengyel, József, 36
Lenin, Vladimir, 36, 55, 57, 61, 69, 74, 95, 162, 183, 235, 259
Lenk, Elisabeth, 21, 108–11, 116–18
Leppert, Richard, 146
Lesznai, Anna, 34
Levin, Tom, 58
Levine, Norman, 250
Lifshitz, Mikhail, 82–3, 88
Ligeti, György, 105, 157
Living Theatre, 93, 105
Lowenthal, Leo, 9, 202–4, 225
Löwy, Michael, 31–2, 38
Loyola (Ignatius of Loyola), 173
Lukács, Georg, 1–23, 105–7, 119, 129, 144, 146, 169, 195, 197, 210, 215, 220–1, 225–9, 244, 246–51, 258–61
  "Aesthetic Culture" (essay), 42–4, 83–4, 96
  "Ariadne auf Naxos" (review), 47–8
  "'Eine Art Freundschaft'" (interview), 252
  "August Strindberg" (essay), 43–4
  "Blum Theses" (essay), 76
  "Bolshevism as a Moral Problem" (essay), 36
  "A Critique of Lassalle's Literary Theory" (essay), 68–9
  The Culture of People's Democracy (book), 55
  A Defence of History and Class Consciousness (book), 3, 6
  The Destruction of Reason (book), 18, 88
  Developmental History of Modern Drama (book), 20, 60, 64–5, 72
  "Emlékeim Rajk Lászlóról" (essay) 229
  "The Form of Drama" (essay), 65
  "Das Formproblem der Malerei" (essay), 87
  "Free or Directed Art?" (essay), 84–5
  "Georg Simmel" (essay), 195
  "Grand Hotel 'Abgrund'" (essay), 18
  Heidelberg Philosophy of Art (book), 33–4, 40–2
  The Historical Novel (book), 20, 63–4, 72–3, 75
  History and Class Consciousness (book), 1, 3–9, 31, 37, 55–6, 58–9, 76, 92, 244
  "Hungarian Reality" (essay), 84, 87, 89
  "Hungarian Theories of Abstract Art" (essay), 89–90
  "Lecture on Painting" (essay), 83
  "Madách tragédiája" (essay), 215
  "Marx and Engels on Problems of Dramaturgy" (essay), 69, 71
  The Meaning of Contemporary Realism (book), 11, 13–14, 16–17, 94
  "The Metaphysics of Tragedy" (essay), 20, 47, 67–8
  "Művészet és valóság" (essay), 87–8
  "On the Fascistically Falsified and the Real Büchner" (essay), 228
  "On the Fetish Character in Music and the Regression in Listening" (essay), 148
  Ontology of Social Being (book), 75
  "The Parting of the Ways" (essay), 43, 83
  The Process of Democratization (book), 3, 98–9, 249–50
  Record of a Life (book), 6–7, 35–7, 82–3, 225–6
  "Reflections on the Sino-Soviet Split" (essay), 14
  "The Sickingen Debate between Marx-Engels and Lassalle" (essay), 68
  "Solzhenitsyn and the New Realism" (essay), 99
  Soul and Form (book), 9, 20, 31, 42, 47
  The Specificity of the Aesthetic (book), 75, 82, 96, 99
  Studies in European Realism (book), 98–9
  "Tendency or Partisanship?" (essay), 69

Lukács, Georg (*cont.*)
  Theory of the Novel (book), 7, 9, 11, 18, 32–4, 36, 59, 63, 84
  "Tribune or Bureaucrat?" (essay), 61–2
  "Új Magyar Líra" (essay), 46
  The Young Hegel (book), 60–1

Machiavelli, Niccolò, 55
Madách, Imre, 215
Mahler, Gustav, 128–9, 135, 147
Mallarmé, Stéphane, 111
Mann, Thomas, 11, 62, 127
Mannheim, Karl, 9, 195
Marcuse, Herbert, 1, 5, 9, 13, 22, 92–4, 170, 175–81, 188, 190–1, 196, 202–5
  "The Affirmative Character of Culture" (essay), 204–5
  Eros and Civilization (book), 175–8
  An Essay on Liberation (book), 93
  Soviet Marxism (book), 13, 92
  "A Study on Authority" (essay), 204
  "The Struggle against Liberalism in the Totalitarian View of the State" (essay), 204
Márkus, György, 67
Marlowe, Christopher, 62, 229
Marx, Karl, 1, 3, 5, 8, 10, 12, 18, 20, 36, 60–1, 65, 68–72, 88, 98, 209
Marx Brothers, 162–3
Masson, André, 115
McKay, Claude, 244
Medgyessy, Péter, 220
Merleau-Ponty, Maurice, 244
Meyer, Agnes, 247
Meyer, Hans, 202
Meyerhold, Vsevolod, 71
Mission to Moscow (film), 239–40
modernism, 3, 11, 18, 20, 31, 81–3, 85, 88, 91–5, 106–7, 109, 119, 124–6, 135, 208
Moholy-Nagy, László, 105, 147
More, Thomas, 39
Morris, Robert, 94, 105
Moscow trials, 13, 22, 163, 225–42, 244–8
Mozart, Wolfgang Amadeus, 147–8

Müller, Heiner, 160–1
Muse, Clarence, 132

Nagy, Imre, 13–14
Naville, Pierre, 119–20
neo-avant-gardes, 93, 105, 110, 117, 208, 217
Neumann, Franz, 13
New Left, 3, 59, 92–3
Nietzsche, Friedrich, 62, 105, 161

opera, 19, 21–2, 57–8, 71, 129, 133–4, 136–40, 144–63, 215
Orbán, Viktor, 210, 215, 217, 220, 258

Pataki, Gábor, 91
perversion, 22, 169–79, 181, 184–5, 187–92
Pollock, Friedrich, 4, 204
Pollock, Jackson, 95, 105
Pontalis, Jean-Bertrand, 177
Pooley, Jefferson, 242
Popper, Leo, 41
Popular Front, 15, 232, 241, 243
postmodernism, 120, 198
potpourri, 132–8, 149
Prague Spring, 3, 99, 249
Princeton Radio Project, 147–8, 242
Proust, Marcel, 151–2
Puccini, Giacomo, 147, 162
Putnam, Hilary, 23, 249

Rabinovszky, Máriusz, 91
Radin, Max, 238–9
Radnóti, Sándor, 32
Rajk, László, 227, 229
Rákosi, Mátyás, 215, 229
realism, 3, 14, 18, 31, 38, 55, 59, 63, 87–8, 92–5, 97–9, 119, 153
  critical, 59, 106
  socialist, 11, 14, 59, 62, 70–1, 88, 91, 93, 95, 110, 217
Reich, Wilhelm, 205
reification, 1–3, 7, 9–10, 12, 59, 87, 92–4, 110, 114, 128, 133, 147, 149–50, 153, 169, 176, 197
Reinitz, Béla, 57
Rév, István, 218–9
Révai, József, 4

Rienzo, Cola di, 71
Rodell, Fred, 238
Rodman, Selden, 245–6
Rorty, James, 241–4
Rorty, Richard, 242
Roudinesco, Élisabeth, 175
Rudas, László, 7, 13
Russell, Bertrand, 15

Sade, Marquis de (Donatien Alphonse François), 19, 22, 117, 169–75, 178–92
Schapiro, Meyer, 234
Schiller, Friedrich, 70, 75, 105, 175
Schlegel, Friedrich, 49
Schneemann, Carolee, 93–4
Schoenberg, Arnold, 62, 105, 124, 135–7, 147–8, 150, 153
Schubert, Franz, 133–4
Sedov, Lev, 233, 238
Seidler, Irma, 40, 48–9
Serge, Victor, 6
Shakespeare, William, 41, 56, 62, 66, 70, 75
Shostakovich, Dmitri, 163
show trials, 22, 163, 219, 225, 227–30
Simmel, Georg, 61, 66–7, 85, 195
Sohn-Rethel, Alfred, 1, 9–10
Solow, Herbert, 242
Solzhenitsyn, Alexander, 99, 217
Sombart, Werner, 64, 195
Spitzer, Alan, 247
Stein, Gertrude, 131
Sternheim, Andries, 202
Strauss, Richard, 147–8, 154–5
Stravinsky, Igor, 112–13, 129, 139, 147
Strindberg, August, 43–4
surrealism, 21, 85, 107–20, 126
Sziklai, László, 260–1
Szondi, Peter, 60–1

Takács, Jenő, 135
Thompson, Virgil, 131

Topor, Tünde, 96
totalitarianism, 12–13, 22, 196, 208–11, 213, 217–20, 227
tragedy, 7, 20, 40, 42, 47, 49, 56–7, 60–73, 76, 85, 229, 247
Trotsky, Leon, 15, 22, 69, 226–7, 230–6, 238, 240–2, 245–9, 251, 259
typology, 59–66, 202, 205
Tzara, Tristan, 105, 114–15

utopia, 19–22, 31–2, 36–43, 47–51, 63, 93, 108, 126, 148, 160, 169–71, 175–8, 181–2, 184–6, 188–92, 209, 213

Valéry, Paul, 105, 111, 151
Verdery, Katherine, 215
Verdi, Giuseppe, 147–8, 158–9, 162
Vezér, Erzsébet, 258
Vienna Actionism, 94, 105

Wagner, Richard, 71, 105, 127, 147–50, 153, 159, 215
Warhol, Andy, 94, 105
Weber, Marianne, 34–5
Weber, Max, 64, 67, 195, 197–8, 209
Weil, Felix, 4
Weill, Kurt, 105, 112, 115, 129–32, 134–5, 137–41, 147
Wiene, Robert, 155
Wiggershaus, Rolf, 4, 203–4
Williams, Emmett, 99
Wilson, Edmund, 237
Wittfogel, Karl August, 4, 202
Wittgenstein, Ludwig, 95, 160

Yakulov, Georgi, 71–2

Zinoviev, Grigory, 6, 234
Žižek, Slavoj, 12–13, 210, 213, 225